WINNING HERE

My Campaigning Life
MEMOIRS VOLUME I

WINNING HERE

— CHRIS RENNARD —

\B^b\
Biteback Publishing

First published in Great Britain in 2018 by
Biteback Publishing Ltd
Westminster Tower
3 Albert Embankment
London SE1 7SP
Copyright © Chris Rennard 2018

ISBN 978-1-78590-337-3

10 9 8 7 6 5 4 3 2 1

A CIP catalogue record for this book is available from the British Library.

Set in Adobe Caslon Pro

Printed and bound in Great Britain by
CPI Group (UK) Ltd, Croydon CR0 4YY

To Ann

CONTENTS

INTRODUCTION

This is a very personal story about my life, from growing up in Liverpool and being orphaned before I was seventeen, to becoming what some people called 'the most important person in Westminster you've never heard of'. Most of my life has been about running successful election campaigns, some of which took the Liberal Democrats to a position of greater strength than Liberals had enjoyed since Lloyd George's coalition government ended in 1922. As a result, the Liberal Democrats were able to participate in a peacetime coalition government at Westminster for the first time in nearly ninety years.

I was organising elections in my teens, and was arguably the most successful constituency agent in the country at the age of twenty-two. I never stood for election, spending my time instead getting other people elected. I did, however, become a member of the House of Lords at thirty-nine and chief executive of my party at forty-three.

Politics is a strange business, and some of the most personal or behind-the-scenes parts of it are not well known. My own story described in these pages coincides with some extraordinary political events, including those concerning the last years of the Liberal Party, the period of the Liberal–SDP Alliance, and the rise of the Liberal Democrats to becoming serious challengers for power. The party that I have loyally supported for over forty years has nearly died on several occasions; including the time, early in the period of my membership, when its former leader, Jeremy Thorpe, faced a criminal trial on charges of conspiracy to murder and there was also a public backlash against the 'Lib–Lab Pact' that propped up a Labour government after losing its majority. In such difficult circumstances, I saw how the party's survival in the 1979 general election depended to a great degree on a spectacular parliamentary by-election win on the eve of that election in Liverpool Edge Hill; a campaign to which I had devoted many months and from which I learned much about how a Liberal could win in the most difficult of circumstances. Above all, it highlighted to me the crucial importance that parliamentary by-elections could play in politics and in the life of a party such as mine.

When the Liberal Party and the newly created SDP came together in the 1980s to challenge the 'two-party system', I had high hopes for it and played a mostly modest role in the series of 'Alliance' by-election victories. At one stage, its national polling ratings rose to 50 per cent after Shirley Williams's victory at Crosby. When the merger of the two parties later became an acrimonious split, I witnessed his despair as Paddy Ashdown believed that the party of Gladstone could come to an end under his leadership. I worked closely with Paddy as the party became more successful, although our relationship was some-times fractious. We ensured the party's survival as we started winning elections again. The revival began with our by-election triumph at Eastbourne in 1990, and which Paddy was initially strongly opposed to us contesting. Our success there was a turning point for the party, with a near doubling of our opinion-poll ratings nationally. Six weeks after that by-election win, Mrs Thatcher resigned as Prime Minister as her MPs lost confidence in her. Politics was changed.

When I was subsequently organising 'target seat' constituency cam-paigns for the party in the 1997 general election, we more than doubled our representation at Westminster to forty-six seats. Paddy's aim, how-ever, was always to join a progressive coalition with Labour, especially once Tony Blair became Labour leader, whilst my (not necessarily contradictory) aim was to ensure that this could not happen without securing proportional representation and that the party did not ever lose the perception of independence from both the other main parties, which was vital to us.

My political reputation was largely based on the series of thirteen parliamentary by-election victories that I helped to oversee for the Liberal Democrats during the leaderships of Paddy Ashdown and Charles Kennedy and the acting leadership of Ming Campbell. I also helped (sometimes significantly) in another six parliamentary by-elections that we won between 1979 and 1987. I obviously describe some of these by-election campaigns in greater depth than others, and I have also tried to focus what I say about them on different aspects of the campaigns. This volume of memoirs covers my political experiences up to 2006, including the resignation that year of Charles Kennedy in very sad circumstances, and dealing with the very difficult crisis-management issues that arose in the aftermath in such a way that the party was able to recover.

Throughout Charles's leadership, he put me in charge of the professional organisation of all the party's election campaigns, and he was largely responsible for my appointment as chief executive of the party. I saw how he coped extremely well (far better than I had feared might have been the case given his health problems) with the challenges of leading the party during the time of the Iraq War. I particularly enjoyed the experience of working with him when he was on his best form, seeing how he understood how people thought and felt, and how he could then be the most effective advocate for Liberal values of all the leaders I worked with. But I was also often engaged in dealing with many of the consequences of the alcoholism that caused his downfall and untimely death.

I spent decades learning about running election campaigns at every level, and I believe that this experience was essential to me as I acquired increasing responsibility for running elections at the national level. I gained much relevant experience knocking on doors, listening and talking to people, writing leaflets and working with hundreds of candidates, campaigners and party activists. This all helped me to understand what might inspire people to vote in the way that they did. Everyone who knows me understands how I loved to win elections. But a consequence of my devotion to the role was that I neglected my health. I led a most unhealthy lifestyle. Sometimes I had bouts of depression and feelings of severe stress as I tried to cope with my sense of responsibility for the fortunes of the party and in particular of its growing number of elected representatives and all its staff (very many more than today).

This book is quite long enough to conclude in the spring of 2006 without including all the events surrounding personal allegations made against me in 2013. All that needs to be said here is that the party referred them to the Metropolitan Police Service, who conducted a thorough and professional investigation, concluding that there should be 'no further action', and they did not send a file to the Crown Prosecution Service for consideration. The party then appointed a QC as an independent investigator, who similarly concluded that there should be no further action as the evidence was insufficient for a disciplinary hearing. In a personal statement in January 2014, I had expressed my regret to anyone who felt any hurt, embarrassment or upset and assured them that this would never have been my intention. In May 2014 I explained that I had accepted Alistair Webster's report saying that there should be 'no further action' as it had been presented to the party, and I apologised 'for any intrusion into personal space', which would have been inadvertent on my part. The party processes, and the original Webster report, were then all reviewed by the independent businesswoman Helena Morrissey, who said in December 2014 that 'every investigation has concluded with no further action to be taken against Lord Rennard' and that 'there is no justification for it remaining ambivalent towards Lord Rennard – he should be just as welcome a participant or guest at party events as any other'.

Through all my involvement in politics, I would still say that I believe without doubt that the overwhelmingly majority of people who engage in politics in any party do so for decent and honourable reasons. I hope that what I have written here helps to demonstrate that.

ACKNOWLEDGEMENTS

By the time I had eventually served six years as chief executive of the Liberal Democrats, been in charge of most of its major election campaigns over a successful twenty-year period, and was also an active member of the House of Lords, I was feeling great strain. My diabetic control had become extremely poor over several years and I was advised in 2009 that I was heading to a significant risk of a stroke or heart attack, unless I changed my lifestyle dramatically. At that point, I stood down as chief executive. My mental health had also been suffering from the stresses of all the various crises that went with the job. Since then, my health has improved, and so I have to begin by thanking everyone who has supported me in this, and in particular family, friends and many excellent NHS professionals for their role.

There are, of course, thousands of activists in the Lib Dems that I would like to thank for working so well with me over all these years and for coping with the great demands made upon them in order to try to bring about the most successful outcomes possible. Huge numbers of people helped in the parliamentary by-elections and far too many people had key roles in them for me to include their names here, but I have included as many of them as I can within the text. Some of my colleagues working with me in the by-elections have also been amongst my best friends and worked with me in many other election campaigns. For the period covered in this book, they include Peter Chegwyn, Pat Wainwright, Paul Jacobs, Bill MacCormick, Paul Rainger, David

Loxton, Candy Piercy, Willie Rennie, Gerald Vernon-Jackson, Shaun Roberts, Hilary Stephenson, Mark Pack and many others.

At HQ, as director of campaigns and elections and then chief executive, I had great cause to be grateful to many people for their tremendous skills and personal support as we built the party up to successful peaks. It is difficult to single out particular members of staff from the twenty-seven years that I worked for the party, but in addition to those already mentioned, I should thank especially Sarah Morris, Kate Heywood, Ben Stoneham and Nigel Bliss, and I should also acknowledge Frances Tattersfield, who worked with me for three years before the 1997 breakthrough and sadly died shortly afterwards. National general election campaigns require professional organisation of hundreds of staff and volunteers and the party could not have achieved its best ever general election results in 2001 and 2005 without the support given to me by my general election managers for those campaigns: Kate Harvey and Alison Suttie. I am also grateful for the support in many of these different campaigns from my friends in the US political consultancy Ridder/Braden. Throughout much of the period covered in this book a good friend and constant support was Tim Razzall, who chaired the general election campaigns of 2001 and 2005. Many other people were generous with their time and with their money. I am sure that the donors still feel that they invested well, and I am very grateful for their tolerance as I kept asking for their support, together with the then party treasurer, Tim Clement-Jones and others, as we raised the funds for our campaigns.

In relation to this book, I am most grateful to Nicola Sangster for her professional skills and encouragement whilst writing it, and to Olivia Beattie and the staff at Biteback for their enthusiasm in publishing it. Iain Dale has been hoping that I would publish a book for at least fifteen years.

Many members of my family and friends have supported me, including in particular 'the Liverpool group', which is based around friends I made in my university days and who have remained close for over thirty-five years. They are partly how I survived all the events in this book. Principal amongst them, of course, is my wife Ann. She has been at the heart of everything written here since the early 1980s and we were both active in the Liverpool Liberals before that. Nothing that I have achieved since that point could have been done without her. She has been one of the super party activists at elections since the 1970s, and I hope that the party may take greater note of the role that she has played in it. Support from her and many people has, of course, also been crucial to me in more recent years.

Finally, I would like to thank the party leaders, candidates and people throughout the Liberal Democrats who gave me the opportunities to serve the party and to be engaged in politics, striving to advance a cause in which I still believe passionately, and also everyone who reads this memoir and who may feel inspired to try to do something for the public good, through whichever party or cause.

CHAPTER 1

AN UNUSUAL INTRODUCTION TO POLITICS IN LIVERPOOL

AN UNUSUAL FAMILY BACKGROUND

Cecil was a Yorkshire lad. He grew up in the town of Bridlington. He spent a good deal of his time standing at the edge of the cliffs, looking out over the North Sea towards Jutland. In the years to come the greatest naval battle of the First World War would be fought in those waters, with great grey leviathans pounding one another with twelve-inch guns.

Cecil came from a family of builders and local politicians, but when he left Bridlington Grammar School he decided to train as a dentist and eventually opened a surgery in Liverpool. He was twenty-five when war broke out, and volunteered to serve as a soldier in the Liverpool Scottish Regiment. In 1917, he went 'over the top' with rifle and bayonet fixed, into no-man's land to attack the German positions. There was a deafening explosion, with much fire and smoke. Cecil was tossed into the air. When he came around, sometime later, he was alone on the battlefield, his body full of shrapnel and his left leg severely damaged. He lay there for thirty-six hours, before being picked up by German stretcher-bearers and taken to a field hospital. He underwent the first of many operations, and his shattered left leg was amputated.

The Germans sent him back to England. He was eventually fitted with an artificial leg and began to work as a dentist again. One Sunday, he went to All Saints', his local parish church. The vicar suggested that he should have felt proud to have had his leg blown off for his country. Cecil never went to church again, unless he could possibly help it.

Cecil's surname was Rennard, and he was my father. His story, and the stories of many others, taught me that there is no glory in war. There is courage, there are heroic acts, and there is self-sacrifice, but no glory.

This was how my elder brother Edward, an Anglican priest, began his Remembrance Day sermon in 2009. My father had been born 121 years earlier in 1888, when Queen Victoria still had more than twelve years left of her reign. Cecil Rennard was twenty-eight when he was sent to fight in the First World War, losing his left leg within a few months. Many of his relatives, including his brother Frank, did not come back. I still have the letter written by Frank Rennard's commanding officer to my grandmother explaining how he died 'instantly and without pain' when a German shell landed in his trench.

By the time that Cecil was sixty-one, he was a widower. He married my mother, Jean Winifred Watson (his second wife), in 1950. Following a prostate operation, no children were expected. But Edward arrived in 1951, I followed in 1960 (when my father was seventy-one) and my younger brother Peter was born in 1962. My father retired as a dentist in 1961, and we moved from the home in Liverpool's Old Swan, which had also been his dental surgery, to a modest, semi-detached house some two miles away in Wavertree.

I have very clear memories of my father, even though he was to die in 1963, aged seventy-four, when I was just over three years old. My mother used to bring him his breakfast of bacon and eggs on a tray, which he would sit up in bed to eat. I sat next to him, watching him enjoy it, and then my job was to wipe the 'eggy plate' with the bread and butter, and this was my breakfast.

I remember standing up on the back seat of his car, an Austin A40, as he reversed it from the garage along the front drive into the cul-de-sac that was Wavertree Green. We visited places like Sefton Park, where I tried kicking a football, but generally failed as the ball seemed to come up to my knees.

It is hardly surprising that someone whose formative years were in the Edwardian era came across to me as a somewhat stern man. I remember only four words that he ever spoke to me. I was playing in the hallway and he was having his afternoon nap in an armchair in the living room. His words were: 'A little less noise.' Afternoons were boring as both my parents slept in front of the horse racing on the TV, and I was disappointed with the new brother I had been promised I would be able to play with, but who turned out to be a baby in a pram that did nothing but sleep.

The shock to my father's body of losing his leg was possibly what brought on his diabetic condition. In the 1920s, he would have been one of the first people saved from death by insulin injections and his relatively long life owed everything to the treatment. But this condition, the fact that he was a heavy smoker, and two heart attacks (the latter one in hospital whilst recovering from the first) eventually took his life.

His funeral stands out in my memory as the day that there were more cars parked outside our house than I had ever seen before. The line of them stretched from our house all the way to the end of the road. Neighbours told me how, for some time afterwards, I used to walk around clinging onto my father's hat, unable to understand where he had gone.

My mother had met my father at a wedding in Leeds, then moved to Liverpool to become his dental nurse, and eventually his wife. She was born in 1923, one of five children of a small builder from Market Weighton in Yorkshire's East Riding. Her own mother had been very ill through much of her childhood, suffering great pain from the cancer that eventually killed her. Throughout and after this illness my mother's eldest sister, my Auntie Greta, did much to bring up her younger siblings. Only one of the five went to grammar school. My mum left school at fourteen, trained as a nurse, and spent the Second World War working at Lloyds Hospital, Bridlington.

My father's death left my mother with three boys, aged twelve, three and one; but not necessarily a house to live in and no real means of support. For reasons that I never understood, my father's will (re-written shortly after his second marriage), gave the house that he owned in Newcastle to the daughter and only child from his first marriage, Marjorie, whilst it then split his remaining assets (mostly our house in Wavertree) 50 per cent between Marjorie and his two grown-up step children from his first marriage, and 50 per cent to my mother. I assume that relations between my mother and Marjorie and 'the other side of the family' must have been very poor as they pressed for their share of the assets to be paid immediately. In this event, my mother and her three young children would have been made homeless.

My mum was not good at dealing with legal and financial matters; she had never done so before. She didn't even understand that when the bank paid various bills on her behalf that it would be deducted from the £1,000 fixed sum left for her in my father's will. The bank also appointed lawyers to act on her behalf and who contested the will. But the outcome of this legal action was very unsatisfactory from our point of view. The sale of the house was put on hold for the 'duration of her life'. The judge did not provide for the possibility that she would die whilst two of her children were still at school and that they would be left without the home in which they were growing up.

My mum died quite suddenly and unexpectedly of hypertensive heart disease at the age of fifty-four, when I was still sixteen and Peter had just turned fifteen. Her death made Peter and me orphaned and homeless. Our elder brother, Edward, was only three weeks away from getting married to a fellow student, Margaret, at Theological College in Lincoln. The 'other side of the family' once again insisted on their share of the proceeds from the sale of the house that we had grown up in and which we called our home.

In the years after my father's death, the stresses on my mother were considerable. She needed to care for us and earn a living to support us. She had one of the two downstairs rooms in the house turned into a nursery, and she became a registered childminder for about ten or twelve children aged three and four, whom she looked after during the day with the help of a young assistant. Next-door neighbours on one side objected to the potential noise from the nursery and organised a petition to try to stop her doing this. But other neighbours said that she had to earn her living somehow and going out to work somewhere whilst bringing up a three-year-old and a one-year-old was hardly practical. She also moved her bed, and the bunk beds that Peter and I slept in, to the front bedroom. This allowed her to let out the back bedroom to lodgers. The garage was also let out as we no longer had a car. Edward's education was disrupted. The private Liverpool College fees could no longer be afforded. But our father had been a Freemason and they ran a boarding school at Bushey near Watford, which was exclusively for the sons of Masons who had died. At the age of twelve, he was packed off there for his secondary education.

Whilst my father had been strongly Conservative in his views and a modest contributor to their funds, my mother was completely disinterested in party politics and apparently took the view that 'politicians were all the same'. That was until one day, not long after my father died, when the local Liberal councillor Cyril Carr[1] knocked on the door. This event eventually proved to be one of the most significant of my life. My mother had been having trouble claiming her widowed mothers' allowance. 'I'll vote for whoever gets it for me,' she said. Councillor Carr made the seemingly strange request of asking if he could come in and use the telephone. He rang the relevant department there and then. When he put the phone down, he said to my mother: 'Well, Mrs Rennard, you have got your widowed mothers' allowance.' She, like many of our neighbours, found him to be the one person that you could trust to 'get things done' and she became a Liberal supporter.

---

[1] Cyril Carr became the first Liberal councillor in Liverpool in modern times in 1962, one of two Liberal candidates who won in the city that year, partly on the back of a surge in Liberal support following the Orpington by-election. He was later to become leader of the city council, chairman of the Liberal National Executive and president of the party.

Peter and I grew up hardly knowing our elder brother Edward (he was nine years older than me and eleven years older than Peter), but we enjoyed an annual trip to London when we went to see him at boarding school. My own primary education was largely a happy experience. Mosspits Lane County Primary School could count amongst its former pupils Edwina Currie (the 'eggs' minister), Derek Hatton (the Militant), Anthony Bevins (the journalist) and Peter Goldsmith (the former Attorney-General). My after-dinner speeches would later claim that 'they must have been putting something in the school dinners'.

With hindsight, I became very aware that I lacked the role model of a father, and regretted that I had nobody to take me to football matches or teach me about DIY or cars. However, I enjoyed activities based around Holy Trinity Church in Wavertree, including the Boys' Brigade, the choir, and their associated football teams. I captained our 'Liverpool 32nd Company' Boys' Brigade team whilst acting as goalie. I was a very keen swimmer, going to the baths in Picton Road most days of the week, swimming a mile aged ten and becoming my school's freestyle champion in the swimming gala. Further along the road from our church was St Barnabas's, where Paul McCartney had once sung in the choir, and this was the area where the Beatles had grown up. As a child, you were always asked if you knew the Beatles as soon as people found out that you were from Liverpool.

Further misfortune struck my mother towards the end of my time at primary school. She developed severe rheumatoid arthritis. This was an extremely painful condition, and she had to close the nursery for a fortnight for hospital treatment (whilst Peter and I were sent to stay with nearby family friends). When she came out of hospital, none of the children returned to the nursery as the parents had (correctly) worked out that her disability now meant that she was unable to run it.

I had always done much of the shopping on my way back from school, but neighbours and church friends now assisted with this as my mother could only get out of the house when I pushed her wheelchair.

6

Peter and I did what we could to help with housework and we were provided with a 'home help' by social services for a couple of hours each week to assist with cleaning.

Our family doctor was extremely good and my mother had all the treatment that could be offered at the time, but it rarely alleviated the pain completely. Occasionally I had to phone Dr Lavelle in the middle of the night and ask him to come and give her an injection. She would have benefited from selling the house and moving to a home that was more suited to her disability. But 'our' home was not our own, and could not be sold as it was in trust as a result of my father's will. I therefore had to stand behind her every time she went up the staircase, pushing the hips that would no longer function. It must also have been humiliating for her that, as her young teenage son, I had to lift her in and out of the bath and wash her feet, as she could not do this unaided, but she never showed any sign of this.

Our financial position was very tight and I was always aware of the stress that this caused. Fortunately, we had a little extra help from the Freemasons and from the Dental Benevolent Fund. This provided for a few treats, such as an annual holiday to Bridlington, where we rented a cheap flat in a house where one of my mother's wartime nursing colleagues lived. I hated counting out the cash that we had for the holiday and dividing it up into the couple of pounds that we could afford to spend each day. In later life, I would think about how many politicians would have had similar experiences of growing up with a single disabled parent, or living on benefits and receiving free school meals.

When I was about thirteen, my mother went in to Liverpool's Broadgreen Hospital to have one of the earliest hip replacements in this country, using techniques and an artificial joint pioneered by Sir John Charnley. Peter and I spent the month of August whilst she was in hospital at our Auntie Greta's in York. But when our mum needed to go back in to hospital for two weeks when I was fifteen, I felt that, as I already did much of the running of the house, I really did not want to go and stay elsewhere. Whilst she was in hospital, I continued living in the house, went to school every day, visited her every evening and looked after Peter. Neighbours kept a watchful eye over us.

If my mother had a bad night with a lot of pain, she would occasionally oversleep. One morning in June 1977, Peter woke me to say that Mum had overslept and he was dashing to get the bus to his school. This was not extraordinary, so I got up and dressed, made my mother her usual breakfast and took it to her room. Then I couldn't wake her. I shook her and there was no sign of breathing. For the first time in my life, I went into shock. I rang the Rectory not far away, where Bob and Rachel Metcalf were great family friends. Rachel soon came over with another friend. I was dazed, sort of knew that nothing was to be done, but I couldn't take it in that she had died. Bob arrived shortly afterwards on his bike. It was clear that they didn't want to confirm what I already knew. In an effort to protect me, Bob told me that 'it didn't look very good'. Nobody told me much whilst I sat in the living room in my school uniform and cried.

An ambulance came, we drew the downstairs curtains and I went to the Rectory. From there, Peter's school was telephoned and he was brought to join me. Edward was contacted at Theological College at Lincoln and he arranged to come to Liverpool immediately. I had a few visitors at the Rectory, including a few school friends. The rest of the week was taken up with contacting people to tell them what had happened and making arrangements for the funeral on the Friday. I didn't know what would happen to Peter or me, but assured him when he asked that we would not have to go and live in a children's home. Holy Trinity Church was completely packed with several hundred people for the funeral. My mother was well known and respected in the parish. As a very kind person, she had become a confidante to many people who needed someone to talk to, and she was always home. Sometimes, when she heard things, she shared the burden of that knowledge with me, knowing that I could always keep a secret. As someone who was largely housebound, she was also willing to let friends drop their children off to be minded, or come to our house after school for a few hours whenever that helped them.

On the night after our mum died, Peter slept in a neighbour's house as he found that easier. The Heeneys were an extraordinarily kind family who lived almost opposite us. Peter was eventually to spend the next year staying with them, but it was particularly difficult for him seeing our old house every day. He also resented being in a more structured household, where he did not have the same complete freedom to do as he pleased that he had previously enjoyed. For some months, I stayed on my own at our old house and spent much of the summer trying to sort out everything that needed to be done there. I did not return to school for three weeks, until after my elder brother's wedding in Northampton.

I did not know what I was going to do. Cyril Carr was a solicitor and handled the legal issues for us. We were unable to avoid the sale of the house as only half of it was ours. The Carr family offered to take me in and let me live with them until I finished my A levels. But I knew that it would be very hard to go from the level of responsibility that I'd had in helping to run a home (at sixteen) to feeling that I was a child again (albeit a welcome guest) in somebody else's family. Our best friends in Wavertree included the headteacher and his wife at the local blind school. Derek and Lillian Marks were simply the kindest, most decent and generous people that you could ever meet. They came up with a suggestion. There were a number of bedsit flats at the back of the blind school intended for members of staff, but which were currently vacant. On the understanding that I would have to move out as soon as a member of staff might require one, I was able to move in.

My secondary school, the Liverpool Blue Coat School, was a very academic institution. My headteacher, Mr H. P. Arnold-Craft, was concerned that I continued to make good academic progress through the second half of my sixth form. Oxbridge was the aim and he said that the school would obviously be worried if my studies suffered from my unusual domestic arrangements. I certainly felt that the other boys in the sixth form had distinct advantages over me in terms of time to do homework. I had to do my own shopping, washing and drying, cleaning (a very small flat), cooking and washing up etc. before doing mine. I was a diligent student at this time and enjoyed working hard on my A level history, English literature and economics courses.

I had to make sure that my studies were not seen to suffer from my domestic arrangements. I had had to miss the exams at the end of the lower sixth as they came immediately after my mother's death and concentration on revision was impossible. But I worked hard for the mock A levels in the final year and came first, first and joint first in my three chosen subjects. I felt that school could hardly say that my arrangements were adversely affecting my studies.

My circumstances were really without precedent and therefore not provided for. A family taking me in would have been able to claim financial support to look after me, but I could not claim such support for looking after myself. My only income was the £7.45 child benefit, which I was now able to collect myself. Collecting it, however, meant that I had to seek the permission of a teacher to go to the post office in a 'free period'. My budget did not stretch to buying *The Guardian* every day. Some years earlier, I had been to our newsagent and cancelled the *Daily Mail* that was my mother's staple reading but which I argued was 'bad for my education'. I ordered *The Guardian* instead (much to her annoyance) but got away with this as I had said that I needed it for school. Once living on my own, and mindful of the 12p that it cost, I stayed behind after school each day to read the sixth form copy before going back to my flat to cook my tea and start my homework.

My interest in politics began with our family friendship with the Carr family. Cyril had fought Liverpool's Church ward for the first time in 1958, losing to the Tory by a very large margin. Over the years he refined his campaigning style to make his election leaflets more about the local issues in the ward. Then he began issuing his 'Church Ward Matters' leaflets outside of election time as well as during elections. His election agent, Alec Gerrard, hit upon rebranding the newsletters as 'Focus'. They were issued regularly in the run-up to the May 1962 elections in which he was first elected.

It was a year later that he knocked on our door and first helped my mother. A smart political operator, Cyril had me (and occasionally Peter) delivering his 'Focus' leaflets from an early age. I delivered them to our cul-de-sac, Wavertree Green, and the near side of the main road as I wasn't then allowed to cross it without an adult. I was happy to do this and he answered my questions about things that I had seen in the news. I followed news programmes fairly intensively from the age of about eleven, coming home from school at lunchtimes to listen to *The World at One*, and whenever I asked my mum to explain things, she often said, 'You will have to ask Mr Carr.'

When I was nearly thirteen, I remember helping in the city council elections that brought the Liberal Party to power in Liverpool – the first major city in modern times to be run by Liberals. Less than a year later, I was standing in my school elections as a Liberal during the February 1974 general election and helping deliver leaflets in Cyril Carr's campaign to try to become Wavertree's Liberal MP. We were disappointed by his result as Liberal efforts were spread very thinly across the country, and local election successes the year before did not translate into a parliamentary win. Cyril satisfied himself by becoming leader-elect of the new city council and suggested that I should come along to one of the local party meetings. I used to say later that it was the 'usual Liberal Party meeting because nobody wanted to be treasurer'. I sat quietly at the back listening when the item of electing a treasurer was raised. After a period of silence, Cyril said: 'Well, Christopher is very good at mathematics at school, I am sure that he could do it!' I looked at the books, decided that 'it was just sums' and so, just before I reached the age of fourteen, I agreed to become the treasurer of the Church Ward Liberal Association. My mother had to be the signatory for the cheques and by the next month they had a printed balance sheet and draft budget for the year.

As a teenager, I enjoyed the company and conversation of adults probably more than that of children of my own age. I could hold lengthy discussions about politics with teachers in lessons, whilst the rest of the class was delighted to avoid dictation. I attended various party events, mostly staying quiet as I was initially quite shy about speaking in formal meetings. But I found that I could organise groups of adults in canvass teams, record the responses that they got on the doorsteps and engage in many of the activities associated with electioneering. This became an enjoyable and interesting hobby that broke up the intensive periods of study associated with my school. I also kept up with the very academic pace there with very good grades in eleven O levels. We were almost all encouraged at school to think of Oxbridge, but my own thoughts prior to my mother's death were that it would never really be practical for me to leave home. My elder brother had already left and got married, my younger brother would not cope in the foreseeable future with all the responsibility of looking after our mum, and I assumed that I would be the one left with the responsibility of looking after her and the house.

Against all this background, my first experiences of real depression hit me in my teens. My life felt difficult as my mum struggled to cope with two growing teenagers at home. I probably experienced the sort of teenage angst that is not uncommon, but I thought that life was particularly unfair to me. My elder brother was effectively a stranger to me as we had only lived in the same house for a few years, when he lived there between teacher training and theological colleges. I fought with my younger brother, as many siblings two years apart would often do, and my mother sometimes despaired. I didn't feel too bad when I was enjoying school, making good academic progress and keeping up with other things such as the church choir and hobbies like astronomy. But school became very difficult at times.

My levels of physical activity declined as I concentrated on homework, and my stress levels increased with the considerable academic pressure at school. I found comfort in the very unhealthy patterns that we had at home. With a lot of weight gain, my self-confidence and self-esteem declined, and becoming significantly overweight at school makes you an obvious target for bullying, together with the fact that you associated and spoke with adults more comfortably than with many of the boys your own age. I remember being ridiculed because I supported what a Liberal spokesperson had said on the radio that morning about there being 'nothing wrong with two men holding hands together in public'. It was much harder to support gay equality at a boys' school in the mid-1970s than it is today. Verbal abuse and taunting could be really hurtful. But sometimes it was more violent. Being hit over the head with a very large textbook sometimes provoked migraines. The experience of bullying gave me feelings of quite severe depression that sometimes didn't lift for several weeks. I didn't recognise this as an illness, but I went through phases of composing letters in my head explaining why I had decided not to continue with life any more. Nobody knew of this, I confided in no one, and I tried to escape the bad feelings by burying myself in books, studying and politics.

Sometimes I also had occasional feelings of anger and resentment against my mother of a kind that may not be uncommon amongst sixteen-year-olds. But I never had the chance to resolve mine before she died three weeks before my seventeenth birthday. Shock and the other emotions that go with bereavement continued for years. But my mental health appeared to improve as I gained my independence in my flat and pursued my academic and political interests with great determination. School also became much better as boys became young men, acquired a greater sense of responsibility, and both verbal and physical bullying largely became a thing of the past for me. Some of my best friends were amongst those who boarded at the school; often because their fathers were in the military serving overseas. They occasionally came over on Sunday evenings to avoid the dreaded boarding school Sunday teas, which had been prepared on Saturday and supplemented by cold leftovers from Sunday lunch. I cooked a good chicken curry or steak and chips – and we dared to share a bottle of wine, feeling very grown up.

I achieved three A grades in my A levels. Whilst some of my fellow pupils who had come behind me academically now headed for Oxford or Cambridge, it seemed to me that this was still not a practical prospect for me. I had retained what possessions I could from our old house and set up my own flat. Going to live in a college hall of residence was a great thing for my contemporaries, but they still had parental homes to go back to outside term time. If I went away to Oxbridge, I would have had nowhere to come home to after the eight-week term. I had to maintain my own permanent home – so doing this and moving away to university was just not something I felt that I could do. So, Liverpool University was my only real option for higher education, and they were very willing to take me.

I considered studying law. With hindsight, I probably should have done that, but I gave up this idea when I realised that I would only really wish to defend the innocent and prosecute the guilty. History was another alternative subject that I should have considered more, but I opted for politics and economics as I thought that this would best reflect my interests and abilities. I found, however, that whilst I was good at maths, I did not enjoy the heavily mathematical and very monetarist approach in the economics department. So, it was hardly surprising that I was more interested in the practical side of politics than the academic one.

Since becoming ward treasurer whilst still thirteen, I had progressed to become secretary of the Liverpool Wavertree constituency at sixteen. I subsequently became chair of the Liverpool Young Liberals and then the University Liberals. The Liberal Party had run Liverpool City Council from 1974 to 1976 and then again from 1978 to 1979. I engaged with relish in the political battle in Liverpool, which was increasingly becoming one between the Liberals and a Labour Party that was dominated by the Militant Tendency.

THE EDGE HILL BY-ELECTION THAT
SAVED THE LIBERAL PARTY

In 1977, the Labour MP for Liverpool Edge Hill, Sir Arthur Irvine, announced that he would be resigning from Parliament in protest at his de-selection and replacement by Labour left-winger Bob Wareing. The constituency was one of the few in the country in which we had come second to Labour in the 1974 general elections and where we had marginally increased our vote share (to 26 per cent in the second one in October). This was the time of the Lib–Lab Pact that was deeply unpopular. Jeremy Thorpe's resignation as Liberal leader following allegations about paying off his former 'gay lover' was headline news. (He was later charged with and acquitted of conspiracy to murder.) The party was regularly being beaten by both the National Front and the National Party (both fascist) in parliamentary by-elections.

Led by David Alton, probably the most energetic Liberal in Britain at the time, the Edge Hill Liberals in May 1977 won three of the four wards in the constituency, in spite of the very difficult political conditions for the Liberal Party that prevailed at the time. Edge Hill was a tiny constituency of just 18,000 houses covering four square miles between the city centre and the suburb of Wavertree. David Alton had come to Liverpool's Christ's College to train to teach. As an active Young Liberal in Brentwood, he was attracted to Liverpool by the constant coverage in the weekly *Liberal News* about councillors Cyril Carr and Trevor Jones.[2] David became close to Trevor, having knocked on his door (wearing a green corduroy jacket as Trevor recalls) offering to help the Liberals. Trevor then led the campaign to 'break out from Church ward' and win seats in other parts of Liverpool, with his wife Doreen standing as the candidate for the next-door Old Swan ward,

---

2   Trevor had joined the Liberal Party when he was opposing a ring-road scheme in the city
    and was first elected to Liverpool City Council in a by-election in November 1968, joining
    Cyril Carr in Church ward.

and leading community-based campaigns based on 'Focus' leaflets, targeted street letters and petitions.

In 1972, whilst still a student, David Alton was himself elected to the city council in the Low Hill ward, then part of Bessie Braddock's old 'Exchange' constituency, but soon to be part of Edge Hill. The following year, he was returned to the new Low Hill/Smithdown ward and helped to ensure that Liberals won every council seat in the Edge Hill constituency. There were forty-eight Liberals on the new 99-member Liverpool City Council. In the meantime, a revolution was taking place in how the Liberal Party fought elections. This was demonstrated by a parliamentary by-election where the swing from Conservative to Liberal exceeded that of the famous Orpington by-election ten years earlier. The by-election was in Sutton & Cheam in December 1972 and the campaign was masterminded by Trevor Jones, with David Alton as his protégé.

The campaign inspired by the Liverpool activists in Sutton was along the same lines as they had helped to pioneer in Liverpool. The first 'Focus' leaflets to be produced outside Liverpool highlighted local campaigns in Sutton. Their techniques were denounced by some of the Liberal Party's 'old guard', but when polling demonstrated the growing support for the local Liberal Graham Tope in the by-election, the national party also got behind it. The swing from Conservative to Liberal was 32.6 per cent – a post-war record. The momentum from this by-election was what effectively rescued the Liberal Party from the near-fatal disaster of the 1970 general election. Three further Liberal parliamentary by-election gains maintained the momentum the following year. Trevor became known as 'Jones the Vote' and was elected president of the Liberal Party.

The hoped-for 'Liberal revival' under Jeremy Thorpe in 1974 did not, however, materialise. Three Liverpool seats – Wavertree with Cyril Carr, Toxteth with Trevor Jones, and Edge Hill with David Alton – had headed the BBC's Liberal target seat list that night. But the results were bitterly disappointing as newfound local-election support did not turn into national votes within just a year or two. Cyril Carr suffered his first heart attack that summer. Trevor (who had originally wanted to fight Edge Hill) tried his luck at Gillingham in Kent for the October election. But David Alton persisted with his campaign in Edge Hill. Whilst I learned about politics from many people, these three men – Cyril Carr, Trevor Jones and David Alton – were my first major political mentors.

The anticipated Edge Hill by-election was my central political preoccupation for two years from 1977, but we often thought that it wouldn't happen. Sir Arthur Irvine never quite got around to carrying out his threat to resign his seat. In the summer of 1978, everyone expected Prime Minister Jim Callaghan to call an election in the autumn. I had finished my A levels that summer and made friends with University Liberals, including Jeff Lamb, who was an active Colne Valley Young Liberal, before coming to Liverpool. I volunteered on virtually every day of that summer in the Edge Hill constituency, working with others to prepare for the expected general election, in which David Alton wanted to give me the title 'campaign director'; I declined, preferring not to have a title. Almost all the leading Liberals in the city were drafted in to the campaign. I knew every road in the constituency well, if not every house, as day after day we knocked on doors, took up local issues and delivered leaflets. Under David Alton's guidance I began writing some of these leaflets, worked on recruiting more local helpers and building the party's local organisation.

One day in September 1977, I was in an office owned by local estate agents,[3] using their ink duplicator to print out all of the instruction sheets for helpers in the forthcoming campaign, when I received a phone call there to say that the Prime Minister was expected to call the general election in a TV broadcast at 6 p.m. The key members of the team gathered at David Alton's house to watch the announcement, immediately before going around all our leaflet distributors. We had

---

3   One of whom was Liverpool Liberal Councillor Richard Kemp, later Leader of the Lib Dems on the Local Government Association.

volunteers lined up to deliver the first leaflet of the campaign across the whole constituency that evening. We had had it printed and sealed in bags to preserve confidentiality in anticipation of the election announcement as we wanted to ensure that we would have the first word in the constituency campaign. We crowded into his living room as we watched Jim Callaghan's broadcast. Then we began to realise that he wasn't going to call an election after all. The subsequent sense of anti-climax was massive. David Alton's small house was effectively the campaign HQ, so some of us then began tidying up the mess that went with trying to run an election out of somebody's home. Others just went to the pub in disgust at the non-election.

The threat of a by-election remained if Sir Arthur Irvine made good his threat to resign. I helped to recruit some fresh blood to the party in the university that autumn, and we all got to know and work with David Alton's continuing campaign. There was little money, no professional agent, but a small grant from the Joseph Rowntree Reform Trust paid for a young man called Robert Littler to be in the small office in David Alton's house answering the phone and helping to deal with the huge volume of casework that our campaigning generated. Then, in December 1978, Sir Arthur Irvine died. If it was possible to step up campaigning, then we stepped it up. Every year in the Liverpool wards with Liberal councillors we delivered Christmas cards from them to every home. 'Focus' leaflets became weekly, reflecting the number of issues being taken up. There were then only eleven Liberal MPs across the country, but most of them now made regular visits. David Alton was also by then chairman of the council's housing committee and was able to make positive announcements and achieve good coverage in the *Liverpool Echo* almost every evening.

Only one thing threatened to derail our plans. David had acted as the election agent for two council by-elections in the next-door Kirkdale constituency in late 1977. We had won them both. But the Labour Party seeking to block his candidature sent sets of all the Liberal leaflets to the police, claiming that he must have broken electoral law by spending more than legally allowed in producing so many of them. It was seen as a smear and on the day that he was formally charged with the election offence, the *Liverpool Echo* led with the headline 'Liberal hits out at dirty tricks'. The case was taken to a committal hearing where David's solicitor, Liverpool's famous E. Rex Makin, was brilliant in demolishing on the witness stand the case of the Labour councillors who had brought the complaint. The printers could back up the election accounts and the case was dismissed by the stipendiary magistrate. Many of David's supporters sat through the court case (and I learned much of what I know about election expense rules from it). When we spontaneously stood up and cheered the magistrate's ruling, we were all threatened with contempt of court and had to sit down promptly.

Two and a half days in court had ended on the Wednesday lunchtime with a full city council meeting that afternoon. So we adjourned to a pub to celebrate, and arranged that David would come in slightly late to the council meeting, at the far end from the Liberal councillors and where I usually sat amongst the public observing proceedings. He would then work his way slowly round to the Liberal benches to take his seat as deputy leader of the city council. Again, we cheered loudly, interrupting proceedings, whilst the Labour members felt incensed by the magistrate's decision and David's stage-managed entrance. When council meetings finished, we often adjourned to the Yuet Ben, Liverpool's first Chinese restaurant. That night, about thirty of us went there, filling three large tables in the centre of the restaurant. Unfortunately, Labour's agent in Edge Hill had arrived just before us hoping for a quiet meal with his wife. How tragic it was that so many of our champagne corks ended up popping in their direction…

As Christmas 1978 approached, we still didn't know if we would get our by-election. It was clear that the Labour government was coming to the end of its life and might fall if the devolution referendums in March 1979 were lost. This would cause the Nationalists to lose confidence in them, and, with the Liberals having brought the Lib–Lab Pact to an end in summer 1978, Labour would be wary of risking defeat in any by-election, but were clinging to the hope that the Liberal MPs would still not want a general election that spring. Fortunately, Alan Beith, who was the Liberal Chief Whip at the time, had enjoyed good relations with his Labour counterparts as a result of the Lib–Lab Pact. He was able to exploit this with an effective sleight of hand. He persuaded the Labour whips that Labour wouldn't lose a by-election in Edge Hill. He said that whilst we couldn't win, we could do well, and that a by-election would damage the Conservatives (who would come third). The Liberal Party, it was suggested, would then be in a stronger position, and would be unlikely to vote to bring down the government. The Labour whips moved the writ for the by-election to be held on 29 March 1979.

The Liberal Party was at just 5 per cent in the national opinion polls (down from the 18 per cent we polled in October 1974 when David Alton had been 6,171 votes behind Sir Arthur Irvine). But canvassing in the by-election was a real joy for me and my fellow Liberals as local people talked about 'how hard David Alton worked' for their community. Voters became very aware of who the battle was between (Labour and Liberal), and we easily got large numbers of posters in people's windows, thereby re-enforcing the message that we could win. We suspected Labour of 'dirty tricks' at the start of the campaign when a man, following a conversation with him in a pub, was tricked into standing with the description 'Gay Liberal', drawing attention to Liberal embarrassment over the scandal surrounding Jeremy Thorpe. The excellent investigative local reporter Ian Craig was able to identify a Labour activist as having arranged the nomination.

National party machines did not run by-elections in those days and with all our experience of election successes, we felt that we knew what we were doing. But we were very grateful for the organisational discipline brought to the campaign by the party's most experienced agent John Spiller (who had been Liberal MP John Pardoe's agent in North Cornwall). I certainly honed my own organisational skills listening to him and watching him in action. Amongst other roles in the campaign, I was in charge of public meetings in an era when many people wanted to see and hear who they might vote for. Sandy Walkington from the Liberal Whips' Office in the House of Commons was sent up to get MPs and peers to speak at these evening meetings and to campaign during the daytime. We held eleven public meetings across the constituency, each with a packed audience, around 1,600 people attending in total.

Liberals across Britain knew that it was a 'must-win' campaign for the party and came to help in their thousands. Accommodating visiting party workers to enable them to help for several days was a massive task. This was organised by Ann McTegart, who had known David Alton in college days as 'the mad Liberal who puts election posters in the window at his hall of residence'. She later taught with a friend of his and was persuaded to become the founding chair of the Edge Hill Liberal Association in 1972. Four people had met in his bedsit and, as David wanted to be the candidate, the rest of them had to be the constituency party 'officers'. For the by-election, Ann persuaded Liberals and friends all over Merseyside to billet the visiting activists. The last week required the use of Holy Trinity Church hall for sleeping-bag accommodation, and which seemed eminently suitable when visited, only for a fight to break out at the Youth Club disco on the night that we were due to take it over, as a result of which most of the windows had been smashed. Young Liberals arriving with sleeping bags wondered what on earth they had let themselves in for.

Trevor Jones wrote most of the leaflets for the campaign, as he had for Sutton & Cheam seven years earlier. I wrote some of the local area specials, as well as printing many of them. Years later, Tony Greaves told me that he had stood at the back of the by-election HQ on the first floor of the old Liberal Club in Smithdown Road and had watched me greeting the visiting helpers, handing them bundles of leaflets and sending them on their way. I was eighteen, so he asked who I was. 'That's Chris Rennard,' was the reply, and, unbeknown to me, the discussion turned into one about how 'he will be chief agent one day'.

I met a lot of people in the party through the by-election. Hugh Jones, the secretary-general of the party, came up for a day and asked what he could do to help. I didn't have a car, and he did, so I got him to spend the day driving me around the local deliverers with bundles of leaflets for them. David Steel arrived much earlier than expected one day when none of the more senior people in the campaign were around. He didn't know anybody in the HQ and was very relieved when I started introducing him to all the helpers after seeing him standing alone for quite a while.

All seemed to be going well, and my own analysis of the canvassing (we were on almost 50 per cent 'definites') suggested that we would get 66 per cent of the vote, but this seemed too good to be true. Our eve-of-poll rally was due to have about half of the Parliamentary Liberal Party speak at it. But that was the night of the vote of confidence in Jim Callaghan's government. Sandy Walkington was able to rope in several Liberal peers to replace them, including George Mackie – a great stalwart of the Scottish Liberal Party in his heyday. He had clearly had a lot of whisky as he told the meeting that he 'loved them all'. But the Edge Hill audience loved this eccentric Scottish lord. Rumours about the result of the vote of confidence went around the meeting. We heard first that the government had won by one vote. This was a great relief as we felt certain of victory in the by-election on that basis, but quite unsure of the effect on polling day if it was also to be the first day of a general election campaign. Then the rumour went around that the government had *lost* by one vote. This one proved to be correct.

The confidence vote could easily have gone the other way. Clement Freud, then a Liberal MP, had spent the last fortnight of the campaign working in the constituency (having booked into the Holiday Inn for the period) and he had invested heavily at the bookmakers on a Liberal win. Some months earlier he had introduced a Private Member's Bill to Parliament introducing 'Freedom of Information'. The Labour government was opposed to this. But the government Whips' Office rang on the day of the confidence vote to say that 'if Mr Freud was able to "accidentally" miss his train from Liverpool Lime Street, then the government would concede to his Freedom of Information Bill'. Freud kept them guessing and did not respond to their suggestion, but returned to Westminster unobserved and hid in a basement committee room before popping out at the last minute to cast his vote; bringing down the government and becoming responsible for the beginning of the general election campaign.

Freud returned to Liverpool overnight and in the morning took over the 'greasy spoon' Italian café opposite the HQ, cooking bacon and eggs for all those who had been on the 'Good Morning' delivery since 5 a.m. He could be either the rudest man I have ever known, or the most charming, when he wanted to be. He particularly hated smoking, but in the smoke-filled pubs of Edge Hill he shook hands with voters and persuaded them that 'David Alton was their man'. He never told me how much he made at the bookies, but it was a substantial sum (he had invested £1,000 on his own by-election win in 1973 at 33:1).

The result of the election was a stunning 30.6 per cent swing from Labour to Liberal, a Liberal majority of 8,133 and a Conservative lost deposit.

Candidate	Votes	%	±
David Alton (Liberal)	12,945	64.1	+36.8
Bob Wareing (Labour)	4,612	23.8	−28.1
Nick Ward (Conservative)	1,906	9.4	−11.3

Even the *Daily Mail* (northern edition) ran the front-page headline 'Liberals by a landslide'. It was the perfect start to the general election campaign for a Liberal Party that had been previously fearing anni-hilation. Opinion-poll support for the party doubled overnight from 5 per cent to 10 per cent. David Steel had newfound credibility based on the win, and his very effective TV performances and high profile during the remainder of the campaign helped increase that share to 14 per cent on polling day.

Eleven of the now fourteen Liberal MPs, including David Alton, retained their seats. David Penhaligon, pursuing a Cornish brand of 'community politics', increased his majority from under 500 to nearly 9,000. The overwhelming sense in the Liberal Party after the 1979 general election was one of relief. I attended the Liberal Assembly in Margate that year, where David Alton was clearly the hero of the party. He even persuaded the delegates to support his motion calling for all public transport to be made free of charge. Clement Freud had spoken against, saying that it was 'nutty' and everyone knew it was unaffordable. But when David Alton waved his parliamentary travel warrant allowing him free travel, the delegates voted for the same free public transport for everyone.

The efforts that I had made studying for my A levels, and in political campaigning, had dominated my mental concentration for the two years after my mother died. I had worked phenomenally hard, partly as a means of blocking out any feelings of bereavement. But with some of the election excitement over, and no longer finding any challenge or satisfaction in academic work, blacker thoughts such as those from my adolescent years returned. I no longer found any sustainable escape from what some people (including Churchill) have called 'the black dog'. That summer, I had had to move out of my flat, and I only had a temporary arrangement to have a room in someone's house. I felt very anxious about where I was going to live and how I could try to keep some of the possessions that I had managed to retain from my old house. I had no close family nearby to support me, my best friend at the university had graduated and moved away, and I felt very isolated.

I think that my feelings of bereavement from two years earlier had been 'put on hold' by all this activity. But they came back when they found a gap in my thinking. I felt that getting up and going into university for lectures was anything but rewarding. I was stressed and couldn't sleep at night and so slept in during the morning, beginning to miss lectures and then finding it harder to keep up with academic work as time went on. It was easier and more rewarding to keep up my political activities and I began to make new friends amongst the University Liberals.

My absences from lectures and tutorials began to be noticed. I received a letter asking me to see my personal tutor. When I went to see him as requested, he had no idea why I was there. I had to suggest to him that it might be because I had missed quite a lot of lectures. He asked why, and I tried to explain something of my feelings of anxiety, depression and isolation. To say that he was unsympathetic was an understatement. He said that worries about where I might live etc. were the sort of worries that all students faced. The fact that I had found my mother dead just before coming to university, had no family support and displayed many depressive symptoms appeared to be of no interest and I was not referred to the student counsellor or offered any suggestion of help beyond experiencing a 'just pull your socks up' approach. This just made me feel worse, and made me even less likely to attend lectures.

I buried myself again in the political work that I enjoyed, felt good at, and provided me with alternative companionship. The senior figures in the party in Liverpool all met weekly to discuss the campaign to retake control of the city in the 1980 elections, when new ward boundaries would mean that every council seat was up for election. Labour had taken control in 1979 when the local elections had coincided with the general election, and we had won few of the wards outside the Edge Hill constituency. We called ourselves 'the cabal' as some of the senior councillors, including Trevor Jones, his deputy Mike Storey, Richard Pyne[4] and David Croft, met with party people like Chris Davies (then a council candidate), Ann McTegart and me. We reviewed likely candidate selections for the target wards, progress against campaign plans based on monthly 'Focus' distribution, number of doors knocked on etc. Potential candidates were pursued, all best campaign practice was shared and responsibility for helping to oversee the campaigns in key

---

4   His surname is Pyne, but this was changed by his agent in Liverpool to Pine for the elections.

wards was allocated. It was a basic model that I was later to adapt for the Liberal Democrats' hugely successful parliamentary target seat campaigns.

The 1980 local elections in Liverpool were most difficult in the more Tory areas. This was because the 'hung' council had failed to agree a budget. After several years had gone by without any increase in the rates, Liberal councillors eventually abstained to let Labour's proposed 50 per cent rate rise go through. The most expensive houses were hit hardest, and there were many of them in the enlarged Church ward where I was acting as the election agent for the three Liberal candidates, including Cyril Carr. It was my first time as an election agent (still aged only nineteen). Because of the rate rise issue, the result was nail-bitingly close; Cyril Carr was re-elected (much to my satisfaction) but our two other candidates in Church ward were narrowly defeated. Across Liverpool as a whole, our plans worked, with our number of councillors increased from thirty to thirty-eight, and we took back control of the city council.

The effort in the elections had been enormous and my studies had certainly suffered. My only attendances at the university in the spring that year had been to successfully organise the campaign to prevent the Trotskyist/Militants from taking over the running of the student union. I was called in again by the university. My tutor now explained that the politics and economics departments had been swapping notes. Whilst each had probably assumed that I was working in the other department, they had eventually put two and two together. They showed me a note from one of my tutors that said: 'Perhaps there has been a mistake with this student's registration as we have neither seen nor heard of this person.'

I tried to explain that I had been busy earlier in the year preventing the takeover of the student union. They said that they were very grateful, but that was not really what I was supposed to be at university for. I then tried to explain that I had been helping to run the city council elections, again keeping the Trotskyists out of power at the town hall.

They said they were even more grateful for that, but warned me of the consequences of neglecting my studies.

At that stage, I might still have been able to scrape through the end-of-year exams if I had felt well. But I didn't. I realised too late that I did want to get my degree, but the exams fell during a period of the 'black dog'. I felt like I had nobody to talk to and I made little to no effort in the exams. I inevitably failed and was told that I had to leave the university at a meeting of the Faculty Progress Committee. At that stage, David Alton suggested that I simply become the paid agent for his Edge Hill constituency. I anticipated that this would be my best course of action, but I had nagging doubts about abandoning university. I got a number of people, including my political mentors, to write to the university asking them to give me a second chance, after which I attended the Senate Progress Committee, which was the final court of appeal.

To my surprise, they accepted that there were reasons why I had felt unwell during the year, though again not offering any support on these issues. I don't think that anybody else had the slightest inkling of any health issues beyond the obvious: that I was putting on a lot of weight, which was through comfort eating and drinking. I certainly didn't want to share my feelings with anyone; nor did I understand that anything might be done to help medically. Nevertheless, I gave assurances to the university that I would keep up with the academic work in future.

My means of doing so, however, was certainly not what they had in mind. I got more involved in some of the student union activities, and in doing so helped to find friends that have been close ever since. I stood for election twice and was elected both to the NUS delegation and to the Student Union Executive. But I did not find 'student politics' wholly rewarding. My contemporaries included Tony McNulty (who later became a Labour MP) and Val Shawcross (a very effective NUS/welfare officer and now deputy mayor for transport in London, but then in the 'Broad Left'). I knew every common room, every bar and the location of every noticeboard across the university campus and the halls of residence. I built an organisation that could turn out students to vote, winning elections at all levels, including those for the sabbatical officers. But in spite of being called 'that bastard Rennard' by Conservative students in one of the many elections when we out-smarted the Tories, many of them were actually quite friendly, very academic, and had good handwriting. They lent me their notes from the many lectures that I missed, enabling me to get through my exams.

I ran the successful campaign at the 1981 Liberal Assembly for Cyril Carr to become party president. He was too ill to attend, but I spoke for him at the hustings meetings. These events and Liberal student con-ferences provided me with my first real experiences of public speaking, at which my confidence grew. In this period, I got to know people like Gavin Grant[5] and Leighton Andrews[6] (who I remember used to argue in the student union bars late into the night about which of them would become Liberal leader first), Liz Barker,[7] and Nick Harvey.[8]

Just before Christmas 1981, Cyril Carr died of a heart attack and I lost my first real mentor. One of my unsuccessful candidates from 1980, Ted Brash, volunteered to stand in the by-election following Cyril's death, and I was again his election agent. It was bitterly cold and there was much frozen snow and ice on the ground throughout the campaign. We won plaudits for our efforts to sustain the weekly 'Focus' leaflets and a full canvass of every door in such bitter condi-tions. My student friends were a great help and one of them, Tony Loftus, drove the student union minibus on polling day. At one point, he had fourteen nuns from a local convent with him in the minibus

---

5   Who later worked for the Liberal Party HQ in a role financed by the Rowntree Trust, was the Liberal candidate for Southend West in the 1980s, and later chief executive of the RSPCA.

6   Who was elected as a Liberal to the NUS National Executive, became Liberal candidate for Gillingham and then defected to Labour, becoming a minister in the Welsh Assembly.

7   Who became chair of the Union of Liberal Students (known as ULS), chair of the Lib Dem Conference Committee, and the party's health spokesperson in the House of Lords.

8   Later elected as MP for North Devon (1992–2015), chair of the party's Campaign and Communications Committee and a highly regarded Armed Forces Minister in the first years of the coalition government.

(that was covered with Liberal posters) taking them to the polling station and back. The statistical dead heat from 1980 now became a Liberal landslide as we polled 62 per cent of the vote.

In July, I went over to Warrington several times to help what seemed to be an unlikely prospect of Roy Jenkins winning the by-election there, but he almost did. A group of Liverpool Liberals led by David Alton took a coach to Warrington early in the campaign. Roy boarded it on our arrival to thank us for coming to support him. We were then treated to a twenty-minute lecture from the SDP's Chief Whip, John Roper, about the purpose of canvassing. We felt that this was a bit strange as two years earlier we had secured a by-election win with two-thirds of the vote. The canvass cards provided were of the old Labour style, allowing us to record voters as being 'For', 'Against' or 'Doubtful'. I intervened in the briefing session to suggest that we should also record specifically anyone supporting the Conservatives in order to enable us to visit them again later and try to persuade them to switch. It was my first introduction to campaigning with the SDP and our visit made an impression on Roy, his agent Alec McGivan and some of the key people in the new party that had come up to support him, including Ben Stoneham (who later became a close colleague and friend).

Later that year, the student union minibus had also been useful for taking my friends from the university and other Liverpool Liberals down to Croydon North-West for the first 'Liberal–SDP Alliance' parliamentary by-election win in October 1981. I spent the last week of the campaign in Croydon learning a lot from the very experienced Liberal agent Peter Chegwyn. The 'Alliance' by-elections in those days attracted huge numbers of helpers. I found myself running one of the eleven 'committee rooms' on polling day from a small first-floor flat, with 160 volunteers working out of it. The challenge of managing volunteers courteously and effectively was always something that I greatly enjoyed.

Much closer to Liverpool was the Crosby by-election contested by

Shirley Williams in November 1982. Shirley has always been one of my greatest heroes in British politics. Her chance to fight the by-election came because of the sacrifice shown by another friend of mine, local Liberal councillor Anthony Hill. I believe that he would have won if he had stood, but Shirley's victory as the first elected SDP MP had the effect of taking the newly formed Liberal–SDP Alliance to its peak level of support, briefly touching 50 per cent in the polls that December. My group of Liverpool University Liberals and Social Democrats helped organise Formby (the second largest town) during the campaign. I was entrusted with this area by Alec McGivan, who was again the agent.

I still had one more major set of elections before facing my final university exams in June 1982. The local elections in May of that year were again expected to be a close-run thing between Labour and Liberals, with a number of SDP candidates also standing for the first time. The Old Swan ward was seen as the key battleground. We were due to defend it, but had lost the county council election there the previous year by over 1,000 votes. It was clear that our sitting councillor, who was not local, was unlikely to win again. At one time, I was thinking of standing myself in the ward (where my father had run his dental practice more than twenty years previously) but it didn't make sense as I didn't at that point want to be tied down to being a councillor. Tony Loftus, who had been born in Old Swan and lived nearby, was keen to stand. We installed Tony as the candidate amongst some controversy as it involved a 'de-selection'. But it was necessary in order to win, and I agreed to be Tony's agent. My friends then all pointed out that this would put my final exams in even greater jeopardy. One of them, Chris Leahy, who had graduated the year before, offered to be agent for this friend of mine he didn't really know. It was a favour to me to help me get my degree. Chris, Tony and their families are still amongst my closest group of friends more than thirty years later.

Despite the understanding with Chris, I still threw myself into Tony's campaign. Tony, Chris and I with a handful of helpers, mostly fellow students, knocked on most of the 6,000 doors in the months leading up to the election, taking up any problem we could and identifying issues for the campaign. Then we knocked on every single door without exception in the last four weeks. Saturdays were the busiest days for canvassing, leaving Sundays largely free for us to deliver a weekly 'Focus' leaflet. Every Saturday followed the same pattern. We met at 10 a.m. and canvassed without a break until at least 1 p.m. We were back at it by 2 p.m. and continued without a break until 5 p.m. Then Tony often had to leave us to run his disco (he acted as DJ in his own mobile disco business to boost his student grant and pay for the campaign). Chris and I would then canvass again from 5.30/6 p.m. until 9 p.m. This meant that the two of us each did at least nine hours' solid door-knocking every Saturday. On the final Saturday, we reached the end of a long road with a most attractive pub at 8.15 p.m. Our feet ached and we looked at each other as we tried to decide whether to go in or not. We decided to toss a coin. We lost, so it was canvassing again until 9 p.m. It seemed worthwhile when Labour's 1,000+ majority was overturned by a Liberal majority of 401. On the same day, another student friend, Peter Rainford, was elected as a city councillor in the County ward by the narrow margin of 132, and the University Liberals were also prominent in the winning of the Arundel ward with one of our members, Simon Hicks, acting as agent. We clung onto control of the city council, winning ten wards (three of them largely with the help of my student friends).

Then it was down to revision for my final exams. Except in my case I was looking at much of the work for the first time. The files of notes that I had obtained, mostly from university Tories, were excellent. But on one of my five courses I had nobody to cover for me and barely attended. I tried to explain to my tutor that there was one course 'I found really difficult' and asked if I could get a degree with very low scores on one of my papers. The reply was to the effect that, with my attendance record, I couldn't possibly get a degree in any event, but since I was asking I must at least get a respectable mark in all five papers. Cramming hard and working twenty-hour days (longer on the day before sitting the exams) got me through most of what I needed to do. But the 'Development Economics' course was a problem, and I hadn't started looking at it at all until forty-eight hours before sitting the exam, when another one had finished. I had to buy the two textbooks (I was too late to get them from the library) and I started working through them, drinking large quantities of coffee as well as taking caffeine tablets to keep me awake. The night before the exam I remember lying down to close my eyes and sleeping for just thirty minutes as I knew that I could not afford to sleep for longer. When I got into the exam room and saw the paper, I was amazed that I had a choice of essays to write and began on the four required.

On the day that the results came out, my group of university friends all met me in the nearby Everyman bistro. It was our regular starting point for an evening of drinking our way through the town centre. They all wanted to buy me a drink and commiserate with me on my failure to obtain a degree (as predicted so confidently by the university). My friends were delighted, however, when I got my 2:2 (having also achieved that standard in Development Economics with only two days of work on the course). I attended the degree ceremony somewhat guiltily, and was pleased that my younger brother Peter came to it. I didn't, however, go to Senate House to collect the certificate that I didn't feel I really deserved.

Thirty years later, I spoke at the alumni reception for Liverpool University graduates held in the House of Lords. I told some of the stories about my academic record, including the non-collection of the certificate, after which the vice-chancellor promptly promised to arrange a special ceremony to hand it over 'in any Liverpool pub of my choice'. I told him straightaway that it would have to be the Philharmonic – the famous pub opposite the Philharmonic Hall where most degree ceremonies took place.

CHAPTER 2

THE LIBERAL AGENT

WINNING FROM THIRD PLACE

I was a graduate, but hadn't found time to do anything about finding a job. I wanted the summer to relax and think about it. My 'rest' after graduation, however, did not last very long.

On 1 August 1982, I became the full-time professional agent for the Liverpool Edge Hill constituency. I had been reluctant to do this at first, thinking that I should really do something else – what one might call a 'proper job'. But disaster had struck the party's hopes of retaining an MP in Liverpool, in the shape of the Boundary Commission proposals to reorganise constituency boundaries. The Commission initially proposed the worst possible outcome for Edge Hill; its four wards would be redistributed into four other existing constituencies. David Alton, having devoted a decade of effort to the Edge Hill constituency, was deeply depressed.

He pressed me to be his agent for a general election campaign in one of the new constituencies. The first task was to try to modify the Boundary Commission's proposals. Our efforts were led by the brilliant local lawyer and party stalwart David Mawdsley. Residents' associations sprang to life (at our instigation) and made submissions. One of them was even called the 'Edge Hill Conservation Society'. I learned a lot during this time about the Boundary Commission processes and their importance. We succeeded in changing the proposals to some extent and the Commission's final proposals were for the Edge Hill constituency to be split in two, with these parts to be subsumed into new, much bigger constituencies. The new 'Mossley Hill' constituency was based on one third of the old Edge Hill seat, with the other two thirds of it coming from constituencies where Liberal support had been at deposit-losing level at the previous general election.

BBC and ITN commissioned studies analysing the new constituencies. Their assessment for Liverpool Mossley Hill was that if it had existed in 1979, the Tories would have been ahead of Labour in it by 9,000 votes. We would have been in third place; 13,000 votes behind the Tories and 4,000 votes behind Labour. But we held nine of the fifteen council seats, with the Tories having five, and Labour one. It seemed very likely that a general election would take place within twelve months and this short timeframe was a significant factor in my agreeing to undertake the role; I didn't intend to make a career of this sort of work. Based in a small office in the Liberal Club, from where we had run the Edge Hill by-election, I began counting up how many helpers we might be able to muster across the five local government wards that comprised the new constituency. Adding up the number of people who would deliver leaflets, knock on doors, help take numbers at a polling station or write envelopes etc., the total number was fewer than a hundred, and well below the number that would be required if we were to mount a winning campaign.

Our previous election campaigns had produced canvass returns indicating some of the people who had voted for us in local elections. The most enthusiastic of them had taken window posters. We also had records of people who had returned petitions or poll cards into the famous 'orange boxes' that we placed near to the entrances of polling stations. I began calling on the doors of these people. The 'strike rate' in finding active helpers was not high, but I was quite successful in persuading some of them to take responsibility for delivering a small bundle of leaflets around where they lived. It was always a small, manageable task, a 'one-off' (in the first instance) and involved profuse thanks from me. Some weeks later I would call again, express my gratitude for their effort the last time and ask if they might manage it again. By the third time that I called, they realised that they were 'part of the delivery network'. Constant thanks and sincere praise for delivering the leaflets with increasing frequency followed.

I concentrated on areas without deliverers, but without a car my progress on foot was slow. I encouraged a culture of volunteers coming in to the office to help with various tasks, and they set about going through the canvass cards showing how people said that they would vote, finding the Liberal supporters and then trying to locate their number in the telephone directory. Years later, this would all be done by computer. I then asked them to produce lists of names and phone numbers, with space on the sheets to record the result of up to three telephone calls, and I began ringing. Calling on behalf of David Alton was always effective with people for whom he was the MP, but elsewhere calls would have been on behalf of a local candidate or councillor. I sounded them out for any indication that their support might lead at some point in the future, even in a small way, to helping us. My first sheet of about thirty names produced three definite leads.

I found that if I then called round personally within 24–48 hours I had a good chance of persuading them to deliver leaflets. But progress was still too slow and I had many other tasks apart from finding helpers. I was working long hours and generally seven days a week. The evenings and weekends were particularly important for working with and finding volunteers. So, I began training a few more people to make the calls. First, they listened to me do it. I devised a simple script and kept it by the phone. When a 'good caller' came into the HQ I could put them on the phone with the script. Mailshots delivered to past supporters also produced a handful of new helpers. Letters to people we had helped with casework (simply asking for help and not mentioning the casework that had been done for them) produced a better response. Above all it was always a question of asking people, not assuming that individuals would just come forward on their own.

My major task was producing the 'Focus' leaflets and other literature for each of the five wards. Some of the local councillors (including Trevor Jones) were keen to control the content themselves, to keep it focused on them personally and their council issues, and to keep material more relevant to David Alton's campaign to the minimum. David Alton, on the other hand, was keen that all the literature should be about him almost exclusively. I had to negotiate my way through conflicting approaches and strike the appropriate balance, showing teams working together. I wrote about what the 'Liberal Team' was doing locally with photographs and contact details for all of them, and about local and national issues as they affected their part of Liverpool. It was time-consuming attending all the ward meetings, talking to each of the councillors and local candidates, discussing what were the issues in their wards, and what to put in 'Focus'. I also spent a lot of time looking at the ideas for possible inclusion that David Alton and his very hard-working London secretary Jackie Winter regularly sent me. In the era before computers and desktop publishing designing the leaflets required using rubdown lettering ('Letraset') for headings, typing on a typewriter and glueing these headings and text onto sheets of paper. Some artistic skill was required but the main priority was always the message – 'What are we saying to these people? How can we get them involved in local campaigns? How can we get things done together? How can we make sure that they know how to get involved?' etc.

The period from the New Year of 1983 to polling day (eventually set for 9 June) was one of the most intensive and hard-working of my life. I didn't take a day off in that five-and-a-half-month period, working seven days a week. We were steadily increasing the flow of 'Focus' leaflets, producing more local area-based newsletters and designing our own tabloid newspapers, as well as knocking on many more doors with survey leaflets. Our campaign gained momentum from a critical by-election held in March that year in one of the five wards. Picton ward's county councillor had resigned. It was one of the old Edge Hill wards that the Conservatives had not taken much interest in since the days when Michael Howard (later to be Conservative leader) had been their parliamentary candidate in 1966. But there were two MPs entitled to claim that much of the new Mossley Hill constituency was 'based on their old constituency': Edge Hill's Liberal MP David Alton and Wavertree's Conservative MP Anthony Steen.

During the council by-election campaign, a battle was being fought between these two Liverpool MPs. The Pexwear factory producing clothing was on the Edge Hill/Wavertree border and was threatened with closure. David Alton took up their cause and successfully persuaded Marks & Spencer to start selling some of their products. Anthony Steen was furious and accused David Alton of 'interfering in another member's constituency'. The row was featured on the regional TV news, with David Alton filmed fighting to save jobs at the factory. In contrast, Anthony Steen's section of the programme showed him calling door to door trying to collect Conservative Party membership subscriptions. When it was then shown that the factory was actually (just) inside the Edge Hill constituency, it was game, set and match to Alton.

The Conservatives, with Anthony Steen as their likely candidate for the Mossley Hill constituency, flung everything into the Picton ward by-election. In order to help 'retain' Mossley Hill, they wanted at least to get a respectable vote in the council by-election; they delivered four leaflets and canvassed thoroughly. But with our much greater canvassing efforts, I knew where just about every potential Conservative voter in the Picton ward lived. I was able to explain to them time and again that the battle there now was between Labour and Liberal. Local residents knew that Liberals worked for them all the year round, whilst the Conservative candidate, imported to a fairly inner-city ward from a leafier part of the constituency, had no local track record. I was conscious of the fact that, at the age of twenty-two, I had to command the confidence of party members and helpers in the constituency. As the agent for the by-election, it helped me considerably when our candidate, Vera Best, polled 65.7 per cent of the vote, whilst the Conservative share fell to 4 per cent. The following week, Anthony Steen ignored the fact that he was supposed to have a national role in the Conservative Party supporting 'marginal constituencies' and applied to be their candidate in the safe seat of South Hams in Devon.

The city council elections of 1983 immediately preceded the general election. I was overseeing the campaigns in the five Mossley Hill wards. There was no complacency in the two wards (Church and Picton) where I had been the agent for the two recent comfortable by-election wins. I knew that the most Tory ward, Grassendale, would be the toughest to crack. We were not helped by the inexperience of the then Grassendale Liberal campaign team. They had designed all their campaign leaflets months in advance of the election, and did not take kindly to me saying that we would have to start again, attract more local campaign issues and casework, and report back on what we were doing in our leaflets, as opposed to simply 'stating our policies'. I went out with our candidate, Gerry Scott, and his agent, Mike McManus, on the first night of canvassing. The electoral register listed roads in alphabetical order, so they tried to begin by canvassing the roads beginning with A, and then driving to the roads beginning with B, and then C etc. I had to persuade them that we should instead canvass the roads that were adjacent to each other in order to reduce time driving across the ward. In 1983, people in Liverpool were generally becoming more aware of the city's politics, specifically, that they were a Liberal vs. Labour battle (with the Militant Tendency at the heart of Liverpool Labour), and this proved to be our most effective message. As time went on, I diplomatically took more control of the Grassendale campaign, and produced a lot of literature targeted at former Tory supporters urging them to switch tactically to the Liberals. On polling day, the 'safest' Tory ward in the constituency went Liberal, with a majority of over 1,000. Trevor Jones held his Aigburth ward, but the most inner city ward, Smithdown, had swung strongly to Labour the previous year, and whilst we halved their majority this year, we did not win it back. The local elections were the turning point for us in the constituency.

When I met with David Alton for lunch on the day after polling day in the Wavertree town hall, his previously fairly depressive mood about his re-election prospects had been transformed. We had polled 49 per cent of the vote across the five wards in the constituency.

The Liverpool City Council elections in 1983 were generally, however, very poor for us outside the Mossley Hill and Broadgreen constituencies. We were not helped by the failure to agree an allocation of council seats between Liberals and our allies in the Social Democratic Party (SDP). Feelings in Liverpool were strongly anti-Thatcher, and a Labour Party that was energised by the Militants took control of the city. They immediately asserted their new style of control by abolishing the position of Lord Mayor. Our campaign in much of Mossley Hill now became one of fighting back against the Militants.

At future training events and in meetings with MPs, candidates and their agents, I often refrained from talking about the scale of the work that we did in the Mossley Hill general election campaign for fear that they would consider it incredible. From having fewer than a hundred helpers less than a year before, by polling day we had increased this number to more than 600. There were just over 32,000 houses in the constituency and I ensured that more than 70 per cent of these households had an identified local person who regularly delivered all our leaflets to them. Between 1 January and polling day on 9 June, every one of these homes received at least twenty-two different leaflets from us. We knocked on every single door at least once during this campaign; two thirds of them for a second time. On the day of the election, all thirty-two polling stations were covered by a person taking voters' polling numbers from 7 a.m. until 10 p.m. and who were organised from eight 'committee rooms'.

Even in the pre-computer era, we did many of the targeted communications to named individuals that became so prevalent in later decades. The constituency had about 700 voters who we could identify as coming from ethnic minorities. They formed our 'E' list and were subdivided into five groups. Each group received a personally addressed letter about David Alton's record and views on issues of concern to these communities and a further letter and leaflet in the relevant languages of the five groups. These were hand-delivered by a member of the relevant community, who would explain the importance of the election when they called. A small central team ran the organisation with me. At its core were my student friends Peter Rainford and Simon Hicks, who, like me, were still only twenty-two years old. Jackie Winter, David's parliamentary secretary, was just a little older than us. We sometimes wondered if the Conservatives realised that they were up against a 'bunch of kids'. As I had run so many local election and by-election campaigns by now, none of our 600+ helpers seemed to have a problem with a 22-year-old being in charge.

During the campaign, the Conservatives, who were heading for a national landslide based in part on Margaret Thatcher's popularity post-Falklands, and having previously represented most of the constituency, fought hard to retain the seat – even though both Liverpool's incumbent Tory MPs had departed for safer pastures. They used the previous 'hypothetical' voting figures and national polls to try to suggest that the race was still between them and Labour. Their candidate, Brian Keefe, made much of his 'strong family background'. The Conservative campaign was largely based on pictures of him with his wife and four daughters and the slogan 'Straight Thinking – Straight Talking: Brian Keefe Conservative – a mature, family man.' As David Alton was then unmarried, the potential inferences were clear. This was only a few months after the controversial Bermondsey by-election, for which I had helped write some of the very early 'Focus' leaflets for Simon Hughes. But I had no part whatsoever in the personal denigration of Peter Tatchell that was largely run by the independent Labour candidate. Of the many thousands of leaflets that I did write over the decades, absolutely none of them would ever appeal to any form of prejudice or make any personal smear on an opponent. I considered the Conservative leaflets in that campaign to be deplorable. Just prior to the general election, we had been assessed by the Liberal Party HQ.

The Joseph Rowntree Reform Trust paid for John Spiller to come and see us. His campaign advice was most helpful. He reported that I was a 'brilliant agent, but it was a shame that my great efforts were being wasted on an unwinnable seat'. I always responded best to a challenge. During the campaign, when I had one of my weekly chats with him to discuss our canvass figures, he eventually agreed with me that we were set to win. On the eve of poll, I thought that our majority would be between 4,000 and 4,500. It was 4,195. We won with a 14 per cent swing against the Conservatives – the highest swing against them in the country, and having come from third place.

But there was a nasty and stressful episode for me that lasted for some years after the campaign. I was never afraid of robust political argument and there was much that needed saying about the Militants in Liverpool. Our leaflets had reminded people that at the height of the Toxteth riots, when there was widespread looting and violence, the Labour Party Young Socialists (dominated by the Militants) issued statements saying: 'We support and defend all those involved in these actions and call for their immediate release and the dropping of all charges.'

Of the thirty-seven different leaflets we produced during the last four weeks of the campaign in Mossley Hill (a lot at the time), I wrote and designed thirty-five of them, Trevor Jones wrote one of them (which I saw in advance) and David Alton wrote another in London that I did not see before it was printed. Unfortunately, the latter of these may have sailed a bit close to the wind about the Militants, but as the legal publisher of all the leaflets I was the one who received a libel writ after the election. A depressing period followed for me and my excellent legal advisers (E. Rex Makin & Co.) had to warn me that my prospects in court might depend upon the political leanings of a jury at the time. We thought that the Militants might drop the case when we first turned up to the High Court in Liverpool to contest their libel writ, but their lawyers on that occasion simply didn't show up, claiming a diary mix up, which was extraordinary. I turned up at the High Court in Liverpool on a second occasion when the case was again postponed. Their claim against me wasn't dropped until about two years after the election. In the meantime, I suffered a great deal of stress over the potential court proceedings in which damages and costs might have bankrupted me. The Militants clearly aimed to frighten me and prevent us campaigning effectively against them. But their reign of terror in the city (which is very well depicted in Alan Bleasdale's televised series *G.B.H.*) needed to be exposed, and we never relented from doing this, even when the national Labour Party and the *Liverpool Echo* seemed reluctant to make public criticism of Derek Hatton and the Militants over what they were doing to the city. It was only much later that they did so.

Whilst David Alton had won Mossley Hill, there had been a bitter fight between the 'Alliance' parties in the next-door Broadgreen constituency. Forty per cent of the old Edge Hill constituency had become part of the new Broadgreen seat, and it was a Liberal stronghold in local government terms. Local Liberal councillor Richard Pyne had been chosen as the Liberal candidate for the constituency, which had eleven Liberal councillors compared to two Labour and two Conservatives.

For the 1983 general election, the Liberal Party and the SDP had real difficulty in agreeing on the allocation of constituencies to be fought by either Liberal or SDP candidates in very few places. Broadgreen was one of them. The SDP wanted a safe haven for Dick Crawshaw, the former Labour MP for Toxteth and one of the first MPs to join the SDP. His existing Toxteth constituency largely merged with the very safe Labour seat of Scotland Exchange. No part of his existing constituency was in Broadgreen, or even bordered it.

As someone very strongly pro-Alliance, I might have supported us standing down for Dick Crawshaw, in return for a deal that the SDP supported Richard Pyne standing there in future. But this was very much a minority view amongst Liverpool Liberals. Most, including the Broadgreen agent Ann McTegart, felt strongly that national leaderships had simply not understood the situation in Liverpool properly.

David Owen's memoirs certainly suggest this, as he referred to Liberals 'fighting Dick Crawshaw [who was] defending his constituency' rather than admitting that he was trying to switch to a completely different seat. The former Liberal Party secretary-general Sir Hugh Jones also appears to make the same mistake, referring to 'Crawshaw's Broadgreen' in his own memoirs.[9]

As a result of both Pyne (Liberal) and Crawshaw (SDP) standing, a constituency that should have been won by the Alliance was actually won by the Militant Terry Fields. Richard Pyne came third behind the Conservatives and Dick (later Lord) Crawshaw came fourth and lost his deposit. The failure of the Liberal Party to back the Liberal candidate in Broadgreen caused ructions in the party and a large protest vote at the Liberal Party Council that summer. It later transpired that with only three constituencies unable to agree whether Liberal or SDP candidates should fight them, Dick Crawshaw had offered to stand down if Broadgreen had been the last constituency to be resolved. Simon Knott, the Liberal in Hammersmith, had offered to do the same thing. But Jeff Roberts, the Liberal in Hackney South & Shoreditch, had insisted that he was going to win and refused to back down. Jeff Roberts polled just 9 per cent of the vote (about half that of the SDP candidate in that seat) and his action prevented complete agreement on the allocation of seats between the Alliance parties in that general election.

A RESIGNATION AND NEARLY ANOTHER ONE

Overall the 1983 general election was a great disappointment after high hopes were raised following the formation of the Liberal–SDP Alliance. Supporters of the Alliance parties had rejoiced at opinion-poll leads for much of the period between the SDP launch in 1981 and the

---

9   Sir Hugh Jones, *Campaigning Face to Face*, p. 207.

Falklands War in 1982. Hopes had been revived with Simon Hughes's great gain of Bermondsey in March 1983, but this was followed by the crash at the Darlington by-election just before the general election, when the SDP's Tony Cook nosedived from first place in the early polls to finish third and offer a reprieve to Michael Foot and Labour. The Alliance polled 25.4 per cent of the vote in 1983, but won only twenty-three seats. It had come close to overtaking Labour, who polled 27.6 per cent of the vote but won 209 seats. Margaret Thatcher was a lucky leader. The divided opposition, with Michael Foot leading Labour and the double-headed Alliance leadership of Jenkins/Steel, helped her to win 397 of the 650 seats, a majority of 144, based on just 42 per cent of the national vote.

If the Alliance had managed to overtake Labour in the last week (as was indicated as possible in some of the polls), then a tactical switch for voters to the Alliance might have developed considerable momentum. The unfair imbalance in parliamentary seats between Labour and the Alliance was to handicap the Alliance in building any kind of base and it led many people in Labour to believe that all that was required for them to win in future was to try harder next time. David Steel's hope of leading a fundamental re-alignment in politics was dashed, as were his hopes that he would be joined in the House of Commons by the likes of Stuart Mole, his principal aide, in Chelmsford (lost by 378), and 'senior advisers' Alan Watson in Richmond & Barnes (lost by seventy-four) and Richard Holme in Cheltenham (lost by 5,518). There had been nothing of the kind of targeted support for these constituencies that I was later to arrange for Liberal Democrat candidates. Perhaps the biggest blow to David Steel was the resignation of Roy Jenkins as SDP leader and his replacement by David Owen.

Roy Jenkins would have been a great Prime Minister, but had not proved to be a popular campaigner in that election. The last-minute attempt to ditch him as the de facto campaign leader, at the 'Ettrick Bridge summit' at David Steel's home, had caused much ill feeling. But Jenkins was clearly a liberal who believed in the two parties working together and he saw the need with the first-past-the-post system for there to be a combined party that did not have rival structures and competing leaderships. David Owen, on the other hand, appeared to hate Liberals and was contemptuous of approaches like 'community politics'. He told Dick Newby (when Dick was national secretary at the SDP) that he was not completely opposed to a merger but that he would not support any party that had the word 'Liberal' in the title and that any new party would have to be based on what he called a 'sensible' (i.e. pro-nuclear) defence policy. The idea of having to work with David Owen for the foreseeable future, with all efforts to bring the two parties closer together likely to go into reverse, was clearly very depressing for an exhausted David Steel. The campaign had been gruelling. Paul Tyler, who organised his tour by 'battle bus' across the country, had to cram in many more visits to far-flung places than any of Steel's successors had to undertake. David Steel had hoped to be in the Cabinet in an Alliance coalition government. But the country was polarised between Foot and Thatcher and he now had to fight off criticism from within his own party. Tony Greaves had published a document listing differences between Liberal and Alliance policies to emphasise the contrasts in a campaign based on the slogan 'Working together'. The Young Liberals had attracted publicity by saying that the Alliance manifesto was not worth voting for. David Alton, Cyril Smith and Simon Hughes wanted to curtail Steel's power by electing a deputy, and the first meeting of the new Parliamentary Party was a very angry one.

David Steel had had enough and resigned as leader. His letter of resignation to the party president was posted at an Ettrick Bridge post box. Fortunately, Archy Kirkwood, his former assistant and the recently elected MP for the new Roxburgh & Berwickshire constituency (containing part of Steel's old seat), became aware of what he had done. Archy waited at the post box the next morning for the postman to come and then begged him to let him have the letter of resignation back. Fortunately, the postman acquiesced, and an alternative to resignation was agreed. David Steel announced that he would take a three-month 'sabbatical' as leader. Alan Beith, as Chief Whip, would take over as acting leader for the summer, with David Steel returning to his duties for the annual Liberal Assembly at Harrogate in September.

I was also feeling extremely tired after the general election, but had to quickly produce 32,000 'thank-you' leaflets and complete the election expense returns. I was a little nervous about the latter as they were very close to the maximum permitted limit; so I also got copies of the Tory and Labour expense returns for the constituency. It was later shown that the election expenditure in Mossley Hill had been the highest average by the three main parties anywhere in the country. Studying the Conservative returns also solved a mystery for me. I had found a very good poster printer and we had had an excellent display of posters around the constituency. I negotiated an incredibly cheap price that will have only just covered the cost of printing them. The Conservatives used the same printer, but paid more than twice as much for their posters. When I queried this with the printer, he explained that he had done my posters at just above cost (perfectly legally) and charged the profit that he thought that he should have made to the Tory account. There cannot have been many campaigns when we took a seat from the Conservatives and they paid for our posters!

A NEAR MISS

On the Saturday after the general election, Michael Young, our candidate from Penrith & The Border who had just lost to the former Conservative Home Secretary William Whitelaw by about 15,000 votes, was driving back down to London. He was stunned to hear news of the Cabinet re-shuffle on the radio, in which it was announced that Margaret Thatcher was sending 'her Willie' to the House of Lords, and that there would therefore be a parliamentary by-election in his former constituency. I was asked to help by acting as Michael's 'minder', which included driving him around the huge Cumbrian constituency in the little car that the Mossley Hill Liberal Association had just acquired, and only a few months after I had passed my test.

When I drove up to Penrith from Liverpool, I took Tony Loftus with me and we did a 'double act' of driving and minding the candidate. We got to know and like Michael very much. A former Tory (he had been an adviser to Edward Heath when he was Prime Minister), he had since become a committed Liberal and was a very strong candidate for the seat. We hoped that he might be a possible link to other Tory defectors who might not approve of Margaret Thatcher. Michael had also played a hugely important role (later the subject of the documentary film *Endgame*) in bringing together representatives of the South African apartheid government with members of the ANC at a secret Somerset location for talks that led to the first elections there in which everyone could vote.

On Monday to Saturday (we didn't campaign there on Sundays), Michael, Tony and I toured the towns and villages, visiting our four local HQs to meet teams, go canvassing, visit the farmers' markets and shows, attend local events, talk with the village shopkeepers and meet parents outside school collecting their children. We had the friendliest reception, and many people commented that whilst they liked Willie Whitelaw, they had never actually met people seeking their votes before, and they were very impressed to meet us. I did wonder what some of them must have made of Tony in his enthusiastic Scouse accent – 'Er… very nice goats there, farmer.' There was a feeling from voters that it had been taken for granted by the Conservatives that they would turn out to vote again, having just elected an MP who lasted for just two days. They evidently didn't like the rather arrogant and complacent view that his replacement, David Maclean, shipped in from Scotland after losing to Russell Johnston in Inverness, and a rather more hard-line Tory, would not really have to fight for the seat.

Tony and I discovered a lot about village life in Cumbria that we had never experienced growing up in Liverpool. We stayed, as did Graham

Watson (David Steel's new principal aide and later MEP), with a very nice old couple called the Walleys in a village just outside Penrith. We were amazed to discover that most cars had the keys left in, front and back doors were left open and there was a culture in which everyone in the village seemed to know how everybody else might vote, and how many pints any of them would drink on a regular basis in the local pub. We found that all the Liberal supporters were keen to seize the opportunity to vote for us in the knowledge that many of the Conservatives would not turn out this time.

Each evening we would take Michael Young to three or so public meetings in the different villages. Audiences were small but enthusiastic about the fact that someone had come to their village to discuss their issues and concerns for the very first time. We got to learn Michael's set twenty-minute speech by heart, and soon decided that once we were sure that he had started off okay and had at least a small audience, we could leave the meeting to go to the pub next door, have a quick game of pool (and a pint, depending on who was driving), get back for the questions and take him to the next meeting. It was a most pleasant, if exhausting, July. David Steel knew Michael Young personally and wanted to break his sabbatical to speak at our main rally in Penrith. So, I met him and his close friends Ming and Elspeth Campbell for a drink before the meeting. David told me that he had been diagnosed with a virus that accounted for his ill health that summer. I also talked to the Campbells about their disappointment in coming close to winning North East Fife that June (Ming had come in second place, 2,185 votes behind the Tories). I am sure that this had also been a significant personal blow to a Liberal leader who needed friends in Parliament, but lacked a party machine capable of helping them to win.

At each of the local HQs across the constituency, we had a short break from canvassing to talk to whoever was there – time that I used to add up the recent canvass returns from that area and to compare them with their previous ones. Nobody else in the campaign seemed to be doing this. Most people there assumed that our prospects were 'slim to none'. But every time I went to the four HQs and did the maths, I found that our percentage of 'definite supporters' and 'probable supporters' was increasing significantly. What mattered most was not the level of support on a particular day, but the trend. The campaign in Penrith was disappointingly low-key. There was no urgent appeal for helpers to come from around the country. I queried what was happening with the very experienced agent Andy Ellis and I wondered why we were not making more effort and trying to get more helpers. Andy thought that the best possible result for us was to lose by 53–38 per cent and that we mustn't 'cry wolf' by trying to get more helpers who would be disillusioned when we didn't come close. On this occasion, I deferred to his greater experience.

On the final weekend before polling day, I met up with friends who had come up from Liverpool, including Michael Key (who had been the canvass officer at both the Orpington and Sutton & Cheam by-elections). I told him that on my reckoning we would lose, but only by a three-figure majority. I was right. In less than two months, the Conservative majority of over 15,000 fell to just 552. There was much frustration in the party that a major alert had not gone out saying that we could win. Michael Young would have made an excellent MP.

It was dispiriting to lose by such a small margin given that we would have won with just a little more effort. It made me think about the scale of effort that had been required to win Mossley Hill compared to what would have been required to win Penrith & The Border in that by-election. The twelve months since I had begun working as a professional agent had been a period without a holiday and hardly a day off. The sense of exhaustion and anti-climax again contributed to one of my periods of significant depression. I knew that I needed a break, and I was invited by a friend to go to the Greek islands, but I simply had no money. The combination of a lifestyle working 'every hour God gave', never being able to shop and cook and paying the inevitable expenses of working in campaigns (which the Liberal Party could not afford to reimburse) left me permanently overdrawn. My agent's salary of £4,000 per annum meant that the £333 monthly payment just about covered the overdraft that I had built up over the previous month. I couldn't afford any kind of holiday. This financial insecurity was another factor that significantly contributed to my depression.

I did, however, spend some time filling in the survey form for constituency agents sent out by the national Liberal Party Organisation. They asked what I thought about their support. What support, I asked? They had generally sent out duplicated policy notes about issues that arrived two days after the issues had ceased to be topical in the election. Where had there been any training that might help anybody to win, I asked? Where was the support that should have come from the party for seats that we might win? Having described their election support as 'bloody useless' (the first time I had or have ever written a swear word on a form), I thought that there was no chance the national party would ever employ me, not that I had any intention of working for them.

My poor state of mind continued through August until September, when I was able to get a break as friends in the German Liberals invited me to campaign there for a few days. I went with Jeff Lamb, his friend Christine and her boyfriend John (who I had got to know as Jonny Guitar during the Edge Hill by-election when he sang lullabies to Young Liberals sleeping on the floor of the HQ in their sleeping bags). John Hemming and Christine Richards were later to be married and then divorced.

In the autumn of 1983, I started thinking about other things to do. I knew a few people who worked in what was then called personnel management and the idea of a career based on negotiating between people seemed quite attractive. A job that began with a reasonable salary and excellent prospects for development came up with Merseyside County Council. Richard Pyne coached me for it and, of the 200+ applicants, I was one of the last three selected for the final interview. But, at the conclusion, the panel said that I was the outstanding candidate but just 'too political'. I found myself typecast at the age of twenty-three.

MILITANT LIVERPOOL

It was a difficult time to find alternative employment in Liverpool, with many graduates seeking jobs. The atmosphere in Liverpool became very dark and threatening with the Militants in control. Their leader Derek Hatton claimed that he was leading 'Liverpool's fight against Thatcher'. Council-paid propaganda regularly attacked 'the combined Liberal–Tory Alliance in the council' even though it didn't exist. The Conservatives were disappearing from the council. The Militants controlled one of the main union branches and therefore the council adopted a policy of granting any appeal against any council decision that was supported by that particular branch. When one of their members shot a foreman, he was of course instantly dismissed. But the branch appealed and he was immediately re-instated. The manager resigned from the council and left Liverpool as it was impossible to manage a workforce in such circumstances. Threats of violence were common and many people were intimidated out of their jobs or out of the city. House prices in the more affluent suburbs fell by 20 per cent in one year alone.

It would be quite a few years before the tide in Liverpool turned against the Militants, and it was only when they began to do significant damage to Labour's national reputation that Neil Kinnock spoke out publicly against them and took action. The *Liverpool Echo* had appeared to give the Militants the benefit of the doubt for much of this time and it failed for several years to expose the scandals that eventually helped to remove them from power. Whilst we had lost control of the city council, the Liverpool Liberal 'cabal' continued to function as we tried to assess which seats we thought that we could win in order to maintain a strong opposition to the Militant-run council. Ann McTegart had become chair of the Liverpool Liberal Party and I had become deputy chair (and chaired the campaign meetings). My university friends remained close and we all continued going out socially. Ann was a regular part of this group and it was in that autumn that our relationship became much closer. But it was another six years before we got married, and she has been my greatest support over the past thirty years.

My close friend Mike Storey said that he would not re-stand for the council that year and would take a break. It seemed increasingly likely to me that I would move on from working for the party in Mossley Hill, and would eventually have to move from Liverpool. I was convinced that our strength as an opposition party in Liverpool would decline dramatically if I moved away and Mike Storey left the council at the same time. I had a 'heart to heart' with Mike, whom I greatly admired. He had become deputy leader to Trevor Jones and had chaired the City's Education Committee. Liverpool needed him. Mike was worried about being seen to do the 'chicken run' that I proposed by moving from a ward that we could not win that year to the much safer Church ward. But I persuaded him that it was vital for him to stay on the council, that he would have to switch wards to do that, and that Church ward was ready for him. I would be his agent and we had volunteers to deliver over 90 per cent of the 8,000 homes in the ward. He agreed. Our campaign would involve taking on one of the remaining Conservative councillors in the constituency.

There were also two remaining Conservatives in the Grassendale ward. Our candidate there, Jeremy Greenwood, also asked me to be his agent. In a very Conservative area and a more conservative period socially, he was well known to be gay, living with his partner, and to be a Quaker. It was going to make for an interesting campaign! But before these local elections, there was a parliamentary by-election in Chesterfield.

THE TONY BENN BY-ELECTION

Following the resignation of the Labour MP for Chesterfield, Eric Varley, Peter Chegwyn was extremely keen that I worked with him on the campaign. Our initial plans for the parliamentary by-election had to be changed when a Labour councillor's resignation meant that there would be a council by-election in Chesterfield's New Whittington ward prior to the parliamentary by-election. Labour had held this ward continuously since at least 1945 and no Liberal had stood there since 1962. There were only six Liberal Party members there, and none of them was willing to stand as candidate. At the Chesterfield party executive, David Stone, a member and local taxi driver, said that he sometimes took fares to New Whittington. That seemed to be our only option and I was not particularly thrilled when Peter Chegwyn announced to the executive (unbeknown to me) that I would be the agent for the campaign.

The ward was on the fringes of the constituency and only consisted of 1,700 houses, so I researched some of the issues there by talking to the few members that we had and scouring the local papers and council minutes. We had no councillors in Chesterfield at the time, but a former Lib Dem councillor was helpful and I was able to produce a first 'Focus' before Christmas. Polling day was set for 28 January 1984. I had to get the nomination papers filled in during the Christmas period as I fought a bad case of glandular fever.

We didn't have many helpers in Chesterfield, or nearby, so I gathered my friends from Liverpool and Jeff Lamb brought his friends up from Leicester, where he was now based, and we did a survey by calling on every single one of 1,700 houses over a weekend, even though there was much frozen snow and ice on the ground. We reported back on the results of the survey in a further 'Focus'. We took up many small local issues with the council in an area where people felt neglected by a council to which the town centre concerns seemed to matter most. One of the biggest issues raised was the lack of a local chemist. We investigated what the council might do to help and asked the council's chief executive to assist. As with many solidly Labour councils, the chief executive appeared to be pretty much under the thumb of the Labour administration; we got a pretty dismissive reply saying that he was looking into the matter. We suspected that he would not be

allowed to respond properly until after the by-election. So, we reprinted the Borough Council crest on our next 'Focus' and in huge headlines
reported: 'The Borough Council's Town Clerk and chief executive is
personally looking into the matter of what could be done to support
the campaign to get a chemist's shop in New Whittington.' Trevor
Jones had told me years before that it was an offence to use a council
crest in this way, but as the offence can only be tried in the Court of
Heraldry, and this had not met since the fourteenth century, I wasn't
too worried when the council complained.

The same group then helped me canvass the entire ward, knocking
on every door over the weekend before polling. It appeared at first that
we had made little progress. Our level of 'definite' support was still
only at about 12 per cent. Over the next few days, Peter Rainford and
Tony Loftus got into some trouble for missing their council meetings
in Liverpool to devote election week to working with me. We split the
ward into eleven areas of between fifteen and 300 houses and wrote a
different letter about the issues raised in the survey to each household
within those areas. Each letter was topped and tailed by hand and put
in hand-addressed envelopes. In addition, the 300 residents who had
mentioned things in our survey all got a handwritten PS mentioning
their particular issues. And then we set out to deliver them all during
the Tuesday of election week. On the Tuesday evening, the canvass returns saw a huge uplift in our level of support as people commented on
the letters. Our level of 'definite support' was now reaching nearly 30
per cent, so I told Peter Chegwyn that we were set to win (he wanted
to double-check my figures) and I now admitted this to the candidate
for the first time, as I feared up to that point that he had only stood on
the basis that there was no chance of victory.

The eve of polling saw our small team delivering eleven area-specific
petitions, with a common petition form in support of getting a chemist to open in the area. These forms could be returned to our helpers at
the two polling stations the next day, and many people did so. We also
delivered a 'Good Morning' leaflet to every house between 5 a.m. on

polling day and 8 a.m. (when the polling stations then opened for local elections). I spent polling day running the local committee room (HQ) still desperately suffering from glandular fever. I had to sleep in an armchair in between knocks at the door from returning activists who were calling on our supporters and telephone calls from people wanting a lift. I felt just about okay to make it to the count. Labour's agent was the council leader Bill Flanagan, who many people had thought would be Labour's candidate for the parliamentary by-election. The surprise selection of Tony Benn instead meant that Chesterfield suddenly got national media attention. I had Vincent Hanna's number on *Newsnight* (he was then the BBC's by-election expert) and I got Tony to ring him from a phone box outside the count whilst the programme was on air to say that we had won. 'How the F**K did you do that?' was his response. Our victory in a council by-election was reported in the programme and it featured in editorials in the *Mail* and *Express* the next day.

We had begun the parliamentary by-election campaign in a poor third place behind the Tories, whose candidate was Nick Bourne (later their leader in the Welsh Assembly and now a minister in the House of Lords). The New Whittington council by-election victory catapulted us into becoming the main challengers to Tony Benn. *Liberal News* that week led with Tony Greaves's report 'Taxi Driver Dave Smashes Labour' and we attracted many more helpers to our campaign. Sadly, our parliamentary candidate, Max Payne, was not a strong choice for us, and his evident weaknesses (he had no real local track record and came across as arrogant and unpersuasive) were eventually exposed in the high-profile campaign. We came from third place (14,000 behind Labour) to second place ahead of the Conservatives but now some 6,000 votes behind Benn. In the process, we added 15 per cent to our vote. It was a creditable result and during the course of the campaign John Spiller got in touch to congratulate me on the council by-election win and sound me out about working for the party nationally. He had taken over as secretary-general, read my comments about how useless the party's national organisation had been at supporting potentially winning campaigns in 1983, and he was inviting me to help try to put this right.

THE LEAVING OF LIVERPOOL

I returned from the Chesterfield by-election to Liverpool to find that the Mossley Hill constituency party officers had decided in my absence that a constituency agent 'was no longer affordable', even on my meagre salary. They did not handle this well and the local party revolted against their plan. But whilst I had huge support and encouragement amongst the local party members and activists, it was clear to me that my only career progression in the party could come from working for the national party organisation. I went down to London to see John Spiller, and the then chief agent John Holmes, for an interview. Ann came with me and waited in the reading room of the National Liberal Club, whilst I went upstairs for my interview. The first 'settling-in' question was to the effect of 'Why would I be mad enough to want to work for the Liberal Party?' I began explaining my commitment to Liberal values, but was quickly interrupted and told: 'Don't worry, we know that and we have seen in detail what you can do. The question is how can we best get you doing this for more of the country, helping the best seats and helping win some parliamentary by-elections?' Their plan was to appoint regional agents who would be employed by the national party, but with each regional party making a financial contribution. They would let me work from Liverpool if I insisted. But my fear was that I would simply be expected by friends there to carry on as before, *and* take on the rest of the region and whatever else they wanted me to do nationally. So, they asked me to consider basing myself in the East Midlands on the premise that it needed a lot of help to improve campaigning, it was a central location, and that it wouldn't be very long before they created a job for me in London.

I later discovered that John Spiller's plan was for me to take over as chief agent when John Holmes retired in a year or two. I accepted their suggestion and told Ann (who was supportive of my career move) that I would be leaving Liverpool in a few months.

But before taking up the new role I still had to act as agent in Liverpool for the two most Tory wards in the constituency in the 1984 local elections with the aim of consolidating our general election success. In Church ward, with Mike Storey, I was confident after the first night's canvassing and told him that we would win with a big majority so should spend our time in helping other 'more marginal' wards. At the end of the campaign, he was elected very comfortably with a majority of 1,650, almost matching the by-election majority of two years previously. In Grassendale, I was more worried. Some of the members came to me saying that they were concerned that people were talking about our candidate being gay. I said that we must simply ignore this, people would talk but that it didn't matter and that we would continue to campaign in our own way on the issues that we thought mattered locally. Our candidate, Jeremy Greenwood, became the local crime-fighting champion in an area with a lot of house burglaries. Through the 'Focus' leaflets, we established the first neighbourhood watch schemes across the ward. We invited the police crime-prevention team to address a public meeting (advertised in 'Focus') and 'Focus' repeated their advice.

We squeezed the Conservative vote in the ward ruthlessly with effective arguments in letters to all their supporters identified from the past three years of intensive canvassing. Many of them then switched to us in response to the letters written on blue paper, in hand-addressed envelopes. There were far fewer Labour supporters in the ward, but I also drafted letters to them, pointing out that within that ward there would be either a Liberal or a Conservative councillor, and that Labour could not win.

The Tories fought back hard. Their candidate was their deputy leader and at one stage during the campaign spoke to the full city council budget meeting for more than an hour, trying to emphasise his importance. We countered with our slogan 'Only the Liberals can beat the Militants' alongside individual photographs of our team: councillor Gerry Scott (elected the previous year), David Alton MP, Sir Trevor Jones and Jeremy Greenwood ('Focus' editor). On election day, having just checked that everything was okay at the count in Church ward, I drove across to Grassendale. I was more than happy to see our huge majority of 1,710. Jeremy made a very nice and very gracious speech. The former Conservative councillor made a long and bitter one and promised that he would not miss watching the cricket in future for the sake of politics! The Conservative Party in Liverpool was effectively dead.

The overall Liverpool election results were again not so good for us. Whilst my friend Simon Hicks won the Arundel ward, other friends like David Croft (a former Sutton & Cheam Young Liberal) lost Breckfield narrowly. But something seemed to me to be amiss. Wards that I thought should be won on the basis of better canvass figures than previously were frequently narrowly lost. I didn't begin to understand why until I reflected on my experience calling on the doors of our supporters in some of the Lib/Lab marginal wards that evening. Whenever I found a Liberal supporter hesitant to go and vote, I would of course plead with them and beg them to let me give them a lift to the polling station. Sometimes the Militant activists were in the same street calling on their supporters. But when they found people who said that they weren't going to vote, the Militants just said thank you and, surprisingly, moved on very quickly. When I analysed the results, it seemed clear to me that the suspiciously high turnouts must have been based on 'personation'. The Militants did not mind the fact that their 'supporters' were not going to vote as they were organising people to vote on their behalf. This was later confirmed in the Labour Party's own investigation into the Militants in Liverpool. Many people in Britain would be surprised to learn how relatively easy it is in this country just to give a name and address and claim a vote. As this was being done on behalf of people who said that they weren't voting, it was very hard to detect. Liverpool's excellent returning officer at the time, Charles Lasham, thought that my suspicions about the scale of the problem did not seem credible. But years later Baroness Joyce Gould, a Labour peer who as Labour's director of organisation had investigated the Militants in the 1980s, told me that my suspicions had been correct. Some of the Militant successes in marginal wards had been been achieved by personation.

My 'leaving of Liverpool' party was a great and emotional occasion soon after those local elections. Very warm tributes were paid to me, but I felt sad to be leaving at a time when the Militants were ruining the reputation of my home city. At the same time, I felt that many of the Thatcher government's policies were inflicting great harm on places like Liverpool, despite tremendous efforts made by Michael Heseltine to push in the other direction. The Conservatives had a majority in the House of Commons of 144. Defeating them nationally would take a long time, but was the only hope for places like Liverpool. I felt that I had learned a lot about making the Liberal Party more electable and I relished the chance to develop these skills in other places, and to see if I could do more to help change national politics.

CHAPTER 3

THE CAMPAIGNER

STARTING IN THE EAST MIDLANDS

The East Midlands region was possibly the weakest in the country for the Liberal Party. John Spiller had considered it to be in need of learning effective 'Liverpool-style' campaigning. There were forty-two constituencies within the five counties, but there had not been a Liberal MP there since the Second World War. There were fewer than a hundred Liberal councillors across the whole region when I arrived. Many constituencies did not have a local party association, and those that did have one were generally very weak, with few members and little income. Until my appointment nobody was really advising the local activists about how to campaign effectively and target their resources. An early visit to a Derbyshire constituency involved me meeting all six active Liberal members. They explained to me that there were ten wards, five of which were fought by the SDP and five by them. This meant that five of the active Liberals were candidates, and the sixth member acted as agent for all of them. Every year, they managed to put out one very dull election leaflet to just over half the households in each of the wards that they fought. They considered this to be the 'best use of resources' and it was a lengthy, painful process, taking many months, to persuade them that six activists working in one ward, delivering half a dozen good leaflets to every house during an election, and several beforehand, would give them a much better prospect of electing a councillor.

The East Midlands Regional Party was considered to be one of the most viable in England because it owned a (near-derelict) terraced house in Loughborough. The house did not even have a functioning loo and visitors had to rely on the facilities at the nearby railway station. This was the regional office and home for the administrative secretary, a man called Maurice Bennett, who also hailed from Liverpool. Maurice made sure that the Regional Executive meetings, Regional Finance and General Purposes Sub-Committee and Regional Council all met regularly and he tried to raise funds to cover his modest salary and the costs of the house by selling a weird assortment of pens, key fobs and party memorabilia, as well as organising draws and sponsored walks. The operation required the limited number of constituency associations to pay into the regional party £200 per year, unless they could plead great poverty. For this fee, they appeared only to have the benefit of being able to buy the key fobs and to send representatives to regional party meetings; meetings I found particularly unrewarding as I listened to them discuss the dates of future sponsored walks and policy issues such as the merits of Esperanto.

There was clearly very little understanding amongst many of the Liberal members about what might be done to campaign more effectively, achieve greater political success and win influence or control over any of the local authorities. I arrived just before the 1984 European elections. With no time to influence the campaign, I set off to try to help the Liberal candidate for Nottinghamshire. He was considered by the region to be a strong candidate because he was a university lecturer and knew some policy. I was less impressed when I got to his house (there was no HQ), waited for some time whilst he mowed his large lawn and then heard him explain to me over a very nice roast lamb dinner (and some good red wine) that there was nothing really to do in the campaign. At dinner, his volunteer agent, who had unfortunately just been made redundant from his professional job, spent the evening explaining how he had written to David Steel asking him to arrange for the party to pay him to be a professional agent. He did not understand the reply that the party had no funds to create a job for him and had no comprehension that he might not be the party's first priority if it had. He had written back offering to 'lend the party the money to pay his salary as agent from his redundancy payment, providing that it paid him back in due course'. He didn't understand the lack of a further reply.

Unimpressed with the Nottinghamshire European election campaign, I set off for Lincolnshire where the two north Lincolnshire constituencies had previously achieved good results. They had more members and some funds, and a higher profile for the party. But the candidate that they had chosen for the European campaign had no profile in Lincolnshire, and had no local supporters willing to do much for him. As I was not seeking to interfere too much too quickly, I sat at the back of a meeting discussing whether or not to hire a helicopter for the last day or two of the campaign. There was no discussion of media profile, or of any potential visit by one of the few Alliance VIPs to support the campaign, or anything that might win votes; just whether or not there was enough money in the budget for a helicopter. After a lengthy discussion, it became clear that nobody was willing to organise the renting of one even if funds had been available.

I decided that I might learn most about this new territory by spending polling day in the town of Gainsborough, where there was a local council by-election in the North ward. This was supposed to be a relative stronghold. The small houses in terraced streets in a Tory-held constituency where Labour was non-existent seemed ideal territory. The Liberal organisation which had helped Andrew Phillips[10] to fight a strong campaign in the general election the year before seemed to have disappeared. There were no lists of supporters – just the list of voters. Numbers were taken at the polling station and subsequently

10   He became the Lib Dem peer Lord Phillips of Sudbury before retiring from the House of Lords but was then best known as Jimmy Young's 'Legal Eagle' on Radio 2.

crossed off on a copy of the voting register, but since we had no idea about which of them supported us, this was of limited value. Towards the end of the day, we went out and knocked on the doors of every single person who hadn't yet voted (not knowing whether they supported us or not). I was told that 'this was how they always did it'.

I set myself four immediate priorities for trying to make progress for the party in the region: training, council by-elections, membership recruitment and making a breakthrough in Leicester. I also decided to get more involved with the Association of Liberal Councillors (ALC) so that I had a more national role. Much of the work of trying to spread the community campaigning election techniques pioneered by people like Trevor Jones had since been taken up by the ALC under the direction of their organising secretary Tony Greaves.[11] Trevor always used to complain to me that they 'owed him royalties' for constantly reproducing headings from the 'Focus' leaflets that he had designed. The ALC also tried to support Liberal councillors in their work on councils and ran training courses in fighting local elections. I felt that I knew a lot about fighting elections, but little about how to train others other than by working closely with them in successive elections.

A weekend in the ALC's Hebden Bridge headquarters was the way in which many Liberal Party activists in the 1980s undertook their 'Training for Trainers' courses. I found it to be one of the most valuable weekends that I ever spent in politics. One of the team of Kingston Liberals, Roger Hayes, who had previously worked with Peter Chegwyn on the Isle of Wight, ran his own professional training consultancy. He explained the maxim of 'what people hear they forget, what they see they remember, what they do, they understand'. For me this was a revelation in approach. I could see how my short pep talks, examples of leaflets and Q&A sessions were of limited value in actually getting party activists to adopt new techniques. The training games and exercises that they devised involved breaking into groups, analysing sets of

---

11   Now Lord Greaves of Pendle.

local people's problems and concerns, deciding what to do about them, and drafting 'Focus' leaflets and sometimes press releases. The canvass role play was particularly hilarious as participants 'ham acted' the parts of canvassers and those being canvassed based on scripts – and our own experience.

On fifteen Saturdays and Sundays over the following year I ran one-day courses in different parts of the region based on what I had learned that weekend. I worked hard at marketing the events, particularly to potential candidates and those involved in the following year's county council elections. Attendances were in the 20–40 range, which meant that around 400 party members (about 10 per cent of the membership in the region) came to one. They were attracted in part by the novelty of this strange new person from Liverpool, who seemed to have a knack of winning elections and was beginning to make an impact in a region where the Liberal Party was not noted for electoral success. I led each day myself in order to develop my relationship with the activists. The days were absolutely exhausting, but hugely rewarding in motivating those there, changing the way in which they fought elections and helping the party to become more successful. Successes at first were most notable in council by-elections.

I had always found council by-elections to provide the best possible means of learning, training and experimenting in campaign techniques. Across the region there were generally several each month. I prioritised them carefully with four, five or six visits to a by-election campaign if I sensed that there was sufficient commitment and willingness to use the right techniques to give us at least a chance of winning. This meant spending several days each week, particularly at weekends, meeting the local activists, seeing what was planned, often persuading them to change much of what they planned to do, and frequently writing most of the leaflets and letters for them. But I rarely adopted this very direct approach to running a by-election in the same council area a second time, despite many requests that I should repeat it. I explained that they had got a 'model' set of leaflets, and needed to learn from what

I had shown them by doing it themselves, with guidance from me, ALC and others. I knew that there was significant scepticism about my role as an 'area agent' working for the national party in the region, but the fact that each month I was responsible for at least one or two council by-election gains, often with spectacular swings, helped me to win friends and made me feel that I was justifying my existence there.

In each of these council by-election campaigns I learned a lot about the local party and in particular who actually did things as opposed to just talking about what should be done. The gender balance of many party events was particularly interesting. I did a round of meetings with almost every 'constituency executive' in the first year. These 'executive' meetings were generally about 85 per cent male and comprised, in my view, people who liked to 'authorise' things to happen. The volunteers who worked at the council by-elections were, however, generally at least 50 per cent female and consisted by definition of people who *did* things. I frequently highlighted this finding at party meetings in future, to the embarrassment of male-dominated gatherings.

The 'Trevor Jones' techniques were invariably successful wherever I tried them, and I added to them as I learned in each council by-election much more about what worked most effectively. In a council by-election in Matlock in early 1985, where a legendary Liberal figure called Peggy Edwards was a councillor, I was asked to help. Peggy had crossed swords with quite a few people in the party, but I was pleased that she seemed to take to me, and I was trusted sufficiently to take over the running of the campaign on polling day. This was usually just a matter of organisation and drive. But it was clear to me from the numbers of people that appeared to be voting for us, and the number of people that appeared not to be, that we were not going to win. Our candidate Steve Flitter's greatest area of support was where he lived on a council estate with the pleasant title of 'Hurst Farm'. Its residents, however, had many problems, including major concerns about a planning issue.

The local party owned one of the old-fashioned duplicators that could splatter ink everywhere (unlike modern equivalents) and I needed a typewriter and a duplicating skin on which you typed and then the ink went through the holes onto the paper. Having got the facts about the local issues from Steve and from Peggy, I wrote a letter in the name of the candidate about 'how proud people on the Hurst Farm estate would be if one of the local residents was one of the councillors, representing them'. The letter spoke of his concern about many of the issues that we listed on the estate. Then he invited them to sign a petition about the planning issue that should be returned to his helper outside the polling station when they voted later that day. Of course, some people had already voted. But after delivery of the letter people started pouring out of the houses on the estate, taking the signed petition forms to the polling station, handing them in to our helper and then going on to vote for us. Very few people in elections in the mid-'80s delivered anything on polling day apart from reminders to vote to known supporters. This duplicated letter made the difference in that campaign, and the members in West Derbyshire took to me overnight as we celebrated a famous victory and the election of a new Liberal councillor.

Quite often it was much more of a struggle persuading local members to follow the sort of campaign blueprint that I proposed. In a Charnwood by-election north of Leicester, I persuaded the team that we needed to do a door-to-door residents' survey at the beginning of the campaign. This has become quite normal practice over the decades since. But it was rarely done then, and the process of surveying was clearly not understood by the team there, who told me that they proposed to put the 200 or so completed surveys in a box and look at them after the election if we won! It took some time persuading them that the hard work was only just beginning, which was to identify all the issues and the areas with particular concerns, and to decide how to campaign on them. But this they did, reporting back on their actions and going on to win. The victory was one of a long series of council by-elections that I helped to win in Leicestershire. The *Leicester*

Mercury ran a story about these Liberal by-election wins, describing how 'Zeal and Expertise is the key to victory'.

I wasn't sure where I would live in the East Midlands. I hoped at first to be able to buy a modest property. But my party salary was not really sufficient to do so on my own, I had little time to look after a property, and I was still living in fear of the Militant libel action possibly bankrupting me. Jeff Lamb had bought a house in Leicester and let out some of the rooms, so he offered one to me. I agreed to move there for a few weeks whilst I sorted out what to do. I moved out four years later. My working days were very long and there was much travel involved. I had borrowed the money from the bank to buy a modest car (a Mark 2 Ford Escort) to enable me to do the job, and the party paid a mileage allowance so that I could run it. In the early days, I tended to go from Leicester to Loughborough to the regional office and then after office hours there was always an evening meeting I had to attend somewhere in the region. If I left Loughborough at 5 p.m., I could be anywhere in the region for 7.30 p.m. If the meeting finished at 10 p.m., I could be back for not much after midnight. Jeff was generally kind enough to stay up with an open bottle of red wine so that I had a little time to unwind.

Jeff had agreed to be the agent in Leicester's Crown Hills ward for the 1985 county council elections. The Liberal Party had not won a single election in Leicester since 1962, but we were determined to see if the 'Liverpool campaign techniques' could also be successful in a city such as Leicester. It was not the ideal ward to try them as it was seen as a 'solid' Labour area. Our candidate was Rob Renold, who I knew about from the Young Liberals nationally. He had stood in the area twice before, including in a council by-election, so there was some initial name recognition. The area was approximately 70 per cent Asian, and about 20 per cent of the electorate did not speak English. Some people got to know Rob as we called round with our surveys and featured his local campaigns in our leaflets. We found that we could overcome some of the language barriers within the Asian community with personally addressed letters in envelopes that tended to be read and discussed in family groups. In the pre-computerised era, this meant a lot of hand addressing that was 'farmed out' to volunteers. Sometimes it was done by groups of the Leicester University Liberal Students who we invited round to drink the cheap red wine that we provided whilst they wrote envelopes until the small hours of the morning – or until the red wine ran out (we generally didn't let it). The letters had a big impact with all voters.

One of our lucky breaks was discovering the poor quality of the food in the university halls of residence on Sundays. These meals (like my recollection of school meals for boarders) were prepared on a Saturday and refrigerated for Sunday lunchtime. The leftovers for Sunday tea were again pretty undesirable. I was generally working six and a half days per week on pure politics and very long days at that (a pattern I maintained for decades). But as a break from campaigning, I was very happy to cook on Sunday evenings. A big curry, chilli, occasionally a casserole or even pizzas could feed a lot of hungry students. In return for this, they delivered a lot of leaflets for us and as they progressed we trained them in door-knocking. We also had a lot of fun with breaks for *Spitting Image*, the political satirical puppet show, and a lot of laughter, except when the red wine got spilt on the neatly written envelopes. One of the students who came along initially for the free food, Paul Rainger, became one of my long-term friends.[12]

One of the ALC training exercises was called 'Evaluating your ward'. You had to assess the relative strengths of each party in each part of the ward, examine the local issues and determine what you needed to do in order to win. It was clear to us that the most heavily Asian polling district based around Moat Road would be more than 80 per cent Labour, making it impossible for us to win unless we did

---

12   Paul Rainger later became a campaign officer and then director of campaigns for the Liberal Democrats. He is probably the best campaigner that I have ever worked with and he later made the difference in electing MPs in a series of different constituencies in successive general elections.

something about it. There were only about 500 houses in this polling district, but they were amongst the most dilapidated in Leicester
and in need of significant renovation. In Liverpool, I had been involved in campaigns for 'Housing Action Areas' to be declared so that
75 per cent improvement grants would be awarded to pay for basic
renovation. This seemed appropriate for the Moat Road area. Public
meetings for candidates are rare events these days, but we decided
to hold one for Moat Road residents to discuss the campaign for a
'Housing Action Area'. Individually topped and tailed letters were sent
out inviting people to the meeting. In households where the adults
did not speak English, the children often read out and translated the
letter line by line and family groups discussed it. In order to make
the meeting interesting, I persuaded Tony Loftus to drive over from
Liverpool, 'borrowing' the city council's slideshow presentation about
Housing Action Areas for the occasion. (We knew that the Militant
regime would not have approved of lending it out for this purpose, but
they weren't to know!) Tony explained the Housing Action scheme,
Rob chaired the meeting, and about forty residents attended and went
home explaining it to their families and neighbours.

On polling day, the Moat Road area divided evenly between ourselves and Labour. Across the ward there was massive intimidation by
Labour supporters at all the polling stations, with up to a dozen Labour
workers telling approaching Asian voters that they must vote for their
Labour county councillor. He was well known within Labour circles
but less so to local voters. Every Asian voter was harangued by these
Labour supporters as they entered the polling station and were firmly
told in Hindi, Punjabi or Gujarati that they must vote for the Labour
candidate on the ballot paper and they were told which number he
was. The intimidation worked to a powerful extent and was Labour's
only real campaign effort. I felt very frustrated running a rural committee room in Lincolnshire that day and receiving phone calls from
Leicester about these tactics, unable to do much about them. When
the polls closed at 9 p.m., I drove back to Leicester in haste to Jeff's

house, which was campaign HQ. I arrived whilst everybody else was at the count and put on Radio Leicester to listen to the results. A local member, Harry Datt, arrived soon afterwards with a bottle of whisky and we decided to have a drink to relieve our stress. He was in despair as the results were coming through and there were very poor Liberal votes in most wards. He assumed that we would do well everywhere or nowhere. As the whisky flowed, I tried to explain targeting to him, that the results that we were listening to didn't matter, and that we must listen out for Crown Hills and the Knighton wards. There wasn't much whisky left in the bottle when the first of these results came through.

Labour had lost Crown Hills; Rob Renold had won by 132 votes in spite of the intimidation, and he had become the first Liberal councillor to be elected in Leicester for twenty-three years. A few minutes later, Anne Crumbie, most of whose leaflets I had designed, was declared as the new Liberal councillor for West Knighton with a 490 majority. Bob Pritchard missed gaining a third Leicester ward by ninety-eight votes in East Knighton that night (where another Leicester student, Iain Sharpe, who was later to be heavily involved in Lib Dem campaigning in Watford, had also been following the style of campaign that I had set for the other wards). It was a great party in the house that night, with Liberals from across Leicester coming over. It is also one of the rare occasions when I remember doing a 'thank-you speech' to the activists, whilst quite drunk, and nobody cared about hangovers the next day.

The fourth priority I had set for myself in the region was party membership. Whilst being a member did not mean that you were necessarily a helper in elections, the number of helpers you had generally correlated to the number of members. Members were not only loyal voters, they contributed financially through their subscriptions and by supporting appeals and fundraising activities. Finance was always a major problem if you wanted to run a proper campaign, and we did not have the sort of funding that the Labour and Conservative parties generally enjoyed. So, the Liberal Party desperately needed more members. This was a national priority for the team of Liberal area agents employed by the HQ, and we were effectively told that we needed many more members paying in if the party was to be able to continue paying our salaries.

A promotional video was made with the production costs being met by Sir Anthony Jacobs, a generous party donor. Our brief was to show it to groups of party members and then take all those willing out on the doorsteps aiming to recruit new members from amongst people who had previously indicated their support. A guidebook for the membership campaign was also needed and after many weeks of laborious work, the director of policy at party HQ produced one. It was completely incomprehensible and was quickly junked before it became a barrier to recruitment. I was asked to write a much more 'activist-friendly' guide and 'Members, Money and Workers' was published through Tony Greaves and the ALC in order to try to get the party's activist core and councillors more involved in recruiting members.

This booklet was followed a year later by 'Keeping Members, Getting Activists', which I wrote with my friend and fellow area agent Bill MacCormick. Bill was brilliant at writing letters, particularly those seeking to raise funds. He and I studied fundraising techniques using direct mail in the United States. In an era when the Liberal Party lacked any national list of members, and before home computers became very common, the booklets were very useful to local associations, and membership numbers grew nationally. Inevitably, we found it easier to recruit in more affluent areas than in poorer ones where people had much greater pressures on their budget. The Leicester students were amazed that we could collect quite large sums of money to join the party in West Knighton, which was relatively affluent, but we struggled to collect subscriptions in the much poorer Crown Hills. We also had success identifying poster sites, potential helpers and people who needed postal votes.

In the first year of this campaign, I could show that I had helped to increase membership in the East Midlands region by about 15 per cent (from about 4,000 members to about 4,600). As with the campaign training days, I ran sessions all over the region doing two or three of them per week on the evenings or weekends when not otherwise committed to party events. Part of the plan was always to engage the new members quickly in party activities. Two new members in Leicester who arrived for an Indian food social evening at Rob Renold's house were asked to 'go and collect the food' and given the address of some local Asian supporters who were cooking the curries. When they got there they very surprised by the dumfounded response to 'We've come for the food'. After several awkward minutes explaining that they were not in fact begging for some of the residents' own dinner, they realised that they had been given the wrong address. The experience did not put them off and Brian and Kay Brown became very good friends, doing a lot of work with us in Leicester before moving to Liverpool where Brian became a councillor.

CAMPAIGNING WITH ALC AND
THE NATIONAL PARTY

Around this time my own role with the ALC developed significantly. At the request of a friend and former Liverpool councillor who worked for the ALC, David Vasmer, I began writing up to a third of the bi-monthly ALC Bulletin. This was sent to around 3,000 party activists (including about 2,000 councillors) and I was elected to the Standing Committee of the ALC with a large vote from their membership. I also started writing a series of campaign booklets which became the main election campaign guides for the Liberal Party in the 1980s. The first of them was 'Winning By-elections', based on my experiences in Liverpool and the East Midlands.

I never took my holiday entitlement in those days; something that I later realised was unwise. A change of role was as much as I managed and I spent some of the summer of 1985 working for the ALC on the *Assembly Gazette* publication for the annual Liberal Assembly that was to take place in Dundee that year. The main aim was simply to raise funds for the ALC through advertising. The last edition had put just over £1,000 into their coffers and I was determined to do much better. With the help of a student volunteer, Simon Jones, we raised £8,500 for the ALC that August/September – the equivalent of my annual salary and enough, therefore, for the ALC to recruit Adrian Sanders, later MP for Torbay, as an additional member of staff the following year.

I enjoyed the work with the ALC, although it brought me into conflict with my paymasters in the national Liberal Party Organisation at my first Liberal Assembly after becoming an area agent. John Spiller, the secretary-general, had taken a big gamble in employing a team of professional agents, hoping that once they were employed, he could raise the finance for their salaries. The only way to provide the funds for our employment was for the national party to get the sum of £2 for each membership card issued, instead of just 50p.

All decisions about matters such as membership subscriptions were decided by the annual Liberal Assembly. There was a fierce debate on this most controversial measure. The reputation of the national party organisation was poor. Local campaigners naturally felt that the money raised locally was better spent locally. The ALC's Standing Committee had decided to recommend voting against the new subscription scheme; even though the ALC depended to a significant degree on a grant from the national party. The ALC's political secretary, Maggie Clay (who I regarded as a friend and great ally in the party), was to speak for the 'campaigning wing' against the scheme. John Spiller told me that I had better speak in favour of the scheme during the debate. I was nervous; I was still only twenty-four and, I had not spoken at anything like the 1,500-strong Assembly before, but his plan for employing me and my new colleagues depended upon winning the debate. With considerable trepidation, therefore, I spoke. I outlined some of what I had done in Liverpool and what I was now doing as an area agent. I said that it was not a choice between money locally or money nationally, but a balance that meant that people like me could take what I had done in Liverpool, and what I was doing in the East Midlands, and help to make the party more successful in more of the country. There was some thunderous applause, especially from the Young Liberals and Liberal Students who knew me well, and from people who had seen something of what I could do in elections. The vote for Spiller's scheme was carried and the party would have a budget for the following year that provided for campaigning.

The annual Liberal HQ Christmas party was a great event in those days, well organised by then finance director Dee Doocey[13] in the historic and appropriate venue of the National Liberal Club. John Spiller took me aside at the party to tell me in confidence that the chief agent of the party, John Holmes, would be retiring some time the following year. I liked John Holmes very much. He had good judgement, had been a brilliant organiser in his heyday, but it was felt by many that he was now burned out and in need of retirement. John Spiller told me that he would want me to be his successor. I was flattered and more than slightly alarmed. I still felt that I had a lot to learn, but I also knew how I wanted to drive the party machinery to make it more successful.

However, the opportunity that John Spiller outlined to me then did not arise – at least not for another five years. I continued pursuing my priorities in the East Midlands, whilst working with the ALC nationally and taking a more active role in the parliamentary by-elections cropping up across the country. In October 1984, the country was shocked by the IRA bombing of Brighton's Grand Hotel. When it became known that Sir Anthony Berry, MP for Enfield Southgate, had been killed in the bombing, there was a debate about contesting the vacancy. Would a by-election be giving in to the IRA? Or would the Tories nominating a successor without a by-election be a defeat for democracy? It took some weeks before the Liberal Party concluded

---

13   Now Baroness Doocey and a former Richmond councillor and member of the Greater London Authority.

that it would actually be 'giving in to terrorism' if the democratic process of letting people choose their MP in the subsequent by-election
was somehow suspended. Because of the time needed to choose a
candidate, the writ for the by-election was moved before a Liberal candidate could be chosen by local members. One of the three weeks of
the campaign was effectively lost in terms of leafleting and canvassing
as no candidate's name could appear before the selection. Our hastily
put together campaign began with a one-bedroom first-floor flat as
temporary HQ, before moving to two 'portacabins' in a pub car park.

Tim Slack was seen as a strong Liberal candidate. The major controversy at the time was the government plans to massively increase
the contributions that parents were expected to make towards their
children's living costs at university. Cracks were also beginning to show
in the popularity of the Thatcher government. We set out to exploit
them and present Tim Slack and the Liberal–SDP Alliance as the alternative to the Tories. The area also had a large Labour vote to which
we could appeal. For the first time in a Liberal by-election, we used a
computerised database, the 'Election Agents Record System' (known
as EARS) devised by John Jefkins, to help produce a lot of material
targeted towards potential Labour supporters urging them to switch to
Tim Slack to beat the Tory (Michael Portillo). A red-coloured leaflet
in the most Labour inclined areas sought to point out the weaknesses
of Labour's position. We printed a campaign newspaper, *The Enfield
& Southgate Courier*, with the headline 'Southgate turns to the Alliance' by Chris Rennard. It was the last time I had my own name on
one of these newspapers as it caused a little embarrassment to David
Steel on the election night *Newsnight* 'Special' when he was shown
the newspaper and asked: 'Who is this Chris Rennard?' In two and a
half weeks, we ran a campaign that reduced the 16,000 Conservative
majority to less than 5,000 and pushed Labour below deposit-losing
level.[14] Of longer-term significance perhaps was the bonding of a core

---

14   The deposit-saving level was then 12.5 per cent.

team working on strategy and literature for the by-election that comprised Bill MacCormick, Peter Chegwyn and me. The three of us all reflected on the lost time in the campaign when the party (unbeknown to David Steel, who wanted to press ahead with a campaign quickly) debated whether to fight the by-election or not. We all assumed that there would be no such debate in future if there was to be such a terrible cause for a by-election again.

The big dip in the popularity of the Thatcher government was also illustrated by the result of the Brecon & Radnor by-election in July 1985. I was only a helper on the periphery of that by-election campaign, but went with friends from Leicester to help. The by-election was seen initially as a struggle between the Liberal (Alliance) campaign and Labour's to demonstrate which party had the better prospect of defeating the Conservatives. I would like to think that if I had been there full-time, or at least at the crucial time, one of the most embarrassing (and I believe disgraceful) episodes in Liberal by-election campaigning would have been avoided. The Liberal campaign drafted a leaflet pointing to the supposed importance of local Liberal candidate Richard Livsey having a 'secure family background'. I have questioned some of those involved in this campaign many times since about what happened. They say that Richard Livsey's 'family man' image was being contrasted with that of the unmarried Labour candidate Richard Willey (in itself quite disgraceful in my view). They claim complete ignorance about the fact that the Conservative candidate, Chris Butler, was gay. The press pack attending the daily press conference was certainly not so ignorant. Richard Livsey was put under great pressure about the leaflet and eventually apologised unreservedly. Apologising in such circumstances was deeply damaging and I feared that the by-election might have been lost because of the leaflet. In questioning the team, I was told that the draft version of the leaflet had the 'secure family background' phrase underlined and the only change felt necessary in the team, and significantly also in London as they considered the draft, was to remove the underlining. Two years after the

Bermondsey controversy over the inference taken from the use of the 'straight choice' phrase, this episode should not have happened, and it caused widespread anger and embarrassment within the party. I was determined that this sort of incident would never be repeated.

Richard Livsey's own character and perceived decency was what probably rescued his campaign from this well-publicised setback. He was a very gentle, very caring man with a great knowledge of the agricultural issues that appealed strongly to many of the Conservatives now having their doubts about the Conservative government. I went to help in the last few days and witnessed some of the best of the old-style Liberal campaigning side by side with some of the most modern. David Penhaligon, the Liberal MP for Truro, was a great character held in much affection by the party. He brought up his old offset litho printing machine from Cornwall and set it up at the back of the HQ. He was an engineer and joked about how he liked to keep his machine going 'with a few "lacky" bands' if necessary. Next to his machine was Paddy Ashdown's brand-new laser printer. This was the first by-election in which we used computers linked to laser printers to mass produce target letters personally addressed to individual voters. The laser printer was much slower at printing than David Penhaligon's old machine, so David delighted in teasing Paddy about how the Truro printing press had produced 100 leaflets, whilst Paddy's laser printer was producing its second one ... and so on.

The letters from Paddy's machine, however, were written as if from David Steel, with personal addresses, salutations and a printed blue signature. It had been quite common in our by-election campaigns to produce a letter from the very popular Liberal leader. This was the first time that we had used a computer program, called 'Polly', to produce them. Bill MacCormick was in charge of this operation and I suggested to him that we varied the PS on the bottom of the letters to make a slightly different appeal to voters according to the information that we held from our canvass. This was revolutionary then, but soon became common practice. People now receive huge numbers of computer-generated letters. But these letters were hugely effective then in an era when people did not expect such things. John Spiller came up to the campaign for a short while and told me how he listened to the conversation in a local pub as one man got a letter out of his pocket and showed it to his friend: 'I've had a letter from David Steel!' he proudly boasted.

The campaign was probably the finest hour in the career of Richard's by-election agent Andy Ellis, a legendary figure in Liberal politics. He made sure that the organisation was much stronger than in Penrith two years previously and thousands of Liberal activists poured into the constituency that became the focus of much media attention. It became clear to me in the last week that our attempt to portray Labour in third place was no longer credible. To his credit, Andy was willing to devolve organisation and the writing of the last-minute leaflets to others. His strong reputation with the media was, however, crucial in persuading them that we were heading towards victory. Although the seat was Tory held, the Conservatives were almost certainly now in third place. With the help of David Penhaligon's printing machine, I designed the last-minute leaflet for all the more 'Tory-inclined' rural areas, urging Tories to switch to us to keep out Labour.

Polling day saw all three main parties competing vigorously. Labour hopes were greatly boosted by an Ipsos MORI opinion poll suggesting that they were heading for a massive 25 per cent margin of victory. The *Daily Mirror* led with this on its front page. But Labour made the fatal mistake of reprinting this and delivering it widely across the constituency on polling day. It encouraged Conservative-minded voters to switch to us to prevent this Labour 'landslide', and it told Labour supporters that they didn't need to bother voting. The southern part of the constituency, Ystradgynlais, was heavily Labour territory. They spoke of the 'Taffia' who ran things locally, and I was advised that we should not have Liberal posters on our cars as people would not travel to the polling stations in such vehicles for fear of hostility from their neighbours. I was sceptical about this claim until I called on a lady on the eve of poll to ask if she could help out at a polling station the next day. She was on a list of supporters, but said no. Later she rang me at HQ to say that she had said no only 'in case her neighbours overheard', but that she was willing to help providing that an unmarked car took her somewhere outside her local area. We were clearly not going to win that part of the constituency, but we knew that every vote might count and I got 93 per cent of the identified Liberal supporters out to vote on polling day from my committee room in Upper Cwmtwrch. I also got to know two young Oxford students who came to help in my committee room that day, Bridget and Paul Fox, who later became Islington councillors and then parliamentary candidates.

As ever, the core team indulged in a little private speculation about the outcome at the end of the campaign. Andy had forecast victory to the media and stuck by it privately. Canvass cards were still analysed manually in those days and Michael Key had this job, as he had in Orpington and Sutton & Cheam. He thought that we would probably narrowly lose. I studied the trends that I had learned to be crucial, and said to Michael that I thought that we would win, by about the same margin that we had lost in Penrith. Penrith had been lost by 552, so I was pleased to be so accurate in my forecast when Richard Livsey won by 559.

Party spirits were high after the Brecon & Radnor win. I drove from Brecon to Leicester and then later that day down to Hastings for the ALC conference to run some training sessions. Paddy Ashdown was also speaking there; many of us thought that he was building support for an eventual leadership bid and so cultivating the support of the 'ALC' constituency of activists was very important for him. That July also saw a simmering row come to a head over the running of the party nationally. Sir Hugh Jones[15] was thought to be widely displeased with the appointment of John Spiller as his successor and with his reorganisation of party structures, which reduced administrative staff

---

15   He was knighted for his services to the Liberal Party in 1984 having stood down as secretary-general.

at party HQ and created instead the network of area agents. As he stood down as secretary-general, Hugh had sought to retain significant power by standing for election as treasurer on a joint ticket with Anthony Jacobs.[16] The election of treasurer in those days was a one-person-one-vote election amongst Assembly delegates. At the 1983 Assembly, many activists preferred to vote for Liverpool's Sir Trevor Jones to be treasurer, but Trevor was unable to attend the Assembly and this probably cost him the election. Hugh then found himself an office within the National Liberal Club and continued exercising influence over the party organisation. This made John Spiller's position as the new secretary-general extremely difficult. The tension came to a head when a substantial legacy of around £80,000 was left to the party. This was in the context of an annual party budget of only around £500,000 at the time. Hugh said that the wishes of the person leaving the money were expressed to him as being for the creation of a 'fund-raising unit' under Hugh's direction. John Spiller wanted to be able to spend the money on campaigning and in particular the area agent network. The National Executive became very divided. Former Bodmin MP Paul Tyler had become chairman of the National Executive and sought to protect John Spiller's position. But John was not good at coalition building and he made a number of enemies, including some of the staff who had lost out in his reorganisation. Spiller became ill through the stress and resigned that summer. The National Executive decided immediately to appoint Andy Ellis as acting secretary-general. When he was appointed permanently, and John Holmes retired as chief agent shortly afterwards, Andy effectively undertook the role of chief agent in addition to being secretary-general. This meant that there would not be a national campaigning position of the kind that John Spiller had intended for me, and I was naturally disappointed by this. There was at the same time considerable concern about the lack of experienced senior management within the organisation and a deputy

---

16   Anthony was a generous funder to the party, was knighted in 1988 and made a peer in 1997.

secretary-general was appointed. Simon Bryceson was a very strong appointment made particularly in order to help with the communications aspects of the general election that was due in 1987.

LOSING BY 100 VOTES

By the spring of 1986, I had been an election agent nine times and won nine times. My work in the East Midlands, the publications I was producing for the ALC and the training sessions I was running at the Liberal Assemblies all resulted in a higher profile for me in the party. I felt that this did me no harm given the relative lack of job security that appeared to go with any sort of career in politics. In March, there was a diary story in a newspaper suggesting that Matthew Parris, the Conservative MP for West Derbyshire, was about to become the next presenter of the very popular Sunday lunchtime programme *Weekend World*, taking over from Brian Walden. Most people thought this an unlikely prospect, but I arranged to meet the West Derbyshire Liberals' constituency executive on Wednesday evening. Christopher Walmsley, who worked for the BBC in Manchester, had just been chosen as their candidate. On that Wednesday morning, the news was confirmed that Matthew Parris was indeed resigning as an MP to do the job. I knew that this would be my tenth campaign as an election agent.

It was clear to me at the outset of the West Derbyshire campaign that the Tories would call the by-election for the first Thursday in May to coincide with the local elections. They were clever and devious enough, however, to brief widely that the by-election would be in the autumn. This made it harder to mobilise many of our helpers who had their own local elections in May and trusted the newspaper reports about the autumn date. Our campaign also began before the Fulham by-election polled and some Liberal, and all the SDP, resources were devoted to Roger Liddle's campaign there. We had hardly started our campaign in West Derbyshire when the Conservative MP for Ryedale died and a Yorkshire by-election was likely to be held on the same timetable. Ryedale was more clearly a two-way Conservative vs. Liberal Alliance contest and was in a seat where local councillor Elizabeth Shields already had a strong vote. She had a tremendous opportunity to become the first woman Liberal MP for many decades and a lot of members chose to help her campaign as a result. My fellow area agent Jane Merritt was the agent for that campaign and we kept closely in touch. The number of helpers that we could muster in West Derbyshire was to be much reduced by the local elections and these other by-elections.

Labour were in a stronger position in West Derbyshire than in Ryedale, and they also had the advantage of having the only local candidate (Christopher Walmsley lived in Manchester and the Conservative Patrick McLoughlin[17] was from Staffordshire). Labour also received a big boost by winning the Fulham by-election convincingly and pushing the SDP into a poor third place. We began quickly by targeting Belper, the biggest town in the constituency and the largest area of Labour support. The decline of the town featured on our first 'Focus' leaflet: 'Ghost Town Fears'. Other editions of 'Focus' followed for each area, with surveys and petitions covering every major settlement in the 400-square-mile constituency.

By-elections tended to have much longer 'run-in' periods in those days. Ten or twelve weeks from date of death or resignation to polling day was quite common. We used the period before the writ was moved to campaign effectively on issues such as bus deregulation (that was thought to threaten many local bus services), rate increases (forced through as a result of central government cutbacks), and for a 'New Deal for Derbyshire' (as our alternative to the government's recent Budget). I had assured David Steel at a meeting in London that we were very keen to avoid any embarrassing issues such as those at Brecon and Bermondsey. We would lead with good positive messages,

---

17   He later became Secretary of State for Transport and was made Conservative Party chairman in 2016.

but would also feature heavily the need for Labour voters to switch if we were to overcome the 12,000 Conservative majority.

Public meetings do not generally get very big attendances these days, but Christopher Walmsley was a very good public speaker and we attempted to hold a meeting in every community, however small, with most of the Liberal and SDP MPs coming up to support us, either at these meetings or by leading canvassing teams. I recall telling one of the daily press conferences I chaired that 'there were only three empty seats in a village hall for one of his meetings the night before. This meant that the other eight seats were all full.' In the middle of the campaign, Mrs Thatcher gave permission to Ronald Reagan for US jets to bomb Libya. The reprisals involved killing British hostages in Lebanon and there was a widespread backlash against her decision, fuelled by the direct linking in news reports of the hostages' deaths with the bombing of Libya (which resulted in about sixty casualties but not the death of Gaddafi).

By tracking the canvass returns we knew that we were making good progress until a week before polling day. The Conservatives were fearful of losing as our posters sprang up across the constituency and Labour voters began switching to us. The BBC's Vincent Hanna was then the 'doyen' of by-election correspondents. He had employed students to conduct a number of opinion polls in the constituency and whilst I had good reason to be very doubtful of the methodology, they had been helpful to us previously. Sometime after the by-election, Matthew Parris told me how concerned he had been that we might win; his party would have laid the blame on him personally since the by-election was caused by his resignation. A week before polling day, he gave an interview to Vincent Hanna and made the 'unusual prediction' that Labour could be poised to gain the seat. The *Newsnight* programme including this interview was then widely picked up by the rest of the media. On the face of it, a former Tory MP predicting Labour to gain his former constituency seemed like an honest admission. But, as he wrote in his memoirs, 'had I not lied in an interview with the late Vincent Hanna, a BBC pollster carrying out a rogue poll which most improbably suggested that Labour and not the Liberal Democrats were the challengers in this by-election, [the Liberal Democrats] would have won. I knew what I said was false.'[18] I knew myself that the latest *Newsnight* poll was subject to a serious attempt to rig it, as one of the academics supervising the students conducting it told me so. The combination of the dodgy poll and the contrived Parris/Hanna manipulation had the desired effect of persuading some of our voters to switch to Labour, thereby dividing the anti-Tory vote and making it harder for us to win.

Just prior to the final weekend, the canvass returns for Ryedale (sent to me every day by my friend Paul Jacobs) showed that we were clearly on course to win comfortably there, with Labour nowhere in sight. In West Derbyshire, I reckoned that we were at that stage some 3,000 votes behind, but with some of our vote slipping back towards Labour. Nevertheless, it was essential to our prospects that we showed confidence in our own campaign if we were to regain momentum. Our final weekend tabloid newspaper therefore led with 'Walmsley set to win!' Labour had been trying to suggest that it was close three ways, but issued bar charts in their own literature showing levels of support revealing them to be in third place, albeit not far behind us. Ian Wright from the SDP, who came up to help me with the newspaper, seized upon this to run a front-page article headlined 'Labour admit they're third', in which I, as the Liberal agent, was quoted as saying that 'it was refreshingly honest for a political party in the closing stages of a by-election to admit this'. We redoubled our efforts in most of the places where Labour voters were most concentrated. We had canvassed Ken Robinson, who many years before had been chairman of the West Derbyshire Constituency Labour Party. He told us he had been Labour all his life, but hated Thatcher and Tebbit and 'would not follow Labour like a lemming'. We used this quote extensively.

---

18   Matthew Parris, *Chance Witness*, p. 348.

We had planned for David Steel to make two visits to the campaign and I begged him to make a third. This proved to be difficult with his diary. He had an engagement in Gleneagles on a Saturday night in the middle of the campaign, but agreed to come that morning if we were able to arrange for a helicopter to fly him from West Derbyshire to Scotland. I don't think he thought for a moment that we would. But his principal assistant Graham Watson[19] (who understood from me the urgency of the task) made intensive efforts to secure a helicopter and was able to persuade JCB to fly the Liberal leader from Matlock to Scotland, enabling him to make another campaign visit. Graham later told me that someone from JCB was personally 'handbagged' by Mrs Thatcher at a Downing Street reception for having helped us out in this way. The leader's 'walkabout' in Matlock and departure by helicopter again secured great media coverage. I asked him to say that we were 'within an inch of victory' and this provided very helpful headlines. The attendances at our public meetings were rising sharply. On the final Tuesday, we planned to hold three of them over the course of an evening with both Alliance leaders. David Owen agreed to speak at all three whilst David Steel did two of them. The combined attendances were well over a thousand people. The donations collected at them just about covered my budget shortfall. In those days, Liberal agents were given a very small amount of cash from HQ to fight parliamentary by-elections, and so had to raise the balance needed for the campaign themselves. As well as organising the by-election campaign, I managed to raise about 60 per cent of the budget for it.

The timing of all this activity proved to be particularly fortuitous in that the final opinion poll to be published by the *Daily Telegraph* was sampled over that last weekend. I was told that their samples showed us at a much higher level of support on the third day of sampling than on the first. The poll was published on the Tuesday morning. It showed us 5 per cent behind the Tories (39 per cent to 34 per cent with Labour

---

19   Later a Member of the European Parliament, and also knighted.

at about 25 per cent). Our printer, a Liberal volunteer, was working through the night and I quickly added to his workload with an extra leaflet. We managed to cover much of the constituency with it. Sadly, some parts of the organisation were not robust enough and we missed out key areas as some people felt that 'we had delivered enough leaflets'. Andy Ellis made periodic visits to our campaign and when I told him that we still needed to get the last-minute tactical leaflet delivered in Bakewell he went up there personally with about twenty volunteers from the Matlock HQ to make sure that this key town also received our leaflet highlighting the latest poll.

I sensed exactly the closeness of the contest. I told Michael Meadowcroft, then the Liberal MP for Leeds West who had taken over from David Penhaligon as chair of the Liberal By-election Unit, two days before polling day that the result would be 40:40:20, with 200 votes either way between ourselves and the Conservatives. During the campaign, I was staying with a local family in Matlock, but was embarrassed about creeping in during the small hours of every morning and getting up at about 5 a.m. to have a shower and get down to the HQ to work on things like leaflets before the morning press conference (daily press conferences were still part of the ritual of by-elections in those days). In the last week of the campaign, Ann took a week's holiday and rented a flat we could stay in near the HQ. This helped, but I did not sleep for more than a couple of hours on the Tuesday night or at all on the Wednesday night as we tried to pull together everything that we could do to try to make the difference. On polling day morning, I was first up in the constituency delivering early-morning leaflets from the Belper HQ from 4.45 a.m. I always believed in leading by example where possible. Our brilliant poster campaign organiser Mike Connors (lent to us by the SDP) also made sure that we had good poster board displays on all the main roads on the way in to the main towns and villages.

At about 6 p.m. on polling day, Vincent Hanna came into my office in the Matlock HQ. His students had been doing an exit poll at polling stations across the constituency. He congratulated me on our win; he said that we were heading for a 1,500 majority, had a lead of about 3 per cent and could not lose (as 3 per cent was the margin of error). Geraint Howells, the Liberal MP for Ceredigion, was with me in my office at the time making calls to sympathetic farmers across the constituency. I thanked Vincent and took over the phone to start ringing all the committee rooms. I had thirty-nine committee rooms across the constituency which were working to get our voters out. I rang each of them in turn to say that 'Vincent Hanna has just been in to my office. You are not supposed to know but we are heading to be 600 votes behind. He reckons, and I agree, that if we can get everyone to run between the doors this evening, instead of walking, we can get enough votes out to close the gap. Please can you pass the message on and make sure that we really pull out all the stops. Sorry I can't talk further, but I have got to ring every committee room.' Word of what I said about the exit poll went around like wildfire. Geraint was impressed with my 'spin' about the outcome, told me that I 'should go far' and started making more calls himself. By ten o'clock, as I was still speaking to committee room organisers, they generally reported that there were virtually none of our supporters still to vote.

The actual exit poll result, showing our 3 per cent lead, was broadcast shortly after the polls closed. Our team at the count was, of course, very happy, and the Tories looked very depressed. David Steel spoke to Christopher Walmsley about his portfolio in Parliament and the media were all convinced that we had won. We knew what target share of the vote we needed in each polling district and examination of the votes from the different ballot boxes confirmed that we were hitting those targets. There were also local elections in Belper, our strongest part of the constituency, taking place that day (with polling for local elections in those days closing at 9 p.m., an hour before it did for the parliamentary by-election). We soon had the good news that we had gained both of the Belper council seats. But around 1 a.m. I got the last of the turnout figures from each polling station. Belper had

had a thunderstorm that day and turnout there had been significantly less than elsewhere, only around 70 per cent. The more Tory-inclined towns and villages in the north and west of the constituency had enjoyed perfect weather and turnouts in them had been around 80 per cent. I suddenly realised that the result was going to be very close, much closer than we had been expecting until then.

When the total votes were first shown to me, we were 182 votes behind. The returning officer thought that this should end the process. I protested that this was very close (out of around 50,000 votes) and that requesting a recount was clearly reasonable. His deputy, the acting returning officer, to whom I had been talking for much of the evening, agreed and counting began again. I quickly briefed our counting agents that we must carefully check that every single vote due to us must be put in our piles, and that any vote that was dubious and was being given to our opponents should be challenged. Word quickly went out to the media that I had asked for the recount, giving a clear sign that we were unlikely to win. Many of our supporters were in a nearby pub which had been an unofficial alternative HQ for the last ten weeks. The landlord later told me that sales were extremely good until about 2 a.m. when the recount was announced, but that after that time he only sold a couple of orange juices.

The second count (and first recount) produced a Conservative majority of just ninety-four. At this point the returning officer thought that I should simply accept the result he now had. I said that I could not yet accept that figure. The returning officer, his deputy (who did almost all the real work), some of the staff counting the votes and all the parties' counting agents adjourned to a side room for a discussion which became quite heated. I argued that a change of eighty-eight votes between counts justified another recount. The returning officer tried to imply that this was an insult to his staff. I had spent the past few hours being incredibly polite and grateful to all the counting staff. I praised their efforts and said I was sorry that it was so close, and I made a particular point of praising the acting returning officer for the overall conduct of the election. This clearly helped when the returning officer consulted his staff and they again agreed that my request was reasonable. By this time, some of our helpers had come down to the school and were looking through the windows into this side room. They described how the returning officer and I were the only two people standing in the room, like a 'Western shoot out', whilst everybody else was sitting down observing us.

The third count and second recount began and this time produced a majority of 100 for the Conservatives. At this point, we adjourned to the side room again. I knew now that victory was a remote prospect. But the possibility remained that some of our votes could have been put in the Conservative pile – or in one of those for other parties. The returning officer was quite exasperated but I maintained my stance as firmly and as politely as possible. I was also mindful that there was no overnight broadcast and that if we went past 6.30 a.m. our result would be live on the TV breakfast news programmes. The fourth count (third recount) was what is more commonly known as a 'bundle check'. I agreed with the returning officer that either Michael Key or I would be allowed to personally inspect every vote cast against us to see if any of our votes were accidentally in the wrong piles, or see if we could find a complete bundle of 100 of our votes in a wrong pile, preferably the Tory one. Sadly, we found none and I had to accept defeat. The result was therefore a Conservative majority of exactly 100 votes for the second time and I could not argue any further. Christopher made the most gracious speech possible in the circumstances. He could refer to our success in Ryedale and our near miss in West Derbyshire. The result was finally declared as:

Patrick McLoughlin (Conservative)	19,896	39.5%
Christopher Walmsley (Liberal–SDP)	19,796	39.4%
Bill Moore (Labour)	9,952	19.8%
Rainbow Alliance	348	0.7%

We came out of the school into the playground just after dawn broke. Many of our supporters who had stayed up all night greeted us as we emerged, many of them in tears. It was a painful defeat for me. Some people blamed mistaken votes for the so-called 'Rainbow Alliance' which confused a few voters. Others asked why HQ in London did not switch some resources from Ryedale to West Derbyshire, given that Ryedale was won by 5,000 votes and West Derbyshire lost by 100. I just decided to learn what lessons I could from the experience. When referring to the by-election in later years, I often quoted the US politician Dick Tuck, who, when he narrowly lost an election to the California State Senate, said: 'Well, the people have spoken ... the bastards.'

CHAPTER 4

THE ALLIANCE AND
ITS AFTERMATH

POST BY-ELECTION DEPRESSION

Over several election campaigns, I came to recognise a pattern of significant depressive feelings following many of them, irrespective of the result. I felt that I had failed personally when we lost the West Derbyshire by-election by just 100 votes and for quite a while I lost much of my confidence. The campaign was the tenth occasion on which I had acted as the legal election agent, and the only time I had been unsuccessful. I believed that a double by-election win at that time would have propelled the Alliance much further nationally. As it was, Mrs Thatcher was able to dismiss the results of the by-elections, saying: 'We won one, we lost one, and the one that we lost we will get back.' The two parliamentary by-election results at least secured the main national headlines, avoiding the Alliance appearing to have been eclipsed by Labour's major successes in the local elections that year. Over the summer, there was much media commentary to the effect that the Conservative position was now so weak that Mrs Thatcher could not possibly call a general election in 1987.

ANOTHER NEAR MISS

Another parliamentary by-election soon followed in Newcastle under

Lyme in July 1986. I had been agitating for some time for the party to prepare for this prospect as the local MP, John Golding, was set to become general secretary of the Communications Union. The constituency was not in my East Midlands region, but in the next door West Midlands. The rigid party structure at the time prevented me from acting as the agent in another region. Despite my urging, the party had failed to prepare for the possibility of a by-election and, when it occurred, it failed to take seriously the prospect of us winning. This was perhaps understandable at first as it was a seat in which we were in third place, with the Conservatives second, less than 3,000 votes behind Labour.

The campaign was very short, but Alan Thomas, a local Liberal councillor, was an excellent candidate for us and we held a number of the local council seats. There was much resentment amongst local people as to how John Golding had manoeuvred to get a highly paid union job, whilst his wife obtained the Labour nomination to be his successor. We had a political campaign team in the by-election comprising me, Peter Chegwyn and a leading Young Liberal at the time, Mike Harskin. Between us, we produced some hard-hitting campaign leaflets suggesting that people were being taken for granted by the Goldings in what we described as a 'dynasty'. We squeezed the former Conservative vote ruthlessly and I believed that we were edging towards a win. When I drafted our final newspaper with the headline 'Alliance Victory Forecast', Andy Ellis (who acted as the agent) asked me: 'Who forecast that?' 'I did!' I said, but I meant it. He had much less belief in the possibility of us winning and the campaign organisation put together at very short notice proved to be very lacking in what we needed for a winnable campaign. Our professional organisation in many by-elections was generally praised. But volunteers in this campaign often had to wait very long periods in the HQ in order to be given anything to do, and then sometimes found themselves delivering leaflets in the same roads as other volunteers delivering the same leaflets. On the eve of poll, I actually forecast that we would lose by about 800 votes. It was the closest forecast I ever made, as we went on to lose by 799, though increasing our vote share by 17 per cent. Once again, the result was a source of great frustration for me, as we had failed to seize an opportunity for the Alliance to regain national momentum.

THE EASTBOURNE ASSEMBLY DEBACLE

National support for the Alliance remained at around 25 per cent throughout the summer of 1986, but it fell to 17 per cent in the autumn following the very poorly managed defence debate at the Eastbourne Liberal Assembly in September. I came to the conclusion following this that the difficulties involved in agreeing major policies, given David Owen's approach to negotiation, made the future existence of the Alliance unsustainable. The Liberal Party did not share David Owen's apparent long-term infatuation with nuclear weaponry. With significant reservations by some party members, Liberals were mostly in favour of membership of NATO (and the 'nuclear umbrella' that went with it). But there was significant disagreement in the party about the proposed Trident replacement for the Polaris submarines introduced in the 1960s when they came to the end of their service. A Joint Commission between the Alliance parties had been set up to decide what could be said at the forthcoming general election. It sensibly concluded in the summer of 1986 that this decision could be deferred beyond the next Parliament, thereby avoiding any split. But this decision was reported as a victory for David Steel, who was seeking compromise; whilst David Owen portrayed it incorrectly as a firm recommendation not to maintain a UK nuclear capability.

The Commission's report was publicly denounced by David Owen. In an attempt to secure an alternative agreement, both Alliance leaders then began promoting a nuclear defence policy which came to be portrayed as supporting a 'Euro bomb'. This would involve the UK guaranteeing to maintain a nuclear deterrent in cooperation with the French. It appeared to be a decision to launch a new generation of nuclear weapons. Preparation by the Liberal Party hierarchy for a debate on the issue at the Liberal Assembly was poor. Those opposed to the 'Euro bomb' proposal kept the leadership informed over the summer of their plans to try to stop it becoming official Liberal policy at the Assembly. The party president at the time, Des Wilson, is absolutely scathing about this failure of party management in his account of the 1987 general election, *Battle for Power*, and David Torrance gives a very good account of the episode in his biography of David Steel.[20] The two-leader structure was unsustainable. An 'Alliance leader' was really needed for the general election, but Owen would not reciprocate Steel's generosity to Jenkins prior to 1983, when the Liberal leader graciously gave way and effectively allowed Jenkins to be the Alliance choice for Prime Minister.

Steel was probably forced, somewhat reluctantly, into advocating the 'Euro bomb' option because Owen (to the anger of many people in the SDP, including Lord Rodgers of Quarry Bank) had vetoed the Joint Commission report. The Liberal Assembly did not feel bound to go along with Owen's alternative. I remember particularly Simon Hughes's passionate and persuasive arguments during the Assembly debate against the proposal. With twelve members of the EU at the time, he described the plan as meaning that there would be 'twelve fingers on the button'. He received a standing ovation for his speech, in which he said: 'We have never voted to replace [an] independent nuclear deterrent. Not only must we not do so now, but our policy must be to do so never and to replace an independent British nuclear deterrent by a European nuclear deterrent, even if that concept was workable, is not an acceptable alternative.'

The Liberal Assembly agreed that consideration should be given to a European defence policy. But the party hierarchy completely underestimated opposition to any commitment being made to renewing our independent nuclear deterrent (especially in this way). It

---

20   *David Steel: Rising Hope to Elder Statesman* (2012)

also completely failed to demonstrate to those voting in the debate that it was not about strengthening our hand in negotiations with David Owen, but about how our policy was perceived. The crucial amendment saying that European cooperation should be 'non-nuclear' was carried by 652 votes to 625. The votes were still being counted as 6 p.m. approached and in those days the party could only afford to hire conference halls during the day, vacating them in time for evening shows, which made a recount impossible. I thought at the time that such a recount might well have produced a different result, if only as a result of people changing their minds, as a signal would have been sent in the debate about unhappiness with the leadership position. But there was no time to count the votes again. The headline on the BBC's *Six O'Clock News* was 'defeat for David Steel's defence policy'. The newspaper headlines that followed were dreadful. Liberal MPs showed little self-control and I stood next to Russell Johnston as he spoke to journalists, saying that he 'had never felt so sick in his entire life'. After a brief period of very professional calmness on David Steel's part, those in charge of the party's media management ensured that the damaging headlines were repeated. In his closing speech, Steel strongly attacked the 'non-nuclear' decision, and those who had voted for it. With very few exceptions (such as with Neil Kinnock's belated attack on the Militant Tendency a year earlier), I have never thought that leaders do well in the long run by attacking their own parties. Good party management skills could probably have avoided the crisis, but those close to the Liberal leadership were not good at this, and were too often contemptuous of 'party activists'. The eventual compromise agreed some weeks later between Steel, Hughes and others could and should have been put in place prior to the Assembly, but the process of securing any agreement was made extremely difficult by David Owen's behaviour. It was a very low point for the Alliance, and from which it did not properly recover. The resulting acrimony over this issue lingered for a very long time and was a major factor in the disintegration of the Alliance following the 1987 general election.

Three further parliamentary by-elections provided the best opportunities for the Alliance to try to get back on track. In November 1986, there was a by-election when Robert Kilroy-Silk quit his safe Labour seat in Knowsley North, just outside Liverpool, to become host of his own TV chat show. I spent the last two weeks of the campaign in Knowsley. Labour's majority was cut from 17,000 to under 7,000, but we didn't win.

THE DEATH OF DAVID PENHALIGON

I was in Liverpool just before Christmas 1986 when I was called from HQ by a friend in tears telling me of the death that morning of the Liberal MP for Truro, David Penhaligon, in a car crash. I had got to know David particularly well through the parliamentary by-election campaigns. He was a very charismatic and committed Liberal who believed, not just in representing his own constituency superbly, but in trying to get more Liberal colleagues elected through by-election campaigns in particular. He described these campaigns as 'providing the life-blood of the party'. He recognised that we would never establish ourselves without succeeding in local elections, and in by-elections, and he had also become a mentor and great source of personal encouragement to me. But I had no idea of his great standing in the country until he died. He had become a very popular and witty speaker, and a star performer on BBC1's *Question Time*, with a technique for making complicated problems seem simple and applying common-sense solutions to them. The BBC's *Nine O'Clock News* that night led with his death, and some very emotional commentary. The item lasted for a full nine minutes. Only then did I really recognise that David would almost certainly have become our next leader. He had much greater public recognition and support than Paddy Ashdown would initially have when he later became leader. David's widow Annette (later made a Dame by Paddy) was an essential part of the Penhaligon partnership that had won the affection of Truro voters, and her book, *Penhaligon*, should be compulsory reading for any aspiring Lib Dems who really want to know what it takes to win. There were many times, such as during the merger negotiations, when his practical common sense would have been of great benefit to the party. His public standing and the affection for him that had spread across the country would have helped the party survive in difficult times. His death was a great blow.

GREENWICH AND TRURO

On Christmas Eve 1986, the Labour MP for Greenwich died. An early opinion poll in January gave the SDP (who were fighting the seat) just 15 per cent of the vote. When I saw the poll, I felt some regret that I had agreed to be part of the by-election team there as it appeared to have little prospect of success for us. But to give great credit to the SDP HQ, they were committed to fighting it with absolute determination. They were also able to throw in massive resources because of the financial backing of David Sainsbury.[21] Sainsbury was an astute businessman who knew the value of doing well in parliamentary by-elections to the SDP's credibility.

The SDP had previously made a major effort in the Fulham by-election in March 1986, but their result there was disappointing and Labour had gained the seat. Their organisation in Fulham had been very professional, but the campaign on the two days that I spent with them (before becoming the West Derbyshire by-election agent) felt very cold. There was little sense of community campaigning based on identifying key local issues, or developing the momentum that a successful by-election campaign requires. Roger Liddle,[22] the SDP candidate, had neither the national standing of Shirley Williams or

---

21   Later a Labour peer and minister and very generous donor to Labour.
22   Who later defected to Labour in order to work with Tony Blair and Peter Mandelson in
      Downing Street and then became a Labour peer.

Roy Jenkins, nor the local credibility of other successful by-election candidates. The SDP team led by Alec McGivan (who had run the Warrington, Crosby and Hillhead campaigns) reviewed their disappointing third place in Fulham. They concluded that in order to succeed in future by-elections, the SDP's very professional organisation also required the sort of local campaigning flair that we more often had in Liberal-led by-elections (but where we generally lacked the scale of resources that the SDP could afford to commit). I had been asked, therefore, together with Peter Chegwyn and Bill MacCormick, to be part of the by-election team at the next big SDP-led campaign, which turned out to be Greenwich.

Winning seemed like a very tall order and would require making a gain from an opposition party, from a third-place position, by squeezing the votes of the party that had almost won. On my first visit there, I was impressed by the scale of intent shown by the SDP in hiring enormous premises (a former car showroom) which had a warehouse at the back into which they had installed three large printing machines, giving us tremendous capacity to print leaflets on site. More importantly, there was an immediately friendly reaction from local passers-by who saw us setting up the HQ and putting posters in the windows. Rosie Barnes was a great candidate to work with. She was a marketing professional and I was pleased that she approved of all my draft election literature and was fully appreciative of the efforts being made by the Liberal team. I also got on well in the campaign with John Cartwright, the SDP MP for the neighbouring Woolwich constituency. With a little difficulty, we managed to integrate the efforts of our Liberal campaign group with those of the SDP locally and nationally. The Conservatives had come close to winning the seat in 1983, but we believed that we could mount a better challenge to Labour. Labour's candidate, Deirdre Woods, faced a hostile press and was identified by it as a left-winger. The campaign brought together the very best of what the two Alliance parties could bring to campaigning. Around sixty of us were working as full-time volunteers out of the former car showroom and Alec arranged for all our names to be shown on a massive chart visible to everyone in the HQ.

Liberal and SDP members from all over the country arrived in their thousands. They included Gerald Vernon-Jackson, a friend I had not seen for some years since we had been at university together, and who was now actively involved in the party. Our campaign targeted former Conservative supporters so effectively that the Tory candidate, a councillor in Blackheath ward, eventually came third in our estimate of the vote shares in his own ward. We captured two thirds of the Tory vote from 1983, when they had come within 1,211 votes of gaining the seat. Throughout the campaign, the media remained sceptical about our prospects, even when an *Evening Standard* poll a week before polling day put Labour on 40 per cent, with Rosie Barnes on 35 per cent. I actually knew then that we would win and I committed the very last of my modest personal savings to this prospect at the local bookmakers. Most days I chatted to journalists attending the morning press conferences trying to raise their expectations of our prospects with the aim of obtaining favourable coverage that we could then use in our leaflets to further increase local belief in us winning. But I had little success. Several times I tried to convince Andrew Rawnsley (covering the campaign for *The Guardian*) that we were on course to win. I was always disappointed to read his reports in the paper following my briefings, as they never suggested that a win for us was even a remote possibility. But on the morning after polling day, I was delighted to see him queuing with me in the local betting shop, collecting his winnings.

There was a raucous victory party in the HQ on the night of the by-election to celebrate the majority of 6,611. David Owen ably demonstrated his own leadership skills by arriving 'impromptu' at the party immediately after the declaration of the result and making a speech about the significance of the result. It made for very good television pictures. A tiny stroke of meanness on the part of someone, however, meant that our volunteer activists were all due to be charged £3 for admission. Fortunately, I found the original invitation ticket left on the photocopier and 'liberally' copied sufficient numbers of them to make sure that all the hardest working volunteers were given free tickets for the party. It was a beautiful sunny morning when we eventually all staggered from the HQ to smarten up before the victory press conference. There was real hope for the Alliance again.

Further momentum for us came just before the 1987 general election, when David Penhaligon's former constituency of Truro was held with a swing to us from the Conservatives of almost 5 per cent and a majority of 14,617. Andy Ellis had overseen another spectacular by-election win. It was a great break for David's former researcher Matthew Taylor, who became the country's youngest MP at the age of twenty-four, and also a great tribute to the memory of a Liberal MP who had previously shown how it was possible for a Liberal to 'buck the trend' in elections.

THE 1987 GENERAL ELECTION

After the Alliance's narrow failure to achieve second place nationally in 1983, we had high hopes, and Labour had real fears, that we could get into second place during the campaign and then become the main challengers to the Conservatives. There was real belief amongst the members of the Alliance parties that fundamental change to the political system could be brought about, involving 'breaking of the mould of British politics', as had been sought in 1981, and that this would involve the introduction of proportional representation.

Sometime before the 1987 general election, I met with the Liberal Party's own general election team. The purpose of the meeting was for me to outline what we had done in the highly successful Liverpool Mossley Hill campaign in 1983, where we had gained the seat (and achieved a much greater swing to us than anywhere else in the country). I spent some time explaining the approach before most of the members present then dismissed what I was outlining more or less out of hand, saying things like, 'It wouldn't work in other constituencies' and that 'it was impossible to anticipate in advance where you might win, as seats popped up unexpectedly as victories in all sorts of places!' The national party devoted none of its limited resources in that election to supporting target seats (unlike the SDP), but some limited funding for them came as usual from the Joseph Rowntree Reform Trust.

I did not have a national role in the '87 campaign, but my jobs for the election included preparing packs of literature for Liberal candidates based on the most successful leaflets that I had produced in the parliamentary by-elections and which many of our candidates then adapted for their own constituencies. I also had to negotiate the standard 'election communication' draft for both Liberal and SDP candidates to adapt for their own constituencies. This involved negotiation with the SDP's Policy Unit. Liberals took a different approach to leaflets and did not see campaign literature as primarily statements of policy. My SDP counterparts for this negotiation were Danny Finkelstein and Andrew Cooper (who both later became Tory peers). It was hardly surprising that we struggled to agree the text on nuclear weapons.

My role during the campaign itself was confined to the East Midlands region and I found this very frustrating as I was unable to help any of our best prospect seats in the campaign. I maintained support, however, for West Derbyshire, where we increased our vote by nearly 1,000 since the 1986 by-election, but the Tories increased theirs by 10,000.

I was also the party's regional media coordinator for the East Midlands, which was really a full-time job in itself, and was a very challenging role given the weakness of both Alliance parties in the region. Nevertheless, I organised a very high-profile launch event at the start of the campaign for 'the two Davids' (as they became known) when they flew into East Midlands airport. What shocked me about this event was that as I ushered both leaders into a private room for a quick briefing before the press conference, they appeared to begin their first discussion about what to say. It was clear that the difficulties of making the Alliance function as a single campaign had not been overcome and there was no agreed script. So, I suggested to David Steel that he could congratulate the campaigners against nuclear dumping in Lincolnshire on the recent success of their campaign, as I had taken him there the year before. I suggested to David Owen he should have a go at Scargill since he had taken a strong line on the miners' strike and the region included the heart of the breakaway Union of Democratic Mineworkers. They were both very grateful to me for my suggestions, but we all had to rack our brains for something to say about the national issues. They rang Des Wilson, who was running the night team at Cowley Street, and who suggested pushing his 'rent a room' scheme to help provide more housing for people who struggled to find somewhere to live. But this was not one of the big issues of the election.

Many aspects of the Alliance national campaign were very professionally organised, and well-resourced compared to previous Liberal campaigns. But this counted for nothing in the absence of a clear and effective message that could persuade people why the Alliance should be supported. This experience taught me much about preparation for future campaigns (when I would ensure that all such scripts were agreed in advance, and when it was somewhat easier, but not necessarily straightforward, with just one leader).

It was also a challenge to organise a large rally in such a weak region, but with effective advertising I was able to get an audience of over 1,000 people in Nottingham for an 'Ask the Alliance' rally. Listening to Bamber Gascoigne discuss the format with the two leaders immediately before the event also convinced me that we were using a poor approach in relation to promoting any message. This involved asking the audience to put questions, hoping that they would be relevant and that the leaders would then produce effective (and compatible) answers, rather than promoting an agreed and effective message that we knew might persuade people to vote for us.

The 1987 general election was the first campaign in which journalists had mobile telephones. Those travelling on either of the leaders' 'battle buses' took great delight in asking a question of one of the Alliance leaders, and then phoning their colleagues on the other bus suggesting that they ask the same question of the other leader to try to get a different response. They were both aiming for the balance of power and a possible coalition. But at one point David Steel explained why it would be effectively impossible to work with Mrs Thatcher, whilst David Owen on the same day ruled out working with Labour because of their nuclear weapons policy. They both got trapped by the coalition issue and, as Roy Jenkins had warned them before the campaign began: 'The problem of aiming for the balance of power is the probability that you will miss.' Such a strategy depended upon people being able to vote for such an outcome. But this option was not one that people could see on the ballot paper and vote for. Achieving the balance of power depended upon the relative numbers of Labour and Conservative MPs elected, which was something that most voters in most constituencies could do little about (even with the Alliance at over 25 per cent in the polls).

In contrast, Labour ran a clearly focused campaign, with effective messages, but which sought to at least retain the support of their most likely supporters and keep their party in second place. Their newspaper adverts on three consecutive right-hand pages in the tabloids featured something like a teacher saying: 'Try telling him that his school has enough books', then a nurse saying: 'Try telling her that her hospital has enough nurses', and then a picture of Mrs Thatcher with the caption: 'Try telling her that she is wrong.' Their message was simple and effective, based on funding the key public services of health and education, which were weak issues for the Tories. The Tory campaign was also based on effective messaging and advertising that attacked Labour. Much of it was the work of John Sharkey, who worked for Saatchi & Saatchi at the time, and who later switched to the Liberal Democrats and helped us from 1997.

The Alliance challenge for second place nationally did not last long in the campaign. For the first time in a general election, parity had been achieved in national broadcasting entitlement (based on the 1983 results). But most media interest in the Alliance soon faded and the phones stopped ringing so frequently in the press office at HQ. The campaign's efforts descended into farce one day when it was suddenly discovered that the party election broadcast to be shown that night would be of ten minutes' duration, not the five that had been expected. This resulted in lots of footage, not originally intended for broadcast, of Rosie Barnes stroking her pet rabbit.

The Alliance national campaign produced a lot of expensively printed glossy colour leaflets, such as one based on the slogan 'Bigger bombs, versus no bombs at all', trying to explain Alliance defence policy. Distributing such leaflets simply stating national policies across a constituency was not really going to help any of our candidates to win, and I was shocked to see the large number of them being ordered at the pre-election Alliance rally held in the Barbican with both leaders. SDP candidates issued campaign newspapers that largely comprised nationally written stories, using generic photographs that were the same for every constituency. The SDP had taken a decision to target its resources on its held and most promising constituencies, and they could do so generously thanks largely to David Sainsbury's financial support. These campaigns were very professionally organised, but there was in my view little understanding in many of them about the importance of the candidate, local community campaigning, or how to encourage tactical voting. Delivering more leaflets with the same ineffective national message (a list of a few national policies) was not going to deliver any more votes, let alone seats. No SDP candidate gained a seat anywhere, and very few came close. Ian Wrigglesworth narrowly lost his seat in Stockton South and Roy Jenkins (who had been reluctant to attack his Labour opponent George Galloway) lost Glasgow Hillhead. Michael Meadowcroft lost Leeds West (in spite of very generous targeted support from the Joseph Rowntree Reform Trust for him). Nigel Priestley narrowly failed to retain Richard Wainwright's seat in Colne Valley and Clement Freud unexpectedly lost his seat in the Isle of Ely. But three Liberals did gain seats, where we had very well established local campaigners able to benefit from anti-Tory tactical voting. Ray Michie won Argyll & Bute from the Conservatives. Ming Campbell gained North East Fife (at the third attempt and helped by Paul Rainger, who was deputy agent to Iain Smith,[23] and who wrote many of the leaflets). Ronnie Fearn finally won Southport (at his fifth attempt), where he was a local councillor and had built his reputation as 'Mr Southport'.

In the aftermath of the campaign, I again felt very frustrated about the Liberal Party's lack of commitment at national level to promoting community campaigning and targeting seats effectively, and about its inflexible regional agent structure. I thought very hard at this point about seeking a role outside the party and began seeking career advice, but I was not enthusiastic about becoming a lobbyist, which was what was most frequently suggested to me (and which would have been much more remunerative). I waited to see how the battle for the future of the Alliance developed. Immediately after the election, David Steel and three of the original members of the SDP's 'Gang of Four' were arguing for a merger, whilst David Owen effectively declared that it would be over his dead body.

THE 'MERGER'

The merger of the Liberal Party and the SDP was eventually democratically agreed by both parties in all member ballots, but not by David Owen and his closest followers. What was intended by most members of the Alliance parties to be the coming together of two separate parties was seen by the public as a major split. The unique selling proposition of the Alliance at its outset had been that it showed how different parties could work together in the national interest. Its most high-profile leaders were now fighting in public against each other, and

---

23   Later a Member of the Scottish Parliament and Business Minister.

with much personal bitterness. David Owen was unable to accept the majority view of the party that he had led. He had not been in favour of the principle of the Alliance at the outset, favouring a 'go-it-alone' strategy for the newly formed SDP. The substantive account of SDP history, written by Ivor Crewe and Tony King, describes how Owen's passionate belief in this strategy 'was not remotely credible'.[24] He was determined to return to pursuing what was an incredible strategy in a first-past-the-post system.

Whilst the arguments between SDP members about whether to merge with the Liberal Party or follow David Owen raged, there was very little that Liberals could do to influence this outcome. During the process of negotiation, opinion-poll support for the Alliance parties crumbled and previous advances in winning council seats were reversed in the May 1988 local elections. My own biggest project in this period was continuing my work with the ALC, producing what would become known within the party as our 'campaign bible', *Winning Local Elections*. With much encouragement from Tony Greaves (who described it as the best campaign book ever written) and Maggie Clay (who took over from him as head of the ALC) this was a compendium of campaigning advice running to 160 A4 pages. It was based on what I had learned in Liverpool, Leicester and elsewhere. Those of us involved in the ALC took the view that whilst the national situation was deteriorating rapidly, we had to preserve our local campaigning strength and council seats if we were ever to recover. We also wanted to persuade active members to buy into this strategy and 2,000 copies of the book were sold at £9.50 each. At a number of party meetings promoting it I even promised people their money back if they did everything recommended in the book but still lost. It was of course impossible to do absolutely everything in the book, and nobody ever asked for a refund.

There were two likely candidates for the position of chief executive

---

24   *SDP: The Birth, Life and Death of the Social Democratic Party*, p. 458.

of the new party, the Liberal Party secretary-general Andy Ellis and the SDP's national organiser Alec McGivan. Alec approached me to say that if he got the job, he wanted me to be the national party's liaison person with the ALC and to take a lead role in the new party promoting grassroots campaigning. But after many of the other staff appointments at the new HQ had been made, Alec decided not to apply. Andy Ellis got the job and, together with the retiring SDP national secretary Dick Newby, they offered me one of the two available positions as an 'election coordinator'. The other such post was offered to Bill MacCormick. These jobs had very vague job descriptions and were not very senior. Andy remained in personal charge of campaigning. Bill and I had no staff to manage ourselves, but we accepted the roles, along with modest salary increases.

Bill and I were both allowed to sit on the 'launch committee' set up to oversee some aspects of the launch of the merged party. The group was far too large (nearly twenty strong), quite unwieldy and not very effective. Its most significant decision was probably to agree with Richard Holme's proposal for a new slogan for the new party: 'The New Choice – The Best Future'. This, he said, was intended to last for the first ten years of the new party. I was a dissenting voice about the slogan, thinking that it was too vacuous, even by the standard of many previous party slogans. I did not believe that anyone would remember it for ten minutes, let alone ten years. Shirley Williams expressed support for my view that it was a poor response to David Owen's approach, which maintained the name, logo and colours of the original SDP. But the group sided with Richard. I was then asked to produce some national leaflets and a national newspaper. I did so, whilst feeling that the whole approach of 'everybody delivers the same national leaflet at the same time' had been part of the problem with the Alliance approach to election campaigning, and that this would not be part of any solution to the problem of the party's low electoral base.

The launch committee was not responsible for some of the other very poor decisions taken by the combined parties' hierarchy at the outset. It was agreed to immediately employ a very large national staff at HQ, on the basis of very optimistic assumptions as to how many Liberal and SDP members were likely to sign up to the new party. A more immediate problem was that the negotiators had been unable to agree a sensible name for the new party. Some people regarded the idea of calling the new party the 'Alliance' as being akin to calling a new ship 'Titanic'. But I could have lived with keeping the Alliance as our title as it was the established brand name for our remaining supporters, who saw the David Owen-led alternative calling itself the 'SDP'.

The eventual compromise party name, 'Social and Liberal Democrats', was simply unworkable. The row over the name of the party (the Liberal side favoured 'Liberals and Social Democrats') led to a walk-out from the negotiations by some Liberal members of the negotiating team, including Tony Greaves.[25] The *Evening Standard* led with the headline 'Walk out over what's in a name'.

The negotiating teams had agreed that there should be a joint policy statement at the launch of the merged party. But there was little con-sultation about the draft, which appeared to be an attempt by young right-wing aides of the acting SDP leader Robert Maclennan to 'out Owen' David Owen. It included hugely controversial proposals to add VAT to food, children's clothing, domestic fuel and newspapers, as well as a strong commitment to the Trident nuclear missile pro-gramme. When it became clear in a negotiating session, which went on until 4 a.m., that the proposed document would not be acceptable to the Liberal representatives, the SDP nevertheless sent a member of their staff in a taxi round the major newspaper offices to hand-deliver copies of the offending document, thereby ensuring its widespread publication. An explosion of rage about these proposals then led to the cancellation of the lunchtime press conference in the House of Com-mons that had been planned to launch it, just as it was due to begin. A

---

25   These events are thoroughly described in *Merger: The Inside Story*, by Rachael Pitchford and Tony Greaves.

hastily re-arranged early-evening press conference then took place at the National Liberal Club. The acting leaders, Steel and Maclennan, were both hugely embarrassed to appear in front of most of their MPs simply to say that the proposed document had no standing. David Steel emphasised the point in a radio interview saying that there was no more life in it than in John Cleese's 'dead parrot' in the famous Monty Python sketch.

The launch of the new party could hardly have been less auspicious. These events led Paddy Ashdown to tell friends that he would now be certain to stand against David Steel, if Steel stood for the leadership of the new party. A private group had been meeting for some time to plan Paddy's campaign. In spite of the problems with the Alliance fallout, my own view was that continuing the 'David Steel' brand for somewhat longer would have initially helped to defend the new party against David Owen's brand as the 'continuing SDP'. But few people believed that David Steel would stand for the leadership of the new party, especially after this fiasco, and he did not.

CIVIL WAR AMONGST THE FORMER PARTNERS

In the year following the merger, three parliamentary by-elections provided the battleground for what felt like a civil war between the 'Social and Liberal Democrats' and the 'continuing SDP'. In July 1988, the Kensington by-election provided the first opportunity for activists from the two parties to fight each other in a significant election. Bill MacCormick was the agent for William Goodhart, a very well-respected figure in the 'original' SDP. Bill and I stayed for the duration of the campaign in the impressive Kensington home of Elizabeth Bingham. We got to know her husband Tom Bingham over breakfast each day, only learning after some time of his status as one of the country's greatest ever lawyers, later becoming Master of the Rolls and Lord Chief Justice. The Goodharts were also frequently very hospitable to us in their Kensington home. But the campaign was difficult as it was portrayed in the media as being about two different contests; one between the Conservatives and Labour to win, and one between ourselves and Owen's party for third and fourth place. Most people naturally chose to vote in the first contest. From the former Alliance vote of 17 per cent, we polled 11 per cent, whilst the Owenite candidate polled 5 per cent (saving his deposit by nine votes). The ruthless streak within the Owenites was shown by their campaign to ban the Caribbean Notting Hill Carnival 'unless it was made safe', a sentiment that appealed to some quite illiberal instincts.

The Owenite SDP was then remarkably lucky about where the next two by-elections came. They had virtually no 'pockets of strength' anywhere in the country. But when the Tory MP for Epping Forest died, the previous SDP parliamentary candidate (a local councillor) was a supporter of Owen's party. Our candidate, Andrew Thompson, was less well known as he had not been the parliamentary candidate. It was difficult for us to gain momentum with the party being so demoralised, and with many people perceiving our campaign as a continuation of an internal civil war that did not concern them. But we seized on the campaign to move the local hospital to Harlow, and various other local issues such as the threat to the green belt, and we began to build support.

Paddy's nervousness about the party's generally precarious position[26] and his tendency to try to micro-manage events was shown at this time by his daily phone calls to Pat Wainwright on the front desk of our by-election HQ to check on how many people had signed in to help that day. I operated from a windowless basement in the HQ, where I designed most of the leaflets. When Paddy wanted a private word with me about the state of the campaign, I asked Ann to leave

---

26   He had been elected as the new party's first leader in 1988 with a large margin over long-serving Liberal MP Alan Beith, but the first two years of his leadership were extraordinarily difficult as the party struggled in the polls against opposition from David Owen's SDP and it suffered very poor election results and poll ratings.

the room. In those days, people still smoked in by-election HQs and as someone used to giving orders, he was surprised that I would not let him smoke in my room. Ann had left her half-eaten Danish pastry on my desk and when she returned she asked what had become of it. I had to explain that Paddy had eaten it as a substitute for not being allowed to smoke. She was then delighted by being able to claim that 'Paddy Ashdown ate my Danish pastry'.

Ann was head of a nursery and children's centre in Reading at the time, and we lived in nearby Earley. She was only able to help at the weekends (or when she took time off, as she did in almost all of the parliamentary by-elections I worked in over the best part of three decades). Late one night she rang me from home to say that a letter had been sent to me by the Prime Minister's Office at 10 Downing Street and should she open it? She then did so assuming that it was some kind of spoof. On my part, I assumed that Mrs Thatcher had taken exception to some of my literature claiming that 'she had gone too far' and that it was a threat of legal action. I tried to listen to her on the phone in HQ (with dozens of by-election workers surrounding me). She began laughing, as the 'spoof' appeared to suggest that I was being offered the MBE, and then she suddenly recognised that it was for real. In those days, party leaders were able to nominate a few party members for such honours in recognition of their political service. I spoke to Paddy, querying his nomination of me and suggesting that there must be others who had served the party for far longer. But he was quite adamant that he wanted to see my efforts for the party recognised.

Andrew Thompson came second in the by-election with 26 per cent of the vote, which was hailed as a success as it was 7 per cent above the Alliance vote in the general election the year before. But his Owenite rival polled 12 per cent in the by-election (somewhat contradicting their last-minute 'spoiler' leaflet claiming to be well ahead of us and poised to win). That 12 per cent share of the vote, added to ours, would have taken us to within around 1,000 votes of victory, and without their intervention I believe that we would have won. The 'Owenite' intervention had denied us the sort of boost that Paddy had really needed for his new leadership.

CHRISTMAS AND NEW YEAR 1988/89

I spent Christmas 1988 at my elder brother and sister-in-law's. Edward was a vicar in Grimsby at the time. Ann had her usual family Christmas at her parents' house in Crosby. It was our last Christmas apart. We had had a relationship, although not continuously, since 1983 and I had lived in her house in Earley near Reading for over a year. We always celebrated New Year in Liverpool with friends. Mike Storey and Carole Cartmell (later Carole Storey) hosted a party at their house in Wavertree for our large group of friends, many of whom I had got to know whilst at university.

New Year's Eve began at Ann's parents' with her telling her father that I would be getting the MBE in the New Year's Honours list the following day. He had already heard of Eric Bristow's award that year and said that 'he didn't even know that I played darts'! There was much delight at the award amongst my friends at the party, and they even conducted an embarrassing mock medal ceremony in the kitchen. In the small hours of the morning of New Year's Day, Ann and I were alone in the front garden. It seemed like a good opportunity to propose, so I got on one knee and she accepted.

The next day, we told her parents and I asked my best friend Jeff to be best man. We basked in the delight of our friends, most of whom admitted to wondering why this decision appeared to have taken so long. Ann's parents were regular worshippers at the nearby Roman Catholic Church of the Holy Family in Ince Blundell, which has a wonderful early Renaissance-style interior. I had been a choirboy and server at my Anglican church in Wavertree, and whilst I knew that I would not be able to receive communion at the service, we wanted to have a Nuptial Mass.

Ann's birthday was two weeks after we got engaged, so I wrote to friends inviting them to celebrate it at her parents' house at what also became an engagement party. Finding a venue for a wedding reception proved problematic as we decided to try to get married in the Easter holidays, just three months away. When we made enquiries of potential venues, several of them asked us if we were enquiring about the following year or the year after that. But Waterloo Rugby Club was available on Friday 31 March, and their main room looked fabulous once marquee style drapes and a chandelier were added, so we booked it.

My elder brother gave the sermon, my sister-in-law Margaret (also an Anglican priest) took part in the service, the Roman Catholic priest conducted it and the registrar formally married us. I had been warned that Ann's younger sister Jane, the chief bridesmaid, was bound to cry, as she always did at weddings. But I did not expect Jeff to cry as well. In thanking Ann's parents in my speech, I was able to tell a number of tales that I had gleaned about their own wedding in 1946. Alcohol had been in short supply during the war, but it certainly wasn't at their wedding, which followed a six-year period when Ann's dad had served in India (not knowing for much of the war if he would return home). Ann, of course, made a speech herself (she wouldn't have had a series of men speaking about her without a right of reply). Her extensive and very close-knit family were amongst the 160 guests. I inevitably felt some personal sadness on the day as neither of my parents were alive to see me get married, and I had lost touch with some family members since my mother's death.

Before the wedding, I had also needed to buy another car after my previous one had been written off in a by-election when I had lent it to one of the volunteers, who crashed it. We took delivery of the new car at the wedding and its first trip was for our honeymoon in France.

We visited Épernay (we are both fond of Champagne) and Burgundy and went as far as the French Alps in our week.

THE RICHMOND BY-ELECTION, FEBRUARY 1989

Whilst preparing for our wedding, my political focus was on the next major parliamentary by-election which resulted from Leon Brittan's appointment to the European Commission. A by-election in his North Yorkshire constituency had been expected since the summer of 1988. There were only about half a dozen places in the country where a number of SDP councillors had followed David Owen. Unfortunately for us, Richmond, North Yorkshire, was one of them. Their candidate, Mike Potter, was a local councillor as well as a local farmer. He also had many farming friends who let him use their fields for poster stake boards.

In the circumstances, we needed a really strong local candidate. I consulted my longstanding friend Richard Wainwright, the former MP for Colne Valley in West Yorkshire, and we agreed that Richmond councillor Angie Harris was who we needed. I drove all the way up to North Yorkshire to help try to persuade her to stand. Unfortunately, she then became a victim of rivalry within the local party. Some members at the other end of the constituency decided that it was not to be her, and they chose Barbara Pearce, who once taught locally but was now based in Leeds. I liked Barbara, but she was no longer a local candidate.

When William Hague was chosen as the Tory candidate, I immediately realised the significance of the fact that Potter would be the only major local candidate, thereby giving him a very significant advantage in the campaign. I sent an urgent memo round the party warning of what might happen in the by-election, and begging for more support. But little help was forthcoming from party HQ, which was by now facing a series of financial crises having been over ambitious about staffing levels. As was normal for us in those days, the by-election agent

(Paul Jacobs) and I had to raise most of the money for the campaign ourselves. One poll towards the end of the campaign gave us a slight edge in second place as challengers, but then a subsequent poll partly commissioned by one of the regional TV companies (who featured it prominently) put us in third place, presenting Potter as the main challenger. The polls were of course impossible to balance properly by weighting according to previous levels of support as there were now two candidates claiming the previous Alliance vote. Whether the final poll was accurate or not, it inevitably meant that the last few days of the campaign were incredibly dispiriting for us. We went from hopes of winning to a realisation that our votes were draining away to Potter.

William Hague eventually polled 37 per cent of the vote (down from the Conservative's 61 per cent of the vote in 1987), whilst Potter polled 32 per cent, Barbara Pearce 22 per cent and Labour just under 5 per cent. A single Alliance candidate would, of course, have won. In response, Paddy attempted to revive the idea of our members and those supporting David Owen's party jointly voting to select by-election candidates. My immediate reaction was strongly opposed to this idea, but Paddy proved to be right as his apparently conciliatory approach took the wind out of David Owen's sails. After the by-election, the *Daily Express* ran the headline 'David Owen rides again!' But my own experience told me that second places do not count for very much at all compared to victories, and that this one, painful as it was personally, would not be remembered nationally for very long.

SURVIVING THE 1989 LOCAL ELECTIONS

The local election results in England in May 1989 were a little more successful for us than the Richmond by-election had been. Whilst we lost 175 county council seats, we still had over 3,300 councillors, retaining significant support in many areas as a result of continued local campaigning. We polled an estimated national vote share of

19 per cent, down from 26 per cent at the high watermark of the Alliance in 1985. The Owenite SDP, however, won less than ten council seats across the entire country. David Sainsbury, who had bankrolled the breakaway party, was pulling out and it was clear that the 'incredible strategy' that David Owen had always wanted was not working. Paddy commented on the results in a press release at the time: 'The period of retreat and retrenchment is over',[27] but he was still somewhat premature in saying this.

The nadir for the merged 'Social and Liberal Democrats' came in the European elections a month later in June 1989. The party HQ had done very little to prepare for the elections, with Andy Ellis eventually asking Bill MacCormick to make some proposals for a campaign shortly before it began. But before he could begin any work on this, Bill's role was switched to overseeing preparations for the Vauxhall parliamentary by-election campaign, which would take place on the same day as the European elections. A hasty deal was negotiated with the 'SDP' to ensure that there would be no 'SDP' candidate in Vauxhall, in return for us guaranteeing not to oppose Owen's parliamentary colleagues Rosie Barnes and John Cartwright at the following general election. Our candidate in Vauxhall, Mike Tuffrey, was a local councillor who went on to become council leader, and he almost maintained our 1987 vote, but still came third. With only a few weeks to go until the European elections, Andy suggested to me that I take charge of them (and even offered me a mobile phone if I agreed!). But my instinct was that I would simply become the fall guy for an unprepared campaign (that still had no budget). I decided instead to go to Cornwall to support my friend Paul Tyler's campaign in the European elections, as I believed that he might have a chance of winning there.

I was soon producing 'thank-you' leaflets for all of our recent council candidates in Cornwall to launch Paul's campaign. With access to the HQ's sole Apple Macintosh computer, but without the benefit of

---

27   Paddy Ashdown, *The Ashdown Diaries, Vol. I: 1988–1997*, p. 40.

email communication in those days, I had to work through the night, and also throughout the following day, to produce over fifty different leaflets, each featuring the relevant local election result. As I drove from Westminster to Reading to send the leaflet designs by Red Star to Cornwall, I remember feeling extremely tired. I woke up quickly when there was a very loud bang as my car went off the motorway and hit a crash barrier. I have often looked at that stretch of the M4 to see how little of it has a barrier. I was incredibly fortunate. The car could still be driven and once I was past the immediate shock, my first priority was to get the package onto the train at Reading. Having done this, I then drove back to Earley and told Ann what had happened. She had nearly become a widow just three months after we had got married. I was probably the only party member who nearly died by working so hard in the European elections that year.

I moved into Annette Penhaligon's Truro house to assist her in her role as agent for Paul Tyler. She was a very kind host to Ann and me. I designed election addresses in different editions for each part of Cornwall and Plymouth, and there was even one exclusively for the Isles of Scilly. We produced the party's first tabloid newspaper in Cornwall, the *Cornish Voice*. This was the Packet newspaper group's biggest ever print run with over 250,000 copies. There was also a *Plymouth Voice* edition. We campaigned on why we were pro-European, but also on the big issue of the 'poll tax' and why Paul was the clear alternative to the Conservatives in the Cornwall & Plymouth constituency.

There was very little of a leader's tour organised for Paddy during the European election. He was also very engaged with events in China at the time (the Tiananmen Square massacre occurred ten days before polling day) and on the weekend before polling, he was in Hong Kong. The party's European election campaign was very weak and the national result was dreadful. We polled just 6 per cent nationally, and were in fourth place behind the Greens, who came third nationally with 15 per cent of the vote. We didn't quite win Cornwall & Plymouth, although we polled 30 per cent of the vote, five times the national average for the party in that election. It was also our only second place in the country. In every other seat, we came fourth or worse.

FINANCIAL CRISIS

In the wake of the results, there were continued internal rows concerning the name of the party as well as some private manoeuvring, of which I disapproved, to see if some accommodation could still be reached with David Owen. I did not believe that David Owen would ever compromise in a reasonable and sustainable way. I became aware of these attempts at rapprochement, which involved Paddy, but did not think that they were realistic and I felt that a war of attrition would continue. Within the merged party, nothing seemed to have moved on from the merger negotiations with Paddy, supported by Bob Maclennan and Charles Kennedy, now backing the short title for the party of 'Democrats'. Many of our MPs were refusing to be described as anything other than 'Liberal Democrats'. There was discussion of a ballot amongst members to resolve the issue of the name, but many feared that this would not solve the party's problems. Paddy was clearly very depressed in this period.

The appalling European election results coincided with the HQ at Cowley Street attempting to renew many membership subscriptions, which indicated poor planning. Few members renewed their membership or contributed financially at this point. Quite a few redundancies had already taken place at HQ and more would be needed.

An emergency meeting of the party's Federal Executive and English Committee considered some senior management changes. The meeting was told that the party officers had decided that Andy Ellis should not remain as chief executive (it was suggested by Paddy that he might become director of campaigns) and that Dee Doocey should switch from being director of finance to become conference organiser. Archy Kirkwood became acting chief executive.

Paddy then finally forced the Federal Executive to agree to a ballot of all the members in order to resolve the 'name issue'. Around the same time, Sir Anthony Jacobs, who was then chair of the party's Co-ordinating Committee for England, proposed a simple, but drastic, plan to rescue the party's financial position. This involved making all but one of the party's campaigns staff redundant, and also reducing the number of policy staff to one. There was a long and difficult discussion that evening, and after almost five hours of arguing there was no consensus about any decisions. At this point the party's Chief Whip in the Commons, Jim Wallace, told the meeting that we only had the room in the National Liberal Club for another ten minutes, and that we had better make our minds up. The most drastic plan was agreed.

I was personally angry about how this had all come about, and I told Paddy that 'getting rid of all but one of the campaigns staff may have finally destroyed the party'. The position of chief executive was now replaced with one of 'general secretary' and Graham Elson, our former leader on Oxfordshire County Council and a tough political operator, was appointed to try to lead a recovery at HQ. His first job on the day after that controversial meeting was to meet with eighteen members of staff (most of whom he had never previously met) and to make them redundant.

DIRECTOR OF CAMPAIGNS AND ELECTIONS

In the circumstances of the party in summer 1989, I was not sure if I wanted to be the one remaining member of campaigns staff, and there was some discussion about whether or not I was to be included in the redundancy programme. However, I asked to be treated in the same way as all my colleagues. I was also asked for my ideas on what was needed for a new national campaigns officer or national agent for the party. In some ways, it was the fact that the party was at such a low ebb that attracted me to the challenge, and I believed that the party's position was not irrecoverable. Four candidates for the remaining campaigns post were interviewed by Archy Kirkwood, Graham Elson and the party's finance chair, Tim Clement-Jones. I made it clear that I was only prepared to undertake the job if it was to be described as 'director of campaigns and elections' and if it would involve directly managing election campaign staff, as and when we could afford to employ any of them again. After some deliberation, they agreed.

As a campaigning team of one, I then sought to work closely with my friends in what had become the Association of Social and Liberal Democrat Councillors (ASLDC, as it was then called), based in Hebden Bridge. Together we sought to galvanise the party with a series of campaigns under the umbrella slogan of 'People First'. Andrew Stunell, then its general secretary, led the political messaging for this whilst I led the promotion of a series of training days in every part of the country, making use of the database of members that we now had at the Cowley Street HQ. Anyone attending these events got a new campaign booklet in return for their registration – a basic guide to local campaigning written by me and Peter Chegwyn. At the events, we trained members in identifying community issues, engaging with people, getting something done about those issues, and then reporting back on what they were doing. I asked our MPs to front these 'People First' campaign training days in order to help attract members, and to assist in lifting their battered morale. The events were also great fun as we had people engaging in mock canvass role play sessions, giving them more confidence and greater skills in knocking on doors. It was then the most closely integrated effort ever between the Hebden Bridge team and the Cowley Street HQ.

Attendances at these events all over the country were generally between about forty and a hundred people. We helped members to get past the demoralising events of the merger, and get working on drafting local leaflets and press releases. The effects of all this activity (and the *Winning Local Elections* book) began to be felt by the May 1990 local elections. This was the year of the poll tax riots, and we were expected by the media to lose most of the council seats that we had won in the 1986 local elections (when the Alliance was at 26 per cent, and we had won Ryedale whilst narrowly missing West Derbyshire).

On election night, I established an elaborate results operation with over fifty volunteers at HQ and people in over 400 counts across the country relaying information to us. Party spokespeople covering every media outlet were provided with minders and equipped with pagers (sometimes they also had mobile phones). Every small achievement that night was spun successfully as a great result. In the end, we lost just fifty seats and came close to gaining as many seats as we lost. On the basis of this, I asked Paddy to say in all his interviews that 'we were back to three-party politics'. The effects of the training and mailings were to be even more pronounced in the following year's local elections, by which time we would also have gained two parliamentary by-elections.

A LABOUR GAIN IN MID STAFFORDSHIRE

In the meantime, our party morale still remained low. In the spring of 1990, we had faced a parliamentary by-election in Mid Stafford-shire. Paddy himself was very demoralised and he initially told me that we shouldn't put up a candidate for it. I didn't know how to argue with him, but decided to quietly forget this view, and I was correct in assuming that he would not sustain it. The party was fortunate that our previous candidate, Tim Jones, was willing to fight the by-election for us. I had no staff to send to the by-election, but I asked Candy Piercy[28] to be campaign manager, and the party's new general secretary Graham Elson also spent much time there. Our campaign was very modest compared to the biggest Labour by-election campaign that I could recall (with Neil Kinnock visiting by helicopter).

---

28   Candy had been working part-time for the party and later became a core of the parliamentary by-election campaign as well as one of the campaign officers helping us to gain a number of seats in 1997.

Amidst some confusion over party labels, two different opinion polls for the by-election put us on 5 per cent, and as low as 2 per cent, whilst the Owenite SDP was at 4 per cent in both of them. But a week before polling day in the parliamentary by-election, there was a local council by-election which we won, retaining our seat. Tim Jones was also the clear winner in a sixth-form debate between the candidates. The result of this debate was enough for me to justify producing a campaign newspaper with the headline 'Tim Tops the Poll!' On polling day, we did much better than had been suggested, polling 11 per cent, just under half Tim's 1987 share of the vote, whilst the Owenite SDP candidate polled just 2.5 per cent, half the support required for him to hold his deposit. Their Richmond 'bubble' had burst after less than a month. When their spokesman on the election night TV programme, Ian Wright, was asked to comment on the result, he said that he had hoped they hadn't noticed that he was still in the studio.

In the aftermath of the Mid Staffordshire by-election, Graham Elson and the party's solicitor were very keen to take legal action against the Labour agent, Fraser Kemp (later a Labour MP), over their by-election expenses. The costs of Kinnock's helicopter had not been included in Labour's expense return (which was extremely close to the legal limit). A file was prepared to send to the police, but when I was invited to a meeting in Paddy's office to consider sending it, I said that we should not. I had used a helicopter myself for David Steel's visit to West Derbyshire and had not seen fit to declare the donated cost of it. I felt that this was unfair and also feared retaliation from Labour if we took action in this way.

KILLING OFF DAVID OWEN'S SDP

The real turning point in the struggle to establish the 'Social and Liberal Democrats' as the only 'third party' in British politics came in Bootle in May 1990. A parliamentary by-election in a seat with a 25,000 Labour majority at the previous general election seemed unlikely to create any headlines. We struggled to find a candidate. Eventually, Liverpool councillor John Cunningham was selected by the handful of local members. He was weak on national politics, but had the advantage of living in Bootle (he qualified to be a Liverpool councillor because of his work as a nurse in the city).

Bootle borders Liverpool, but can be fiercely proud of its independence. Ann's family lived in Bootle for many years and knew many members of the Bootle Labour Party, including Simon Mahon, who was the MP for twenty-four years until 1979. I was personally very aware of how Bootle residents passionately believed that they lived in Bootle, not just a part of Liverpool. Most of them expected Labour to choose the long-serving local Labour councillor Joe Benton to be their candidate and many of them had never warmed to Allan Roberts, the previous MP, who hailed from Manchester. Instead, the Labour Party chose Michael Carr, who was Bootle-born, but now lived over the Liverpool border and had sought to be the Labour candidate in Liverpool Walton. The Conservatives chose James Clappison, a barrister from Yorkshire.

Our campaign budget was as always in those days extremely modest. The party had very few employees at this point and I was still the sole member of campaigns staff. Ray Atkins was one of the few party agents still earning a living working for the party, and he agreed to act as agent, whilst I wrote the literature and tried to oversee the campaign with occasional visits. Challenges to our campaign came from opponents from both the splinter groups that had emerged from the Alliance post-merger. The Owenite SDP's National Committee had not wished to fight such unpromising territory. But, spurred on by the party's relatively recent success in Richmond, Jack Holmes put himself forward for the so-called 'continuing SDP'.

The 'continuing Liberal' splinter group, supported by the former Liberal MP Michael Meadowcroft, was a mirror image of David Owen's party. It was also unwilling to accept the democratic decision of the party's merger ballot. This so-called Liberal Party contained a very small number of activists, most of whom seemed to have simply had a falling out with other members in their local parties. But it did have a major financial backer. Party treasurer Tim Razzall told me that, despite his efforts, one of the party's previous backers, David Blackburn, had felt snubbed by the new party. I understood that he had given the 'Liberal Party' some £20,000 for the by-election campaign (approximately double what I expected to be able to spend).

There was little national media interest in the campaign, but I had huge sympathy for our candidate when a local journalist asked him at one of his few press conferences whether he was gay or not. He answered honestly that he was. Unfortunately, this was news to some of his family, who did not all take the news well. I am not sure that such a question would still be asked, or that it could have so much significance to a campaign in most seats these days. Candidates, in my view, could say 'yes', 'no' or 'mind your own business', but had to be ready for the consequences of any answer.

David Owen supported his candidate by speaking at a public meeting in the Crosby part of the Bootle constituency. This area had been part of the seat won by Shirley Williams in the 1981 by-election. In Shirley's campaign, nine years previously, over 1,000 people attended her meeting at this school, and she and other Alliance speakers had to address two overflow meetings in other halls. I was now one of about thirty people who attended David Owen's public meeting this time, and I could recognise at least twenty people present as being members of different parties, who were there only to watch the spectacle. It was to be David Owen's last appearance at an election 'rally' and it was dominated by questions about his stance on the merger ballot. This event must have helped demonstrate to him the folly of maintaining a continuing SDP, even if he would never acknowledge the folly of having set it up, or apologise for the terminal damage that he had done to the careers of most of his followers.

Our campaign focused on the fact that John lived locally ('Bootle deserves a Bootle MP') and that, unlike Labour, we had an alternative to the deeply unpopular poll tax. Areas such as Bootle had lost out heavily from the change from 'rates' (based on the value of properties) to the flat-rate 'poll tax' (through which every adult paid the same amount). We put forward 'local income tax' as our alternative, as it would be based on ability to pay. My belief that we could achieve second place was greeted with some scepticism in the Leader's Office, but we eventually fell short of second place by just forty-one votes, polling 3,179 (8.9 per cent).

The major significance of the result, however, was the relative performance of David Owen's SDP to that of the Monster Raving Loony Party. Owen's candidate polled just 155 votes (0.4 per cent). Lord David Sutch polled three times as many votes (418), narrowly behind the Liberal (Kevin White) on 474. Labour had their expected landslide win, but all attention focused on the imminent demise of David Owen's party. *The Sun* reported that 'Owen's in Sutch a state because he can't beat the loonies'. The SDP National Committee met shortly afterwards and wound up the 'national party'. Ian Wright, initially a backer of Owen (who subsequently switched to the Lib Dems), kept us informed of progress in their deliberations. Owen became an independent MP and stood down at the following election. Both of his parliamentary colleagues stood again (without opposition from the Liberal Democrats), but lost their seats.

Throughout this very difficult post-merger period, I had always maintained my belief that the new party would only be able to thrive when it could contest elections without having the distraction of a party able to maintain the old SDP branding (and which was led by one of the people who had led the original SDP). My party's branding was weak in comparison, and Paddy had yet to establish himself as a national leader. David Owen's role had proved simply to be a wrecking one. There were others in the merged party who believed that some compromise could have been reached with Owen. On the same day as the Bootle by-election, a senior Ashdown aide and former SDP staffer

Mark Payne met with a leading Owenite councillor, Chris Clarke, to see if they could persuade their leaders to discuss electoral pacts. Paddy himself met Owen to explore reconciliation. But, in the end, the Owenite SDP was only brought to an end by being humiliated by us electorally. For two years they had prevented the Liberal Democrats re-establishing a bridgehead. The way forward for the Lib Dems would now be much clearer, as and when a suitable opportunity arose.

THE 'DEAD PARROT' TWITCHED IN EASTBOURNE

I did not expect that there would be the prospect of a potentially winnable by-election for us quite so soon after the demise of David Owen's party. In the summer of 1990, the party's position was still very precarious and we stood at around 8 per cent in the national opinion polls.

At the beginning of August that year I was working on a new publication, *The Campaign Manual*. I wanted to produce a guide to help our parliamentary candidates in the run-up to the general election by providing them with a best-practice manual. This would complement *Winning Local Elections*, which had proved so helpful to our councillors and council candidates. Whilst working on the text, I heard on the radio that a bomb had exploded outside the home of the Conservative MP for Eastbourne, Ian Gow. The news soon emerged that he had been murdered by the IRA. It was a shocking crime and revealed again the willingness at the time of this group to kill their opponents, rather than engage in democratic debate.

After the experience of the Enfield Southgate by-election in 1984, I did not expect there to be any thought that we would not fight Eastbourne. I attended the Federal Executive to discuss the campaign (Paddy was not present) and there was no suggestion at the meeting that we should not fight it. I spoke to Archy Kirkwood, who was chair of the Campaigns and Communications Committee at the time, and confirmed our plans to fight, then began thinking seriously about how we would go about doing so after the funeral.

We had outpolled the Tories in the Eastbourne borough elections that year. But in parliamentary terms, the Conservatives had a 16,000 majority. We were certainly not in a strong position to mount a winning campaign, and the campaigns department still comprised just me. My aim, however, was to do for the party what Trevor 'Jones the Vote' had done and win a parliamentary by-election creating the sort of revival for the party that followed his masterminding of Sutton & Cheam in 1972.

I was working at home writing the new handbook when I received a call from my friend John Ricketts, then head of the Lib Dem Whips' Office in the Commons. He thought that I ought to know something. Paddy's leading advisers Alan Leaman and Mark Payne were both away on holiday, so Paddy had asked John to draft a press release saying that we would not be contesting the Eastbourne by-election. It was to be released in twenty minutes.

The general secretary, Graham Elson, had been consulted, as had the chair of the English Party. But although my new job had put me in charge of parliamentary by-election campaigns, I had not been. John, however, thought that I should know about the imminent statement. I was acting in haste, but knew that I had to stop that press release going out. I faxed Paddy with what in hindsight was a most intemperate memo. But there was little time, and I felt that I had to act swiftly and strongly to (at least) delay the statement being made.

It is greatly to his credit that Paddy included much of the text of the memo in his own memoirs, together with a fulsome recognition that he had been wrong. He said that I was very brave to risk being sacked by saying what I felt in this way. This was the fax:

Dear Paddy,

I'm appalled if I understand correctly that you were thinking of issuing a statement about the Eastbourne by-election without consulting the person responsible for organising the party's by-election campaigns i.e. me.

At least when you had the crazy idea that we should not put up a candidate at Mid Staffordshire, (Remember that one, just before Christmas), you explained the idea to me and then you forgot about it over Christmas.

No decision needs to be taken about whether or not to fight the by-election for some time (certainly not before the funeral). Any statement or recommendation from you would be tantamount to a decision. How could a local party fight a by-election if it was known publicly that their party leader opposed them fighting?

The reason the Labour Party are terrified by this by-election is that they know that we would probably win and that their PPC for Eastbourne is a Militant.

Of course, the Tories would prefer to nominate an MP instead of risking losing an embarrassing by-election.

Your job is not to do what the Labour and Tory parties want, but to stand up to them!

It will not be seen to be bold and courageous to recommend not fighting – it will make you a laughing stock in Walworth Road, Downing Street and eventually in the quality press that you threw away this chance.

Let me remind you:

* All the arguments about fighting were well rehearsed after Sir Anthony Berry was blown up by the Brighton bomb in 1984. The logical conclusion was that it is the right of voters in any constituency to choose their MP and we should not let the IRA interfere with that right.
* In the resulting Enfield Southgate by-election, the major controversy was student grants (not the Brighton bombing) and we polled 35% coming within 4,000 votes of winning.
* After Enfield Southgate David Steel complained vociferously that the constituency had been too slow in selecting a candidate whilst they

awaited guidance on fighting (Tim Slack was not chosen until after the writ was moved). We would have won a better prepared campaign.

* Eastbourne was one of the seats which you personally predicted would have been won by the Liberal Democrats on the strength of the local election results.

* On May 3rd, Liberal Democrat candidates polled 13,619 votes to the Tories' 11,712 whilst Labour polled 5,411.

* If we fight this by-election, we will have the best base of support which we have had at any by-election since Liverpool Edge Hill in 1979.

* The swing to win Eastbourne would be considerably less than the combined Lib Dem/SDP swing achieved at either Epping or Richmond.

* In August 1972, the Liberal Party stood at 7% in the polls. In August 1973, it stood at 28% as a result of a string of by-election successes.

* We can win Eastbourne (unless Ian Gow's widow fights – press speculation is that she will receive a peerage) – providing that we have the determination to resource it.

* Nobody at the Federal Executive on Monday spoke about not fighting it.

Yours, Chris Rennard

I sent Archy Kirkwood and Graham Elson a copy of the fax, with a request for Archy to ring both Paddy and me. Archy then told me that the leader was determined to issue his statement, that he was of course very angry about my fax, and that he had just spent twenty-five minutes 'scraping Paddy off the ceiling', but that in view of what I had said, he did agree to speak to me before issuing the statement.

It was, of course, a very difficult conversation that I then had with Paddy. I suggested to him that the consequence of us not fighting the seat would be to give the Greens a chance. It had taken over a year for them to fade from their Euro-election breakthrough in June 1989. If we didn't stand, they would be in a position to garner the anti-Tory vote in the constituency, restore their fortunes and put us back to the position behind them where we had been in June 1989. Paddy admitted that he hadn't thought about the Greens fighting the seat.

I then said that I thought that it should be the Eastbourne local party's decision as to whether or not to fight the by-election, or that they should at least be consulted before a decision was announced. Paddy then agreed that they could, at least, have their say. I then argued with him that it would be impossible for them to decide to fight the by-election *after* he had told the press of his opposition to us standing. I suggested that every press conference we held in the campaign would be dominated by the question: 'Why are you standing, when your leader thought you shouldn't?'

Again, Paddy said that he hadn't thought about this. He agreed at least not to release his statement until *after* the Eastbourne members' meeting, which was to be held the following Monday. In the meantime, I was in discussion with local members in Eastbourne, and with John Ungar, the local party chair, in particular. He said that members there who knew about Paddy's proposed statement were generally shocked. He said that they were now feeling frightened that if they went ahead and fought the by-election that they would not get proper national support for the campaign.

I, somewhat mischievously, told John to regard Paddy's view as an initial one only. I promised that if they agreed to fight the seat, I would personally relocate to Eastbourne, that I would not leave until after the by-election, and that I would move heaven and earth to galvanise the entire national party behind a campaign to win. This was enough for the local members; they decided to fight the by-election, agreed not to mention Paddy's view (it never leaked out), and Paddy's statement was never issued.

This row with Paddy (subsequently settled amicably) made the actual campaign an extraordinarily stressful experience for me. It also came at a very difficult time. Ann and I had been married for about eighteen months. We both loved children, Ann worked all her professional life with other people's babies and children, and we hoped to have our own. Following stressful medical investigations, we discovered that I could almost certainly not be a father. Couples who do not choose to be childless often suffer great anguish and we have felt this very greatly. Our lives would have been very different if we had been able to realise our hopes. It did not seem fair. Around this time, I also lost the last vestiges of any religious beliefs.

At the Lib Dem conference in Blackpool that September, members received an emphatic call to arms that I had drafted for Charles Kennedy (then party president) for his introduction to Paddy's speech, and they responded. I felt that the future of the party, as well as my own, was very much at stake. Fortunately, Paul Jacobs was again willing to be agent for the by-election, and he was a first-class organiser. Pat Wainwright, who had run the office in many of our most successful by-elections, moved into the HQ that we established in the town centre. Candy Piercy was due to become my first appointment in the campaigns department and she came down to handle the media. Paul Burstow then worked for the Association of Liberal Democrat Councillors (ALDC) and was seconded to the campaign in a very successful collaboration to help me with the major leaflets. Norman Baker, then a Lewes councillor and environmental campaigner for the Lib Dem MPs, handled the casework, and John Ricketts took holiday from the Whips' Office to take charge of target letters.

We researched the issues for the constituency, ward by ward, polling district by polling district. We began from a low base of support. An early poll that we conducted with the help of my US political consultant friend, Rick Ridder, put us on just 11 per cent, so Paul and I kept the figures to ourselves. Our professional team worked well with the Eastbourne Lib Dems (many of whom are still very good friends). At my first meeting with local members, there were several mentions of anger in the town about the introduction of car-parking charges at the District General Hospital, although they all said that this would not be a by-election issue. I disagreed on the basis of what I had been told, and our first leaflet launched a petition against these charges.

Within weeks we had collected over 5,000 signatures. Many letters sent in response to the campaign described the trauma of visiting relatives at the hospital whilst people felt frightened about having their cars clamped, or being fined for overstaying the parking periods. Our campaign reflected general concern about the NHS and the local hospital.

David Bellotti was selected as the candidate. He had fought next-door Lewes in the two previous elections, but had stood in Eastbourne in 1979, allowing us to highlight local connections and to refer back to issues on which he had campaigned over a decade ago. In contrast, the Conservatives made the kind of mistake that I hoped they would make. They chose Richard Hickmet, who had lost his seat in Scunthorpe at the previous general election, which allowed us to make a great contrast between them in terms of local connections. Our tabloid newspaper (designed with the help of Mike Harskin) featured a story headed 'Ex-Scunthorpe MP fails to impress'.

The Conservative media guide for the by-election included a list of local hospitals. Unfortunately for them, one of these hospitals had recently been demolished. We took a photograph of the rubble and then put out a leaflet showing it, which was headed: 'The Conservative calls this a hospital!' It suggested that the Tory candidate did not have a lot of local knowledge about Eastbourne.

My fear of Paddy's reaction to a bad result meant that I sometimes felt so physically sick that I had to leave the office for a few minutes' fresh air in order to avoid anyone else observing how stressed and worried I was. I knew that it was always crucial in campaigns for me to *appear* self-confident if I was to be able to encourage belief in others about the prospects of success.

There was also some fun in the campaign. David Bellotti's mother sent me a copy of *Old Moore's Almanac* – an astrological guide published many months earlier which predicted that 18 October (which happened to be polling day in Eastbourne) would be a good day for the 'Democrats to win a by-election'. It just seemed to be an incredible coincidence. The article suggested that the stars were due to be in a propitious disposition for us. Over the final weekend, our tabloid newspaper featured a back-page article entitled: 'Can our stars predict the future – by Eastbourne's resident star gazer – Chris Rennard.'

In the article, I drew attention to the way in which *Old Moore's Almanac* claimed to have predicted the assassination attempt on Pope John Paul II, the Hiroshima bomb and the winner of the 1,000 guineas horse race that year. I attributed a quote to our candidate, David Bellotti, saying that 'his confidence was in the voters – not in the stars – but that if what the voters were telling him was true, the stars would be correct in their forecast!'

The only published poll during the campaign put us on 26 per cent, far behind the Conservative, but well up on the initial 11 per cent, and by-elections are all about momentum. A week before polling day, my own estimate of our canvass returns still put us about 8,500 votes behind (compared to 16,000 in the general election). I even feared at that time that Paddy might have been right. But on the Tuesday before polling day, I completed my own analysis of the canvass trends and concluded by then that we were just 1,700 votes behind. I knew that with this momentum we would be ahead on polling day and told Paul that the only question in my view was whether or not we could get to 50 per cent of the vote.

In the last few days of the campaign, we re-canvassed 'soft Labour' and 'soft Conservatives' to find that around 50 per cent of them were already supporting us. We organised petitions on numerous local issues on which we were campaigning and invited people to return them to our helpers at the polling stations. For the first time in a parliamentary by-election, we used the telephone very extensively to remind our supporters to vote and to switch soft supporters of other parties. Our poster and garden stake board display on all the main roads was fantastic. Kenneth Baker, then Tory chairman, told me that he was given a 'cast-iron assurance' by Conservative Central Office that the Conservatives would win by not less than 5,000 votes. But he changed his mind about the outcome when he saw our poster display as he was being driven into the constituency on election night.

On polling day, I told the media to expect recounts. At the count itself, I was trying to keep the media in suspense in order to increase the sense of shock when we won. David Bellotti became the first person to gain a parliamentary seat as a Liberal Democrat, winning with 51 per cent of the vote and a 4,550 majority.

Ann and I drank a lot of champagne that night with hundreds of supporters in Eastbourne's Cumberland Hotel, where we had held our daily press conferences. At 3 a.m., I spoke to Paddy, who apologised profusely for his error at the outset of the campaign. I told him to forget it. However, I had since discovered that his London advisers were telling him not to come to Eastbourne the next day and to comment on the victory from the studios in London, reflecting their lack of experience in how to 'milk' the coverage of a by-election win. I told him that if he wasn't in Eastbourne the next morning to claim credit for the astonishing victory, then I would never forgive him.

He came, and the celebratory pictures of him with David Bellotti on the balcony outside the hotel on Eastbourne's seafront ran extensively in the media for almost a week. Paddy described this as 'his best day as leader'. The reaction in the party was euphoric as our national opinion-poll ratings went from 8 per cent to around double that within a week. The shock amongst the Conservatives was considerable. A safe seat had been lost to a party that Mrs Thatcher herself had recently branded as 'a dead parrot'. Asked about this, Ken Baker said that 'the parrot has twitched', and this made the *Standard*'s front-page headline. During the campaign, Paddy had predicted that if we won, Mrs Thatcher would fall. Six weeks later, she resigned as Prime Minister.

CHAPTER 5

RECOVERY AND SURVIVAL

A 'SHOCK WIN' IN RIBBLE VALLEY
KILLS THE POLL TAX

The consequences of the party's budgetary cutbacks in 1989, and in particular making all campaigns staff other than me redundant, were shown by our inability to immediately capitalise on the Eastbourne breakthrough. A by-election in Bradford North followed just three weeks after the victory, but the staff that we had 'borrowed' from other parts of the party for Eastbourne had to return to their jobs and we simply could not have moved them up to Yorkshire for the next by-election. After Bradford North, Paddy was angry that we hadn't deployed more staff to that campaign. Always slightly fearful of him, I had to point out that the staff that he had wanted me to send there had all been sacked the previous summer, and that I had warned him of the consequences.

Despite the lack of national party resources, David Ward[29] capitalised on his local popularity and his team benefited from the significant bounce provided by Eastbourne. They gained second place with 25 per cent of the vote. David was a local councillor representing Idle (the 'Idle Working Man's Club' was of course referred to in many media

---

29   David was eventually to win the redrawn Bradford East constituency in the 2010 general election, but was dropped by the party after his selection to fight the seat in 2017 and then stood unsuccessfully as an independent. He is now an independent councillor there.

reports of the campaign). He pushed a noticeably weak Conservative candidate, who had allowed herself to be pictured in a local graveyard in her election address, into a poor third place.

This was the signal for Michael Heseltine to announce that he had a better chance of securing a Conservative victory at the next general election than Mrs Thatcher, and I have no doubt that he was right. Many Conservative MPs had suddenly become more fearful of retaining their seats after the Eastbourne by-election (and Labour's earlier triumph in Mid Staffordshire). They knew that their party would benefit from a change of leader, but personal loyalty to Mrs Thatcher remained strong. Heseltine made much of the damage being done to the Conservatives as a result of the poll tax. Although he failed to beat her in the first vote of Conservative MPs, it became clear that her position was untenable. She resigned on 22 November 1990, exactly six weeks after polling day in Eastbourne. I believe that Michael Heseltine would have been a very formidable Prime Minister. He ran a brilliant campaign for the Tory leadership, chaired by the supposedly 'wet' but very effective Peter Walker. I am sure that, had he won, he would have had the sense to go to the country very quickly on the back of the Conservative recovery which their leadership election campaign brought about. He would probably have won a landslide victory. But the deeply divided Conservative Party could not stomach the idea of Mrs Thatcher's assassin, and a pro-European, leading the party. The much weaker but essentially decent John Major became their leader instead.

Major lacked the courage to call a general election himself at this point. He failed to capitalise on the key messages available to him at the time: 'new' and 'change', which are two of the most powerful words in politics. He would have had a comfortable Conservative majority in an immediate election, especially if he had been committed in it to abolishing the poll tax. Instead, he blundered badly by appointing the right-wing Home Secretary David Waddington to the House of Lords, thereby triggering a by-election in Lancashire's Ribble Valley constituency. Waddington had a 19,000 Conservative majority and Major assumed that this was impregnable. But I was very aware that the constituency would have been a big loser from the introduction of the poll tax, and the Conservatives were not yet committed to replacing what Mrs Thatcher considered to be 'the best tax ever invented'. I went up to Lancashire and drove around the constituency with Tony Greaves, himself a Lancashire county councillor. It was clear to us both that the small terraced houses which dominated the constituency, particularly in the main town of Clitheroe, would be ripe for classic Liberal community campaigning, and a very strong emphasis on the issue of the poll tax.

Tony rapidly set about producing a series of 'Focus' leaflets for the different parts of the constituency that were to be the springboard of our success in the campaign. He was very happy to work with Michael Carr (who had fought the seat twice before for the SDP, coming third each time). In the New Year of 1991, my main focus of attention was on trying to assist our MPs in vulnerable seats and our target seat candidates and their teams prepare for a general election expected later that year. I therefore took a back seat for much of the by-election campaign, again appointing Paul Jacobs to be the agent, whilst still overseeing the fundraising and resourcing of it, and keeping a careful eye on what we were saying. Candy Piercy, now employed by me in the campaigns department, worked on strategy (including trying to persuade the press that we could win) and on writing some of the major leaflets. Our North Cornwall agent, Willie Rennie, led the management of volunteers; David Loxton, on leave from the Whips' Office, acted as Michael's minder; and Bill MacCormick again returned to the fray to oversee computer and direct mail operations.

As I had become used to expecting, I encountered great scepticism from Paddy's office and the party hierarchy about my determination for us to try to win the campaign, especially as we were now preparing for war in the Gulf following Saddam Hussain's invasion of Kuwait. But Paddy himself was now more willing to trust my judgement, as were our MPs. I was keen for David Steel to visit and we were able to encourage the former leader by offering him the opportunity to take a Maserati for a test drive in order to get there! The first polls had put us in third place, but Tony's early leaflets, and our strong campaign, meant that later polls put us second. The Conservatives had once again made an error in their choice of candidate for a by-election. Nigel Evans was a rising star in their party, but as a West Glamorgan county councillor who had fought Swansea West (where he ran a newsagent's shop), he was not an obvious choice for a 'safe' Tory seat in Lancashire. I christened him 'the Swansea newsagent' in our literature (whilst we made sure that nothing we said could be seen in any way to refer to rumours about his private life).[30] Labour chose Lancashire county councillor Josie Farringdon (now a Labour peer), but they were slow off the mark in the campaign, which also helped us to rise to second place.

On the Monday before polling day, Tony Bevins, the first political editor of *The Independent*, rang me excitedly when their latest poll put us a strong second. Many people treat polls such as this one as a forecast of the result, rather than the 'snapshot' of opinion that they actually represent. The Conservatives remained very confident, but by then it was clear to me, and I persuaded Tony Bevins that news of their poll would be sufficient for us to squeeze the third-placed Labour vote much further, and for us to win. *The Independent*'s report of the poll helped us by listing the swings to us in previous by-election 'earthquakes' such as Orpington, Sutton & Cheam and Eastbourne, providing a clear indication that another was in the offing. Bookmakers William Hill still made us 6:1 against, and I advised a few friends to make an investment. My own stake resulted in Ann and me being able to purchase some very good teak garden furniture, which we considered having engraved with the words 'Ribble Valley by-election memorial'.

I had not been full time in the campaign, and so did not expect to attend the count. But I was there on polling day when it emerged that

---

30 He came out as gay in December 2010.

'Miss Whiplash' of the 'The Corrective Party' did not need her full allocation of places to attend it. I therefore attended the count on her behalf. Nigel Evans had already been photographed in a winning pose for the next day's *Daily Express*. I felt sorry for him as I witnessed his arrival at the count, immediately being surrounded by his team who were telling him that he had lost. We overturned the 19,000 majority to win by 4,356 with a 24.7 per cent swing. As a result of my car getting stuck down a slope in the school car park outside the count, I arrived well after the declaration of the result at our victory party in a local Clitheroe pub. It had no champagne in stock, but by the time I got there, Ann and Gerald Vernon-Jackson had been round to the Clitheroe Conservative Club to successfully enquire whether, as they probably wouldn't need all their champagne, they could buy a case of it, which they did!

After Eastbourne had restored the party's opinion-poll ratings, they had fallen back again during John Major's honeymoon period after his election as Conservative leader and Prime Minister. The Ribble Valley by-election brought an abrupt end to this, and once again restored the Lib Dems to around 18 per cent in the national opinion polls. Our win meant the death of the poll tax, with many papers running pictures of tombstones inscribed with the words 'Poll Tax RIP'. Exactly two weeks after polling day, Michael Heseltine announced that it was to be replaced. In the meantime, the Chancellor Norman Lamont raised VAT from 15 per cent to 17.5 per cent in order to cut all the recently issued poll tax bills by £140, requiring every bill to be re-issued.

MONMOUTH, AND THE LOCAL ELECTIONS OF 1991

The Eastbourne and Ribble Valley by-election successes and the 1991 local election gains restored the party's self-confidence and demonstrated that the new party led by Paddy could win. The belief in our capacity to win was often the missing 'magic' ingredient needed for successful Lib Dem campaigning. Following the by-election success, more members were willing to come forward as candidates, membership of the party was steadily increasing (it reached 100,000 during the 1992 general election) and we were again able to raise significant funds for the general election campaign. In the meantime, we had actually been kept afloat by a generous loan of £200,000 provided by a mysterious benefactor in the Midlands and arranged by Paddy. Such an anonymous loan would now be illegal, but it wasn't then. The money had been lent to us when banks were unwilling to help us any more, given the risk of the party collapsing. There were no rules about disclosing the source of donations or loans in those days. Graham Elson tried to glean what he could about our mysterious supporter, and the two of us even speculated about whether or not this might have been Paddy himself lending the money via a trusted contact! It was eventually returned in stages as our financial position improved under Graham's stewardship of HQ, and with Tim Clement-Jones's oversight of party finances.

My main focus as director of campaigns and elections, apart from the by-elections, was endeavouring with very limited resources to support and bolster campaigning in our target seats. These were the constituencies that we held but considered to be in jeopardy (which was most of them), and those where we considered that we had some real prospect of gaining. The general election was then expected in the autumn of 1991. By the summer of that year, I had been able to employ a small campaign team comprising Candy Piercy, Derek Barrie (who had been a major figure in Ming Campbell's success in North East Fife), Tim Payne (the son of Paddy's aide Mark Payne), and for one day a week Paul Rainger. Our budget to support the key seats (including the cost of employing these staff) was extremely modest (just £120,000 for campaigning over about eighteen months).

The party had yet to 'buy in' properly to the concept of targeting constituencies. The thinking at national level (where I still had little influence) was much more about national advertising etc. Our campaigns team organised training sessions at conferences and in the key constituencies (based in part on what we had shown worked well in parliamentary by-elections). We spent most of our time in these target constituencies helping where we could with their local council elections and by-elections and we allocated modest funding for agreed items of additional campaign expenditure in them. In 1987, the SDP had had a very much larger fund available for target seats and distributed it following agreed plans. I discovered, however, that some of this money was still sitting in local party bank accounts years later, and that some of it had been spent on projects other than those agreed. All payments from us were now authorised by our campaign officers only on the basis of receiving receipts for the expenditure and copies of the locally produced leaflets. We distributed copies of the best leaflets, together with those that we had produced in the by-elections, to all our other candidates. Our aim was to identify and spread best practice, and support the seats that we could directly in ways that were most helpful to them.

In presentations about future strategy, we used academic research about opinion polls to show that our party's significant increases in ratings generally came from by-election successes. Donors to the campaigns, as well as helpers, were on a database that I established (the helpers' one was based on the signing-in books used in each campaign). After a campaign, we sent everyone who contributed financially to a successful by-election campaign a copy of the election address.

The first major by-election after Ribble Valley was Monmouth in south Wales. A very early poll there gave Labour a 1 per cent lead over the Conservatives in a Conservative-held seat. We were a poor third on 16 per cent, making it very difficult for us to present ourselves as challengers, or to avoid being squeezed. Peter Mandelson ran the very high-profile Labour campaign, whilst our agent Tim Payne was constrained in the campaign by a much more modest budget, which was also made more difficult because there were local elections in most of England and Wales during the middle of it. We got a boost in the by-election by targeting and winning a seat in Monmouth itself, but there were difficulties in the local party and it was not possible to persuade all the local council candidates to do what was needed to win more seats. One of them even threatened to resign if some of our carefully worded letters were delivered where this person was standing. I tried always to be very sensitive to local views, but from time to time I was frustrated by an approach which was basically: 'I will try to block someone else succeeding if I don't get my way.'

Our campaign also received an enormous boost from the results of the local elections elsewhere across England and Wales. The BBC's Huw Edwards clearly thought that he had drawn the 'short straw' when I first spoke to him on local election night, as he was assigned to broadcast from Cowley Street. Eventually, he had the best story to tell of any commentator that night as the scale of our success surprised him and everyone else (including most Lib Dems). With a similar results operation in place to the previous year, I was able to feed him a constant diet of Lib Dem success stories as we made net gains of 407 seats (compared to 584 gains for Labour) and we achieved an estimated national vote share of 22 per cent. The 'People First' campaigns, booklets and training days paid real dividends for us. We were able to set the tone for the evening's media coverage and the next day's papers very early on when Tim Razzall (in charge of number-crunching on the night) first forecast our 400 gains. Paddy should, of course, have been jubilant, but he often tended towards pessimism. He sat outside my office late that night bemoaning 'how on earth are we going to defend all these gains in four years' time'. He then took my mocking criticism of this response to a stunning set of gains in good humour. It was clear from these local election results that we had at least restored the party's fortunes after the merger debacle. It was the Conservatives who were now to have serious worries, as these were their worst local election results since 1973, and a general election had to be held within a year.

The Conservatives' problems were exacerbated two weeks after the local elections when Labour secured a 2,406-vote victory over them in Monmouth. Our candidate, Frances David, increased her share of the vote from 16 per cent in the first opinion poll to 25 per cent on polling day. I considered this to be a very creditable result as we had avoided being squeezed, but we did not achieve the win that Paddy had clearly hoped for at the outset. Labour were delighted with their win, but their level of support actually dropped compared to the first poll, whilst Conservative support had dropped even further.

LIVERPOOL WALTON AND THE 'POSTPONED' ELECTION

Whilst at Monmouth, I was also worrying about the next potential by-election. I was always anxious not to appear ghoulish or disrespectful, but senior people in political parties are always mindful of the state of health of various MPs. Labour's MP in Liverpool Walton, Eric Heffer, had been quite ill for some time and died two weeks after the Monmouth by-election. At this time, there was no process in place in the party to distinguish between those prospective candidates who might cope with the rigours of a parliamentary by-election and those who might not. A local councillor for one of the wards in Walton, Richard Roberts, was determined to stand for us in the by-election. I did not consider that he had the potential to handle national media questioning, and I feared that he and the party would be severely embarrassed under such scrutiny. So, I arranged for him to go down to London for some media training. Christopher Walmsley (our former West Derbyshire candidate and who still worked for the BBC in Manchester) kindly agreed to put him through his paces. Archy Kirkwood and David Loxton assisted the training in a mock media conference by posing the sort of questions that Richard might face from journalists in the campaign. At the end of the process he felt very bruised but agreed that he should withdraw from the selection. He admitted to me in colourful language that he had made a bad mistake in thinking that he should stand, but it had taken a day of intensive media training before he realised this. As a result of this experience, I persuaded the party to introduce a further tier in the vetting process to approve parliamentary by-election candidates. This meant in future that representatives of the Candidates Committee, the Parliamentary Party and the relevant Regional Party would have the power to interview potential by-election candidates and determine whether or not they were credible enough to go forward for selection.

The lack of such a process at the outset of the Walton campaign meant that the writ for the by-election to be held on 4 July was moved in the House of Commons before we had a candidate in place. On my advice, Paddy rang Paul Clark (our former candidate in the constituency, a local councillor, and someone who would handle himself well in the media spotlight of a by-election). Paul was on holiday in Portugal, and I also rang him there, pressing him to respond positively to Paddy's call for the sake of the party. He agreed to do so, despite having finished 23,253 behind Heffer at the previous election. Paul was the Leader of the Opposition on the city council, and I persuaded his deputy, Mike Storey, to be his election agent. They were both brilliant at briefing the media about the political scene in Liverpool, whilst I acted as the campaign manager, drawing on advice and support from my former candidate David Alton (then Lib Dem MP for Liverpool Mossley Hill) and my former mentor Trevor Jones (still a Liverpool councillor).

By 1991, the political tide in Liverpool had turned against the Militants, and their domination of the city's Labour Party had been brought to an end. The Militants stood their own candidate, Lesley Mahmood, against the official Labour candidate, Peter Kilfoyle, their North West organiser, who had recently been employed to root out the Militants. Alan Bleasdale's seven-part series *G.B.H.* was running on Channel 4 at the time, starring Robert Lindsay in the Derek Hatton role and Michael Palin as the teacher being bullied by the Militants. Many people asked me about it, and if things could really have been as bad as portrayed. I could only say that it had actually been much worse. Ann would have been able to vouch for this as her personal experience of the Militant era included being one of 31,000 council staff declared redundant by the Militant council when she was a teacher in inner-city Liverpool. As a known opponent of the Militants, they had also blocked any career progression for her, which meant she had to leave the city to gain a headship elsewhere.

The unpopularity of a 'bin strike', when Liverpool's council workers had refused to collect domestic refuse, had really damaged Labour across the city in the local elections of 1991. The unpopularity of the continuing strike was the big issue on which I believed that a winning campaign could be based. Our first leaflets had pictures of the emergency rubbish tips on waste ground and suggested that the 'evidence was mounting up' against Labour locally as the council failed to resolve the strike.

The media, however, focused relentlessly on the Militant vs. Labour battle, even though the Militants were now a hated and spent force in the city. It was a struggle within the party and the media to suggest that we were the challengers, not the Militants. Perceptions were not helped by an early BBC report about the by-election which was filmed on the very edge of the most Labour part of the constituency, and on its border with Everton (an even more strongly Labour part of the city). The report was based on interviews with passers-by (many of whom would not live in the Walton constituency) and claimed that *nobody* at all could be found who was voting for us. It was later the subject of a complaint that we made to the BBC. Labour of course encouraged the media's misguided belief that the by-election was a battle between them and the Militants.

The media perception about our poor prospects was initially generally believed by our own party members outside Liverpool. This made it more difficult for us to attract helpers from outside the city, but those within it worked incredibly hard. It would have been a hugely significant result for us to have gained a seat from Labour less than a year before the general election. But fortunately for Labour, the key issue of the bin strike was resolved before polling day.

The media coverage, including the initial BBC report, had been completely wrong, as we came a strong second with 36 per cent of the vote. We cut Labour's majority from 23,356 to 6,860. Lesley Mahmood, who had been portrayed by Labour and the media as the main challenger, polled just 6.5 per cent of the vote. Our efforts to squeeze the Conservative vote reduced their candidate Berkeley Greenwood's vote to just 2.9 per cent, which was a record low for the Conservatives in a by-election in England. Peter Kilfoyle's well-earned reward for helping to take on the city's Militants was to become the MP for what would now be a very safe Labour seat.

Most expectations in the summer of 1991 were that John Major would call a general election in the autumn. I was not one of the biggest players in our national campaign, although Des Wilson made sure that I was a full member of the General Election Planning Group and I concentrated my team's efforts on supporting the target seats. But John Major didn't call the election as expected, and I was surprised to find that I was amongst the first to know that this would be the case. I was at an academic conference that September bringing together politicians, commentators and pollsters at Nuffield College, Oxford. Duncan Brack, director of policy, was also there and we were both chatting to Robert Waller, a very nice guy and then one of the country's leading pollsters whose role at the time involved briefing John Major on the opinion polls. Waller told us that he had advised Major to call a general election at that point, and that he would win. I was inclined to agree, but Waller then described Major's cautious nature, and despite being warned that things would probably be worse in the spring, Major decided against an autumn election. I rang Des that night. He was in a highly excited state about the imminent election campaign that he thought he was about to run for us. I had to let him know that it would not be so soon. This 'extension' of time meant that the Lib Dem campaign was also to be in a much greater state of readiness by the spring of 1992 than it would have been the previous autumn.

BECOMING THE SECOND PARTY
IN SCOTLAND (TEMPORARILY)

The last three parliamentary by-elections before the general election were all held on 8 November 1991. Kincardine & Deeside was the most significant of them. It was long expected and the constituency was also a target seat for us in the general election. Our candidate was Nicol Stephen, who in 1982 had been elected as Scotland's youngest councillor aged twenty-two. He had come within 2,063 votes of winning the seat in 1987, having been the election agent for it in 1983. By the time of the by-election, I had got to know Nicol, and his partner Caris, quite well through regular visits there to advise on the forthcoming general election campaign. I arranged for the employment of a young local activist, Ian Yuill, to assist with election preparations.

The by-election was triggered by the death of the very popular Conservative incumbent Alick Buchanan-Smith, who had been in poor health for some time. Once again, I asked Paul Jacobs to be the agent in an effort to score his 'hat-trick' of by-election wins. Willie Rennie came back up from North Cornwall to lead the management of volunteers in the 'front-of-house' area of our HQ (a former car showroom in Peterculter). Tavish Scott[31] took holiday from our Commons Whips' Office to be the press officer. Bill MacCormick again ran the computer operation and he worked with me on the most sophisticated direct mail operation that we had run since Greenwich. Paul Rainger came up from St Andrews and worked on local targeted leaflets, Sheila Ritchie (a leading councillor and longstanding friend) oversaw the casework operation, and key organisers included Derek Barrie and Sir Bob Smith (who later became MP for much of the constituency). The local party, with whom we had an excellent relationship, were quite adamant that they wanted this team to be in charge. They wanted us to bring to the constituency all our experience of running successful

---

31   Later MSP for Shetland and leader of the Scottish Liberal Democrats from 2008 until 2011.

parliamentary by-election campaigns in all parts of Great Britain. This, however, left some of the Scottish party officers at the time more than a little miffed not to be in control of it.

Kincardine & Deeside was the first parliamentary by-election in which the Lib Dems used opinion polling very extensively. Archy Kirkwood helped us to obtain finance from the Joseph Rowntree Reform Trust to pay for this, and Rick Ridder oversaw it. Our first poll showed that our party support had declined substantially since 1987. The 'Nicol Stephen brand' was very strong, but the 'Lib Dem brand' was initially very weak. Nicol was associated locally with campaigns such as that in support of the electrification of the Aberdeen-to-Edinburgh rail line. He was also known for campaigning on issues such as hypothermia as he highlighted the large number of elderly people dying in the cold winters of North East Scotland compared to far fewer 'winter deaths' in much colder Scandinavian countries.

The biggest issue for our campaign was the controversial proposed 'opt out' of the Foresterhill hospitals in Aberdeen, involving leaving existing NHS structures to form a new 'NHS Trust'. There was much scepticism about the formation of these Trusts (although Paddy was in favour of one relating to the ambulance service in his constituency) and the phrase 'opt out' generally rang alarm bells. A formal consultation about the proposal was underway during the by-election campaign and the decision had to be taken by Ian Lang as Secretary of State for Scotland. He avoided taking it during the campaign period, and only gave the controversial go-ahead for it after the by-election. We launched our campaign with Charles Kennedy, and he and Nicol were pictured together by a Foresterhill hospital sign with large piles of petition forms opposing the opt-out.

An early blunder by the Conservative candidate Marcus Humphrey played into our hands. In a media interview immediately after his selection, he was somewhat flustered and declared his support for the 'opt out' proposal. When its considerable unpopularity became evident, he tried to deny that he had ever said this, and now claimed that he was opposed to it. His problem, however, was that Nicol had taped the original early-morning radio news programme. So, at one of our morning press conferences I got Jim Wallace, then our MP for Orkney & Shetland, to play the recording of this interview. For good measure, we gave out tape cassettes and a transcript of the interview to every journalist present. The news bulletins that day all featured Jim playing the tape recorder and exposing the Conservative candidate's contradictory statements. It was a significant turning point in the campaign.

We did, however, have some problems of our own as a result of our party's apparent enthusiasm for increasing tax on petrol as one of our environmentally friendly policies. I was sceptical of our own claims that the number of miles driven in private cars could be reduced significantly by increasing petrol prices, but Paddy and many others in the party were keen on it at the time. There was a lot of public hostility to the policy, as most people considered their own journeys to be necessary, and thought that the costs of making them could increase significantly. This was felt particularly strongly in rural areas with little public transport provision. The Conservative Party chairman Chris Patten and all visiting Conservative ministers made much of the issue and our response was sometimes shaky. Fortunately, Ming Campbell came to our rescue at the height of this controversy when he was challenged about the issue at one of our morning press conferences. These were held on a daily basis in by-elections until about 1997 and were often 'gladiatorial'-style events, as journalists did battle with candidates and visiting party dignitaries. Ming put a firm stop to the questioning with the answer: 'If you think that our party would be so stupid as to propose significant and sudden increases in the cost of motoring in the sort of rural areas that we often represent in Parliament, then you can just think again.' In a private aside to me immediately afterwards, he said that 'of course some in our party could be that stupid'.

I decided to not include much Lib Dem branding in Nicol's first leaflets, attracting some criticism within the party and the press, but I included it rather more when further polling showed that our campaign was significantly boosting support for the party in the constituency – polls that rattled the Conservatives. The by-election had particular significance in Scottish politics because it would determine whether the Conservatives or we would become the second largest party in Scotland in terms of Westminster seats. The Tories had ten Scottish MPs prior to the by-election occurring, whilst we had nine. Labour had fifty seats at the time, whilst the SNP had three. It was felt that Conservative authority to govern in Scotland would be challenged even more forcefully if they no longer had the second largest number of MPs in the country. We were therefore determined to become the second party in Scotland.

The *Press & Journal* reflected these Conservative fears and its eve-of-poll edition was probably the most biased local newspaper coverage that I have ever seen of a by-election. Their lobby correspondent was up for the campaign and I later remonstrated with him about how it had run seven prominent stories about the by-election that day, all of them appearing to be very crudely based on the final Conservative campaign press releases. Our own campaign literature, however, had much more powerful messages and the *Press & Journal* coverage had no discernible effect on the campaign. Nicol won with 49 per cent of the vote and his 7,824 majority was sufficient to make sure that this result dominated media coverage of all three by-elections occurring that day. It was a severe blow to the Conservatives in Scotland and I was highly amused by the way in which the *Press & Journal* then had to put Nicol's 'Boy Wonder Win' all over its front page, to the obvious chagrin of their lobby correspondent, who brought copies to our victory party and who was trying to be friendly as he would now have to work with Nicol as a local MP.

On the same day, we also managed very respectable results in the by-elections at Hemsworth (second place with 20.1 per cent of the vote) and Langbaurgh (third with 16.1 per cent). But our own handling of the Kincardine & Deeside result was something that we sadly misjudged. We had said very little about the potential of a Scottish

Parliament during the campaign as our polling confirmed that there was actually little support for it there at the time. But it was a key issue for the Scottish Liberal Democrats, and the result was used to advance demands for it. We gathered our ten Scottish Lib Dem MPs together (flying some of them in at considerable expense) for a group photo, and we used the event to suggest that with the Conservatives now third in Westminster seats, the result had provided a mandate for the long-hoped-for Scottish Parliament. With hindsight, the switch to claiming that the by-election had been about the Scottish Parliament, and not the issues on which we really fought it, was a significant factor in the reversal of the result in the general election five months later.

1992 GENERAL ELECTION

Our three parliamentary by-election wins since the merger and local election successes of 1990 and 1991, together with Paddy's increasingly successful profile, had restored the party's poll position from 4 per cent in 1989 to about 15 per cent prior to the 1992 general election. This was a base from which we expected to build during the campaign as our party profile would increase, particularly in the broadcast media. We had much greater self-confidence in our general election campaign than we could possibly have expected in 1989. Significant credit for this must go to Des Wilson, who was not popular with many of the MPs (and the feeling was mutual) but who worked incredibly hard as an unpaid chair of the campaign, providing great inspiration to many party activists. He had the task then of building a general election campaign organisation based largely on volunteers, as our staff at HQ was still only around twenty strong at this point. The focus of our campaign was what became known as the 'five Es': Economy, Education, Environment, Europe and Electoral Reform. A document prior to the election that launched our policies in these five areas was also privately regarded as a potential negotiating document for coalition talks.

With the polls in March giving a slight advantage to Labour, it appeared that the nature of the campaign was going to become very unpleasant as the Conservatives feared defeat. Paddy's diaries describe how an edition of the *Sunday Times* led with 'Kinnock, the Kremlin connection', picturing him with a red flag.[32] Paddy also knew at this stage that the *News of the World* had obtained a document which had been stolen from the office of his solicitor Andrew Phillips. He had only recently discovered that there was any such document and it noted his discussion with his solicitor about his affair some years previously with his former secretary Tricia Howard. An injunction had been obtained to block publication by the *News of the World* of material from the stolen document, but other newspapers spread rumours of impending political scandals with clear hints pointing in Paddy's direction. A wide-reaching injunction had then been taken out to prevent them running the story. This injunction, referring to the stolen document, confirmed the details to them all, and gossip spread quickly. An unusually high number of press photographers began following Paddy around.

Affairs between MPs and staff were not unknown in Westminster. But here was proof of one involving a major party leader, just before a general election. The timing of the break-in, and the burglary of a very secure safe, seemed very suspicious. The manner through which the media became aware of the story gave rise to significant sympathy for Paddy, and his deft handling of the crisis won him significant respect from many people. The facts of the story had been established, and Paddy knew that the detail was bound to be broken soon in the media. It was actually broken by *The Scotsman*, as Scottish papers were not covered by the injunction. But by then Paddy was about to have it lifted as, if he didn't, he correctly believed that coverage of the story would break out in a more damaging way.

Paddy's planning for significant events was often meticulous and he arranged precise timings for a press conference announcing the lifting

---

32   *The Ashdown Diaries, Vol. I: 1988–1997,* p. 137.

of the injunction, whilst making every effort to avoid being 'door-stepped' by the media. His appearance at the press conference started slightly late, which was most unusual for him. He had been delayed after taking a phone call from John Major, who was supportive and appeared to want to re-assure Paddy that the Conservative Party would not seek to capitalise on his personal situation. I believe that this was a genuine, well-intentioned attempt to provide some comfort at a time of considerable distress for Paddy. The Prime Minister's call was later judged less charitably, however, by some people, when Edwina Currie revealed her own affair with Major.

In the packed Jubilee room, just off Westminster Hall in the Houses of Parliament, Paddy made a short and very dignified announcement explaining that he was lifting the injunction. It was to be his only statement on the issue for some considerable time. He explained that it had been a brief affair, before he was party leader, and that the event should have remained private to those directly involved. Paddy demonstrated what Roy Jenkins sometimes used to describe as 'grace under pressure'. It was a difficult day for all of us in HQ to continue working on preparations for the imminent election campaign, unsure about whether or not we could be certain that Paddy would still be our leader for it.

I had to spend much of that day working on the standard candidates' election address, which many of our candidates would use in the general election. I struggled with the design, knowing that it was possible that all the pictures of Paddy might have to be replaced with those of someone else. I faxed Paddy a brief note of personal support and spoke to him that afternoon. He was quite emotional, but now determined, as he had said to the press, 'to get on with his job'. It is not, I think, widely known that he did offer his resignation to the Chief Whip Jim Wallace, but his parliamentary colleagues, taking a lead from David Steel at their weekly meeting, were supportive of his position of carrying on as leader and did not want to put him under any pressure.

The Sun's infamous headline the next day was 'Paddy Pantsdown'. Paddy referred to this as being 'dreadful – but brilliant'.[33] Coverage was extensive in all the papers (about ten pages in *The Sun*) and it continued for many days. The media were, of course, encouraged to try to investigate any other potential allegations or rumours of affairs involving Paddy, and to try to unearth any other scandal. Many calls were made to former female members of his staff and other women involved with the party. The husband of one of them opened the front door to be confronted by a journalist saying: 'We have come to talk to you about your wife's affair with Paddy Ashdown.' It was a 'fishing exercise' with no basis and there were many such speculative and misplaced attempts to find further scandals and keep the story running. Paddy was to suffer from threats and rumours throughout the campaign, and for much of his leadership. It was not possible for him as party leader, with an imminent election, to duck out of sight from the media. He and his family had to cope with a large media entourage wherever he went, and they were besieged at both his London flat and Yeovil home. Whilst always being polite to the journalists when he encountered them, he maintained his professional resolve not to add anything to his earlier statement, and to avoid 'giving legs to the story', which is the golden rule of crisis communications.

It entered into political folklore afterwards that the party's opinion-poll ratings increased as a result of the scandal. What happened in my view was that Paddy's overall standing as a leader grew as he demonstrated real political leadership skills, and that this eventually helped him to boost the party's ratings. But, without ever telling him, I discreetly added a couple of questions to opinion polls that we were conducting in a few constituencies at the time (and kept the results private). This polling showed that there was neither a significant 'bounce' for the party nor any net loss of support as a result of the publicity. But we did find that some older women were slightly less inclined to vote for us,

---

33   *The Ashdown Diaries, Vol. I: 1988–1997*, p. 141.

whilst some younger men were slightly more so, effectively cancelling out their different reactions.

Attempts to find further scandal about Paddy continued throughout the campaign, keeping us under pressure. After the election, Kelvin MacKenzie claimed in *The Sun* that an unnamed Conservative Cabinet minister had been encouraging the media to make further investigation of allegations about Paddy's private life. John Major later promised to look into this story. Paddy was also led to believe that there was an organised 'dirty tricks' campaign which may have involved right-wing operatives from the US.[34] Their role was allegedly to disrupt opponents' campaigns by distracting those running them.

The fear that any further allegations about Paddy might be made caused real stress to our campaign at national level. On the Thursday before polling day, I was talking to Des very late at night before driving overnight to north Wales and the north-west. He told me of the latest rumours doing the rounds suggesting that allegations about Paddy could be published in a German magazine to avoid the threat of legal action in the UK. Each day, and particularly at the early-morning press conferences, Des feared that someone would ask unpleasant questions or make allegations. This was particularly so in the run-up to publication of the Sunday newspapers, and Saturday evenings involved nervous waits whilst people were sent out to get the first editions. The tabloid papers had a much greater presence on his 'battle bus' tour than their interest in his political views might have justified. In his memoirs, Des described how 'the scare stories came to dominate my role in the campaign. It was a nightmare.'[35]

---

34 'An interesting piece in the *Sunday Times* today about the so called "NERDS", a group of scandal hitmen who operate in America and are said to have been active here – for the Tories, of course. Their technique is to set a piece of scandal running, often totally unfounded. This disconcerts the opposition, makes them spend time rebutting it and so puts them on the back foot. Some of it sticks in the minds of the press and of the electorate. Real Goebbels stuff. Their job is to destroy people's reputations if they can, but failing that to unbalance them. I wonder if this is what happened to us over the election?' 17 May 1992, *The Ashdown Diaries, Vol. I: 1988–1997*, p. 166.

35 Des Wilson, *Memoirs of a Minor Public Figure*.

Our strategy in the last week of the Lib Dem campaign caused internal controversy. I believe that one of the reasons that we failed to respond correctly to the changing story of the election in the last week was that our campaign was distracted by all the rumours, which proved baseless, about further allegations to be made. I also believe that these rumours were stoked by political opponents. The last week of the campaign was always bound to be a difficult one for us to handle because the overwhelming majority of polls in the months before polling day had suggested a hung parliament. Paddy had been preparing for this possibility with a discreet hung parliament or 'HP' team that was really looking for a deal with Labour on the basis of a commitment to proportional representation in future Westminster elections (to be obtained by threatening to do a deal with the Conservatives if Labour did not accede to this). Paddy also wanted four Cabinet places for the party, with three of his senior colleagues being considered for these roles. Alan Beith would become Chief Secretary to the Treasury, David Steel would hopefully have become Foreign Secretary and Ming Campbell would also be included. The demand for proportional representation at the following election was something that I always regarded as essential in order to protect our interests as a smaller party in any such coalition. We would inevitably be squeezed and suffer significantly if the first-past-the-post system continued. This might all have come about, because after the general election, Neil Kinnock admitted that he had become a convert to the cause of proportional representation. But it was not to be as the party's public demands for a coalition backfired.

I always doubted that very many people really wanted a hung parliament and was mindful that even those who did so could not vote for it as an outcome. The prospect of a hung parliament always depended on the unpredictable distribution of seats between the parties. I also thought that openly advocating a coalition as our desired outcome would result in some squeezing of our own vote because people who might have supported us otherwise might not like one or other of our potential coalition partners. I raised these fears with Des as I felt that we would be particularly damaged in our main Conservative vs. Lib Dem battleground seats if the impression was given of a deal being prepared with Kinnock. The Labour leader was being subjected daily to savage media treatment in the Tory-leaning press, and I feared that the effects of this could rub off on us. Des agreed that I should raise my concerns at the strategy meeting on the penultimate Sunday evening of the campaign, which was held over dinner at the National Liberal Club. The 'hung parliament strategy' was, however, pretty much set in stone, with Paddy and his key advisers Richard Holme and Alan Leaman having determined a course of action in which others concurred, whilst I would have felt more comfortable simply arguing for the election of more Lib Dem MPs and not focusing on coalition. The consequence of there being more Lib Dem MPs might well have been a coalition, but this prospect would have arisen after people had voted. Raising it as an explicit public aim actually made it less likely.

Richard arrived prepared for the discussion with a sheet of paper listing five reasons why we should be arguing for a coalition in the campaign; and five reasons why we might not. He made the suggestion that we should quickly accept the five reasons in favour of the proposed strategy, move on and work as a group on how we would overcome the arguments behind the five reasons why we might not support it. I raised my concerns about this less than objective approach to consideration of the issue, and what this strategy might do to our prospects in the target seats. The discussion became quite heated, with Richard shouting at me, claiming that I did not understand what he was saying, and me replying that I did understand, but I didn't agree with him. Des saw that I had little vocal support in the meeting, and most of the group acquiesced to Richard's strategy. The decision was taken that we were going ahead with arguing for a coalition in the last week of the campaign.

One thing I didn't know at the time was that the Conservatives were aware of Labour's private plans to attract votes from us in the last week by supporting some of our constitutional reform agenda, and explicitly saying that they would consider electoral reform. The

Liberal Democrats were to be invited to join the commission that they had established to consider the issue of proportional representation. They latched on to the fact that Charter 88, a constitutional reform campaigning organisation, planned to hold a large series of 'Democracy Day' events to make electoral reform a big issue in the last week. Around eighty public events across the country, exactly a week before polling day, were to promote messages such as the need for proportional representation. Labour planned to respond positively to these events when they took place.

Roy Hattersley had been briefed on Labour's last-week strategy over lunch in the restaurant at Smith Square, near all the party HQs. A former aide told him that Labour planned a bold statement for 'Democracy Day' saying that they would at least consider introducing proportional representation. Unfortunately for Labour, the Conservative director of communications, Shaun Woodward (who later defected to Labour), was sitting at the next table, carefully noting it all down on a serviette. He was able to brief Chris Patten on Labour's plans that afternoon.

In response to this proposed strategy, John Major put great emphasis on how he would, in all circumstances, rule out proportional representation. Many of us wondered why he was apparently departing from the Conservative script for the campaign. It was in fact a very clever and carefully pre-planned move. He was responding to Paddy's demand that no other party leader should 'pick up a phone to talk about coalition without accepting proportional representation'. Paddy had described the choice between working with the Tories or with Labour as like the 'choice between being run over by a train or by a bus'. But Major's tactic deliberately left Paddy without the potential choice of working with the Tories. The Conservatives had realised that the PR issue meant that the only apparent coalition option for us was one with Labour. They knew that most voters who were considering voting for either us or the Tories would be hostile to a Lib–Lab deal. Major made it clear that the only alternative to a Lib–Lab deal was a Conservative majority. This appealed to the Con/Lib Dem waverers in most of our target seats. At the academic conference at Essex University later that year, I heard John Wakeham (a key player in the Tory campaign) describe how their strategy was to 'line up their two principal opponents and shoot them with a single bullet'.

On the last Sunday of the campaign, Paddy made his final party election broadcast. The opening six minutes were brilliant, played to his strength of character and featured his military background, showing him in khaki uniform hacking his way through a jungle (something that he had rejected doing at the outset of his leadership). But then any positive effect was destroyed as his script began: 'So, you have settled on a hung parliament in the election.' In fact, people had not settled on this outcome at all. It may have appeared as a likely possibility, but that was not the same as being the outcome that most people desired. People were effectively invited to reject a hung parliament, if they wanted to, by voting Labour or Conservative. The following morning, Robin Oakley, then of *The Times*, had been briefed to report that the Lib Dems wanted four Cabinet places. His front-page story reflected how we were now seeking to negotiate a coalition. This was when it appeared that it could only be possible with Labour, led by the unpopular Neil Kinnock.

The effect in a significant number of seats, that we were otherwise set to win, was dramatically negative. I was in the Conwy constituency in north Wales on the final Friday before the election when Paddy addressed a large crowd in Llandudno, its largest town. It was a memorable afternoon in the campaign for me. Paddy's plane had been delayed, and the waiting crowd was kept in place with a series of messages saying that his arrival was imminent (as opposed to telling them the truth, that he was more than an hour away). One of our 'advance team', Allan Biggar,[36] helped to keep the crowd waiting as our candidate, a local Methodist minister, Roger Roberts, found a busker

---

36   Who had been one of my fellow area agents for the Liberal Party in the mid-'80s.

to perform with his guitar on the back of an open-top lorry and led the singing of hymns such as 'The Old Rugged Cross'. Only in Llandudno, I thought. When Paddy eventually arrived, I told him that we were ahead in the constituency, and that Roger was going to win. I did not usually give him such forecasts, but I was confident here and in other places where I had all the canvass data and was close to all aspects of their campaigns.

On polling day, however, we lost Conwy by 995 votes. I had also been confident that we were ahead in Hazel Grove, with just a week to go. I had written most of the major leaflets for Andrew Stunell's campaign, and he shared the view that he was ahead on the final weekend. But on the Thursday, he lost by 929 votes. Donald Gorrie failed to capture our main Scottish target seat of Edinburgh West by just 879 votes, and Mike Hancock failed to regain Portsmouth South by 242 votes. My reckoning had been that we were ahead in over thirty seats on the final weekend of the campaign. But we went on to win just twenty of them, one more than when the merged party had been launched by nineteen MPs. My impression was later confirmed when I heard about how some of the Conservatives' private polling had put us ahead in target seats such as Taunton a week before we went on to lose them.

On election night, we knew that we had survived the post-1987 traumas, but it was a very disappointed party in the National Liberal Club. We lost all three by-election gains and three other seats (Ceredigion, Brecon & Radnor and Southport). Many people felt that the Conservatives were becoming invincible after their fourth consecutive general election victory. Our main consolation was that we did gain four of our target seats in the south-west of England. Paul Tyler gained North Cornwall (where he followed through on our success there in the 1989 European elections). Nigel Jones won Cheltenham (where Richard Holme had stood in the 1980s). And in a personal triumph and without much support from the party nationally, Nick Harvey won back Jeremy Thorpe's old seat of North Devon. Our most prominent success, however, was in Bath, where Don Foster defeated the Conservative Party chairman Chris Patten.

BATH

Nine weeks before the general election, it had seemed unlikely that we could win the Bath constituency. The candidate we had selected there had recently resigned, and Don Foster had only just replaced him. We had had a very strong candidate in Bath in the 1980s in Malcolm Dean, a *Guardian* journalist. But Malcolm was not fighting again. The Conservatives did not consider that the candidate first chosen after Malcolm posed a great challenge to them. Otherwise it was rumoured that Patten might have moved seats. But Don was an entirely different character. When I first came across him, he was a councillor in Bristol, famous for his energy and known to local Lib Dems as 'Don Faster'. As soon as he was selected, he wanted me to do a presentation to his campaign team indicating what I thought they had to do in order to win.

The experience of almost all Lib Dem MPs was that it took many years, and often more than one parliament, to get elected. Malcolm Dean had come within 1,412 votes of winning in 1987, but we had lost much momentum since then. My advice to Don's team was that they had to do in nine weeks what could normally only be done in a parliamentary by-election with a huge influx of helpers from elsewhere. I outlined the successful Eastbourne parliamentary by-election campaign. I expected resistance to my proposal that the seat be fought like that, but Don tolerated no discussion about either the ambitious scale or the manner of the campaign that I outlined. He simply announced that this was now *the* plan to which they would work. He moved quickly to begin a collection for his campaign fund, going around the room asking for donations to help finance it. Ann said afterwards that

Don was clearly the sort of candidate who 'would not sell his grand-mother, but would give her away' if that was what was required to win.

Bath was one of a small number of constituencies in that election for which we were able to conduct a constituency poll using a tele-marketing company, whose staff had been trained by Rick Ridder. The firm was new to the business, however, and I told Des Wilson that we could not therefore release any details of these polls. But the result of the one in Bath, showing us just 1 per cent behind, was too good for Des to ignore. He needed a headline for a national press conference just before the start of the campaign and decided to publicise this poll finding. I knew that the *Bath Evening Chronicle* would be furious if the story appeared in the national media before they could cover it, so I rang Don and told him what Des would be doing. Don said that he was due to have lunch with the editor of the *Chronicle*, but that would be too late for coverage in that day's paper. So, Don rang him that morning with the story. The editor, of course, rang Chris Patten seek-ing his views on our poll. It was actually a fortunate coincidence for us that the Conservative Party chairman was attending Cabinet, which then met on Thursday mornings. Our poll finding provided the front-page headline for the *Bath Evening Chronicle*, giving a flying start to Don's campaign, and the paper had to report that 'Chris Patten had been unavailable for comment'.

The Conservatives were very sceptical about our poll findings, but it was difficult for them to maintain that position when the regional news company, HTV, published a constituency poll the day before the election putting Don 1 per cent ahead. The eve of poll was also Don's birthday, so the *Chronicle* front page showed him celebrating it in our HQ blowing out the candles on his birthday cake. In the afternoon of the day before polling day, Chris Patten chaired the final Conservative press conference of the campaign at Central Office in Smith Square. I wanted to make sure that everyone there knew about the potential Lib Dem gain, so I had a hundred copies of the *Chronicle* sent to me on a train from Bath. A small team of volunteers from our HQ, including

Ann, then went over to Conservative Central Office to give a copy of it to every journalist entering the press conference. I don't know what effect it had on Chris Patten to see them all reading it during the press conference, but we were pleased that we ensured successful national media coverage of our likely gain in Bath, making the point that the Lib Dems could not be written off. In the end, Don won with a majority of 3,768. Chris Patten then became Governor of Hong Kong, a job which had apparently been previously promised to David Owen, who had lent his support to Major in the campaign. I am not sure that he ever thanked us for this opportunity.

CHAPTER 6

FIGHT BACK

THE CHARD SPEECH

The result of the 1992 general election created feelings of despair for most non-Conservatives. John Major had won re-election with an overall majority of twenty-one in spite of Labour's huge leads over the Conservatives in the mid-term polls, and more modest leads in polls during the campaign. Almost every poll in the six months before the election had pointed to there being no overall majority for any party. Many people felt that if the Conservatives could not be defeated after three terms of office, then they simply could not be beaten.

The year following the general election was one in which the Liberal Democrats largely disappeared from the national news as the party appeared to have little relevance at Westminster. Paddy's sense of disappointment was clearly considerable, but his response to the result was not to reflect on how the potential association with Labour had damaged us in the campaign, but to consider instead how such an association might develop more fully in future to provide the country with an 'anti-Tory alliance'. The problem with this strategy, as with David Owen's a decade previously, was that it would only really be viable in a proportional representation system, in which the resulting squeeze in the party's vote would not be fatal in terms of lost seats. But if the first-past-the-post system remained, the loss in support for the party resulting from such an alliance, with the inevitable loss of independence and distinct appeal that it would involve, could cost us many seats. There were signs in the aftermath of the election that Labour could move on the issue of voting reform, but for change to happen, Labour had first to get back into a position of power and become fully committed to making a fundamental change to the voting system. It only ever achieved the first of these two propositions.

During the 1992 campaign, Paddy had tried to maintain a position of apparent 'equidistance' between the Tories and Labour. This was on the basis that he (and most of the party) would have really preferred a deal with Labour if there was to be a hung parliament. But the only way of ensuring that such a deal could be achievable was to threaten the possibility of a deal with the Conservatives if Labour wouldn't deliver proportional representation. This meant actually being prepared to go into coalition with the Conservatives if PR was not conceded by Labour, and making this prospect appear credible.

The direction in which Paddy now wanted to take the party was clear to me at the Parliamentary Party's immediate post-election meeting, which was held at the National Liberal Club. Paddy announced that he had asked Richard Holme to review the campaign that had been run by Des Wilson (who, like me, had expressed reservations about the promotion of a coalition in the last week of the campaign). This meant that Des's arch-rival would review the campaign that he had chaired. It showed the power of the leader to appoint whoever he wanted for such a role, without reference to any of the party's professional or governing structures, and I saw it as a clear indication of Paddy's intended direction of travel over the next parliament.

Paddy's plan was to set out a bold proposal to state explicitly his aim of working with Labour in the future, rejecting any possibility of working with the Conservatives. Over the next few weeks of meetings with his parliamentary colleagues, he set out various drafts of what he wanted to say about this proposed strategy to a forthcoming meeting of members in his constituency. But there was much resistance to the plan as many of the MPs knew that we had recently suffered significantly from our perceived association with Labour, and they did not fancy facing their more conservatively minded electorates again with such an explicit proposition. The arguments were fierce; Paddy was persistent, but he had to accept some of their points, at least temporarily, and each draft of the speech gradually watered down his proposed text.

The local elections in 1992 were held three weeks after the general election and they confirmed the superiority of the Conservatives' position nationally. Paddy avoided making his speech about his new strategy during the local election campaign, knowing that it would have had damaging electoral consequences for us, and for this reason I thought that he should not make it at all. I tried to persuade him that it was not necessary to reveal his thinking in this very public way. Paddy argued with me that he had to be completely honest about what he felt should be the party's position. 'A poker player is not being dishonest if they don't reveal all their cards to the other players,' I argued back. But Paddy did not want to pursue a covert strategy, which was the alternative I suggested to him, and he eventually made the speech outlining his intentions to party members in Chard, near Yeovil, on the Saturday after the local elections.

The speech was high profile, with much media commentary about how it would divide the Labour Party over how to respond. But it was also very divisive within our own ranks. Those people in the party whose principal opponents were Labour were overwhelmingly against a national strategy based on appearing to 'line up' with Labour. Liz Lynne, who had just retained Cyril Smith's former Rochdale constituency, against many expectations, was furious, as were most of the MPs. Charles Kennedy, in contrast, representing a rural constituency in Scotland with the Conservatives as his main opponents, was notably warmer to Paddy's strategy at this stage. Charles only became more hostile to it much later in Paddy's leadership. Paddy had to admit that most of the reaction he was getting within the party was strongly hostile as its independence and distinctiveness appeared to be put in jeopardy. Paddy's general approach to such hostility was simply to see it as a challenge to be overcome, rather than any reason to reflect on his position. He explained to some of us that he would make temporary tactical withdrawals from advocating the strategy that he really wanted; but that once the party thought that some compromise had been reached with him, he would later seek to 'move on again' in the direction he wanted.

At the ALDC conference in Eastbourne that July, the hostile reaction when Paddy described his proposed strategy was very clearly expressed. It was again evident at the party conference at Harrogate in September. I opened the strategy consultation session there by pointing out that our achievement in the general election had been to survive, but that increasing our number of MPs from nineteen to twenty over four years was a rate of progress that would only see us winning a general election by the year 3232, suggesting that we needed to change the way in which we fought elections. I wanted the party to make the kinds of campaigning approaches that had elected so many of our councillors, and increasingly a number of our MPs, more universal and to target more effectively at the Westminster level. Although I was not explicit about it in my speech, I did not see how appearing to line up with another party would help us in a first-past-the-post system.

The formal debate on strategy a few days later might have resulted in a humiliation for Paddy, but nobody in the party considered this desirable. A face-saving motion leaving the leadership some 'wriggle room' was eventually proposed as a result of much pressure from Paddy to change the motion that had initially been agreed by the Conference Committee. Tony Greaves, Andrew Stunell, Liz Barker and others worked with Alan Leaman from Paddy's office to draft something more acceptable to him. There were only a handful of people in the debate who spoke in support of Paddy advocating closer association with Labour (including Leighton Andrews, who later joined Labour). Tony Greaves was amongst those who rubbished Leighton's amendment to the main motion, calling it the 'cosying up to Labour amendment'.

The overwhelming defeat of the 'cosying up' amendment in the debate made the feelings of the conference clear, but did not amount to an outright rejection of all that Paddy wanted to do. It certainly wasn't the successful endorsement of his proposed strategy that he recalls in his diaries. There was, however, little media attention devoted to the debate as it took place on 'Black Wednesday', when, after temporarily raising interest rates to 15 per cent, the UK left the European Exchange Rate Mechanism. The Tories finally lost their reputation for economic competence on this day. For the rest of his leadership, Paddy steered a precarious path on strategy, seeking some sort of arrangement with Labour, and meeting secretly with John Smith, Tony Blair and others.

Meanwhile, after the 1992 general election, John Major's government was able to govern with their majority of twenty-one. But after recovering from the shock of a fourth consecutive Conservative victory, some people began to wonder if that slender majority could survive a full parliament with evident splits amongst Conservative MPs. It would take eleven Conservative defeats in parliamentary by-elections (or defections from Conservative MPs to opposition parties) for the Conservatives to lose their majority. This seemed improbable in 1992, but was to happen eventually, with the Lib Dems playing a significant role gaining four seats from the Conservatives in by-elections and with the defection to us of two Conservative MPs.

NEWBURY

The first by-election of the parliament did not occur until a year after the 1992 general election. Newbury was considered to be a Conservative safe seat with a majority of 12,000, and the timing of the by-election was well before the supposedly dangerous 'mid-term' for governments defending by-elections. No Conservative government for over fifty years had lost the first by-election that it had had to defend. The economy had, however, taken a turn for the worse since the general election and Black Wednesday.

It was late on a Friday evening in February 1993 that I returned home to an answerphone message from Tim Payne (whom I had previously employed) 'offering to help in the Newbury by-election'. I assumed at first that this referred to a council by-election and wondered why Tim would be interested. I soon discovered, however, that Judith Chaplin, a rising star of the Conservative Party, had died unexpectedly during an operation. Amongst many conversations that quickly followed, I spoke to David Rendel, our candidate there at the last election. He explained that he was due to go away the following morning for a week-long family holiday. I advised that he should go, as these might be his last few free days for several months.

David was a well-established local candidate, having fought the seat in 1987 and 1992. He was popular in the local party and had a good profile as a district councillor based on his coverage in the *Newbury Weekly News*, which had huge penetration throughout the constituency. He had originally been chosen as the parliamentary candidate before he had any local connections, to the evident dismay of Paul Hannon, a Newbury councillor who had expected to be chosen. Paul had been the leader of Newbury district council until recently and would have liked to have been the candidate for the by-election, but he had little support in the local party. Alternatively, he was keen to be in charge of the by-election campaign. There was also a paid agent in the constituency who wanted to be the by-election agent. I could not cede control to either of them on behalf of the national party, however, as I saw parliamentary by-elections as national campaigns, and not just local ones. I believed that fighting them successfully required a great deal of experience garnered in previous parliamentary by-elections in many different places and over many years. I was not prepared to risk putting someone in legal charge locally who might not understand this. Most of the local party agreed, as did David Rendel.

The potential stresses of the campaign became apparent over that first weekend, when the local party chair Paul Walter (who subsequently became a good friend) felt that he could not cope with the pressure of that position during the by-election campaign, but I had to persuade him not to issue a press release announcing this. He and most local members were very strongly of the view that David Rendel should be reselected as our candidate as soon as possible, and that my decision to appoint Tim Payne (who they didn't know) as the agent for the by-election should be respected. In order to help the local party understand what was about to hit them, and prepare for their involvement in it, Tim and I invited all local members to a meeting at a Newbury hotel on the following Saturday afternoon. Our presentation to them demonstrated our experience from successful Lib Dem by-election campaigns from the last parliament, and involved showing them on an overhead projector some of the leaflets from Eastbourne and elsewhere. We then involved them all in a discussion of the potential by-election campaign issues in which I effectively acted as the moderator of a large focus group.

The by-election campaign followed immediately after Norman Lamont's Budget in which the Conservatives' promises of a year ago not to increase taxes were clearly broken. In particular, he announced that they would add VAT to domestic fuel bills. In a strategy paper on the by-election prepared for Paddy and others, I proposed that we could become the voice of national anger over these broken tax promises and how the VAT plans would hit pensioners and people with lower incomes particularly harshly and unfairly. I explained in the paper the need for us to try to win by focusing on what I considered to be 'bread and butter' issues, as opposed to what I called the 'chattering class issues' which sometimes preoccupied my party but did not seem very relevant to people's major concerns at the time. Matthew Taylor, who had been appointed by Paddy as chair of the Campaigns and Communications Committee, was extremely supportive of this approach and helped us to stick to it in the daily press conferences which he chaired. Tim Payne was also extremely keen that we were seen to fight on the big national issues, and not just local grievances, so that the campaign would provide a national platform for the party and not just be seen as a local success if we won.

An early opinion poll for the *Mail on Sunday* put the Conservative lead at 18 per cent (exactly as it had been in the general election). We conducted our own poll which found that 'jobs and the economy' was the biggest concern to 57 per cent of our potential voters. Our polling in those days showed that only about 15 per cent of the electorate said that they would never consider voting for us, so we were most interested in the views of the 85 per cent who didn't reject us totally. We asked about the recent Budget and 70 per cent of our sample of potential supporters thought that it was bad for their family (9 per cent didn't know). The proposal to add VAT to domestic fuel bills made 71 per cent of them less likely to vote Conservative (with 51 per cent of them much less likely to do so). The poll confirmed emphatically the effectiveness of the messaging on which we wanted to base our campaign.

The Conservatives chose as their candidate a Somerset councillor, Julian Davidson, who had stood against Paddy in Yeovil in the general election. Paddy was highly excited by his selection and the morning after it he had rung me to discuss it three times before 7.30 in the morning. Julian Davidson had been commenting on the Budget for his local radio station, 'Somerset Sound', and we noted carefully how he described the unpopular Budget tax increases as 'modest and appropriate'. We then made sure that this statement about the Budget was the first thing that most people in the constituency knew about him. Our poll showed that 78 per cent of the sample was less likely to vote for him because of his support for the Budget (51 per cent of them were much less likely to do so).

Other prominent issues for local people in our poll included crime, education, health and the environment. With the economy as the first local concern, it clearly confirmed that these were the five biggest issues for us, and it was helpful in persuading Paddy that we should fight on these points. It was obvious that the Conservatives would try to rebut our accusations about broken promises by saying that the economy was recovering, and that they would play upon continuing fears about our potential association with Labour. At the time, we were working with Labour on Berkshire County Council and we were attacked by the Tories for 'living in sin' through this arrangement. The fear of our potential national cooperation with Labour was clearly shown in the poll to be a problem for between a third and half of our potential voters. Paddy, however, was keen to try to use the by-election to seek endorsement of the strategy that he had begun outlining in his 'Chard speech'. The poll showed, however, that there was absolutely no advantage in it for us to do this – whilst there were many dangers. Although he pressed me very hard to make his desired national strategy part of our campaign, I successfully resisted this.

Paddy even travelled to Newbury for a private meeting to discuss his case for pushing his new 'Chard' strategy during the campaign. This was to David Rendel's evident surprise, as is clearly seen in the TV documentary that was made about the by-election, when David was told that Paddy was about to arrive. In the face of the overwhelming poll evidence, Paddy was persuaded that we could not risk helping the Conservatives in the by-election by advocating this strategy during the campaign. This was one of many occasions when I expressed my view that it was an unsound political strategy for us to be overtly associated with one of our main rivals. Throughout the campaign, Paddy was also very nervous about the strength of our opposition to the addition of VAT on fuel bills as he was seeking to strengthen our credibility on environmental issues. But the idea of adding VAT to domestic fuel bills was actually something that we had ourselves earlier considered and rejected, recognising that it would be seen as being grossly unfair, rather than environmentally friendly.

We were helped in the campaign by the fact that Labour's candidate from the general election publicly disagreed with his party's decision to contest the by-election. Richard Hall had polled just 6 per cent in the general election a year previously and now called on Labour not to stand, saying that Labour members would 'have their fingers crossed' for a Liberal victory. After the shock of a fourth consecutive Conservative general election triumph, there were a small number of people in both Labour and the Liberal Democrats who favoured an electoral pact between the opposition parties. But Labour nevertheless decided to fight the by-election and John Smith sent Peter Mandelson to be my opposite number in the campaign. My strategy document argued that we needed to use the by-election to show how Labour supporters' only hope of defeating the Conservatives in such seats was to vote for us; and at the same time show the Labour leadership that they should effectively leave us alone in similar contests in future, even if they had to stand candidates.

Paddy's personal ratings were shown to be very high in our poll, even at the outset of the by-election campaign. This helped us to persuade him of the validity of the other poll findings. Noting this, I learned to begin all future poll presentations to him with demonstrations of his popularity (which he modestly had to accept) and then to present him with findings about strategy, messaging and positioning, which he then found harder to claim were unrepresentative of our potential voters. This approach also helped to overcome the vehement opposition to the use of opinion polling that Paddy had expressed in his first years as leader. Paddy's net favourable rating in the poll was a massive +43 per cent. John Major still retained a positive rating of 11 per cent, whilst after the Budget (and our campaign in the constituency attacking it), Norman Lamont now had a staggeringly unpopular rating of -64 per cent. We were able to build our campaign around issues such as David Rendel's opposition to the VAT proposal, his support for a new Newbury hospital, and his petition for more police locally. David's own net favourable rating was +56 per cent.

Julian Davidson had swung the Conservative selection in his favour with a speech vigorously attacking 'the Liberals'. This meant that former Conservative Cabinet minister John Maples probably had a lucky escape. Journalists afterwards told me about the shock on the faces of Conservative officials when the result of their selection was made known. The Conservative campaign then blundered further by letting an unprepared Julian Davidson conduct an impromptu press briefing. In this he made a series of statements which included the fact that he had previously 'only visited Newbury on a few odd occasions'. It was something that we repeated frequently to the Newbury voters.

In the very early stages of the by-election, we also placed an advertisement in the *Newbury Weekly News* including a petition form opposing the imposition of VAT on domestic fuel bills. Eighteen people came into our office on the Thursday that the paper was published with signed copies of the form. This indicated that there would be a massive response to the petition, which we then also printed in our local leaflets. We wrote to everyone who signed the petition, asking them to collect more signatures, and then again to those people whose signatures we received, also asking them to collect more signatures, and so on. In this way we amassed over 5,000 signatures across the constituency in a few weeks. All of these people now had positive reasons to vote for us.

In the early stages of the campaign, I was approached by the BBC's *On the Record* programme, which wanted to film a 'fly-on-the-wall' documentary. I was instinctively hostile to granting such access because of the obvious risks involved. It was also clear to me that what they were hoping for was to expose the kind of 'dirty tricks' that had been alleged to be behind previous 'unexplained' Liberal by-election successes. But, after some reflection, I agreed to let them do this as a 'one-off' on the basis that we had nothing really to hide, and that by allowing such unrestrained access we might be able to show that there were absolutely no 'dirty tricks' involved in our campaigns. I hoped also that their documentary would portray Paddy as a major force in what I believed should be a successful campaign. If Paddy could be given significant credit for what would be a remarkable win, then his standing in the country would be significantly enhanced and the evidence of previous by-election wins was that our party poll ratings would rise.

On reflection, I underestimated the inconvenience to me, Tim and others of being followed by a TV crew filming and recording almost everywhere that we went for the next few weeks. I estimated that the BBC spent more money making their twenty-minute documentary than the Liberal Democrats did in the campaign (our budgets remained modest, though bigger than previously). There were risks to us from the fly-on-the-wall approach, but in those days of daily by-election press conferences, I did not consider that we were adding greatly to my risk assessment. The *On the Record* team filmed many of our internal discussions, including one about how to make the Tories admit that they had broken their major election promises on tax. We sent Nick South (later Paddy's principal speech writer) to their opening press conference in order to distribute a copy of a letter to every journalist just before it began. The letter was from David Rendel to Julian Davidson challenging him to admit to the broken promises. This then resulted in a somewhat flustered Tory candidate responding to a question from BBC Radio Berkshire's Terry Dignan (soon to join *On the Record*) that he would only respond to the challenge to be honest about broken promises 'in due course'. Our challenge, and the weak response to it, set the agenda at the outset of the campaign and featured strongly in the coverage of the Conservatives' campaign launch press conference.

A few days later our own campaign hit some difficulty at one of our press conferences when Sheila Gunn of *The Times* questioned us about ideas in an old Lib Dem discussion document, 'Costing the Earth', which itself had suggested putting VAT on domestic fuel bills. Fortunately, Malcolm Bruce, a skilful media performer, was at our morning press conference that day. He was able to explain that the idea had indeed been considered whilst he had been our environment spokesperson, but that it had been rejected by our party on fairness grounds.

The final opinion poll four days before polling day (again for the *Mail on Sunday*) gave us a 12 per cent lead over the Conservatives (50 per cent to 38 per cent). Tim rang Paddy to let him know the result. Up to that point, Paddy had been phoning every fifteen minutes or so on that Saturday afternoon to ask if we had heard the result. Tim was filmed by the *On the Record* team laughing loudly as he listened to

Paddy screaming excitedly down the phone and then suggesting our response. Tim had to tell him that I had already given out the quote in his name that 'all that is clear from the poll is that it is between the Lib Dems and the Conservatives'. We wanted to avoid any complacency amongst our supporters, Paddy, or anyone in our campaign, and to keep up the pressure on Labour supporters to make them switch to us tactically. The *On the Record* team were of course delighted that they appeared to have been documenting a by-election sensation. They found no 'dirty tricks' whilst interviewing all members of our campaign team and many helpers from all over the country as well as in the constituency. Many people who watched the programme remarked on the youth of our campaign team, most of whom were in their twenties, whilst I was now described as a 'veteran' of by-elections at the age of thirty-two.

The result was a landslide victory, with a 28 per cent swing to the Lib Dems from the Conservatives:

David Rendel (Lib Dem)	37,590	65.1%	+27.8%
Julian Davidson (Conservative)	15,539	26.9%	-29.0%
Steve Billcliffe (Labour)	1,151	2.0%	-4.0%
Lib Dem majority	22,055		

Paddy had asked to be woken in the middle of the night to be told the majority, and famously shouted back on discovering that it was '22,055' that he wanted the majority, not our vote! Labour's lost deposit and 2 per cent share of the vote was a humiliation for them, which I did not mind highlighting, even though Charles Kennedy told me that Labour had been in touch with him 'asking us not to be too hard on them'.

Robert Shrimsley of the *Daily Telegraph* asked me at the count how I could account for this extraordinary result. I wanted the Lib Dem campaign to block the addition of VAT on domestic fuel bills to succeed, and for this to be recognised as a significant achievement for the party. So, I pointed to Norman Lamont's recent Budget as being to blame for many of the Tories' problems, and perhaps rather more cheekily described his visit to the constituency as a turning point in the campaign. The Chancellor of the Exchequer had been asked at one of the Conservative press conferences whether he most regretted claiming to see 'the green shoots of recovery' or 'singing in his bath when Britain left the Exchange Rate Mechanism'. His reply – '*I je ne regrette rien*' – was not just ungrammatical, but added to the sense of ridicule surrounding him at the time. He was sacked by John Major just three weeks later and became an angry critic of the Major government for its remaining time in office, describing it in his resignation speech as 'being in office, but not in power'. His memoirs[37] make it plain that he thought blaming him personally for the catastrophic Conservative loss in Newbury was most unfair, and had cost him his job. I later became aware that his special adviser at the time, a young David Cameron, would not have warmed to the Liberal Democrats as a result of this by-election campaign.

CHRISTCHURCH

The media coverage that resulted from the Newbury by-election took the Lib Dems to 25 per cent in national opinion polls, within just 2 per cent of the Conservatives' rating at the time. The campaign in Newbury had also helped us to make widespread gains in the county council elections that year, depriving the Conservatives of control of every county apart from Buckinghamshire. 'There's only one Tory council, one Tory council!' had been the heartily sung refrain of hundreds of our supporters at the Newbury count. The result also meant that we were immediately seen as credible challengers in the next by-election when Robert Adley, the Conservative MP for Christchurch, died the following week. He had had a 23,015 majority a year earlier and for us to win there would previously have been considered most improbable.

---

37   Norman Lamont, *In Office*.

But I saw it as an opportunity to try to recreate the kind of by-election-led momentum that the Liberal Party, and then the Alliance, had obtained in 1962/63, 1972/73 and 1981/82, which had made us appear as credible challengers for power at those times.

Quite a few of our party members also saw this as their opportunity to become a Lib Dem MP, and I was soon receiving calls from all over the country from people volunteering to be the Liberal Democrat candidate. The local party was clear, however, that it expected to be able to choose someone from at least Dorset or Hampshire (Christchurch was in Dorset, but at one time had been in the same constituency as Lymington in Hampshire). The party's by-election panel (that I had asked to be set up after the Walton by-election) met during the spring conference in Nottingham that May and it decided that our 1992 candidate would not cope with the national pressures of the campaign. The combination of the constituency's shortlisting and the national by-election panel's decision meant, however, that local members were only presented with one choice of candidate to consider in Diana Maddock (then the party's Hampshire & Wight organiser), but they warmed to her immediately. As soon as she was selected, I sat with all the members at her selection meeting to listen to their views on the campaign issues and again acted as a kind of 'moderator', treating them as a focus group, for our first discussion of issues.

Diana's campaign attracted enthusiastic backing across the party, and which I was easily able to encourage as it clearly wanted to support a woman in a high-profile and winnable by-election. The national momentum now behind us was such that we could gloss over her quite limited local credentials, something that we could not do in many by-elections. The Conservatives again obliged our campaign by putting forward a defeated MP from elsewhere in the last general election. Robert Hayward[38] had lost his seat in Kingswood, near Bristol, and was now seeking another chance in Dorset.

---

38   A leading Conservative psephologist and campaigner, who was made a peer by David Cameron in 2015.

I asked Willie Rennie, then working for me as the party's regional agent in Devon & Cornwall, to be the by-election agent and he was a fantastic motivational organiser. Our press officer was Vicky Young, previously our party agent in Falmouth & Camborne, and who has since pursued a successful career with the BBC. Many of our successful themes from the Newbury campaign were continued, and the issue of VAT on domestic fuel was felt particularly strongly by the very large elderly population in Christchurch. Our private polling showed that people overwhelmingly felt that the Conservatives had lied to them in order to win the last general election. Our five best key themes were again confirmed by the polling to be the economy, education, the environment, crime and health.

It was clear, as the recession was ending, that there was now a need nationally to reduce the then £50 billion budget deficit. The Conservatives had reduced the basic rate of income tax from 33p in the pound in 1979, and introduced a new 20p rate in their pre-election 1992 Budget. In response to the evident need to reduce the deficit that had been accumulated, the Conservatives now began talking openly about ideas such as introducing 'hotel charges' for staying in hospital, and making everyone (including pensioners and children) pay for prescriptions. Michael Portillo (then Chief Secretary to the Treasury and seen at the time as a hard-line right-winger and the clear Thatcherite choice to take over from Major) would only insist that no decisions had been taken about these ideas, nor about cutting invalidity and unemployment benefits. Few people thought that what they were considering was fair. There was a sense of them becoming arrogant and out of touch in the fourth term of a Conservative government and threats to privatise the Forestry Commission suggested to many of their traditional supporters that they were now 'going too far'. Robert Adley had also been a noted opponent of railway privatisation, and so the plethora of issues on which we could campaign against the Conservative government created a perfect storm.

Faced with these considerable difficulties, the Conservatives in

Christchurch launched a 'survey' about capital punishment, and we picked up the gossip being spread verbally in the constituency about the Liberal Democrats 'opening the floodgates to more widespread immigration'. We were mindful of the fact that 65 per cent of voters in the constituency took either the *Daily Mail*, *Daily Telegraph* or *Daily Express*. But there was little that the Conservatives could do to defend their record nationally, or their candidate for that matter, who was personally targeted in public protests by disabled people's groups in response to his having blocked a civil rights bill for disabled people by filibustering in a Commons debate when he had been an MP.

The weather that summer was extremely pleasant, Diana Maddock won the confidence of both the media and the local voters as she challenged the Conservative's national record, and our evening meetings attracted very large crowds. The halls were so full that many people had to stand outside in the school grounds where Diana, Paddy, Shirley Williams and others had to repeat the speeches that they had made inside. This also allowed more informal questions and discussion in small groups afterwards and Shirley Williams in particular excelled at this format and also allowed a compromise between my view, that there should be no questions after the set speeches, and Shirley's, that this was an affront to democracy. At our first rally, I had tried to ban questions in the hall, but Paddy had insisted on taking them and the first (obviously planted) question was about capital punishment and meant that the local newspaper coverage of the meeting was all about hanging, as opposed to our campaign messages.

In Christchurch, I felt free of the high degrees of stress that I suffered from in most of our successful campaigns, because I never really doubted the result. My confidence was almost given away to the party by the fact that I was away from Christchurch on the Saturday before polling day, attending Paul Rainger's wedding in St Andrews. I flew up to Edinburgh and I was only away for twenty-four hours, so everyone in the campaign was briefed to say that I had 'just popped out of the HQ' when helpers asked where I was.

A month before polling day, an opinion poll for the *Bournemouth Echo* put us in the lead with 32.5 per cent of the vote, compared to 28.3 per cent for the Tories and 8.3 per cent for Labour. We were determined, however, not to claim victory prematurely, and not to be complacent. Matthew Taylor, who again chaired many of the press conferences, said that we would 'not take the people of Christchurch for granted', which at one time would have seemed ridiculous in a seat that we had lost by 23,000 votes at the previous general election. We wanted to push for a decisive outcome and told local voters that they could 'speak for Britain' in demanding a fairer approach than that which was now being proposed by a desperate government. As well as protecting the poorest people in any deficit reduction measures, we remained committed in our campaign to invest more in education and raise the basic rate of income tax by 1p in order to fund it, as well as safeguarding what we considered to be the principles of the NHS by rejecting both 'hotel charges' for hospital visits and making everyone pay for prescription charges.

Fifteen months after their largely unexpected general election victory, we had the Conservatives on the ropes. The scale of their defeat in Christchurch came on the back of other trouble for John Major, as he had unwittingly admitted to a live ITV microphone that some of the people he had appointed to his Cabinet were 'bastards', and this resulted in international headlines. The Tory majority of 23,015 was turned into a Liberal Democrat one of 16,427. The swing of 35.4 per cent exceeded even that of 32.6 per cent when Graham Tope won Sutton & Cheam in 1972. The national news bulletins featured Diana's speech from the count, in which she told John Major to 'change your policies or get ready to change your job'. The following day, Paddy posed with her on a playground swing which we christened the '35 per cent swing'. It was the biggest turnaround of support in a parliamentary by-election since Liverpool Wavertree in 1935.

The Tories had timed the by-election for immediately after the start of the summer recess in the hope that coverage would be minimised.

But their objective was hard to achieve given the scale of their crushing defeat. The boost that we achieved from the Christchurch campaign coverage that summer took the Liberal Democrats to level pegging in the national opinion polls with the Conservatives on 28 per cent each, with Labour in the lead on 40 per cent. In Christchurch, however, Labour lost their deposit, polling just 2.7 per cent of the vote. In a *Guardian* ICM poll conducted after this result, only 5 per cent of people now said that they were against the idea of the Liberal Democrats being in government.

EASTLEIGH AND EUROPE

The third of our four parliamentary by-election wins in the 1992–97 parliament was in Eastleigh in Hampshire. I heard of the death of the Tory MP Stephen Milligan whilst I was driving up from London to Rotherham, where a by-election was also pending. I was with the then chair of the Yorkshire regional party, Julian Cummins, and we were heading up for a meeting with local activists to set up the Rotherham campaign. My car phone kept ringing on our journey as my friend and Cowley Street colleague Keith House, leader of the Lib Dem group in Eastleigh, updated me on reports that Stephen Milligan, who had been elected as MP there for the first time in 1992, had died. During the course of our journey, Keith told us that the police were outside the former MP's home and that there were rumours that he had been murdered.

It transpired that his secretary had found him dead, naked apart from a pair of stockings and suspenders, with an electrical flex tied around his neck, a black bin liner over his head and a segment of an orange or satsuma in his mouth. The bizarre details continued to emerge and some people blamed the police for the leaks. Within a few days it was confirmed that the death was accidental and had been based on 'autoerotic asphyxiation'. Stephen Milligan had been well liked, was previously an SDP candidate, and then a BBC correspondent, before becoming a Conservative MP. Norman Fowler, who had visited the house on the evening that his body was found, said that the incident was so 'freakish, so private and extraordinary that it could happen in any party'.

Nobody wanted to make political capital out of the tragedy. But the media made much of the circumstances of his death, because this was the period following John Major's call for his party to return to a 'Back to Basics' approach (which was mistakenly taken to be a call for a return to more old-fashioned 'family' values and the avoidance of sex scandals). There were wild rumours at the time about gay sex rings in Parliament, with MPs leading double lives, and a number of extra-marital affairs involving MPs did come to light. These 'scandals', together with allegations such as 'cash for questions', led to accusations that the fourth-term Conservative government was mired in sleaze, and that John Major was not in control.

The period from Stephen Milligan's death to polling day was a very long nineteen weeks for me. Most by-election campaigns then lasted under three months. It was clear from the outset of this campaign that Labour were determined to avoid the sort of public humiliation which we had inflicted on them in both Newbury and Christchurch. Leading Labour figures immediately highlighted the traditionally strong Labour base in the town of Eastleigh itself, and in the part of Southampton that was then contained within the constituency. They announced very publicly their determination to win the Eastleigh by-election and to mount a very large campaign to achieve this. Labour's home affairs spokesman, Jack Straw, and John Denham (who had recently gained Southampton Itchen for Labour) were prominently engaged in the campaign from the outset, and we were aware of reports of fifteen Labour MPs campaigning in the by-election even before Stephen Milligan's funeral had been held.

The Guardian prominently reported a poll at the time claiming that it gave Labour leader John Smith 'a 25 per cent lead nationally and victory in Eastleigh'. This was based on taking a national poll and extrapolating the results to the Eastleigh constituency, something to which I strongly objected. Labour were confident that they could win, and John Smith made a public promise that they would. Our party was therefore very unnerved by the confidence of the Labour campaign. This was in spite of the fact that the first poll in the constituency put us in the lead in a seat where the Conservatives had had an almost 18,000 majority at the previous election. We were, however, aware of how much could change during a campaign, and we were initially in awe of Labour's efforts. I felt the need to provide reassurance to our team that we knew how to overcome them.

The combined effects of the Newbury and Christchurch wins the previous year had raised our national opinion-poll ratings and given us an initial lead in Eastleigh. But this frontrunner status was not a comfortable position. Having previously run campaigns that demolished very large opinion-poll leads, I was certainly not taking anything for granted. I was very aware that the Labour Party had far greater resources than we had, and I also felt that it might be difficult for us to win if the campaign became a 'three-horse race', free of helpful tactical voting considerations.

Our candidate selection involved Keith House, David Chidgey (who lived just outside the constituency but had fought the seat in 1992) and Jenny Tonge (who had recently failed to gain Richmond Park). Unfortunately for Keith, he fell victim to a lack of time to prepare for interviews before coming under scrutiny from *Newsnight's* Michael Crick. Michael was aware of how I had positioned our previous by-election gains as significant national achievements, not just local successes. Eastbourne had got rid of Mrs Thatcher. Ribble Valley had killed off the poll tax. Newbury had secured the removal of Norman Lamont as Chancellor and together with Christchurch had forced the government to rethink plans for VAT on domestic fuel bills. Michael outlined some of these achievements in an interview with Keith, and then asked what the Lib Dems winning Eastleigh would achieve. Keith had not prepared an answer, waved his hands in front of the camera and asked for time to prepare one. The resulting, repeated, coverage of this clip may well have cost him the selection, which was won by David Chidgey.

The campaign was very bitterly fought by Labour. Unflattering photographs of David Chidgey were published in Labour leaflets. Claims were made that Labour were on course to win; at one point, they even hired a small room as a press office at one of our rally venues announcing that they were there to 'counter the lies that our speakers would make at the rally'. Their leaflets even publicised the wrong date for our main rally and I assumed that this was deliberately done in order to confuse and annoy people and reduce attendance at the event. This rather unpleasant tactic evidently failed as we attracted almost a thousand people to the Fleming Park Leisure Centre for a rally addressed by Paddy, who was by now seen as a strong national leader, and he was an enormous asset to our campaigns.

The local elections in Eastleigh preceded the parliamentary by-election and I was determined to use them to remove the perception, which was strong in the media, that Labour could win the parliamentary by-election. The Conservatives, as the largest party, ran Eastleigh borough council without a majority, with the Lib Dems in opposition and Labour in third place. Labour had five councillors in the borough and also held the largest ward in the constituency, which was part of Southampton council.

The scale of the Labour challenge in the parliamentary by-election meant that we had to focus much of our effort in the local elections on the Labour vs. Lib Dem battleground wards. From the large and most impressive town centre premises that Gerald Vernon-Jackson had found for us, we organised very strong community campaigns based on identifying the key issues within each of the wards, promoting our local candidates and showing that we were the challengers to the Conservatives for control of the borough (and to Labour in Southampton's Woolston ward). Our campaign team included Matthew Clark (then a Southampton councillor who said that he had won his ward simply by following my 'yellow book', *Winning Local Elections*), Candy Piercy and Keith House, with Mark Payne (Tim's father) as the agent.

On the night of the local elections we gained every single Labour council seat in the constituency (including their 'safe' Southampton ward) and prevented them winning a single ward anywhere in the Eastleigh constituency. We won every ward that we possibly hoped to win, came within 200 votes of wiping out the Conservatives in their two strongest wards and took control of the Eastleigh council, with Keith becoming council leader. Labour's by-election campaign was killed stone dead by these results, which were a major embarrassment to the Labour Party given that John Smith had pledged that they would win the parliamentary by-election.

On the same day as the council elections it had also been polling day in Rotherham. A brilliant but small-scale campaign run by Paul Rainger had managed to secure second place for us there with almost 30 per cent of the vote. Labour's Denis MacShane was based in Geneva at the time of the by-election, enabling us to promote our candidate, who lived in Rotherham, as the only local choice. But for having had to concentrate almost entirely on Eastleigh, we might even have won the 'very safe' Labour seat of Rotherham on that day.

Just a week after the local elections, the Labour Party leader John Smith died suddenly of a heart attack. This was also four weeks before polling day in the European elections. All national political campaigning was suspended for a week by mutual agreement. But the European elections were not postponed, and the timetable for the Eastleigh parliamentary by-election would have to coincide with them, or else people in Eastleigh would complain that they would have to vote three times in five weeks. There followed some unseemly squabbles about what was defined as 'national campaigning' as we delivered leaflets in Eastleigh thanking people for their support in the local elections; and Labour had to reprint millions of leaflets for the European elections as those already printed all had John Smith's picture on them.

The Lib Dem European election campaign in 1994 was chaired by Tim Clement-Jones and my main role in helping him was to coordinate support for our two target euro-constituencies of Cornwall & Plymouth and Somerset & North Devon, whilst continuing to work in Eastleigh for the by-election. There were also four other parliamentary by-elections on the same day as the European elections, three of them in north-east London, and one in Bradford South. All the different elections across the country (including local elections) greatly stretched our campaign resources. Eastleigh had become a 'must win' for the party, although our number of helpers was very sparse because of the other competing election campaigns. We hoped to win more of the south-west Euro-constituencies based on the strength of our local election successes that year, and we came very close in two more, but we lacked national finances to support them as I would have wished and I couldn't persuade the national party to part with any more money. My own attention still had to be concentrated on Eastleigh.

This was still the era of daily early-morning press conferences in by-elections, and ours were at 8.15 every morning, with the Conservatives at 8.45 and Labour at 9.15. The stress on the campaign of preparing for these conferences, with potentially significant damage if they went badly, was always considerable. A great deal of preparation was undertaken to prepare for potential traps, identify issues of the day (the main papers were bought and studied several hours beforehand) and ensure that our candidate and a daily guest MP were well prepared. I had asked Paddy to let me have Nick Harvey as campaign manager as I wanted to use his considerable skills in handling difficult media; he also had local knowledge, having been brought up there, and his parents and sister still lived nearby. I persuaded Alan Beith to let his excellent researcher, Jeremy Browne,[39] act as our press officer.

Inevitably, Paddy's visits to Eastleigh attracted media questions about the European election campaign at least as much as about the

---

39   Jeremy later won Taunton for the Lib Dems in 2005 and became a minister in 2010.

by-election. Paddy was making much of his belief in the need to try to justify rule changes to permit more 'qualified majority voting' in the European Union, and he was very knowledgeable about the subject. However, I considered this issue to be far too technical for most people, and far from being amongst our best themes for either the European election or the Eastleigh by-election. The problem with the issue became evident when he was asked about it at one of our press conferences, and his answer to this single question lasted over ten minutes. It also fed into a national Tory attack suggesting that he wanted to 'hand over power' to Europe.

One of the most bizarre events ever in a parliamentary by-election then took place on the eve of poll when our candidate in Newham North East, Alec Kellaway, defected to the Labour Party. The first I heard of this was when George Dunk, a veteran helper, rang me to say that the press had rung him claiming that Alec was in a car on his way to Westminster to announce his defection. I immediately arranged for people to try to intercept him at every entrance to the Palace of Westminster in order to seek a meeting to try to talk him out of it. But the pressure from Labour had been too great on him and he had not been coping well as the sole non-Labour councillor opposing sixty Labour members on Newham Council. The publicity from his defection was very damaging to us and was so unusual that it continued running in the broadcast media throughout polling day.

We inevitably lost our deposit in Newham as Alec's name could not be withdrawn from the ballot paper. Notwithstanding this, in Eastleigh we overturned the Conservatives' near 18,000 majority for David Chidgey to gain the seat by 9,239 votes. The Kellaway defection had helped Labour to squeeze into second place, with the Conservatives coming an embarrassing third. The coverage of our by-election win was the dominant story of all the elections declared both that night and on Friday, including the local elections, in which we made 400 gains. I hoped that these successes would help to mask what I feared would not be seen as brilliant European election results. When they were declared on the Sunday night, we had gained both our target seats, making Graham Watson and Robin Teverson our first ever directly elected MEPs. Winning both Cornwall & West Plymouth and Somerset & North Devon was very satisfying, and a great relief after much effort over a long period of time. Success in these two European constituencies was part of a longer-term strategy I was pursuing to try to win several of the Westminster constituency seats contained within them. But it was disappointing that I had not had the resources to gain at least two more MEPs. Adrian Sanders was cheated out of winning the Devon European constituency by just 700 votes when a man called Richard Huggett stood as a *Literal Democrat* and effectively stole 11,172 votes from Adrian. A longstanding Liberal in Michael Meadowcroft's breakaway party, David Morrish, also stood as a 'Liberal' candidate, attracting nearly 15,000 votes that otherwise would have largely gone to Adrian. The fourth European constituency for which I had held out hope of winning was Dorset, where Philip Goldenberg (with Gerald Vernon-Jackson as his agent) came within just 2,264 votes of victory.

It had been obvious to me throughout the European election campaign that we would win between two and four seats. We failed, however, to persuade the media that our strength in local election votes across south-west England that May would not automatically translate into a dozen or so MEPs. There was a failure to appreciate that we always did much better in local elections than in European ones. The odds at the bookmakers on Lib Dems winning between two and four seats, therefore, worked out at 50:1. So I advised friends at HQ to place bets accordingly (only modest ones were allowed). Charles Kennedy was amongst those who followed my advice. Unfortunately, he did this in person and was recognised in the betting shop. With the party president having bet on what was seen unfairly to be a 'flop', the story of his bet made the front page of *The Sun*.

I considered our 400 gains in the local elections that May, seeing off Labour's challenge in Eastleigh, electing our first two MEPs (nearly electing another two) and our 17 per cent of the vote in the European

elections (nearly three times our share in 1989) to be reasonably successful. But I also felt more exhausted than I had ever felt after any
election, and my overwhelming tiredness continued throughout the
summer. I had based myself in Eastleigh for nineteen weeks, with
only occasional day trips to London for meetings about the national
Euro-election campaign. I had been working in Eastleigh every single
weekend throughout that period (but for the one after my father-in-
law died and when I went up to Crosby for the funeral). The by-election
lifestyle and diet throughout these nineteen weeks was most unhealthy
(as it was for me much of the time as I worked very long hours in
London, or in by-elections for many months at a time or travelling
round the country visiting target seats or holding training events).
During the Eastleigh campaign, I had woken twice every night to go
to the toilet. I put it down at the time to the stress of this particular
campaign. But the by-election lifestyle had finally caught up with me,
and that autumn I was diagnosed with diabetes, aged thirty-four.

CHAPTER 7

THE BIG BREAKTHROUGH

TARGET SEATS

By the summer of 1994, we had achieved six Liberal Democrat parliamentary by-election gains since 1990, and they had propelled us significantly upwards in the national opinion polls. We had made gains in every round of local elections for the last four years, adding 1,286 council seats, taking our total number to over 4,551. We had also elected our first two MEPs (in spite of the first-past-the-post system) and their successes pointed towards us winning many of the Westminster seats within the boundaries of these European constituencies, helping to make the south-west of England our 'golden triangle'.

At this point, I felt that there was a significant change of attitude at the top of the party towards me. From being something of an outsider, and not really a part of Paddy's inner circle, these results meant that I was now included in his confidential discussions much more frequently, and my advice was being sought on an increasingly regular basis. Paddy later said how he regretted not including me more at an earlier stage in his leadership. At the Parliamentary Party away day in Oxfordshire that July, I was able to open their strategy session by presenting a paper on the themes and messages that we had found to be most useful in our by-election campaigns. Paddy was rightly always concerned that we should be 'principled' and not to be considered simply 'populist', but his early opposition to the use of polling to help us to become more 'popular' had now disappeared. He had seen how polling had been used to confirm key issues in these constituencies and to help us craft effective messages about them.

The biggest barrier to us winning elections was often simply the belief that we couldn't win, and we were now overcoming this by winning. In doing so, we were creating a national platform for Paddy and our other MPs and achieving power at least at local level, with overall control of twenty-nine local authorities.

I also felt that the by-election successes, and the resulting increases in national opinion-poll ratings, greatly enhanced Paddy's personal confidence. As with leaders in any role, performance is linked to self-esteem. He was now seen nationally as a successful leader, as opposed to the failing leader of a failed party in his first two years as leader. He had the confidence of our MPs, especially those who had gained their seats in 1992 and in the recent by-elections, and who were also very supportive of my approach to party strategy.

Nobody in the party knew, however, how much thought I had been giving to my own future around this time. I had felt very frustrated by not being more included at national level in previous years. I had by then been working for the party at this level for ten years, had helped to bring about much electoral success, but never felt as if I was in the leadership's 'inner circle'. If this had continued to be the case, I would have sought to change my career in some significant way to take on new challenges. I was also very conscious that I wanted to achieve things in politics, and to be able to argue for Liberal Democrat principles and policies more directly myself. So, my thoughts turned again to the idea of being a candidate and standing for Westminster. During the Eastleigh campaign, I had realised that there might well be a change of candidate in the nearby Winchester constituency, and I considered putting myself forward as an alternative to the incumbent candidate Tony Barron, although I was not keen on 'deselecting' anyone. I liked Winchester (as did Ann), and it would have been possible for us to live there and for her to commute to her Early Years Centre in Reading, where she was the headteacher. Although the Tory majority in Winchester was over 8,000, I believed that the seat could be won.

My private dilemma, however, was about the alternative national role which I believed that I might now be allowed to play. I thought that a properly run and significantly funded target seat campaign, based on backing candidates with good community campaigning profiles and many of the techniques that we had pioneered in the by-elections, could produce the really significant breakthrough at national level for the party that I had sought since I first began devoting my energies to politics. Such a prospect would also require a supportive national campaign with messaging based on the sort of themes that we had favoured in these by-elections, and which avoided a repetition of what I saw as the mistakes from 1992. The 'bigger picture' would be to try to bring about this national breakthrough, but it would obviously have to be at the expense of any personal ambition to be an MP.

Not long after the Eastleigh by-election, I had a call from Tim Razzall, who was party treasurer at the time and had the primary task of raising funds for the general election. His call was to say that a potentially very significant donation might follow from the receipt of a plan to carry out such a programme. He warned me that it was a very speculative approach, but said that it was worth spending time on. It took a lot of work, but Tim kept encouraging me that it could be worthwhile to draft such a plan. The donor had observed the successes that I had helped to bring about, and he said that he wanted a plan which gave us a '90 per cent chance of winning thirty-five or more seats at the next election'.

I soon discovered that the person who wanted the plan was Sir Anthony Jacobs. He had been generous to the party in the past, but had become disillusioned with its lack of any electoral progress following his donations to pay for major HQ-inspired projects. I produced a lengthy paper for him identifying a number of constituencies that I assessed as being ones that we could gain. This was based on consideration of many factors, including the previous general election result, the more recent local election results, my knowledge of their organisational strength, the perceived weaknesses of the incumbents, and above all the likely determination of the candidate and local team to run the sort of campaign that we had by now proved would maximise their prospects of success. All of these potential target seats required a swing of less than 6.5 per cent to win (this was the largest swing that we had achieved in any seat in 1992 with Paul Tyler's win in North Cornwall). More significantly, I set out the scale, style and costings for campaigns that would be required to win at least thirty-five of them in a likely 1996 election. We were still in the early days of using computers in elections and the plans then had to include provision of personal computers and printers as well as commitment to use them effectively with the software that was being developed. The plan also required detailed supervision of the campaigns in each seat, ensuring that both the style and the recommended scale of the campaign would be achieved and a commitment to sharing between all these seats everything that we were learning in them, and in by-elections, about best practice. This would mean employing some of the best and most successful agents and campaigners from the previous general election to help manage the people now to be employed within the targeted constituencies as organisers or agents.

I thought that the exercise of producing the paper might be wholly academic, but it wasn't. The budget that I was allowed for target seat support for the 1992 campaign had been a meagre £120,000 spread over more than a year prior to the election. I now suggested that we needed to spend at least £400,000 per annum (for perhaps two and a half years over the remainder of the parliament). My plan would also depend upon the skills of our candidates and trained activists in the constituencies, the value of which could not be quantified in monetary terms. The financial cost of the proposal was extremely modest by recent standards, but it would require a revolution in the party's campaigning approach and election budgets.

I was most surprised, therefore, when Tim came back to me to say that he had spoken to Richard Holme, who was now chairing the general election campaign, and that they had both agreed that this plan was the way forward, irrespective of the hoped-for funding from Sir Anthony, and that it must be financed as I suggested. As it happened, Anthony liked the plan (almost to the point of claiming authorship of it) and was interested in supporting it, whilst not giving any guarantees as to the level of finance that he might provide. The decision by Richard and Tim (subsequently agreed by the party and described at the time as 'throwing the kitchen sink' at the issue of funding targeting many years in advance of an expected election) made up my mind as to my future intentions and was also to change the direction of the party substantially. By stripping out many other costs in previous general election budgets that were now considered to be of much lower priority (such as national newspaper advertising), they decided that the plan could be financed. The budget bid to the donor became the actual battle plan for the target seat campaign, and my task became delivering it.

The first residential training event for the new target seat campaign took place in Dolphin Square in London that summer. I wanted to outline to the agents, organisers and representatives of the seats that we invited how we had campaigned in by-elections such as Newbury. I aimed to indicate the scale of campaigning, and the methodology required to win, and to show that what we had done in by-elections with many outside helpers in a matter of weeks could be done in con- stituencies over several years if they built their organisational base. This was effectively what I had done in Liverpool ten years earlier. My style of presentation was possibly too didactic, but I wanted to command their confidence and give an illustration of where I wanted their campaigns to go. It was followed by a series of training games and exercises more along the lines that I had first used with ALC over ten years previously. National campaigns officer Candy Piercy also began running a series of 'Training for Trainers' events (still running today) and I required all campaigns staff to undertake the weekend course so that we followed best practice in conducting our training events. More residential weekends followed for either agents/organisers or candidates at the Great Northern Hotel in Peterborough.[40] We then held much bigger training events for both candidates and agents at hotels in Bristol and in Perth. Much of the best training, however, came from involving people in the parliamentary by-election campaigns, where many people benefited from 'under fire' experience and being a part of those campaigns, many of which were very successful.

The core team of 'target seat officers' was quite small. Candy Piercy had been employed by the party since just after the Eastbourne by-election. Paul Rainger now became full-time. David Loxton (a veteran also of SDP by-election campaigns and their target seat programme) joined us from the Whips' Office in the Commons. Willie Rennie moved from being North Cornwall's organiser to take charge of our target seats in Devon and Cornwall. Paul Schofield moved from Birmingham Yardley, which had been nearly won in 1992, to Somerset. Derek Barrie continued to cover target seats in Scotland, whilst the former Conwy agent, Mel Ab Owain, now covered target seats in Wales and the West Midlands. We could not afford to provide campaign officer 'cover' across all regions as we prioritised 'clusters' of nearby target seats. The necessary financial arrangements to employ these staff were achieved following a pattern first agreed with Matthew Taylor when he had chaired the Campaign and Communication Committee. Matthew had been instrumental in changing the distribution of the party's Campaign Fund (financed by standing orders to party HQ) from a system in which regional parties all made bids for project funding (on top of their share of membership money and twice-yearly fundraising draws) into one which financed target seats directly.

I spent much of my time in this period travelling around the target seats myself (driving well over 20,000 miles per year), usually

---

40   The hotel was owned by party donor Peter Boizot, who gave me a heavily discounted rate for the use of a business hotel at weekends.

accompanied by the relevant target seat officer, covering in most cases between four and six seats. Each of these people had a 'hands-on' role, writing much of the literature in many of their seats, based very largely on the local campaigns that the candidates within them were running, and supporting the agent or organiser. I was most anxious to avoid a repetition of my own earlier Liberal area agent experience when regional boundaries were rigid, and the roles expected of the staff within them were far too wide for them to have any real impact on winning seats in a general election. Local elections and council by-elections within the seats were a very high priority for direct campaign staff support and they had ring-fenced budgets to assist with them. Targets were set for membership (we had shown that in most seats gained in 1992, there were around 500 members), production of the by-election-style newspapers based on local issues (three times per year), regular 'Focus'-style leaflets (at least six per year in urban areas), canvassing/data collection, targeted letters and media releases. It was a sophisticated system of key performance indicators that directly related to prospects of winning and which I monitored very closely.

Despite the significant uplift in funding, we were not able to support as many seats as I would have liked. The target seat officers were allocated budgets to support the local campaigns in their seats; but we could not afford to allocate a dedicated member of the campaigns department to all the seats that I was now beginning to believe might be winnable. We sought, however, to assist a wider pool of seats by including them in all the training events and mailings. We were not yet into the age of social media, and email communication was in its infancy, but it soon became crucial to the networking within the seats. We established confidential online conference sites in order to enable discussion between those working in the seats and the team employed by the HQ. They were used for the downloading of literature from other seats and organisational information. It was as much a bottom-up approach as a top-down one, as everyone learned from each other. We certainly didn't have a monopoly on wisdom at the centre, and with so many candidates and their teams doing good things, our job was to share their best ideas with the other seats.

The year 1994 ended with an enormous boost to the party following the defection from the Conservatives of Emma Nicholson, then MP for West Devon & Torridge. There had been rumours of Emma's unhappiness with the Conservative Party for some time that autumn. At first, we simply didn't believe them and were unsure if she was joking when she told Nick Harvey in the Commons tea room that he should speak to Paddy about her joining us. After some private discussions between Emma and Richard Holme, she then met Paddy on the Friday before Christmas at a secret rendezvous (the Devon home of Graham and Jane Elson, who were away at the time) and it became clear to us that she was deadly serious, if agreement could be reached. She wanted to know that she would at least be able to stand for us in the European Parliament elections, now to be held on the basis of proportional representation. Her defection was then planned with the sort of military precision that I became used to working with Paddy. Surprise was essential to the success of the operation in seeking to dominate the media in the crucial few days between Christmas and the New Year, when we thought we could get the best headlines. Emma was extremely keen that the key local party officers in her constituency were informed in advance of her defection, as well as John Major. Personal letters explaining the situation were therefore delivered to the homes of these Conservative Party officials just before 9 p.m. on the Friday by Lib Dem volunteers from the neighbouring North Cornwall and North Devon constituencies. I stood next to Emma at the fax machine in Paddy's office as she sent through her resignation statement to 10 Downing Street. Her interview with the BBC's political editor Robin Oakley (recorded earlier) took up the first six minutes of the BBC's main evening news that night and there was tremendous coverage of it during the following week. With our by-election gains, it took our number of MPs to twenty-four, and our opinion-poll rating rose from 16 per cent to 22 per cent.

LITTLEBOROUGH & SADDLEWORTH

The fourth and the last of our parliamentary by-election victories in the run-up to the 1997 general election was at Littleborough & Saddleworth in July 1995. It had long been known that the sitting Tory MP Geoffrey Dickens was seriously ill with cancer. It had therefore been very important to be sensitive about political activity in the constituency, although the Lib Dems had been campaigning there for decades. Saddleworth, which is proudly in Yorkshire, was until 1983 part of former Liberal MP Richard Wainwright's Colne Valley constituency. In 1985, my friend Chris Davies, a former Liverpool councillor, was selected as the candidate for Littleborough & Saddleworth. He brought great energy to local campaigning, using many of the techniques that we had pioneered in Liverpool to help us win most of the council seats in the constituency. Three of the constituency's eight wards were within the Rochdale borough, and campaigns which Chris led resulted in us winning two of them, and taking control of Rochdale council.

The local council elections in 1995 were particularly hard-fought across the constituency, with all the parties knowing that a parliamentary by-election was probably going to take place in the not-too-distant future. Paul Rainger spent the entire local election campaign there, overseeing the production of leaflets and helping us to win seven of the eight wards within the constituency. Labour narrowly gained one ward from us, whilst the Conservatives failed to win a single ward in the constituency that they had held since it was formed in 1983. A week after the local elections, Chris Davies rang me to say that Geoffrey Dickens had died.

There were some immediate problems for us. One of the regular local Lib Dem surveys had asked people their voting intention in a general election. This question had been misrepresented in the media as being a question about by-election voting intention, anticipating Geoffrey Dickens's death. Labour tried to make much of this, suggesting that campaigning in this way had been in bad taste. Such considerations did not, however, prevent them speaking to the *Manchester Evening News*'s lobby correspondent three times on the day that Geoffrey Dickens died to assure him that Labour would win. To counter the accusation of campaigning prematurely, we went to great lengths to remind people there of our many years of 'all-year-round campaigning' locally, and in particular the ten years of local 'Focus' leaflets since Chris had become the parliamentary candidate. Our launch event for the by-election campaign was branded as a birthday party marking ten years of the local 'Focus' newsletters. We held it in our headquarters, a disused mill in Shaw, with a large birthday cake suitably decorated in Lib Dem colours and designed as a 'Focus' leaflet. This was intended to contrast with how 'New Labour' and their candidate had only 'newly' arrived on the scene for the by-election.

Over the past year, there had been a breakdown in the previously good working relationship between Chris Davies, who was initially supportive of Paddy's 'Chard strategy', and Cyril Smith, who had been MP for neighbouring Rochdale until 1992, and who was vehemently opposed to it. Our own constituency polling showed that Cyril was far and away the most popular local or national politician in the constituency. We had no idea at the time about the very serious allegations against him that would emerge years later, so we very much wanted his endorsement for Chris and his support for the campaign. Fortunately, I was able to heal the rift between them at the outset of the campaign, helped by the fact that I had known Cyril since the Edge Hill by-election. It seems clear to me with hindsight that Labour must also have known nothing substantive about the later allegations, otherwise they would undoubtedly have surfaced during the by-election campaign. Cyril campaigned for us extensively and he spoke together with Richard Wainwright and David Alton at Chris's adoption meeting in Upper Mill. This was exactly the same line up of speakers as we had had for the Edge Hill by-election adoption meeting sixteen years earlier.

A major issue for us was the fact that Chris was an outspoken candidate and well known to have argued strongly for the decriminalisation of drugs. This led Labour to encourage media questions suggesting that he must either be, or have been, a user of illegal drugs. This was of course completely untrue. I was personally conscious of the fact that Chris's father had died as a result of lung cancer and I knew that he had never even smoked tobacco. Nevertheless, Chris wanted initially to fight the by-election strongly in defence of his belief in drug liberalisation. I had to persuade him that this emphasis would needlessly put the result in great jeopardy. I was confident, I told him, that we could secure a win in spite of the apparent upsurge in Labour support, providing that we fought on similar campaign themes to those in our other successful by-election campaigns. I could not guarantee success otherwise.

Labour seized every opportunity to attack Chris personally rather than the Conservative government. Chris had run a business in Liverpool that had failed in the recession a few years previously, and he was not personally to blame for this. But Labour soon ensured that suggestions to the contrary were running in the Liverpool press, and they sought to get national press to follow it up. Much of our time in the campaign was spent fire-fighting and rebutting such attacks.

Following the 1992 general election (when he had come second), Chris had spoken on the local radio about the need to reverse some of the Tories' tax cuts in order to fund public services. He actually used the phrase 'hefty tax increases'. Chris's candid approach to such issues was not necessarily what I wanted for the by-election, and Labour seized upon them. Our press officer David Loxton and his 'minder', a Cowley Street colleague Garry White, worked closely with Chris to ensure that his views could not be presented out of context during the campaign. He gave them his mobile phone so that he was not constantly interrupted by journalists asking mischievous questions planted by Labour. Sarah Gurling organised Chris's campaign programme.

Despite Chris having lived in Saddleworth for ten years, Labour tried to brand him as 'the councillor from Liverpool', rather than the local councillor he now was within the Littleborough & Saddleworth constituency. Labour's campaign was noted by all concerned for being extremely negative and personalised, branding Chris as being 'soft on drugs, high on taxes'. It was hardly a progressive Labour campaign.

Our own campaign concentrated rather more positively on local issues, such as trying to reverse the decline of the local town centres, the future of NHS services, investment in public transport and the need for more and better policing. Above all, we emphasised how Chris was the strong challenger to the Conservatives, who had been the dominant force in the constituency's recent general elections.

It became a very difficult campaign for us as Labour's massive effort, in a very strong region for them, gained ground, and the smear campaigns against Chris began to have some effect. In the penultimate week of the campaign, our daily canvass returns showed our support slipping significantly, and Labour's rising. Our apparent 'frontrunner' status was no guarantee of victory. The Conservatives had previously triumphed in the constituency thanks in large part to the split in the vote between ourselves and Labour. We warned strongly against this possibility recurring. I also decided at this stage that we had to fight back rather more strongly against the Labour Party's very personal and negative campaign. Labour's candidate, Phil Woolas, had a Lancashire accent but had only moved up to the constituency from where he lived in London at the start of the by-election campaign. He had, however, advertised his 'local' address on letters to voters, with a local phone number, suggesting that this was where he lived. When looking at one of his leaflets, Ann recognised the address shown as that of a small holiday rental cottage that we had looked at renting for ourselves for the last few weeks of the campaign. I then produced a leaflet headed: 'Who can we trust for Saddleworth?', highlighting the contrast between where he claimed to live in the constituency and his 'real' London address, 'as shown on the official nomination form for the election'.[41] As a trade union official who had not initially appeared sympathetic to Tony Blair's New Labour project, we suggested that he might not be quite what he seemed. Paddy was never

---

41   Election law now permits such addresses not to be disclosed in this way.

keen on 'negative campaigning', and some people in his London office were aghast at my change of tactics. On his next visit, Paddy asked local members about their concerns over my change of strategy and 'how far it would backfire'. But they all told him that they considered that what I had done to be a very mild rebuttal compared to what was normal politics in that part of the world, and suggested that perhaps I should have been more hard-hitting at an earlier stage. Paddy initially also objected to my drafts of letters to voters in his name, referring to some of the alleged 'dishonesty' in Labour's campaign. I faxed him some of Labour's leaflets and he immediately called me back wanting to toughen up the language I was proposing.

Hundreds of Labour MPs canvassed in the constituency, spending a considerable amount of time with individual voters, and seeking to persuade them that only Labour would have any role in removing the Conservative government. My fear was that if they succeeded with that argument in this by-election, then it would also prevail in many of the seats that I believed we could otherwise win at the general election. We understood that Labour's campaign had hired an entire hotel and a fleet of cars for their very large campaign staff. Labour's deputy leader John Prescott was prominent in their campaign, but managed to offend local sensitivities by swearing loudly at the organisers of the Saddleworth Festival when they would not let his campaign bus, covered in Labour posters and red balloons, enter the non-political event. He was furious that Chris Davies was part of it (without any party colours) as he was participating as a local fell runner. Given Labour's constant onslaught on us, I persuaded David Alton, still the Lib Dem MP for Mossley Hill, to bring his great skills and experience to chairing what were quite tricky daily press conferences. Labour's were presided over by my opposite number for the campaign, Peter Mandelson. Whilst we had significantly fewer helpers in our campaign than Labour, our volunteers worked as hard as in any campaign that I had experienced, with my good friend and local councillor Howard Sykes acting as the by-election agent and motivating the local party.

I felt so stressed at many points in the campaign that I was frequently thinking that I could not continue with my job, and must give it up afterwards. I had woken up at 4.15 a.m. every day, partly because of the stress, but also because of the sound of a milking machine next door to where I was staying. As I then drove in to the HQ with David Loxton (he, Paul Rainger and I all stayed in the same place), I feared that all our efforts in the previous parliamentary by-election campaigns could be undone if we failed in this one. At the HQ, however, I knew that my role required considerable self-discipline to ensure that my body language reflected confidence in our campaign. An image makeover for Chris, by the leading consultant Mary Spillane, also helped maintain his confidence as he was constantly pilloried by Labour's campaign.

We began polling day with our traditional 5 a.m. delivery of a 'Good Morning' leaflet. We were suspicious about what the pro-Labour *Daily Mirror* might print on polling day, and we even prepared to buy up large quantities of the paper if we thought that it would be significantly damaging to us. To our great surprise, the first editions did not say much about the by-election. But then vans started arriving in the constituency with tens of thousands of copies of a free polling day special edition of the *Mirror*, which featured Labour's campaign extensively over the front page and three inside ones. They were distributed to every local newsagent to give out free to every customer, whilst the paid-for *Mirror*s were taken away.

Our plan to 'buy up' copies of the *Mirror* if necessary then became a plan to simply scoop up all the free copies from these newsagents. There had been no instruction to the newsagents about how many copies each person could collect. As they were free, we sent volunteers round all the newsagents to collect several hundred copies each. A local volunteer called Sarah stored many thousands of copies at her parents' house.[42] In this way, Labour's crude propaganda device (which

<hr />

[42] Sarah went on to work for Chris Davies as an MP, then for Richard Allan in his Sheffield office and then for me in London, shortly after which she married Mark Morris, a former researcher for David Chidgey.

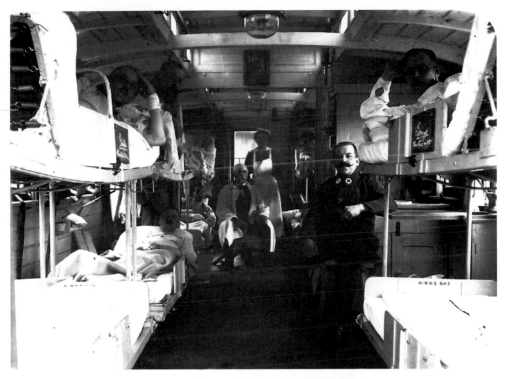

ABOVE After spending thirty-six hours wounded in no-man's land, my father (top left bunk) became a prisoner of war when his battalion was overrun during the Battle of Cambrai in November 1917. His left leg had to be amputated and he was repatriated in May 1918 on this hospital ship.

LEFT My father retired as a dentist when I was one and died when I was three.

LEFT Aged five with my mother and brothers Edward (fourteen) and Peter (three) on holiday in Bridlington in 1965.

BELOW With the Young Liberals at a seminar of the International Federation of Liberal and Radical Youth near Barcelona in 1979.

ABOVE The Church Ward by-election in January 1982 following the death of Cyril Carr (for whom I had been the successful election agent aged nineteen in 1980). Now aged twenty-one, I was successful again as we won with 62 per cent of the vote. The count was held at Mosspits Lane School and our group of helpers includes Liverpool friends Ann McTegart, Carole Storey and future MP and MEP Chris Davies.

RIGHT With Ann at Buckingham Palace receiving the MBE in 1989.

LEFT At the Eastbourne by-election HQ in October 1990 the morning after the 16,923 Conservative majority had been overturned for the Lib Dems to win by 4,550. Paddy had opposed us fighting the by-election, but then described our victory as his 'best day as leader'. Six weeks later, Margaret Thatcher was ousted as Prime Minister.

BELOW Opening the consultative session on party strategy at the Lib Dem conference in Harrogate in 1992.

ABOVE With the newly elected Lib Dem MPs at the 1992 Lib Dem conference: (l–r) Nigel Jones, Don Foster, Liz Lynne, Paul Tyler and Nick Harvey.

LEFT *The Campaign Manual*, published in 1995, showing some of the headlines from our by-election wins. The photo top left shows me with Paddy Ashdown, Chris and Carol Davies and others on our campaign bus the day after the Littleborough & Saddleworth by-election win that summer.

Peerage for Lib-Dems' elections mastermind

THE Liverpudlian who masterminded the Liberal Democrats' general election success has been made a life peer.

Chris Rennard is now Lord Rennard.

Lord Rennard, 38, ran David, now Lord Alton's campaign, when he was first elected Liberal Democrat MP for Liverpool Mossley Hill.

Since moving to London, Lord Rennard has been responsible for many of the Liberal Democrats' successes in by-elections.

But his finest hour was in the last general election, at which the party took an unprecedented 46 seats.

'Delighted'

Lord Rennard said last night: "After 25 years of political life, I'm delighted.

"It was discussed with Paddy Ashdown, and he said he couldn't have had a valedictory honours list without including me.

"He thanked me for my work over the last 11 years and said that I had helped secure eight by-election victories plus 46 seats in the last general election."

Lord Rennard added: "I hope it's a nice thing for the people of Liverpool, especially Liberal Democrats.

"I also hope it will be pleasing to my friends, former neighbours and my brother Peter, who is a Liverpool taxi driver."

Lord Rennard's father died early in his childhood and the remainder of his early life was devoted to

By Penny Fray
Daily Post Staff

caring for his severely disabled mother. After her death, he moved into his own flat at the age of only 16.

Academically he was very bright, coming top in all his A-levels at the Blue Coat School.

The school was the foundation of his later successes.

He said: "I was always a determined individual. I didn't want to live with another family when my mother died. I had looked after her during her confinement to a wheelchair, so I decided I could look after myself.

"Having taken on a lot of responsibility as a child helped me do responsible things at a young age."

The Liberal Society at Liverpool University won almost all the elections it contested under his leadership.

The society played a key role in the campaigns which made Liverpool a Liberal stronghold between 1980 and 1983.

Lord Rennard was made deputy chairman of the Liverpool Liberal Party when he was only 21 and now is the youngest Liberal Democrat life peer ever.

Of his future role in the Upper House he said: "I'm committed to nursery education, especially since my wife is a nursery teacher, and to raising issues of international human rights and the alleviation of poverty in third world countries."

TOP In the Cowley Street boardroom during the 1997 general election when the campaign poster boards arrived.

RIGHT How the *Liverpool Daily Post* reported my peerage in 1999.

LEFT My view of the scene at the Brent East by-election HQ on the night in September 2003 when Sarah Teather and the Lib Dems came from third place (15,260 behind) to gain the seat with a 1,118 majority (Labour's first loss in a parliamentary by-election since Greenwich in 1987).

ABOVE With Charles Kennedy outside Cowley Street after the Lib Dems had polled 27 per cent of the vote in the May 2004 local elections.
© PRESS ASSOCIATION

LEFT Speaking as chief executive to the Lib Dem conference in September 2005 after the Lib Dems won sixty-two seats in the general election that year.
© ALEX FOLKES

Bringing Charles Kennedy back to campaigning and helping to win the Dunfermline & West Fife by-election with Willie Rennie in February 2006 after a series of difficulties, including Charles's resignation and controversy surrounding Mark Oaten and Simon Hughes, had hit the party.
© PRESS ASSOCIATION

Speaking in the House of Lords, 2017.
© HOUSE OF LORDS 2017 / PHOTOGRAPHY BY ROGER HARRIS

we considered to be a breach, at least in spirit, of election laws) did not have the effect on the campaign that they desired.

On polling day, there were thousands of Labour activists competing with several hundred of ours, and what appeared to be only a few dozen Conservatives, trying to persuade our respective supporters to turn out and vote. As the polls closed at 10 p.m., I spoke to Nick Harvey, who was appearing as the Lib Dem on the election night TV programme. In previous parliamentary by-election campaigns I had been able to speak very confidently at this point about the need to 'play it cool to begin with', in anticipation of very large majorities being confirmed as the count progressed. On this occasion, I told Nick that I had not had time during the day for much 'number crunching', but that my instinct was that we would win by about 2,000 votes. 'Oh, f**k,' he said. 'You mean that we might lose?' I had to admit that I couldn't guarantee that we were beyond any margin of safety this time, but that I didn't think that the draft lines for the media that Paddy's office had prepared to explain away our defeat would be needed.

At the count, I was shocked seeing the level of Labour support in some previously strong Conservative areas. But it soon became clear that we were ahead of Labour across the constituency, and that the Conservatives would finish third. Chris and his wife Carol had been told to wait at home until advised to come to the count, where I would advise them as to the outcome. Whilst they were on their way, I went around our hundreds of supporters in the public gallery telling them that we needed the most enormous cheer when Chris and Carol arrived. The media at the count remained uncertain as to the outcome, and I wanted the result to be effectively announced by the huge ovation that we would create for Chris and Carol when they entered the counting area. Somehow my message to Chris that he had won was not clearly relayed to him, and he arrived still uncertain of the outcome, to be shocked and then stunned by the tremendous sound of hundreds of cheering Lib Dem supporters. The live broadcasts from the count could not continue because of the noise, and that was how people watching ascertained that we had won. Our majority was 1,993. I had been seven votes out in my forecast.

A bitter row within Labour then followed about their negative and right-wing tactics, and over who was to blame for their failure. Labour MPs openly criticised their party's campaign. Richard Holme wrote to me afterwards to say that 'the party is, as so often and even more so now, greatly in your debt'. Paddy wrote in a letter of thanks that 'L & S was, in my view, your greatest triumph. We are all much in your debt.'

The result in Littleborough & Saddleworth proved that the Lib Dems could win, even when there was an enormous tide running for Tony Blair's New Labour. It also showed a number of Lib Dems that their putative partners were not always as nice as they purported to be. This was something that many of us with long experience of fighting Labour in the parts of the country where it is strongest felt that we had always known.

THE 1997 CAMPAIGN

By the autumn of 1996, our target seat campaign was very well prepared for the expected general election. We had used the successful parliamentary by-election campaigns to provide models for each of the target seats showing how, over a rather longer period of time than we had had in those by-elections, they could emulate them in order to win.

I had been much less involved in preparations for the national campaign and the so-called air war to be fought in the national media. An advertising agency (Knight Leach Delaney, who went bust shortly afterwards) had approached Richard Holme, and he had taken their advice about national slogans and positioning. Their advice, however, seemed to me (and also to many experienced campaigners in the party) to be quite bizarre. Had there been a general election that autumn, we would have fought under the slogan 'Take Courage for the Future!'

Neither the agency nor Richard seemed to know that this had been the slogan for Courage beer and that it still appeared on many pubs. I didn't warm to the idea of telling voters that they 'had to be brave to vote for us'. The advertising agency also latched onto the distinctiveness of our party colouring. Even though this was not really yellow, they produced posters and products for the party conference that autumn with the slogan 'We're yellow, we've got courage!' All my instincts told me that this approach was extremely poor and was devoid of any persuasive messaging. I had not been invited to the crucial general election team meeting in Paddy's office which had approved the agency's work. I was assured, however, that their approach had been validated by market research, which I therefore asked to see. I found no reference in the reports of the research to the proposed slogan and messaging. I was then told that the supportive comments were all in the detailed comments of the participants in the focus groups, so I sought the detailed transcripts; only to discover that there were no supporting comments of any kind, and only derogatory references to the new slogans when they had been discussed. I spoke to Derek Martin, a longstanding professional market researcher and Lib Dem councillor who had conducted the focus groups, and he expressed his astonishment that any of the research that he had conducted had been cited as being in support of the 'Take Courage' campaign.

I was still very junior to Richard in the party hierarchy and felt nervous about approaching Paddy to explain my concerns about the general election slogans etc. But, armed with these facts about the market research, I told him of my basic concern that the 'messaging' as proposed provided no discernible reason for voting Lib Dem. I advised him that he appeared to have been seriously misled about the market research. After this meeting, there followed an almighty row between Paddy and Richard Holme, in which Richard actually resigned as chair of the general election campaign. Shortly afterwards, however, he agreed to resume the role with Paddy insisting and Richard agreeing that I be brought in on the strategy and messaging side of the national campaign, and from that point on Richard and I worked extremely well together.

Nearer the election, Richard also brought in the former chief executive of Saatchi and Saatchi, John Sharkey, who assisted greatly with our revised approach to messaging. Richard always expected great loyalty to be shown to him in public, but in private now became very much more amenable to discussion about how the campaign should be conducted. I was by then conducting approximately one constituency poll per week testing out the key messages of each of the main parties in our target seats and gave Richard the results. The result of this polling later became crucial in determining how we positioned ourselves in relation to the other parties.

The most difficult area to resolve before the election was the issue of potential coalition, and our approach to Labour in particular. Ever since the Chard speech, and in spite of our 'bust up' with Labour at Littleborough & Saddleworth, Paddy had been wedded to the idea of arguing publicly for a post-election arrangement with Labour, preferably a full coalition, as an explicit part of our general election messaging. He had been reined back from expressing this view at an earlier point as a result of widespread opposition to it within the party. But he kept making strong public hints about his desired aims, particularly in conference speeches where he made reference, for example, to us being part of the 'scrum on the playing fields'. The media were briefed that these were clear pointers towards his aim of being part of a coalition, rather than an opposition party. Paddy often took great delight in including such hidden messages in his speeches, and some of them were not very well hidden. Richard and Paddy's most senior political adviser, Alan Leaman, was firmly wedded to this strategy, as were most of Paddy's advisers who he brought together in what he called the 'Jo group'. It met in order to discuss progress on what was discreetly referred to by some as 'The Project'. Meanwhile, Paddy was generally denying to the party's Federal Executive that he had any plans at all to prepare for a coalition with Tony Blair. Some of those around him saw little problem in making his aims known via the media. But at one of our target seat training weekends with leading candidates in the summer of 1996, there was real anger expressed in the room when *The Observer* contained quotes from 'a senior party strategist' suggesting that the aim of the Lib Dems was 'a ten-year partnership with Labour'. Some of the candidates present had been victims of the 1992 backlash against a potential coalition with Labour, and almost all of them understood how damaging a repetition of this prospect would be in the next general election.

Many of the existing MPs also had great reservations about this potential approach to the election. In the summer of 1996, and before I was more fully brought into the national campaign, the Parliamentary Party held a two-day event in Oxford to prepare for the election campaign. I knew that my presence had at the time only reluctantly been conceded by Richard in response to demands from the MPs. In a long discussion after dinner, the pros and cons of advocating the case for a coalition with Labour during the election campaign were discussed. Archy Kirkwood, a close ally of Paddy at the time, knew of significant opposition to Paddy's intended strategy and had gone so far as to warn me of the danger that Paddy might simply walk out from the event and resign as leader if he was not allowed to pursue the strategy that he wanted. Archy considered it essential that, if Paddy resigned, the remaining MPs should not be allowed to leave the room until they had agreed to nominate his successor; and that it should be Ming Campbell.

I took the opportunity, in the after-dinner discussion, to explain my view that the Labour Party very much welcomed the public suggestion that the Lib Dems wanted to work with them inside a future Labour government, as this provided helpful endorsement for the 'New Labour project' and would reassure some of those people wavering about supporting them. I then described how the Conservatives would also very much welcome this approach, because it had helped them greatly in 1992; they always wanted to be able to say, 'Vote Lib, get

Lab' in order to persuade voters wavering between us and them to vote Conservative. I concluded the explanation of my views by asking: 'If it is in the interests of the Labour Party for us to pursue this strategy, and if it is in the interests of the Conservative Party for us to pursue this strategy, how could it possibly be in the interests of the Liberal Democrats?' I was applauded by a number of MPs, particularly Malcolm Bruce,[43] who knew that my contribution would not have been welcomed by 'pro-Project' supporters and that it was a brave statement to have made.

Subsequently Paddy continued to make great efforts personally to persuade me of the merits of his proposed strategy. At a very convivial dinner cooked by Jane at their Vane Cottage home in Somerset that September, he outlined his proposed 'heads of agreement' for a coalition deal with Labour. It was a document that he worked on frequently. I reflected carefully on all of his arguments (and noted his view that some of the sceptics would be won round by the prospect of ministerial positions), but in a long memo afterwards I once again explained that the problem was not the policy objectives, but the message; the fact that your aim was basically to work with one of your main rivals could not be a helpful one to us in the campaign.

Richard had previously commissioned polling asking people their attitudes towards different potential outcomes of the general election. It was clear from this that people did not like big majorities, and that Lib Dem supporters may be more amenable to hung parliament scenarios than those of other parties. But the problem with these conclusions was that nobody could use their ballot paper to determine what size of majority a particular party might have, nor to ensure that the Lib Dems would be in a position to do a deal with a party that might be acceptable to them, but not with another one.

The origins of our own constituency polling had been a series of conversations that I had had over the summer of 1996 explaining to

---

43   Former Leader of the Scottish Liberal Democrats and MP for Gordon.

Anthony Jacobs that one of the greatest problems remaining for us in relation to the forthcoming campaign was the need to hone our messaging in the key seats. Some of our candidates remained wedded to strange ideas about what were the major issues in their constituencies. I also told him that we appeared uncertain as to how to approach the messaging for the national campaign. In response to this, he agreed to finance a polling operation to be conducted from the basement of our Cowley Street headquarters. With his help, we recruited over thirty callers (paying them £5 per hour) and two part-time supervisors, and we purchased thirteen personal computers, linking them to telephones with headsets.

Rick Ridder then spent ten days training the callers and supervisors, and advising on use of the polling software. With the help of John Jefkins, whose election software was used by the Lib Dems in most constituencies, we were able to obtain very good samples of 400 voters in each of the seats that we were polling. We also collected copies of all the leaflets being distributed by all parties in our target constituencies, and I had a team monitoring the weekly press coverage in all of them. In this way, I was able to devise questionnaires testing the messaging from all the major parties, as well as the relative popularity of all the candidates and all the leaders, and to confirm the biggest issues for our potential voters. We conducted one poll each week, and I was able to present most of the individual seat findings to the relevant MPs, candidates and campaign teams myself, with support from the team of target seat officers. We persuaded a number of them to focus rather more heavily on issues such as health and education, which were consistently proving to be the biggest issues of concern in these constituencies.

The aggregate information from these polls proved to be critical to the national campaign. By asking similar questions in each of the polls we could prove the validity of my proposal to concentrate on what I called the CHEESE issues (crime, health, education, the economy, sleaze and the environment). Paddy in particular had been very reluctant to campaign on the issue of the NHS, believing that 'it was a Labour issue', and that we should leave it to them. Our constituency polls, however, consistently found that it was the single most important issue at the time in those seats. I was able to send Paddy a set of different tabloid newspapers from more than twenty target constituencies leading on NHS issues. They showed him the relative importance of the issue and suggested how our national 'air war' campaign needed to support the constituency 'ground war' campaigns with consistent messages. My point was that successful integrated campaigning needed to be more 'bottom up', taking into account what worked locally rather more than was sometimes understood by those working solely on national campaigns.

We also used this constituency polling to test out the proposed positioning messages about coalition. We were particularly interested in the views of those who had voted Conservative in 1992, but who might now be prepared to vote Liberal Democrat. Many of these people were very disillusioned with John Major's government. They understood and agreed with Paddy's approach that 'if the Conservatives lost the election, and were booted out from the front door of Downing Street, then we should not put them in again via the back door'. But much to Paddy and Richard's initial disappointment, this group of voters was also most unwilling to support us if we stated *explicitly* that our aim after the election was to form a coalition with Labour. The vast majority of these former Conservative supporters made it clear that if this became our stated election aim, then they would revert back to the Conservatives. Paddy had always told me that he would not insist on his proposed strategic messaging if it was going to be damaging to the target seats. I finally proved to him that it would be.

On the final afternoon of the autumn 1996 Lib Dem conference, I sat down with Alan Leaman to spend a couple of hours going through the poll findings in the Mid Dorset & North Poole constituency that he was due to fight. His prospects of winning were strong. At the end of our questionnaire the findings suggested that he and the Conservative would both be on 41 per cent of the vote.[44] The poll findings about coalition strategy, however, showed Alan that we needed to change tack about the proposed coalition with Labour if he was to have a chance of winning. I then made it my business to share the overall poll findings in relation to this issue with each of the other members of Paddy's 'Jo group'. Richard asked me to leave it to him to speak to Ming, as they would both approach Paddy about the necessary change. Paddy was personally disappointed that the messaging he had been working on for some years would not work in terms of winning seats from the Conservatives (even though this had also been the case in 1992). On the other hand, he recognised that I had been consistent in my view of this issue.

Richard had previously believed that a pro-Labour coalition strategy would be of assistance to us and had discussed the issue with Peter Mandelson, who was running Labour's campaign. In order to make it easier for us to change tack and explain why we would now need to differentiate ourselves more strongly from Labour, Richard shared our poll findings with Peter Mandelson, who later expressed his surprise to me about these conclusions. But Labour's election mastermind had to accept that as Liberal Democrats we would defeat more Conservatives by keeping more distance from Labour than if we were 'packaged together'.

After the surprising outcome of the 1992 general election, many people still had doubts as to whether or not the Conservatives could be defeated in 1997. I was personally optimistic about our prospects in many of the seats that we sought to gain from the Conservatives, but my instincts and our polling showed that a large Labour vote in these constituencies would be a major barrier to our success. A number of people on the Labour side were also aware of this. A discussion about tactical voting took place over a private dinner organised by Neil Sherlock,[45] whose employers were happy for him to arrange a dinner

---

44 Alan eventually missed winning the seat, polling 39.5 per cent to the Conservatives' 40.5 per cent.
45 Neil worked at the time for KPMG and later came close in that election to winning the 'safe' Conservative seat of South West Surrey, even though it was not targeted.

discussing issues with representatives of the main opposition parties. Amongst the attendees were Dick Newby, Alan Leaman and myself, and on Labour's side Peter Mandelson, Neal Lawson and Ben Lucas. We discussed the similarity of the issues that we would seek to raise during the election campaign, and how our anti-Conservative message would therefore be very similar and helpful to each other in undermining the Conservatives. I had to explain, however, that whilst squeezing the Labour vote in Lib Dem vs. Conservative constituencies was always helpful to us, it was not always helpful to Labour for the Lib Dem vote to be squeezed because this could result in as many former Lib Dem votes going to the Conservatives as to Labour. The suggestion that we might in certain seats want our supporters to back Labour would also be deeply damaging to us in other seats amongst Conservative/ Lib Dem waverers. Suggestions that Labour voters might vote for us tactically against the Conservatives were not so damaging to Labour.

What I really wanted was to get some help from Labour to encourage, or at least not to resist, tactical voting in our favour, particularly in seats where it was clear that Labour could not win, but where we could defeat the Conservatives. I knew that the following week Paddy was meeting David Montgomery, then editor of the *Daily Mirror*. I asked Peter Mandelson if Labour could give a signal to him that the *Mirror* should endorse the principle of their Labour-leaning readers voting for the Lib Dems in at least ten constituencies where we clearly provided the only real challenge to the Conservatives. Paddy was subsequently delighted when Peter Mandelson's influence with the *Mirror* was demonstrated as David Montgomery evidently knew all about the idea when they met and agreed to exactly this proposition. I was later to work with the *Mirror's* political editor, David Seymour, about which constituencies would be listed. With some effort, I persuaded him to increase the number of seats to be featured, and the *Mirror* eventually listed twenty-two constituencies that I suggested. The Labour-leaning paper gave advice to Labour supporters to vote Liberal Democrat tactically in those seats. We were eventually to win twenty of them. The two that we didn't win were Mid Dorset & North Poole (lost by 600 votes) and Hastings (which had also appeared on the list of where Lib Dem supporters should vote Labour). The *Mirror*'s approach to tactical voting was not endorsed by either party, but it undoubtedly helped both to win seats from the Conservatives. On polling day, we reprinted the *Mirror*'s advice in seats such as Sheffield Hallam where it helped us to gain the only Conservative seat in the city. There was absolutely no agreement that the Lib Dems would back off in any seat that Labour was trying to gain, but we tried, of course, to get our helpers to work where their activity would be most to our advantage. We also asked Labour not to make effort in those seats where it would clearly be counter-productive to their aim of removing the Conservatives from office. I provided a discreet list of such seats in the guise of an independent academic's research.

After the Lib Dem conference, I was due to visit the United States in order to observe the 1996 Presidential election campaign. I had been to the Democratic Convention in 1992 at which Bill Clinton and Al Gore had accepted their party's nominations and I have always taken a close interest in US elections. This has been partly in order to help ensure that the Lib Dems were keeping in touch with the most modern and sophisticated election campaign and fundraising techniques. When it became clear that there would be no UK autumn general election, I was free to spend three weeks in the US. Paddy was anxious to speak to me before I went because of an initiative that he wanted to launch in my absence. The key to eventual future cooperation with Labour was clearly tied to constitutional reform, and proportional representation in particular. Labour had accepted the need for PR in future elections for a Scottish Parliament, a Welsh Assembly and the European Parliament. Following the 'Plant Commission', Labour had also agreed that there should be a referendum to choose between a proportional representation system and the present first-past-the-post system for Westminster elections. If the Conservatives lost the general election, it would inevitably be more difficult for any new government to legislate for these and other measures if they were acting on behalf of just one party. Some cooperation would be desirable if Labour won the election, irrespective of whether they had an overall majority.

Paddy believed that Tony Blair was moving to endorse PR for Westminster and would do so before the general election. He thought that this would become clear through the process of having a joint committee between Labour and the Liberal Democrats to consider the implementation of a programme of constitutional reform post the 1997 general election. This committee was to be headed jointly by Labour's Robin Cook (a well-known supporter of PR for Westminster) and Bob Maclennan (our constitutional affairs spokesman and former Lib Dem president). Paddy wanted me to be the joint secretary of this committee on the basis that my doing so would reassure other Lib Dems that the committee would not be acting against the interests of our party in the forthcoming election. My opposite number in this role was Pat McFadden.[46]

After I returned from the US in October 1996, the committee began work. Its membership included Jack Straw, the late Donald Dewar, the future minister Liz Symons, Baroness Taylor of Bolton, Lord Robertson of Port Ellen, and Lord Plant, together with Lib Dem peers Lord McNally, Lord Lester and Lord Wallace, and Nick Harvey. We were supported by an impressive array of constitutional experts, including Robert Hazell from the Constitution Unit. Our first meeting at the St Ermin's Hotel in Westminster saw both sides lined up for formal introductions. It was the first time that I had met Jack Straw. I knew that he had referred to me in a conversation with a journalist during a parliamentary by-election campaign some time ago as 'that bastard Rennard'. I resisted the temptation to shake his hand and say: 'Hello, I am that bastard Rennard'.

Our meetings proceeded in business-like fashion, but Jack Straw was obviously keen to block any attempt to agree a full move to PR

---

46   Then Tony Blair's adviser on constitutional matters, and later a Labour MP and minister.

for Westminster. He even suggested that as they could not commit to any additional public expenditure in their first two years in office, there could not be a referendum in this period because of the cost of holding it. In one of those strange conversations that occasionally occur between men standing next to each other during a 'comfort break', he suggested to me that he was not opposed to the Alternative Vote (AV) system, which preserved single-member constituencies, but which is not proportional. The committee helped to prepare for the rapid introduction after 1997 of legislation for the creation of the Scottish Parliament, the Welsh Assembly and the London Assembly (all of which would use forms of proportional representation), as well as the incorporation of the European Convention on Human Rights into British law, and the introduction of Freedom of Information legislation. The committee's work was then reflected in the Labour Party manifesto of 1997, which stated: 'We are committed to a referendum on the voting system for the House of Commons. An independent commission on voting systems will be appointed early to recommend a proportional alternative to the first-past-the-post system.' Over the months in which the committee met, Paddy reported back to the 'Jo group' on his hopes that Blair would explicitly state his support for PR prior to polling day. This would naturally make it very much easier to work with Labour if the circumstances were right after the election. Paddy knew my strong view that the Lib Dems could not afford to enter a coalition without the safeguard of proportional representation to protect our numbers in the House of Commons at the level justified by our votes, as opposed to the numbers that we might be left with under first-past-the-post if our vote was badly squeezed. At one point, Paddy explained to me his view that Blair would back PR, but could not do so prior to polling day because of the attitude of the right-wing papers. The explanation was that many of these papers might tolerate a one-off Labour victory to bring down Major's government (in which they had little confidence) but that these papers would not be so tolerant of this result if they believed that a Labour victory would also mean the introduction of a system of PR which might prevent the election of a right-wing Conservative government in the future.

Our campaign polling in the target constituencies continued to demonstrate Paddy's enormous personal popularity. It showed how as leader he could promote very effectively the distinctive messages that set us apart from both the other main parties. We therefore featured Paddy very extensively in all of the constituency literature, and particularly in targeted direct mail campaigns. As the election approached, I felt that our anti-Conservative messaging was proving to be effective, and the Conservatives had given us many targets to hit, but I was worried that our messaging was also too similar to Labour's. The danger to us would be that the difference between us and Labour could simply appear to be that they were a much bigger party, and more likely to succeed nationally. At this point, we appeared to have similar approaches to the big issues of funding public services such as health and education.

The polling told us that the single most common reason for people who had voted Conservative in 1992 switching away from them was the perceived underfunding of these services. Shortly before the general election, Labour announced their commitment to stick to Tory spending limits for at least two years if they formed a government. We made no such commitment, and indeed we were committed to much earlier action in order to restore funding for them, including our pledge to increase spending on education by adding 1p in the pound to income tax rates. This meant that we were able to say that the Lib Dems would 'make the difference', and this became the title of our manifesto. We reached a position with which I was very comfortable, showing clear and distinct differences with both the other main parties, and for which we had considerable public support.

Paddy's campaign tour in the general election was brilliantly organised by Sarah Gurling (later Sarah Kennedy). We made twenty-eight gains and Paddy had visited twenty-seven of those seats, showing how precisely we targeted them. The one 'exceptional' gain was

Kingston-upon-Thames, which was only added to the list of target seats a week before polling day and which Ed Davey went on to win by fifty-six votes after four recounts.

The morning press conferences in Church House, Westminster, made much of our traditional theme of ending the 'Punch and Judy' style of British politics, and Alison Holmes[47] arranged to have a puppet show there to make the point. We repeatedly emphasised the difference that we would make in relation to the 'CHEESE' issues and Paddy frequently made visits to schools and hospitals in support of our public-service-orientated messages. Whilst we had to stick largely to our 'grid' of issues and visits, Richard was generally able to ascertain in advance what Labour's themes of the day would be, and we ensured that we also addressed those issues on the same day in order to maximise our profile in the main media headlines.

Major hoped that a long six-week campaign would enable him to get past the barrage of criticism that had come the way of his government in relation to sleaze allegations. We (and Labour) were determined that this would not be the case. Attention focused in particular on Neil Hamilton, the Tory MP in the very safe seat of Tatton, who had been accused of taking money from Mohamed Al-Fayed for asking questions in the House of Commons. Parliament later published a devastating account of Neil Hamilton's conduct. With a 16,000 majority at the previous election, he refused calls from within his own party to stand down, and he confidently believed that he would be re-elected, if only because his opposition would be split.

The suggestion was then made that, in these unique circumstances, there should be agreement on a single candidate to oppose him. There was much media speculation about the possibility of such a candidate. The difficulty in identifying a suitable person was reflected by reference internally to such a person as the 'Archangel Gabriel'. The prospect of someone standing against Neil Hamilton helped to keep the focus

---

47 Richard's hard-working and very dedicated general election planning manager, who had undertaken a similar role for Des Wilson in 1992.

of the election campaign on the sleaze scandal. As the controversy raged, former BBC journalist Martin Bell (formerly a Young Liberal) suggested to Alastair Campbell that he would put his name forward. Richard Holme then rang me to ask how we could bring this about. It was the first Friday evening of the campaign and I had gone out with the party's press team to the Barley Mow pub in Horseferry Road for a short break.

Standing on the pavement outside the pub, discreetly using my mobile phone, I explained to Richard that we would need the agreement of the Tatton local party and that the view of our candidate there would be crucial to their consideration. I undertook to speak to him in confidence. I knew that there would be significant concern, and outright opposition from some figures in the North West regional party, to the suggestion of a 'Lib–Lab candidate'. When I spoke to our candidate, Roger Barlow, I therefore asked him in the first instance not to discuss the issue with anyone other than his wife. He had clearly hoped that Labour's enthusiasm for a single anti-Hamilton candidate might lead them to support him. I had to explain that Labour would not withdraw for a Lib Dem. Whilst disappointed by this news, he was also magnanimous in understanding the national importance of being able to keep the general election campaign focused on sleaze by having a single anti-Hamilton candidate. I explained the Martin Bell proposition to him, and asked for his help in getting it agreed locally. I suggested to him that a local party executive needed to be convened, without any prior knowledge of Martin Bell's potential candidature, in order to allow a decision to be considered without any publicity in advance that would damage the prospect of agreement. He agreed to convene such a meeting at his house on the Sunday morning in order to discuss the situation.

In the meantime, I agreed to arrange for Martin Bell to be available to attend the meeting in Tatton, and I hoped that when the local party executive members met him that they would agree to his standing on the basis that Roger was supporting this proposition personally.

Events did not go quite according to plan as Richard could not help hinting in advance to the Sunday papers that a potential candidate for Tatton had been found. This resulted in a flurry of calls from senior figures in the North West region concerned that they were being kept out of the loop. This was in fact the case because I knew that Cyril Smith would be vociferously opposed to the proposal and that it would leak in a damaging fashion, and that the issue must in the first instance be a matter for the Tatton members. I had arranged for Martin Bell to be driven up to Tatton early on the Sunday morning, with Tim Clement-Jones as a senior and experienced party figure to accompany him. Once they arrived at Roger Barlow's house, however, the meeting decided that it was not prepared to see Martin until after its decision was made about the possibility of supporting him. Martin had to wait in the kitchen for several hours whilst they deliberated, and then by five votes to four they agreed to support the idea, in spite of some annoyance at the potential 'bounce' having been revealed in that morning's papers. A later members' meeting ratified the decision unanimously, and the party was greatly indebted to Roger Barlow for his leadership and selflessness on the issue. The high profile of Martin Bell's campaign then meant that Major's difficulties in suppressing the sleaze issues continued to dominate the campaign. A major figure in Martin Bell's successful campaign was my friend Bill Le Breton, a former chair of the Association of Liberal Democrat Councillors and with whom I had worked closely in some of the recent Liverpool council elections. Volunteers from many parties, and of none, flocked to Tatton to support Martin, who overturned Neil Hamilton's 16,000 majority to win by over 11,000 votes. It was one of the most remarkable results in a general election campaign that featured many of them.

In early 1997, the bookmakers William Hill had offered odds of fourteen to one on the Lib Dems winning thirty-two or more constituencies in the general election. I made my own investment and passed the tip on. It featured in Des Wilson's diary in the *New Statesman*, which suggested that he remained bitter about his fallout with Paddy, but expressed some confidence in my forecasting a very significant Lib Dem breakthrough. The constituency polling that we had conducted was a new experience for me, but the methodology that we used in conducting twenty-eight constituency polls (in held and target seats) in the six months prior to the election was shown to have provided a reliable forecast of the results in twenty-seven of them. Cash constraints prevented us supporting a small number of additional seats that could perhaps otherwise have been won that year (including Norman Lamb's in North Norfolk). I was confident in advance that election night would be very good for us and the general election team created an excellent party atmosphere at Peter Boizot's 'Pizza on the Park'. I was updated there throughout the night by text messages from our agents in target seats across the country. We were confidently able to forecast publicly many of our gains some time before the official declarations, and to feed these pending results through to the media and to our almost delirious supporters, who were seen to cheer each gain as it was announced. At about 4 a.m., Paddy joined us, having been driven from his count in Yeovil, where he had been returned with a thumping 11,000 majority. By the time that all the results were declared, we had made twenty-eight gains and elected forty-six Lib Dem MPs, the largest number elected 'in the Liberal tradition' since 1929. Paddy's televised speech to us all emphasised the clear majority in the country for constitutional reform.

The last count to declare was the most problematic of the campaign. I had briefly returned to my flat in Dolphin Square for a thirty-minute sleep, shower and change at about 6 a.m. on the Friday morning after polling day. I had been asleep for about five minutes when Gavin Grant called me from Cowley Street to say that Mark Oaten, our candidate in Winchester, had just rung in to say that the count there had been suspended amongst some chaos; it was not clear who had won, and counting would be resumed at one o'clock. I immediately rang Candy Piercy and told her that she needed to get the next train from Waterloo to Winchester, that there was no time to explain properly, but that

I would speak to her as soon as she was on her way. When she was on the train I told her what I knew about the recount. She then decided to ring some of the most experienced party agents in the region and ask them to get to Winchester in time for the recount. She was therefore able to replace the Winchester counting agents, who had been up all night, with a fresher team of experienced counting agents who were able to challenge any vote incorrectly counted and ensure that every vote fairly given to us was included in the piles of ballot papers for Mark Oaten.

Throughout the Friday afternoon Paddy kept ringing me to ask if I had news from the Winchester count. It was clearly so close that Candy was unable to give me any information until the very end of the process. Some of the party's senior figures were due to meet in Paddy's office in the House of Commons at 6 p.m. in order to review the results and in anticipation of potential coalition discussions. As I crossed the road to Paddy's office from Cowley Street, Candy rang to say that we had won – by just two votes! As I walked into Paddy's office he said: 'I don't suppose that we have heard from Winchester?' The whole room cheered as I announced Mark's two-vote victory. It was also clear to me, however, that the result might be subject to challenge by the defeated former Conservative MP Gerry Malone. The meeting was something of an anti-climax in spite of our electoral successes, because Paddy told us that Tony Blair's suggestion of including us in a coalition arrangement, even in the event of a Labour overall majority, was clearly not going anywhere. Labour had won a majority of 179, Blair had apparently spoken to Labour's 'big beasts', including Gordon Brown, John Prescott and Jack Straw, and had then explained to Paddy that any previous suggestion of a coalition was a non-runner at present. Archy in particular looked most disappointed, having been amongst those most enthusiastic about the coalition prospect, and having come down from Scotland for a meeting which lasted no more than fifteen minutes. Most of the Cowley Street general election campaign team then spent the rest of the Friday evening celebrating in a Pimlico restaurant which had become the late-night place of choice for dining during the campaign.

On the Saturday night after the election I was still working at my Cowley Street desk at about 10 p.m., when Paddy rang in something of a panic. His election agent had just rung him to say that he had only just realised that Paddy's nomination form had been filled in incorrectly. Instead of Paddy being described as Jeremy John Durham Ashdown, which is his correct name,[48] as the form read 'John Jeremy Durham Ashdown'. Paddy now feared that this error might have invalidated his nomination and that he would not therefore be the MP for Yeovil. I quickly reassured him that the nomination paper had been accepted by the returning officer and that I had heard the formal declaration making him the MP. To provide him with further reassurance, however, I rang Piers Coleman, who was then acting as the party solicitor, and asked him for a legal reference in order to satisfy Paddy, and make sure that he could go to sleep knowing that he was officially one of our forty-six MPs.

The following week, the new and much larger Lib Dem Parliamentary Party met for the first time in a much larger House of Commons committee room than that used previously. I was a couple of minutes late for this gathering and was instantly greeted by the loud banging of desks and much cheering as I entered the room filled with many of the people that I had worked so closely with as candidates over the past few years, and who were now MPs. Politics had dominated my life for the past twenty years, and I felt then that this was by far the happiest and greatest moment of my political career.

48　The nickname 'Paddy' was acquired when he moved to school in England, as a result of his Northern Irish accent, and stuck with him.

CHAPTER 8

ASHDOWN TO KENNEDY

CONFERENCE '97

The Lib Dem conference at Eastbourne in September 1997 maintained a euphoric atmosphere throughout the week. I spoke at a number of meetings on the conference 'fringe' discussing the recent general election campaign. At a meeting organised by ALDC, I outlined what I thought had been the key factors behind our breakthrough.

I explained the mantra first taught to me by Trevor 'Jones the Vote' – who said that 'the object of the exercise in any election campaign is to find out the issues on voters' minds and to deal with those issues' – and how our polling had shown that the number-one issue of concern in our target constituencies was health. I described how this issue was named as the most important issue by 34 per cent of voters in our sample, whilst the second biggest issue of concern to them was education (most important to 18 per cent of voters). We had therefore successfully focused on health and education, whilst largely excluding from the campaign some of the issues that we had previously focused on such as constitutional reform (which we found was the biggest issue of concern to only 0.6 per cent of voters in our target seats).

Polling had helped to confirm our messages and when we asked people if they were prepared to pay a penny more on income tax to pay for more investment in education, most people (54 per cent) said that they would be *more* likely to vote Liberal Democrat because of this. At the same time, 47 per cent of our sample of voters was much less likely to vote Conservative as a result of their policies on the NHS. I explained how much our success was owed to the energy, self-discipline and communication skills of Paddy Ashdown. Our polling showed that he had been far and away the most popular party leader in our target seats.

My speech outlined five key elements in this strategy:

First, campaigning in these seats did not stop after the last general election. Just as the classic ALDC route to success in local elections is campaigning all the year round – success in parliamentary elections depends upon campaigning over the lifetime of at least one parliament.

Secondly, the campaigns in these seats were geared to the concerns of the voters within those seats, and we sought to demonstrate that the Lib Dem candidate was campaigning more effectively for local people than the sitting member. A candidate has to be seen campaigning to get things done locally – acting as a good constituency MP before the election in order to win on election day.

Thirdly, we had to build the organisation within those seats. We lack the support of major national newspapers and we lack time in broadcast coverage to convey our message adequately. This means that we need an army of helpers to convey a message, to deliver the leaflets, to knock on the doors and to raise the funds. There is a very clear correlation between a high and active membership and winning at parliamentary level. Of course, outside help and resources were required to help gain many of the target seats – but it was the building of organisations capable of delivering eight leaflets in four weeks and completing a full canvass that largely brought about the success in these seats.

Fourthly, was the building of the local government base. Convincing people that we could win depended in large part on winning a dominant position in the council elections. Twenty-five of our twenty-eight gains were in seats which we had not represented in Parliament before 1992. Twenty-two of those twenty-five gains were where we controlled the local council – or held almost all the council seats.

Fifthly, I would identify our determination to pursue tactical voting where it helped us. Some people consider this to be somehow dishonest or underhand. What I think is dishonest and underhand is the electoral system which makes it necessary. This time round, it was possible to make a powerful case to Labour supporters to switch to us where we were clearly best placed to defeat the Conservatives. And with their help we contributed to the Conservatives' worst election defeat since 1832.

The final event of the conference was always the leader's speech, then on a Thursday afternoon. This was immediately preceded by the financial appeal as almost all representatives would be in the hall. Earlier in the week, Tim Razzall had asked me if I would make the appeal for funds that year. I felt some trepidation about doing this, but Tim gave me a gracious introduction as I walked to the rostrum and to my great astonishment the entire hall then rose to its feet to give me a standing ovation. Paddy, waiting in the wings of the conference stage to deliver his own speech, was clearly taken aback by the scale of the ovation for a member of party staff making a financial appeal. Even many of the stallholders watching on monitors in the exhibition area rose to their feet as I began the appeal by suggesting that they all seemed to have had a very good lunch.

WINCHESTER BY-ELECTION

The summer after the general election had seen intense legal activity over the Winchester result. Mark Oaten's declared victory by two votes had come as a complete shock to the former Conservative MP Gerry Malone, who was determined to challenge the result in court. His election petition was based on the fact that a number of ballot papers (fifty-five) had not been correctly stamped at the polling stations. They had been disqualified from the count 'for want of the official mark'. The recount, supervised by a High Court judge, showed that there were four more such votes for Gerry Malone than there were for Mark. There was, therefore, some technical justification in Gerry Malone's case as, but for a number of administrative errors at the polling stations, he could have been declared to have been re-elected by two votes, as opposed to being defeated by two votes. But the greater injustice had been done to Mark by the intervention of Richard Huggett, who had repeated in Winchester his spoiling tactic from the Devon European elections. By standing as a *Literal Democrat* he had, in the view of any fair-minded person, fraudulently obtained 640 votes, very largely at Mark's expense. This had led to an angry scene at the count where Mark went so far as to say that he could 'kill' Mr Huggett for what he had done. As Mark was later on declared to be the MP, the police had to investigate Huggett's complaint that his life had been threatened, before dismissing it as something that should not be taken so seriously.

At the High Court, a judge had to order a rerun of the election. This proved to be a pyrrhic victory for Gerry Malone as there was little public support for his challenge to the result, and he was generally perceived to be 'a bad loser'. We described him to the media as being 'like the batsman given out by the umpire, but refusing to walk'. The description stuck.

Throughout the summer, Mark, with the support of the Winchester Lib Dems, and as much help as we could give him, demonstrated to the people of Winchester what a superb constituency MP they now had. His energetic approach to constituency issues contrasted sharply with the general perception of his predecessor's approach. We knew that Gerry Malone had been complacent in the general election because he and his wife had cast their votes in the marginal Aberdeen South constituency, where they had a home, rather than from their home in 'safe' Winchester! Had they voted in Winchester, the returning officer would have had to toss a coin after the counting of the votes in order to determine the winner. I asked Candy Piercy to be the by-election agent and to lead a team of the party's most experienced organisers. Many of them had been involved in several of our recent parliamentary by-election successes. My role was, therefore, to concentrate on ensuring that we had the team in place, the finances to run a £100,000 parliamentary by-election campaign,[49] and sufficient help from members all over the country. Many of our members greatly sympathised with Mark's predicament in having to refight what was now the most marginal seat in the country. I had anticipated the date of the poll based on the timing of the High Court hearing and was able to arrange for us to have a national party political broadcast on the eve of poll. I then found myself subject to a complaint from one of the independent candidates that this broadcast breached election law (because the cost of it was not included in our expenses), but this claim was quickly dismissed by the police.

One of the obvious concerns for Mark, and for his wife Belinda, was that they had incurred a lot of expenditure, as well as losing income during the general election campaign. Both of them were suffering great stress and Mark would now be without a salary from the time of his formal disqualification as an MP by the High Court until at least polling day, when it would begin again only if he was re-elected. I suggested a means by which he might address their immediate problem. I told him that on the day the writ was moved for the by-election, the bookmakers would advertise odds for the campaign. I promised to ring him immediately that they were known, and advise him exactly how much money he needed to place on himself to win in order to recover his lost salary during this period. 'If you place any more money on yourself to win than that,' I said, 'that is entirely up to you. I don't want to know, but you won't lose your money.' I then explained that as part of this deal, he must then ring me back immediately and I would feel able to place a bet myself. When all this happened, and I rang to place my bet, the odds on Mark's winning were of course significantly less generous than when I had rung Mark, so I assumed that he had

---

49   The legal expense limit for a parliamentary by-election was now £100,000, but there are other costs to a campaign that are not included within the items of expenditure subjected to this limit, including many activities before the candidate is in place.

followed my advice. I did not, however, want my confidence in the outcome to be known and my advice remained strictly confidential, though it was later something for which Mark and Belinda were very grateful.

Our own poll in the constituency had suggested that the result could be close again. But my strong instinct was that with a by-election campaign of the kind that we had by now become used to running, Mark's incredible hard work as Winchester's new MP, and the Conservatives in disarray nationally and locally, we should be able to win again quite comfortably. A big factor in helping to decide the outcome of the by-election would be that the closeness of the result in the general election put great pressure on all non-Conservative supporters to back Mark this time, and put the result beyond doubt. I wanted an emphatic victory to maintain the party's momentum from the general election, and to show that our gains were not a 'flash in the pan'. The key to this would be keeping everyone's perception of the campaign focused on Mark's narrow two-vote margin in May. I briefed Paddy and our newly enlarged group of MPs accordingly.

Labour's by-election campaign was very low profile, as we had hoped, and as I had discussed with Labour officials privately. They were more concerned with trying to secure a gain for themselves in the Beckenham by-election that was to be held on the same day. Paddy discussed mutually desirable outcomes with Tony Blair. I was even offered information by Labour as to where we could most easily find Labour voters to target for tactical voting messages. But I considered ourselves best able to do this without receiving any of Labour's private information, and I certainly did not want to suggest that there could ever be any reciprocal arrangement.

I generally wanted the party to adopt either of two different approaches to parliamentary by-elections; if I thought that we could win I set out to move heaven and earth to do so, and if I thought that we could not, I set out to at least maintain our share of the vote from the previous general election. Our overwhelming priority at this point was winning Winchester, and trying to do so as emphatically as possible. This meant that we could not devote significant resources to Beckenham where we had a good candidate in Rosemary Vetterlein. I knew Rosemary through the Scottish party, her parents still lived in Beckenham, and she later married the Liberal Democrat MP Malcolm Bruce. With minimal support from the party nationally (I had complaints from within our own party that we should have done more, and from people in Labour that we should have done much less), Rosemary successfully maintained our general election vote share at 18 per cent, in spite of Labour's campaign attempting to squeeze our support.

On the final Sunday of the campaign in Winchester, we delivered one of our by-election campaign newspaper specials. I branded this one as *Hampshire on Sunday* and it led with the headline: 'Oaten Edges Ahead'. We wanted to keep up the pressure to force people to choose between either keeping Mark as the new hard-working local Lib Dem MP, or returning to the days of Gerry Malone, who we portrayed as an occasional Conservative spokesman within the constituency. Paul Rainger led the drive to target Labour supporters. We identified most of them individually and he produced a series of targeted leaflets aimed at them, whilst I produced a series of direct mail letters from Mark and Paddy. By polling day, we were able to reduce Labour's support from 10.5 per cent in the general election to just 1.7 per cent.

On polling day, I did not realise that Mark was actually listening outside the slightly open door of my office in the HQ as I was briefing the people running our local campaign headquarters about the potential closeness of the result and the need to step up all our efforts. This then led Mark and Lembit Öpik[50] to adjourn to a room to draft a concession speech in the event that this might be needed. But as soon as I discovered them, I told them not to be so ridiculous and to go back out knocking on doors, which would be much more rewarding and enjoyable for them.

---

50 Relatively recently elected as the Lib Dem MP for Montgomeryshire and who was very supportive in the campaign.

As the counting took place, Mark was duly summoned by Candy to attend as his victory became clearer. When I spoke to him, he did not yet appreciate the scale of his impending landslide until I told him that his majority was already over 10,000 and rising very rapidly as more ballot boxes were opened. I had tried to keep the media focused on the potential closeness of the result for as long as possible in order to maximise the impact of our eventual victory. Some of them were by now used to my approach at by-election counts, and they soon had a very clear idea as to what was happening. None of them, however, expected our majority of 21,556. Mark had obtained 37,066 votes (68 per cent), compared to Gerry Malone's 15,450 (28 per cent). Over various by-elections I always compared the canvass analysis from different campaigns and I had noted the remarkable similarity between our canvass returns in the Newbury by-election and those now in Winchester. It was not a surprise to me therefore that the eventual results were almost identical. Gerry Malone was now the defeated candidate, having been the Conservatives' campaign manager in Newbury, where four years earlier his candidate had lost to us by 22,055 votes.

BECOMING A PEER

In the five years before the 1997 general election, my tiny bedsit in Dolphin Square had enabled me to work extraordinarily long hours at Cowley Street (when I was not away at by-elections and other party events). But it was far too small to be any kind of home. In spite of our electoral successes, the 'post-election blues' also returned and that summer was the first time that I sought professional counselling help to try to deal with them. A contributory factor to my state of mind was undoubtedly the way in which I had led a most unhealthy existence over the course of the previous parliament. My only exercise was an occasional swim in Dolphin Square's basement pool. I was often at early-morning meetings, or at my desk until very late in the evening. My habit in those days often included getting to the 'Top Curry Centre' in Pimlico just before it closed at midnight, sometimes accompanied by Graham Elson. Ann and I had intended to find a London property over the summer, but a holiday, and then spending our weekends in Winchester, delayed our search.

I was very mindful at this time of a conversation that I had had with Paddy shortly after the general election whilst we walked over Lambeth Bridge to Westminster following one of the meetings held at his Methley Street flat. Paddy had asked me about my future plans. I admitted to some personal frustration that whilst I had now helped to elect many other people to the House of Commons, I had not been able to seek election myself as I had previously considered doing. He said that he had always wondered if I wanted to stand, having given so much help to many candidates and MPs (including him). I told him that I was thinking again it was possibly time that I sought my own parliamentary career. In a very strange tone, he then said that this 'could be a disaster for the party'; and quickly explained that he was talking about the damage that could be done to the party's overall standing and election prospects if I had to give up running our campaigns in order to try to become an MP myself. He immediately suggested, pointing across the bridge to the House of Lords, that there was a way in which I could play a role in Parliament *and* continue running elections for the party. This idea, of course, had many attractions for me, because I did want to be able to pursue political issues in Parliament, but I was also conscious of the fact that my best opportunity to win a seat as an MP might have just passed with the 1997 general election. I had also seriously considered standing for the European elections in the East Midlands where I would have stood a very good chance of selection having been a popular regional organiser there for four years. But I gave up consideration of this prospect when Paddy suggested combining my campaign job with being in the House of Lords. I subsequently briefed Nick Clegg on the East Midlands prospect for him as he was unlikely at this point to find a Westminster seat and was looking for somewhere to stand in the European elections.

My longer-term strategy for the party was always based upon trying to help get enough Lib Dem MPs elected to hold the balance of power in the House of Commons, and force one of the other major parties to concede the principle of proportional representation. We had not achieved this yet, but I felt also that quite a few candidates who hadn't quite made it in 1997 (like Norman Lamb) could make it in future, and that the national tide would eventually turn against Labour. I wanted to continue helping the party to grow, but I also had to recognise that the party was unlikely to be able to provide me with any further career progression, or a salary akin to that of the party's chief executive, let alone anywhere near to that of my many Lib Dem student contemporaries who had gone into public affairs. At this time, my salary was little more than half that of the MPs I had helped to elect. Working as a peer would enable me to help pay the cost of a London property, and doing so would be necessary if I was to attend the Lords regularly and continue working for the party.

I was not included in the first list of eleven Lib Dem peers announced on 1 August after the 1997 general election. Four more appointments were made the following year. It was not until Paddy was preparing to stand down as party leader almost two years later that he was able to make another seven appointments to the Lords. He said that he was now keen to thank me for my efforts for the party whilst he was leader of it by including me in that list. At many Lib Dem constituency dinners and other party events afterwards, people asked how I had become a member of the House of Lords. I joked that Paddy was determined to prevent me from leaving my job running elections to try to become an MP myself. I explained that there were legally three ways in which you could be prevented from standing as an MP: you could be declared insane; you could be sent to prison for a year; or you could be made a peer. I therefore said that I was lucky he chose the latter route!

I was introduced to the House of Lords in July 1999, and held a big party (together with the also newly ennobled Baroness Liz Barker) on the terrace of the National Liberal Club for all staff colleagues, our MPs, existing friends in the Lords, and of course friends and family who had supported me so well over all the years.

THE 'PROJECT' AFTER '97

In spite of Labour's 179 majority, Paddy still lived in hope that there would be a coalition with Labour in that parliament, and with it a change to proportional representation for future Westminster, as well as for other elections. It would be completely unfair, however, for anyone to suggest that this was a matter of Paddy's personal ambition rather than a real desire to achieve political reform. In early discussions about the subject, Paddy had explained to me his plan for other Lib Dem MPs to become Cabinet ministers, whilst he remained outside the Cabinet as party leader in order to demonstrate that any coalition was not about him, and in order to help preserve the party's independent position on key issues. Much later on (2007), he was offered a place in Gordon Brown's Cabinet as Secretary of State for Northern Ireland; and this could have led to him later being appointed to more senior positions in Brown's government. But Paddy was always clear to me that any coalition would require an agreement on major policy areas and delivering proportional representation, and that it would never be about his, or anyone else's, personal ambition to be in government.

In the summer following the 1997 general election, Paddy and Tony Blair agreed that a Joint Consultative Committee (JCC) would be formed between Labour and the Liberal Democrats, and it was generally considered to have the status of a formal Cabinet Committee. It was a significant step in the Lib–Lab relationship, but was well short of coalition. It had the stated aim of taking forward the work that we had done in the Cook-Maclennan Committee prior to the general election.

But Paddy's intention to extend the JCC's remit beyond constitutional issues was clear even before it met. At the 'Jo group', both Bob Maclennan and I expressed strong concerns that we might, if we went beyond cooperation on constitutional matters, be unable to maintain distinctive positions to those of Blair's government. We were not alone in this feeling, but those who shared our reservations about the process were not always able to express their concerns at these meetings. Most of the MPs did not know of the existence of the 'Jo group', but many of them became aware of where Paddy was trying to take the party with the new JCC and felt less constrained about expressing their concerns at Parliamentary Party meetings. Some of the MPs not included in Paddy's loop were angry to discover indirectly what was happening. Much of the programme agreed by the Cook-Maclennan Committee was successfully legislated for in the first eighteen months of the Blair government, but there was also some significant backtracking by Blair about what we had agreed. We felt bounced, for example, by his sudden announcement that there would be referendums to approve the creation of the Scottish Parliament and the Welsh Assembly. In Scotland, the creation of the Parliament had previously come to be regarded as 'the settled will of the Scottish people'. Jim Wallace was furious about this particular change to Labour's earlier agreement to simply get on with the legislation for the creation of the Parliament, and our Scottish MPs came close to opposing the Bill to provide for the referendum there.

The Scottish referendum was held on 11 September 1997 and the principle of establishing the Parliament was supported by 74 per cent of those voting. Blair also insisted on a separate vote for it to have tax-raising powers and this was agreed to by 64 per cent of those voting. The Welsh referendum was then held a week later with the hope that Wales would not wish to deny itself an Assembly, if Scotland had a Parliament. The vote, however, was only won by the narrowest of margins, with 50.3 per cent voting in favour. Blair's caution in insisting that there be these two referendums nearly meant that Wales had to do without its Assembly. The narrow victory there may also have been a factor in his waning enthusiasm for referendums.

The creation of the JCC gave our party some credibility, with Conservatives like Ken Clarke openly expressing his fears that this step was consigning his party to complete irrelevance. But there was also opposition to it within Labour's ranks, and concern about it within our own. Most Lib Dems adopted a pragmatic approach, hoping that it would help deliver our much-desired constitutional reforms. One of its members, Alan Beith, spoke of the irony of having to sign the Official Secrets Act when he joined it in order to promote causes such as Freedom of Information. Labour was later to significantly water down what we expected to achieve in relation to that issue.

Charles Kennedy, who had always been somewhat distant from Paddy (despite being president for four years whilst Paddy was leader), spoke for many party members in his interviews at the September '97 Lib Dem conference when he said that we were 'in danger of pulling punches against Labour'. Charles spoke of how the JCC should be confined to constitutional affairs and of 'blood on the carpet' if Paddy tried to take the party into a coalition. This was also Charles positioning himself to be an alternative leader, after some years in which he had been much less engaged with the party. On this issue, Charles was also positioning himself differently to Ming Campbell, with whom Charles had had a very good relationship in the past. Many people assumed they had effectively agreed that if Paddy stood down early in the parliament, Ming would receive Charles's support; and vice versa if Paddy stood down later in the parliament. Whilst there was never such a pact as that supposedly agreed by Blair and Brown, there would inevitably have been some problem with such an agreement between them in any event, as Paddy eventually stood down close to the mid-point of the parliament.

The setting up of the Commission to recommend an alternative (proportional) voting system was crucial to Paddy's coalition hopes. This was eventually established in December 1997, with Roy Jenkins, a longstanding supporter of PR, as chair, thereby giving us great hopes about the potential outcome. But the negotiations over establishing it revealed that Blair was a long way from conceding that there should be a proportional system for Westminster. It had been easy for him to make very sympathetic noises to Paddy about the prospect prior to the general election, but I don't think he gave much thought to what it actually meant. He simply knew how important the concept was to Paddy and that he wanted the Lib Dems inside his 'big tent' if possible and that he needed the Lib Dem voting strength in the House of Lords in order to get legislation through.

There were lengthy discussions about the remit for the Commission. The Cook-Maclennan Committee, and Labour's own manifesto, had clearly referenced a referendum on a 'proportional alternative to first past the post'. It now appeared from our dealings with Peter Mandelson that Labour hoped that an eventual referendum might instead be on the 'Alternative Vote' system, which is far from proportional. Peter Mandelson's own memoirs[51] show that he believed that AV was as far as Blair would ever have been prepared to go. One of the ironies of the discussions between Blair and Ashdown about electoral reform was that neither of them appeared to understand very much about it. I heard an account of how Andrew Adonis[52] had to explain to his surprised boss how this meant linking the proportion of seats to the proportion of votes. Paddy reported back how Blair was personally hostile to any system that would, for example, have denied Mrs Thatcher her overall majority in 1979 with 44 per cent of the popular vote. Blair himself had obtained just over 43 per cent of the vote in 1997.

Whilst many people have accused the Lib Dems of being obsessed with electoral reform, Paddy himself knew very little about electoral systems. When I was assisting him with the writing of his diaries he sent

---

51   Peter Mandelson, *The Third Man*, p. 257.
52   A former Lib Dem candidate who had defected to Labour in order to get a job with Tony Blair in Downing Street; later became a very successful minister and then a crossbench peer before returning to Labour.

me a draft footnote explaining what he considered to be the differences between various systems. I had to say that I had never read a less accurate account of them! I feared that their discussions were, to use the old cliché, 'the blind leading the blind'. A draft of the proposed Commission remit sent to Paddy by Jonathan Powell on behalf of Blair even suggested that *any* voting system could be considered by it, presumably meaning that first past the post could be retained. A compromise was eventually agreed over the remit saying that the commission was required to take into account the need for 'broad proportionality'. This watering down was also accompanied by requirements not previously agreed to consider the need for stable government and the maintenance of a link between MPs and geographical constituencies. These latter points were of course the arguments most used by proponents of first past the post for their opposition to proportional representation. Before accepting the position as chair and agreeing the remit for the Commission, Roy Jenkins (with Paddy) dined with Tony Blair at Downing Street and at the end of the meal asked to meet with Blair alone. I have no doubt that he asked for a basic assurance that Blair intended to support the findings of his commission, before agreeing to undertake the role. He was later to be bitterly disappointed, having had such high hopes initially and having acted as a mentor to the New Labour Prime Minister.

It was clear in the early spring of 1998 that the party's strategy would be the subject of great controversy at the Lib Dem Southport conference in March. A week before the conference, Paddy's diaries describe how I went to see him immediately prior to a dinner that he was to have with the Blairs. I had sent him a memo in preparation for this which highlighted what I considered to be backsliding on progress towards PR, and therefore to express 'concern about the pace at which we are moving to TFM [The Full Monty]'.[53] I once again explained my view that PR was an essential prerequisite for any

---

53   Paddy Ashdown, *The Ashdown Diaries, Vol. II: 1997–1999*, p. 173. 'The Full Monty' was used by him as an expression describing a coalition and was a reference to the film that was very popular but considered somewhat risqué at the time.

coalition arrangement. But Paddy now appeared to be of the view that PR could follow coalition being formed, and shown to work, rather than an agreement on PR leading to the formation of a coalition. This was a significant shift in what many of us in the 'Jo group' had previously considered to be Paddy's 'bottom line'. Paddy's diaries described how he told Tony and Cherie over dinner that '"the project" is all that is keeping me in politics'. Paddy was pressing for a date for the PR referendum, assuming that the Jenkins Commission would report by the end of October, and Blair apparently suggested that it could possibly be held on the same day as the European elections i.e. June 1999.

In a follow-up note after the dinner, Paddy reiterated to Blair his understanding that November 1998 would be the target date for forming a coalition, and that the referendum on PR for Westminster would be held in 1999. He wanted a small group, including David Laws and Alan Leaman, to work on a policy prospectus for the coalition and another group, including Nick Harvey, David Walter and myself, to work on detailed planning for it. Shortly afterwards, I received a call from Pat McFadden in Downing Street suggesting that we should both talk about some of the difficulties in particular geographic areas that coalition between the parties might expose and which we would need to try to resolve. I took this as meaning that Labour were possibly rather more serious about the prospect than I had previously realised and I reported back to Richard Holme, who with Peter Mandelson would have had general oversight of the preparations. Richard had his own doubts about the viability of the project, and told me that the real danger he saw for us was that we could become part of a coalition, but fail to achieve PR. Lib Dems outside the 'Jo group' knew virtually nothing of all this, and nor, of course, did many people in the Labour Party, but there was some well-sourced media speculation. When asked about these issues at meetings such as those of the Federal Executive, Paddy often attacked those he considered to be 'conspiracy theorists'. I noted that his style was never to provide a direct denial, whilst leaving many people with the impression that he had done so.

There was no indication on Labour's side that Paddy's note was agreed by them. Throughout these events, I feared that Paddy might be hearing what he wanted to hear. Tony Blair appeared to have some skill in achieving this with many people, without there being palpable falsehoods. When Paddy sometimes showed me extracts of his diaries, I feared that there was more detail about the wine served at private Downing Street dinners (often Sancerre) than there was about agreements on proportional representation.

Paddy's public position to the party on the coalition issue was simply that we should 'rule nothing out, and rule nothing in', i.e. keep all options open whilst privately pursuing one of the options most vigorously. These private machinations were endangered by the potential of public debate. Julian Astle[54] prepared a strategy paper for discussion at the party's spring conference at Southport in March 1998. This was titled (somewhat ambiguously) 'No Glass Ceilings' in order to reflect our ambitions for future political success. The resulting motion for debate was not in itself controversial, but was bound to be subject to significant amendment.

Some weeks before the conference, I had had lunch with Charles Kennedy at the Millbank restaurant along the corridor from his Commons office, and he told me how he was considering tabling an amendment to the strategy motion ruling out the principle of a coalition during this parliament. I had to maintain some professional neutrality on public support for any proposition, but Charles understood my view that consideration of coalition options would best follow a PR election. I could see the very significant level of support within the party for the position that Charles was now considering taking, but I also recognised that if it was to succeed at the conference, then this would probably force Paddy out. I do not think that Charles, or the party generally, wanted that outcome at this point, and he did not table such an amendment.

---

54   Formerly a researcher for Nick Harvey, who worked with me at Cowley Street, and later with Nick Clegg as Deputy Prime Minister.

Paddy prepared for Southport by telling the 'Jo group' that if the party tied his hands on the coalition issue, he would indeed have to go. At the same time, there was a strong feeling in the party that it wanted some democratic constraints on his freedom of manoeuvre. As at the MPs' away day event in Oxford some years earlier, I feared that there might be a sudden and damaging resignation.

The proposal tabled at the conference for there to be some measure to ensure that the party was consulted on any 'significant shift in party strategy' was code for 'entering a coalition'. It was drafted by Gordon Lishman, a longstanding senior party figure, and it became known as 'the triple lock'. Gordon's proposal suggested that any such shift should require the approval in the first instance of three-quarters of the membership of the Parliamentary Party (MPs) and also of the Federal Executive. In this event, there would clearly have been little controversy over the proposal. But if this figure of 75 per cent was not achieved, then the approval of two thirds of the representatives voting at a party conference would be required (66 per cent). And if this was not achieved, a ballot of the entire party membership would be held requiring a simple majority (50 per cent). Most leaders could be expected to achieve majority support amongst the members in any postal ballot (although David Owen had failed to achieve this in the SDP when he tried to block the SDP/Liberal merger). But all these processes provided for the party to have some say on the principle, before the party leader and the MPs could act.

There were many discussions taking place within the party about how all this could be handled as I drove Paddy up to Southport (via a brief stop in Liverpool to welcome the defection to us of a Labour councillor, which was the lead item for the north-west regional news). I was regularly in touch with Liz Barker in the run-up to the debate, and she was using all her diplomatic skills as Conference Committee chair to ensure that it would be fair and democratic, but preferably did not result in anybody walking away. I talked also to one of the great critics of Paddy's project, the hereditary Lib Dem Earl (Conrad)

Russell, in order to try to gauge where we might be able to achieve sufficient consensus and avoid significant damage to the party that weekend. As I and others worked with Paddy on the final drafts of his conference speech for the Sunday (these often went through twenty to thirty drafts before being finalised), he spoke to us all of how this one might end up as a very short speech, announcing his resignation.

Great effort was made by all those around Paddy to persuade him that the 'triple lock' proposal was one that he should be prepared to live with. With much diplomatic manoeuvring behind the scenes, the proposal was carried by the conference, without any further or more specific proposals limiting what Paddy could do. But very early on the Sunday morning all members of the 'Jo group' were woken by telephone calls at about 6.15 a.m. to advise us of a meeting in Paddy's hotel room at 6.45 a.m. Paddy had had one of his sleepless nights. He had been persuaded the day before to accept the 'triple lock' proposal, but now he said that he felt he had been 'stuffed'. Richard Holme, who could be masterful in managing party leaders in difficult circumstances, now sought to calm him down, and we all sought to persuade him that this was not the end of his political ambitions, and that it was not unreasonable for him to be expected to have to carry the party with him to some degree. He controlled most of the levers of power within the party and almost all the means of communication with members, and this would help him to get his way if need be. He eventually made his speech later that morning as it had been prepared, and with little reference to the controversy of the previous day's debate.

The Jenkins Commission eventually reported in September 1998. Roy himself had favoured a proposal that had been put forward by the Speaker's Conference on electoral reform in 1917. This would have meant adopting the Single Transferable Vote (STV) for multi-member constituencies in urban areas and the Alternative Vote (AV) in rural areas and which would retain single-member constituencies for them. This proposal would have met the objectives set out in the commission's remit. Blair apparently did not like the idea that this would again enable Conservatives to win seats in the urban areas from which they had been largely wiped out in 1997, suggesting that he could not really accept the basic concept of proportional representation at all. The fact that Blair appeared to have vetoed this proposal showed that the Commission was somewhat less independent than was sometimes suggested.[55]

A rather strange system (to be known as AV+) was finally proposed by the Commission. This scheme was really 'barely proportional', let alone 'broadly proportional'. But whilst some people in the party wanted to insist on a more proportional system, and Paddy had possibly led them to believe that he had a hand to play in negotiating the system, I knew that in practice 'beggars could not be choosers', and that this was the best that we were likely to achieve in the foreseeable future.

Hopes were initially very high amongst supporters of electoral reform that there would soon be a referendum putting forward the Commission's alternative to first past the post. I had spent much time that year in meetings with the Electoral Reform Society Council and the nascent 'Yes' campaign to win the referendum (known as 'Make Votes Count'). But within days of the government press conference announcing the conclusion of the Commission, it seemed obvious that the proposal was going nowhere. Roy Jenkins had told the press conference of his recognition that his report 'would not excite the country in the same way as the 1832 Great Reform Act which had caused many riots and the death of three protesters in Derby', but I do not think that he was prepared for how little interest in it would be shown by the government that had commissioned it. Tony Blair's statement about it was at best noncommittal, saying 'that it made a powerful case for the system that it advocated'. In the aftermath of its publication, the 'Jo

---

55   Other Commission members such as the Labour peer David Lipsey opposed this proposal because of the difficulty involved in explaining in a referendum that there would be two different voting systems in the same election, even though voting in both cases would have been by 1, 2, 3.

group' was regularly told by Paddy that Blair would make some 'warm words' more firmly in support of the Jenkins proposal. So keen was Paddy to hear them, that when Blair said something about the report in the House of Commons, he tried to suggest to us that these were indeed the hoped-for 'warm words', but Hansard confirmed that this was clearly not the case.

Labour soon began suggesting to us again that the Alternative Vote system may instead be acceptable to them, and asking us to support it. Peter Mandelson addressed a 'Make Votes Count' rally of electoral reform supporters, telling the organisation that had been set up to support whatever Jenkins recommended that it should now change its objective to favour the Alternative Vote. AV would make it easier for the largest party in an election to obtain an overall majority, and if it had existed in 1997 Labour would have won by an even larger majority, so it was hardly surprising that they might support it. The Conservatives would have won even fewer seats under this system in 1997. It would, however, have protected the position of the Liberal Democrats (whilst we remained the third party and reliant on tactical voting to win many of our seats). Several times in Paddy's office I argued strongly with him that we should now accept the offer of AV, at least on the basis that 'a bird in the hand is worth two in the bush'. In response, he would only keep repeating that 'Roy Jenkins is not in favour [of us now accepting such a compromise]'. In turn, I kept saying that this in itself 'is not a reason at all'. Roy himself later considered that not accepting AV when it was being offered at this point was one of the greatest mistakes of his political life.

A referendum at this time, if it had been strongly backed by a popular Labour government (whose support rose to over 60 per cent in some polls), with the Lib Dems also remaining in a very popular position, and with the Conservatives marginalised, would have been won. But we failed to seize the opportunity that we had then. Fourteen years later, and in very different circumstances, AV was heavily defeated in a referendum, and after the loss of forty-eight Lib Dem seats in the

2015 general election, Nick Clegg admitted to the Lib Dem peers that he had underestimated the importance of trying to achieve at least this measure of electoral reform if the Lib Dems were to survive serving in a coalition. Not trying to achieve the introduction of the Alternative Vote system for Westminster in 1998 was later to prove a costly mistake.

In spite of what I felt was the most disappointing response to the Jenkins Commission, and the offer of AV only, Paddy remained wedded to his hopes that we could still make progress on proportional representation by working closely with Labour. He argued that we needed to win Labour's trust by demonstrating to them that we would not simply use the power that PR might give us to do a deal with the Tories. He felt that we needed to show that we could work with Labour in a stable arrangement before they might concede anything further on electoral reform. It seemed to me that fairer representation might be conceded by Labour for the House of Commons, providing that the Lib Dems could only make deals with them, and undertake never to exert any leverage through use of the 'balance of power'.

In November 1998, Paddy tried to force the pace again in the direction of a closer alignment with Labour, and in the hope that a coalition could still be formed. He and Tony Blair produced a 'Joint Statement' saying that they would extend the remit of the JCC to more policy areas. In planning for this, Paddy had even spoken of the idea of our MPs turning up for their regular weekly meeting, and finding Tony Blair there to speak to them about the proposal. He potentially saw himself sitting in the Cabinet Room as members of it arrived to see how Blair was in turn bouncing them into an agreement. Paddy described this process as 'undressing in public'. Whilst Blair never addressed our MPs, and Paddy never turned up to a Cabinet meeting, there was indeed much 'blood on the carpet'. There were very fiery meetings of the Parliamentary Party and the Federal Executive, where I observed that the protagonists in the arguments were relatively evenly divided, but with Paddy having to depend for support largely on what might have been called the 'payroll vote'. The leader in such circumstances always holds most of the aces if only through powers of patronage. It was a sign of some desperation that Paddy brought in Roy Jenkins to address the rebellious MPs and plead for them to support him. When it was proving difficult for Paddy to win agreement, it was even suggested that there should be a ballot of all party members about the principle of being able to extend the remit of the JCC. I felt that this proposal could degenerate into farce, and would not settle anything as arguments would then continue over which particular policy areas its remit could be extended to.

The public aim of the Joint Statement, according to Paddy and to Tony Blair, was to help end the 'destructive tribalism' of the past. They denied that it was about a merger, a coalition, or a pact, but it was highly suggestive of the direction of travel that they might be seeking. I had been comfortable in the past with necessary cooperation on constitutional reform issues. But in the absence of proportional representation, I feared damaging consequences to the party if we had, as Labour suggested, 'similar cooperation on health, education, modernising the welfare state and pushing towards European integration'. Paddy's position now, as he explained it to me, was that he believed we had to demonstrate how partnership government worked, before people would vote for proportional representation in a referendum. But they were never to get that chance.

Much internal discussion by Lib Dem activists in those days took place through an internet conferencing network.[56] I had promoted this heavily throughout the party as a means of rapidly disseminating information and exchanging views. Those subscribing to Lib Dem conference networks were verified by the membership department as being party members. Paddy was obsessive about electronic communication, and to his credit took seriously the many hundreds of persistent postings on this network expressing reservations about what would happen if we had similar policies to Labour on issues such as health, education and welfare. For a few days Paddy appeared to work through

56 Known as CIX (originally Compulink Information eXchange), an online-based conferencing discussion system.

much of the night trying to answer his critics' concerns. He recognised the scale of party resistance, but as ever believed that he could take the party so far, that things would settle down, and that he could then move the party further again.

In spite of Paddy's hopes, the more fundamental problem was that Blair was clearly not moving towards either PR or bringing Lib Dems into his government. Blair remained at best unpersuaded about PR, with Robin Cook being the only enthusiastic proponent of it within his Cabinet. There remained considerable hostility to the Lib Dems within Labour, many of whose members were still angry about the SDP 'split', and they saw absolutely no need to include 'their enemies' in a government which had such a large majority in its own right. Peter Mandelson appeared to be one of very few people within Labour taking a more pragmatic approach and who saw the benefits to them of silencing one of their major critics, and establishing a kind of 'in-surance policy' in the event that things eventually turned sour for the Labour government. Other Labour figures seemed to take the view in discussions with me that Labour was in any event now invincible, and so not in need of an arrangement of any kind.

Although Paddy had narrowly won the key votes amongst the MPs and Federal Executive about extending the remit of the JCC, it was a pyrrhic victory, as it soon became clear that there was to be no real movement towards either PR or coalition. Paddy told Tony Blair, sometime before he began to confide in fellow Liberal Democrats, that he would soon stand down as leader. His mood at this point was very low and he at least temporarily lost confidence in the sustainability of the Liberal Democrats as an independent party. His 'project' had not succeeded in the way that he had hoped, and he seemed to me to have also temporarily at least lost his self-confidence. He no longer seemed to recognise his own significant role in helping to bring about an end to eighteen years of Conservative government, and then helping to achieve some very significant measures of constitutional reform with far-reaching consequences.

Paddy held many of his most important meetings in the early morning at 8.30 a.m. (or earlier), and the most confidential of them at his Methley Street flat in Kennington. There were now a series of 7.30 a.m. meetings there as he asked some of us for advice about when and how to announce his forthcoming resignation. Discussing his plans felt quite emotional for those who had worked with him so closely and for so long. There was no persuading him out of the principle that he would resign and not lead the party at the next general election. He wasn't sure, however, whether to quit quite quickly, or to stay on as party leader for the European elections in June 1999. I took the view that we really needed him to lead us then, and that if he resigned before the Euro-elections people might assume that it was because we were going to do badly. I did not think that anybody else would want to be leader before then, and it would be difficult for any new leader to pick up the reins just before important national elections. He considered keeping his plans to resign secret until after June. I knew, however, that a secret such as this was unlikely to last very long. I advised, therefore, that he announce his retirement in the New Year, but saying that it would take effect immediately upon the election of his successor after the European elections.

Eventually, 20 January 1999 was chosen as the date for the announcement that he would be resigning. Roy Jenkins was one of those taken into his confidence, and Roy assumed that Ming would have been too. But this was not the case, and when Roy spoke to Ming about it, Paddy then went to some length to tell Ming rather disingenuously that he was staying on. As was typical with Paddy's preparation for any significant event, a planning grid was drawn up for him to inform key individuals privately on the day that his resignation would be announced, and then for the Parliamentary Party to be informed collectively at their weekly meeting. In order to try to make sure that members of the party were properly informed in a positive way, I asked Deirdre Razzall to 'hold the front page' of the *Liberal Democrats News*, which was always printed on a Wednesday evening. This would now be the evening of Paddy's resignation statement. The timetable for the day of the announcement also listed that at 6.20 p.m. 'CJR' departed for Australia. This was actually a long-planned visit to speak at the Conference of the Australian Democrats, and I was quite glad to be away for the first week after Paddy's decision became public.

I had previously advised Paddy that in the event of his resignation Charles Kennedy would be likely to attract approximately 50 per cent of the vote of the members, with the remaining 50 per cent of the vote split between any other candidates. Paddy had actually done very little by way of succession planning, although he had no obvious desire for Charles Kennedy to be his successor. He had observed Charles re-engaging with the party, and in response he told me that he had sought to promote Nick Harvey as 'campaigns chair' in order to let Nick speak more frequently for the party and raise his profile as a potential successor. Nick was not, however, an unequivocal supporter of the project and Paddy's inclusion of him in his most confidential discussions was not consistent. Paddy had clearly worked on the assumption that Ming, who was much less equivocal about 'the project', would not wish to be a candidate in a leadership election. In this, Paddy miscalculated. Richard Holme was advising Ming on his putative candidature and Paddy asked me if I could also get involved with his campaign, if he stood. I said that I couldn't, as this would not have been at all appropriate because members of staff were expected to be strictly neutral once such election campaigns were underway.

Before very long, the potential field of candidates for the party leadership multiplied rapidly. David Rendel rang me in Australia to seek my advice about standing. I thought that I had been very tactful in our conversation by telling David that we had worked very well together in his by-election campaign, and that my advice to him now was to ring round as many party members as possible in order to gauge his level of support. On my return, I discovered that he had indeed spoken to many party members, but that they were completely unaware as to why he had called them. He had therefore misread their politeness on the phone for potential support and he misunderstood my message that I did not think he had sufficient standing amongst the membership to be a serious contender.

Simon Hughes's candidature was widely anticipated and he, like Charles, had never been part of Paddy's inner circle. Jackie Ballard entered the race as the only woman prepared to do so (she was one of only three female MPs that we had at the time). The strangest candidature appeared to be that of Malcolm Bruce, as he was a close friend of Charles, and Malcolm had chosen Charles to be his best man when he married Rosemary. I knew, however, that Malcolm had seriously considered standing in 1988, when Paddy had outpolled Alan Beith, and that Malcolm was now more than worried about Charles's state of health and whether or not this would really permit Charles to undertake the role. Another potential candidate with considerable ambition was Don Foster, who wished to stand on a strongly 'pro-project ticket'. In frustration with the growing number of candidates, and their inability to agree amongst them who was best placed to stand, Paul Tyler also threatened to throw his hat into the ring (which made him the ninth of our forty-six MPs to declare themselves publicly as the potential successor to Paddy).

For some years, most people had anticipated a Charles Kennedy versus Simon Hughes contest. Nick Harvey's hopes had rested on him being the clear alternative to either of them, and when this was obviously not going to be the case he withdrew from the contest, effectively saying that Ming would now be his first choice for leader. Before long, Don Foster also realised that he did not have sufficient support. Eventually Ming himself also stated that he would not be standing, saying that the party appeared to be seeking a rather more 'emollient choice' i.e. Charles Kennedy. Ming, Nick, Don and Paul together with Archy Kirkwood, who had all been senior lieutenants under Paddy, then agreed that they would all act together in relation to the election, and having secured a statement from Charles that he would not rule out further cooperation with Labour in future, they all agreed to support him.

There was, however, some unpleasant media briefing against Charles. In my experience, the major problems with leadership elections invariably result from the actions of overzealous supporters of the rival candidates. These people know that if they are on the winning side they are likely to play a major role in the party in future. There were many people (including me) who had concerns about Charles and alcohol, but would never have indulged in media briefing about it. It was quite damaging to the party when some of these people raised their concerns with the media in a way that significantly damaged both Charles's reputation and internal relationships when he became leader. I was also aware of how Simon Hughes had tried to bring together Jackie Ballard and David Rendel with some of their supporters to agree that it would be better to have a single 'centre-left' candidate i.e. allow Simon a clear run against Charles. The meetings were inconclusive, on the basis that David Rendel in particular was unrealistically confident about his prospects.

The official campaigns were not allowed to begin until after the local and European elections of that year, when there were eventually five candidates for the leadership: Charles Kennedy, Simon Hughes, Malcolm Bruce, Jackie Ballard and David Rendel. As a staff member, I could not be involved in the leadership election campaign. Nevertheless, one of our party activists, Alex Folkes, decided to approach all five of the leadership campaign teams to explain privately that he would vote for whoever Chris Rennard really supported as 'this person was bound to be the best candidate'. He later told me that he had received assurances from all five campaigns that I was privately supportive of them! I cast my own vote for Simon Hughes whilst recognising that Simon could sometimes offer inspiration and frustration in equal measure, and that he would have been very difficult to manage as leader, but like his friend Malcolm Bruce, I doubted if Charles could do the job without dealing with his alcohol problem. I was probably not right in this calculation, but it was a difficult one.

When the votes for the five candidates were counted and the result declared by Diana Maddock as president of the party in early August 1999, Charles Kennedy had polled 45 per cent of first preferences (close to the result that I had first forecast to Paddy). Simon Hughes had run a much stronger and even more energetic campaign than many people anticipated, and he finished second with 32 per cent of the first preferences. When David Rendel's, Jackie Ballard's and Malcolm Bruce's votes (in that order) were then transferred, Charles was ahead of Simon by 57 per cent to 43 per cent, a comfortable margin, but certainly not the landslide that some of Charles's supporters had anticipated. I had agreed to the hiring of the basement room in the Commonwealth Club and a film crew to record Charles's acceptance speech in the belief that it would be very useful footage for future party broadcasts. Unfortunately, the room was rather warm and Charles sweated profusely whilst making his speech, and I felt that this was a further indication of the health problem that he needed to overcome. Charles's sense of humour was a great asset to him and to the party, but his willingness to make a good joke, rather than a good political point, was not always welcomed by me. On this occasion, he departed from his script to say that 'it would be downhill all the way from here'. Despite my reservations, I was determined to support him personally and try to help him use his natural communication ability to fulfil his ambitions for the party. I never told him about my own vote, although I think that he was a little suspicious about it.

The timing of Paddy's resignation statement allowed the new leader some time to find his feet without immediately having to fight a major election. Whilst the leadership election had been taking place, my own focus of attention had been on the local elections in May in Scotland, Wales and much of England, and the European elections in June. My partner in planning 'Campaign '99' was Kate Fox, who I had now persuaded to work with me and Nick Harvey (who she later married) coordinating the efforts of the Campaign and Communications Committee in its role preparing for the party's major election campaigns.

The local elections that year saw us gain an extra 383 council seats across Great Britain. The financial support of the Joseph Rowntree Reform Trust had been instrumental in supporting the party's recovery through local election successes since 1990. But one of my concerns when this support came to an end a few years later was that some of the advances that we achieved with their support might be reversed. Some of the richer regions of the party (generally those in the south of England, where membership income was substantially higher) might have been able to finance their own independent schemes for supporting the local elections if they had wanted to, and some of the strongest supporters of 'regionalisation' within the party wanted every region to be left to its own devices to decide whether or not to help support local council candidates. The problem was that some of them were in a much weaker financial position, and many of them were unwilling to do so, even if they had the funds. When the Rowntree grants had ended, I had therefore proposed and won agreement for a scheme in which all parts of the party contributed, and a committee was created to make grants to support particular local campaigns. This approach helped us in 1999, for example, to gain control of Sheffield.

The local elections were followed five weeks later by the first European elections in the UK to be fought using proportional representation. The 'closed list' system that Labour introduced for these elections was not one that Liberal Democrats would have chosen, but our attempts to amend the Bill in Parliament to provide for greater voter choice did not succeed. The list system did, however, allow the party to take a very significant step in ensuring that the outcome of the election, in terms of seats that we won, would be gender balanced, and I was a strong supporter of this principle. Nick Harvey, who then chaired the Candidates Committee, and his deputy, Helen Bailey, had driven forward a proposal through the Federal Conference to introduce a system known as 'zipping'.

This involved creating separate lists of women and men for our party members to choose as candidates in each region. Each of the regions had to be ranked in order of winnability according to the results within them at the previous general election. An exception was made for the South West region, where the sitting Lib Dem MEPs Graham Watson and Robin Teverson were defending their seats. The list for the most winnable region, the south-east of England, therefore, had to be headed by a woman. We would have equal numbers of women and men at the top of each list and a gender balanced outcome however many seats we won.

The scheme was not without some controversy, however, and I had to help Nick, Helen and others fight to ensure that we could achieve the desired gender balanced outcome. Firstly, it was challenged by one of the men who hoped to head the West Midlands list, John Hemming, who had narrowly failed to win Birmingham Yardley in the general election. He took the first steps to begin proceedings at an employment tribunal alleging sex discrimination. This was on the basis that the ordering of the lists that had been determined by previous general election results meant that only a woman could head the list in that region, and this blocked his employment prospects.

The Candidates' Office was amongst my responsibilities at HQ at the time, and I had to work hard with the excellent Candidates Officer Sandra Dunk to get the plan implemented and to ensure that we resisted any challenge robustly in legal terms. This involved securing legal advice from one of the leading QCs in the field, Cherie Booth. At one of Paddy's meetings with her husband Tony Blair around this time, this advice was mentioned, and Tony expressed the hope that a large fee was paid! It was in fact a very reasonable one, although some people in the party opposed us taking the advice. When we revealed her conclusion, which confirmed the ultimate legality of our approach, but not the advice in full, our 'zipping plan' was strongly challenged by some party members who doubted the veracity of the legal advice, and wanted it all to be made public. Our problem was that Cherie Booth advised that we would eventually win any action at the European level (so we were in fact acting properly and legally) but that the cost of defending such an action could have been over £250,000 and may have taken some years, and we might have lost actions in the UK courts in the meantime. In response to the controversy we had to share the full legal advice with the Federal Executive, even though this might have assisted legal challenges to what we were doing. In the end, John withdrew his objections when he saw the calculations behind the allocation of the lists.

We then faced challenges to the process from some of the regions in England, who tried to suggest that they agreed with the gender balance mechanism across the country, but wanted variation in their own region to help choose a particular favourite candidate. This was not always a male candidate, but the problem was that once one region decided to opt out of the carefully constructed arrangement, others made it plain that they would do so also. I then had to oversee negotiations with some of these regions to enforce the zipping agreement and prevent 'opt-outs' leading to the unwinding of the whole system.

The 1999 European elections were Paddy's last national election campaign as party leader. I had booked the Playhouse Theatre by Embankment station for his last rally as party leader and we packed it out with nearly 1,000 supporters to give him an emotional farewell. The election results were seen as a success for him, and for the party as it prepared to elect a new leader. We won ten of the eighty-four seats in Great Britain; electing five female and five male Lib Dem MEPs. In each of the three European elections in which I was most closely involved, we elected between ten and twelve Lib Dem MEPs, with gender balance each time. The results showed how the introduction of proportional representation, with supporting positive action, can produce gender balanced outcomes.

The run-up to the election in which Charles became party leader also coincided with a very difficult time period at the party's Cowley Street HQ. Graham Elson had retired as general secretary at the end of 1997. I had been elected as the staff representative on the appointment panel to choose a new chief executive. Elizabeth Pamplin, his successor, had an impressive-looking CV, including having worked for the Cabinet Office at one point. The job now was supposed to be a very different role from Graham's.

After the 1997 general election, I had also been the staff representative on a group appointed to undertake what was termed a 'medium-term review' of the party organisation. A 'short-term review' had already recommended some immediate economies that had to be made in the aftermath of the general election, including the abolition of Alan Leaman's post of director of strategy and planning. The medium-term review group looked at the post-election structure of the headquarters. It reported to the Federal Executive (FE) following a consultative session at the autumn conference, and concluded that the weaknesses at HQ were largely related to HR, admin, finance and IT. It was therefore decided to seek a chief executive whose role would be largely confined to those areas, as opposed to the running of the election campaigns, which had become my own major responsibility.

The impressive growth of the party in electoral terms was to be sustained by allowing the professional campaign structure to continue growing, changing the previous assumption that our general elections would have to be run very largely by volunteers from outside that structure (and working in the time that they could take off from their regular work commitments). Consideration was given to changing my job title to something like 'political director' to reflect the fact that in future I would effectively be the 'chief executive of the election campaigns', overseeing them at both constituency and national level. I decided, however, that I was comfortable retaining the title of 'director of campaigns and elections'. With hindsight, this was possibly a mistake, as some people were evidently unaware of how the senior management structure had been changed.

Our breakthrough in the 1997 general election had been followed by further local election gains in May 1998 and in May 1999 (when at the same time we elected seventeen members of the Scottish Parliament, and six members of the Welsh Assembly). In June 1999, we elected ten members of the European Parliament. At this point, Tim Razzall was still party treasurer and I assisted him with the fundraising that paid for these campaigns, principally by producing campaign plans for potential donors. These were then agreed with the Scottish party (where Willie Rennie was now chief executive), with the Welsh party (with Chris Lines as chief executive) and with the group that I'd helped to create to support local election campaigns. Our successes, however, created some jealousy about the power that went with working with major donors on election plans, and some people thought that funds provided by the donors (including the Joseph Rowntree Reform Trust) could be diverted away from the agreed plans supporting candidates, and spent as various parts of the party organisation would have preferred. This would, of course, have led to a major drop in donations in future. I also noted that whilst a few years previously people were grateful for every penny that they ever received towards their election campaigns (never having received anything to support them in the past), some people now became jealous about what they thought others received.

Elizabeth Pamplin and the then chair of the Federal Finance and Administration Committee, Denis Robertson Sullivan (the pro-independence treasurer of the Scottish party), seemed to think the major donors would be happy for their contributions to be simply apportioned between the various national and regional party bodies. The successful national campaign model would therefore be dismembered.

In the run-up to the elections in May and June of 1999, Paddy was preparing to appoint his final list of peers, and included me. This new role was not an alternative to my job of running our election campaigns, and was intended to ensure that it continued. Standing for election as an MP, or as a councillor (as some members of staff had done previously), would have caused a real problem for me. But unless, or until, the House of Lords was reformed, I could not have faced the potential conflict of organising my own election campaign and those of the party's other candidates at the same time. Our leader in the House of Lords, Bill Rodgers, was happy with the role that I would play there.

After the elections, I organised the thank-you party for staff and volunteers in the national campaign, and this was held in the back garden of our Stockwell house. Such events to which all staff, volunteers and their partners were invited were always very popular and I felt it important to acknowledge properly all their efforts and contribution to the party. By then, Diana Maddock, as president, was able to make a speech thanking them all for their efforts. She closed her remarks by telling them that it would be announced the following day that I was to join her in the House of Lords. There was an enormous cheer from them all, whilst the press office team jokingly chanted, 'Embargo!' as the announcement was not officially to be made before midnight.

After some discussion, and following a meeting of the Finance and Administration Committee at the end of July, Elizabeth Pamplin left her post to seek other roles, and the Financial Controller that she had appointed also moved on shortly afterwards.

On the Friday after Charles Kennedy's election as leader, I met with him and Tim Razzall at the Congress Club, then a private dining restaurant in Great Peter Street (around the corner from Cowley Street). Charles quickly confirmed that he definitely wanted me to continue with my role leading the professional team preparing all the party's election campaigns. I confirmed that I was willing, but only on the basis that that was what he wanted. Tim had clearly moved quickly to make sure that this arrangement was in place before any of us departed for our holidays in August, and before the autumn conference. The lunch was a most enjoyable occasion and Charles was in great form. Over about four hours, however, we consumed five bottles of wine, and I realised that I could not personally manage many lunches like this. Ann rang me as soon as I got back to my desk in Cowley Street and suggested that I should refrain from speaking to anybody else for a while, given the state that I was in after lunch!

Charles had always relied on a closely knit and very small team of people, some of whom were not very involved with the party at national level prior to his election. Central to this team, and everything

Charles did, was Anna Werrin, who had worked part-time for Charles since he became an MP in 1983 and who was, until Charles's election as leader, a member of the Labour Party. She quickly joined the Lib Dems and moved from the part-time role organising the life of someone who had often not really been a full-time MP. Charles also relied heavily on Richard Grayson, who had become the party's director of policy, for speeches and policy ideas. The turnover of staff when leaders changed often meant the loss of much corporate memory. Paddy's staff all left, with the sole exception of James Lundie, who was (rightly) considered by Charles's team to be both very talented and very loyal.

Charles had built much of his personal reputation on his great sense of humour, displayed by the style in which he performed on programmes such as *Have I Got News for You*. These appearances were not without controversy within the party, as some people considered that he shouldn't do them anymore. But I was not amongst them. I believed that such exposure could be positive for the party, and helped to ensure that the Lib Dem profile did not fade when Paddy retired as leader, as many expected that it would. Charles's character on such programmes was not so easily demonstrated off camera when he was with groups of people that he did not know well, and whom he was unsure of trusting personally. He liked, therefore, to keep decision-making within a quite small, discreetly chosen group of people (sometimes meeting more formally with a few additional members as the 'Office Group') rather than with party structures, including the Parliamentary Party. Once he knew his direction of travel, however, he recognised the need to take people with him, and he had great ability in ensuring that they felt that they could follow him. It had been agreed as part of the medium-term review after 1997 that the chair of the party's future election campaigns should be the chair of the party's Campaign and Communications Committee (CCC). This was in order to provide some democratic accountability to the election role, whilst recognising that the party's Federal Executive would not elect someone to this position who would be unable to work with the party leader. In due course, Tim Razzall was elected as chair of the CCC. Whilst I was not chief executive of the party, Tim chose to style my role as 'chief executive of the general election campaign'. This recognised the respective roles of chair and chief executive that applied in many organisations. I then appointed Kate Fox as general election manager in charge of the logistics for that election. This was a job that she did superbly well, although she was regrettably not always included in Charles's inner circle.

Charles's first year as party leader was certainly difficult. He had been fortunate in the first instance to find an extremely capable interim chief executive who quickly took over on a temporary basis from Elizabeth Pamplin. Ben Stoneham restored good order and morale within Cowley Street and the wider party. Charles had known Ben well in SDP days as one of only a tiny handful of SDP parliamentary candidates who had come close to Charles's unique success in gaining a seat and becoming an SDP MP. We had discussed Ben's offer to help the party out over our lunch at the Congress Club. Sadly, however, Ben was only able to undertake the role temporarily in between being chief executive of a newspaper group and then becoming director of operations with responsibility for most of the business side of News International's operation in the UK. Ben helped to find another good interim chief executive (Alan Cole, a businessman from whom I also learned a lot about management in a short period of time) before another recruitment process resulted in Hugh Rickard (a former Navy Rear Admiral) becoming the next permanent chief executive. Hugh had the remit outlined in the medium-term review, but his first problem was that we had to move out from Cowley Street temporarily for major refurbishment to take place. We were only able to move back just prior to the 2001 general election campaign. Hugh handled the logistics of the move, and networking the HQ for the first time, extremely well. But I would not myself have chosen to move back to Cowley Street, which was far from ideal as a modern HQ. Hugh's logistical role allowed me to concentrate on the next general election campaign.

By the spring of 2000, the party's opinion-poll ratings and public satisfaction levels for Charles had drifted downwards. Charles was keen to try to reverse the situation and committed himself, for example, to devoting one day per week to Susan Kramer's campaign to become Mayor of London. This was agreed by his office, however, with little thought as to what he would actually do on those days, and what this would actually achieve. The events were low profile. His enthusiasm for the London campaign waned as he began to realise how difficult it would be for him and Susan to make much noticeable impact across London's seventy-four constituencies and standing against 'big gun' candidates Ken Livingstone, Frank Dobson and Steve Norris. He needed a result that would reverse the growing perception that he was not making a success of being party leader.

CHAPTER 9

THE KENNEDY
LEADERSHIP

ROMSEY

The opportunity for a Lib Dem leader to establish their reputation, and boost that of the party, has often come as a result of
the unfortunate demise of a fellow MP. I first heard of the potential
for a parliamentary by-election in Romsey as a result of several very
early-morning phone calls on 24 February 2000, from one of my then
deputy directors of campaigns, Gerald Vernon-Jackson. A friend's call
to Gerald in the middle of the night had alerted him to the fact that
the home of the Conservative MP for Romsey, Michael Colvin, had
burned to the ground. We had no idea at this point if he or anybody
else might have been inside, and it would have been most inappro-
priate to make any enquiries about this. But, as the media coverage
developed, we had to give thought to the possibility of a by-election.

Only three times in the last hundred years had the Conservative
Party in opposition lost one of its seats in a parliamentary by-election.[57]
Trying to win Romsey from the Conservatives in opposition would not
be easy. I appointed Gerald as the agent, and we were both determined
to try. The 1997 general election had seen the Tories' worst national

---

[57] Londonderry in 1911; Roxburgh, Selkirk & Peebles in 1965; and Winchester in 1997,
although Winchester was not technically a parliamentary by-election, but a rerun of the
general election contest there.

performance since 1832. But in the Romsey constituency, they had still maintained a majority of 9,623, polling some 46 per cent of the vote, with us a fairly distant second with just under 30 per cent. When the Conservatives had last won a majority nationally in 1992, they had a majority in Romsey of 22,000. The Tories had a new party leader in William Hague, who was successfully campaigning on populist issues such as immigration, 'saving the pound' and the Tony Martin case, in which a Norfolk farmer had been jailed for shooting a burglar in the back whilst he had been running away from his farm.

I did the maths and saw that if we could shave a little off the Tories' 1997 share of the vote, and manage to squeeze the Labour vote almost as effectively as we had done at Winchester, then a win for us became possible. I saw nothing to be lost by going for it. The weekend after the fire, and when Michael Colvin's death had become known, I travelled to meet Gerald and others in Romsey and we set in place the beginnings of our campaign. I had been immediately impressed by a newly approved parliamentary candidate there, who was also a local councillor, Sandra Gidley. The previous parliamentary candidate had also applied to stand, but he somewhat mysteriously withdrew. I was under some pressure to say that the selection should then be reopened, thereby allowing him to change his mind and re-enter the race, but I had no powers to do so, nor any instinct to try to persuade the local party to do this. As was often the case, a local councillor from within the constituency was to prove a very strong candidate for us and Sandra was a joy for Gerald and me to work with in the campaign.

There was once again great scepticism within the party about my view that Romsey could become another famous Lib Dem gain. After I briefed the Parliamentary Party about our initial plans to try to do so, I discovered that Mike Hancock, then a Hampshire MP and a former leader of Hampshire County Council, had spoken after I left the meeting and told his fellow MPs that my judgement about this was simply ridiculous, and that we could not win there. Charles was naturally nervous about overstating our prospects, and in particular how we might conduct the campaign, and I reassured him by agreeing to spend the entire six-week period in Romsey from mid-March until the likely polling day on 4 May.

We began our usual pattern of conducting surveys, delivering 'Focus' leaflets in many different editions, and taking up as many local problems as we could using our very good local councillors for information. Matthew Clark, a former Southampton councillor, came back down from Scotland to assist our campaign, and Cheltenham's highly experienced 'Focus' writer David Fidgeon also spent a lot of time with us, as Paul Rainger again oversaw much of the local campaigning.

The Conservatives struggled, as was so often the case in crucial by-elections, with their choice of candidate. I had expected them to choose the local chair of the Conservative Party. The succession of by-elections along the M3 and M4 over the past eight years meant that I was well-connected with the local media, and I was told that she was the likely choice. Instead, the local Conservative Party members chose Tim Palmer, an Eton-educated farmer and a Tory councillor from next-door Dorset. Bruce Parker, the legendary editor of BBC South, was quite shocked by the Tory choice and he interviewed Tory members as they left the selection meeting, one of whom remarked that she had voted for Tim Palmer 'because she liked his hair'. On such judgements by-elections were sometimes decided. The Tory members' decision confirmed my view that we must fight to win, even though most of the media assumed that an increased Tory majority was the very likely outcome.

Against this background, Gerald was superb in persuading our much-enlarged group of MPs that they must allow their staff to spend their spare time working in Romsey, and that their own constituency party staff and activists were needed to provide the core of our by-election workforce. I shared an office with Gerald in our Romsey HQ and his persistence on the phone ringing Lib Dem friends and contacts from all over the country has never been bettered in a by-election, and we could not have won without it. By-elections often also provided the best possible training 'on the job' for many of the party's MPs, candidates and organisers and we pointed this out to them at every opportunity. Jo Swinson, who five years later became the MP for Dunbartonshire East, often spoke of the essential campaign experience that she gained in her first proper by-election campaign as a helper at Romsey.

Our campaign gained some momentum from an early council by-election in Stockbridge, in the very Tory northern part of the constituency. We had no prospect of winning a council by-election there, but the swing that we achieved (from a negligible base) was theoretically sufficient for us to gain the Romsey parliamentary constituency. A small story that we managed to get in the *Daily Telegraph* to this effect then provided big headlines for our own leaflets across the constituency, suggesting that we were strongly challenging the Conservatives in the seat.

We conducted more market research for the Romsey by-election than in any campaign since Kincardine & Deeside nine years previously. This all confirmed the validity of maintaining the arguments that had proved to be so powerfully effective in our target seats in 1997, and showed that they were likely to prove effective again at the general election expected in 2001. The campaign hit out at Labour's record in failing to deliver in terms of local health and education services, policing, support for post offices and pensioners (who had been angered very recently by an increase in their pensions of just 75p per week). We blamed the Conservatives for many of the problems connected with the underfunding of public services locally, said that Labour had failed to remedy them, and put forward positive proposals of our own.

Romsey was a rough and bitter campaign in many ways. The stakes were very high as the next general election was approaching. William Hague appeared to be doing well at the time, and he wanted to confirm that the Tories were again challenging for power nationally. For us, I wanted to establish Charles's reputation as a successful leader following in Paddy's footsteps. He really needed a by-election win to prove that we were on track to retain and gain seats in the general election.

Our market research showed the much greater power of the likely main messaging that we proposed to use, as compared to that of the Tories. We asked our sample of Romsey voters which of the following two statements was their greater priority; either *A: Our next MP must make saving the pound and stopping Britain joining the single currency their 1st priority* (21 per cent) or *B: Our next MP must make getting more money for health, education and pensions their priority* (79 per cent). It was a crude test, but it gave me confidence that the Conservatives were not on the right track in their campaign. Our research also helped us to produce a great deal of direct mail segmented to different audiences within the constituency by geography, age and gender.

A few Conservative-leaning people in the constituency were fired up by the Tory campaign, but the tone of William Hague's attacks on 'bogus asylum seekers' backfired with others. The clarity of Charles Kennedy's opposition to this approach also helped to drive some Labour supporters towards voting for Sandra.

We were also helped by a few Conservative tactical blunders. Their attempt to disrupt a photo-opportunity with Charles Kennedy, Sandra Gidley and twenty-five Lib Dem MPs on the eve of poll backfired badly. Thuggish Young Conservatives held Tory placards a few inches in front of the cameras, blocking them from seeing our group photo – but coverage of these antics simply revealed their desperation and fear of the Lib Dems. An elderly lady featured on the TV news condemned this Conservative hooliganism. Few people would have known that she was Mrs Harvey, mother of Nick, our MP for North Devon, and who, with her husband Fred, had been in our HQ almost every day of the campaign. It was only when I discovered their identity that I realised why Nick himself was so well informed about what we were doing. It was always part of my routine to break off from writing leaflets etc. to spend significant time with all the volunteers, and I always considered it time very well spent.

A last-minute letter sent by the Conservatives to large numbers of Lib Dem supporters also backfired for them. It purported to be from a local Lib Dem councillor who had decided to back the Tory candidate 'in protest at the failure of Liberal Democrat MPs to resist government plans which threatened the future of many post offices'. We were able to rebut this, pointing out in our early-morning delivery on polling day that the 'local councillor' was not a Romsey councillor at all, but served on a Wiltshire council and had different reasons for defecting. We reiterated the facts about our defence in Parliament of local post offices.

At every stage of our campaign, we could point out the merits to people in the different parts of the Romsey constituency of having Sandra Gidley as an energetic and active local MP championing their cause. In contrast, we were able to suggest that the Conservative candidate was not someone in whom they could place their trust. His leaflets said that he was a local candidate 'born in Hampshire'. We were suspicious of this claim and obtained a copy of his birth certificate from Somerset House, as well as the copy of *The Times* announcing his birth, proving that he was born in London! The issue of trust has often proved crucial in such campaigns.

Our survey asking residents' views on the NHS was delivered to over 36,000 households and produced a posted-back response from over 6,000 of them. This was a staggering response for a direct mail campaign, but was in line with our experience of campaigning on this issue in target seats at the last general election. In spite of Gordon Brown committing additional funds to the NHS in his recent Budget, our polling and the survey showed an overwhelming feeling that the NHS was still seriously underfunded (68 per cent disbelieving claims that the government was now spending enough money on the NHS). The Lib Dem proposal to boost education spending by raising income tax by 1p in the pound, if necessary, still found strong resonance, with 54 per cent of our sample of Romsey voters more likely to support us because of this, and only 16 per cent less so.

The 'blue letters' that I drafted for Sandra Gidley were in five editions for the different parts of the constituency, using the approach that I had first found very successful in a council by-election in Leicester in the mid-1980s. My drafts, which were handwritten by Sandra, were then printed in blue ink on blue paper, with matching blue envelopes that were hand-addressed by volunteers using matching blue ink pens. The work involved was laborious and supervising the writing of these envelopes was a task sometimes undertaken in the by-elections by Ann, who would sometimes hear volunteers jokingly saying, 'Who invented this bloody idea?', knowing full well the answer to their question. Sandra's letters, written from her home address in Romsey, contrasted how she would be a local MP fighting for this particular part of Hampshire, whilst the Conservative candidate was a farmer in Dorset already representing the Conservative Party on local councils there. She could emphasise how her own family depended upon local NHS services and schools. She described how her daughter hoped to go to university next year and how she did not support the plans to introduce tuition fees. Sandra concluded by drawing attention to our latest estimate of support for the main candidates in the campaign which was:

Conservative	40%
Lib Dem	37%
Labour	6%

The letters were hand-delivered on the Tuesday before polling day and, with hindsight, my reckoning of support over the final weekend must have been fairly accurate at the time, given the switching to us in the last two days.

The canvass analysis of people who had voted by post in the week before the polling stations opened confirmed that there was a significant Tory lead with a few days to go. Unfortunately, Sandra saw these figures whilst sitting at Gerald's desk writing out the text of the blue letters. I was unaware of this at the time and did not realise that she therefore assumed that she would not win. The Conservatives remained very confident in the last week and William Hague was not the first Conservative leader in such circumstances to have been assured that his party could not lose. I was not at all concerned about the Conservatives being in the lead for almost all the campaign, even on the Tuesday before polling day. What mattered more was creating the momentum to win in the last week, and being in the lead on polling day itself. Our hard-working poster team had created a great display giving credibility to our claims about growing support and victory being in sight. Only in the final week did we talk up our prospects in the media (whilst emphasising how close the result was likely to be), and our final campaign newspaper led with the headline: 'Sandra Gidley set to win!' Unfortunately, our eve-of-poll media coverage was marred by a report in *The Times* quoting a senior Lib Dem source suggesting that we would not win. I immediately began investigating where such an unhelpful comment might have come from, as it was soon being reproduced in the Conservative leaflets. I quickly discovered that it was Charles himself, who had tried to be honest and downplay expectations when talking to a journalist 'informally', but who had on this occasion 'not been on message' and had not thought that his comment would ever appear in print.

When the polls closed, I told our team that I was really not sure of the outcome. I knew that it could not be the sort of landslide that we had achieved in Newbury or Christchurch. I wanted to say that we had won, but I actually lost my nerve. I remembered how I thought that we had won in West Derbyshire, and didn't, so I downplayed my hopes as the polls closed, suggesting that I simply didn't know. I remained optimistic during the first stages of the count, whilst others in our team were much less so, and the atmosphere was very tense. By midnight, however, it became clear that Sandra would win and we wanted to get the news onto the front pages as newspaper deadlines were now passing. I wanted the party, and Charles in particular, to be able to exploit the victory to the full, so I told Gerald to let Charles know that we would win, and that Sandra should now come to the count. Our by-election team had become quite used to stage-managing our candidates' victorious arrival at these events. Labour activists there also seemed to be delighted by our success and the imminent Tory humiliation, but I had to ask their candidate to allow Sandra to enter without Labour supporters also surrounding her. Some hours before the returning officer declared her victory, we got Charles to telephone Sandra on her mobile phone inside the count in order to congratulate her on her stunning success. This provided one of the main photos for the next day's papers, and ensured that the result was on the front page of them.

Sandra won with a 3,311 majority:

Sandra Gidley (Liberal Democrat)	19,571	50.6%
Tim Palmer (Conservative)	16,260	42%
Andy Howard (Labour)	1,451	3.7%

We had shaved 4 per cent from the Conservatives' 1997 share of the vote, in spite of their apparent revival in opposition under William Hague, and we had taken 80 per cent of Labour's previous share of the vote, leaving them with a lost deposit. The result provided a huge boost to both Charles's self-confidence and his standing in the party and the country. It had allowed us to test out the major themes that I wanted to use in the general election and provided a model campaign for other target seats to follow whilst enthusing the whole party.

The by-election took place on the same day as local elections in much of England. The Conservatives recovered many of their losses from the 1996 local elections, gaining over 600 council seats. But their defeat in Romsey prevented the local election results being seen as a great triumph for them, and, indeed, there was virtually no mention of these successes in the national media as news of our unexpected parliamentary by-election triumph dominated the coverage. On the

Friday morning after the by-election, Charles was driven from London by Tim Razzall for a victory parade in the town centre. Charles and Sandra were able to pose with the front page of *The Times* leading on their success. Earlier in the campaign, a leader in that paper had said that the seat was 'a most improbable target for Mr Kennedy' and had predicted that 'the Conservatives' share of the vote should increase substantially'. They were proved wrong. Charles enjoyed his seventh visit to the constituency, having helped to secure it, and in turn his reputation, and that of the party.

In the period after Romsey, I was aware that this latest victory had again strengthened my hand and that of my team significantly in continuing to advise the party on the running of election campaigns. It had previously been assumed by many people that by-elections could generally only be won in protest against governing parties, and that further Lib Dem gains from the Conservatives would not be possible at the next general election.

2001 GENERAL ELECTION CAMPAIGN

In planning for the 2001 general election campaign, I was determined to avoid a repeat of the process I had witnessed in previous campaigns in which much time was wasted with internal discussions about who would sit where and who would be allowed to attend which meetings. This was all about jockeying for position within the campaign rather than what the campaign needed to be about in addressing the voters. In the first campaign for which I was acting as 'chief executive of the general election', I wanted to ensure that the principal focus of attention of those involved would be on the general election message, which I described informally as 'what the bloody hell we would say to get people to vote for us'. I then wanted us to focus on how we could repeat this message frequently and effectively. Only then did I want us to consider logistical issues, including arrangements for meetings.

My mantra of '1. The message. 2. Repeating the message. 3. Organising everything else' became the opening part of many presentations I made about election planning.

Our Campaign and Communications Committee meetings, chaired by Tim Razzall and organised by Kate Fox, became all-day planning sessions held on Sundays at the NUT offices near Euston station, with a sandwich lunch at a pub across the road. The members of the committee appointed by the Federal Executive (FE), together with key staff and co-opted members of the general election team, met regularly from February 2000 onwards to plan the campaign. At our first such meeting, I explained the mantra about priorities and how Tim, Charles and I felt about the overall positioning of the party for the forthcoming election. We knew that the greatest threat to the retention of the seats that we had gained in 1997 was any measure of Conservative recovery. We wanted therefore to use the campaign to constantly remind people of the Conservative failures in government, notably lack of funding for services such as health and education. We knew that this would chime with what Labour was also likely to be saying, and we were happy to be taking part in an argument which would involve two major parties arguing against one of the others. This became known as the 'two against one strategy'. But we also wanted to show how we would be distinct from Labour through our willingness to raise slightly more in taxation than they would in order to provide more funding for public services such as health and education.

We wanted a persuasive overall message that could be expressed in not much more than thirty seconds (suitable for the news bulletins), in a slightly longer five-minute format (suitable for set-piece interviews), or in an hour if necessary (in order to brief the serious commentators). My first stab at drafting the shortest form of this message came very close to the form of words that we eventually agreed for what we called the 'Palace Day' statement i.e. the one that Charles would make to a crowd of supporters outside Cowley Street on the day that Tony Blair went to see the Queen to formally begin the general election campaign.

Our general election slogan – 'A real chance for real change' – was the only substantive later addition to my initial form of words, and it was provided by the 'banc' advertising agency who had volunteered to work with us on the message. I suggested that Charles would say:

Everyone will remember that the Conservatives left health and education seriously underfunded and pensioners lost out. William Hague's Conservatives would be a disaster, but people are disappointed that Labour has really failed to make many things any better.

The Liberal Democrats will invest more quickly in education to reduce class sizes, provide more books and equipment and scrap student tuition fees throughout the UK. We will recruit more doctors and nurses to reduce waiting times. We will increase pensions and provide free long-term personal care for elderly people throughout the country. And we will put concern for the environment at the heart of our approach.

The Liberal Democrats offer a real chance for real change – and we are confident of winning more support.

GROUND WAR

My aim for the national campaign, which I called the 'air war', was to provide a supportive background for the 'ground war', which was aimed principally at retaining the seats that we had won in 1997, gaining as many of those seats in which we had a realistic prospect of success in 2001, and also bringing on further seats to a point from where they could be won in future. After the 1997 general election and following the medium-term review, I had appointed two deputy campaign directors: Paul Rainger became deputy for the north/midlands; whilst David Loxton assumed responsibility for the south of England and the south-west (before becoming head of membership, marketing and fundraising at HQ and being replaced by Gerald Vernon-Jackson).

I was determined to build on the successful approach that we had developed within the campaigns department and which now comprised almost twenty staff. This team continued running a highly successful series of residential training weekends, and other training events for all members at our twice-yearly party conferences. The conference training programmes, coordinated with various party bodies by Sarah Morris, allowed members attending the sessions to benefit from our work in developing best-practice campaign techniques in by-elections and in the target seats. The training programme became so popular that the Conference Committee wrote to me expressing concern that many of the formal debates were becoming sparsely attended as a result of the training sessions, and asking me to hold them at other times. I replied to say that our training events were making a big difference to the party and jokingly suggested that they should organise debates when they didn't clash with our training sessions (which ran simultaneously in at least six different rooms around the conference centres). Surveys of conference representatives showed that very many of them had a very good experience at our interactive training sessions, and that they did not enjoy sitting in the hall all day listening to debates. We therefore agreed a compromise that we would try to avoid them clashing with major debates and Sarah worked hard to ensure that we had a training programme at our party conferences that was the envy of all the other parties.

When asked when an election campaign began, Sir Trevor Jones always replied: 'The day that the last one finishes.' By retaining key staff in the campaigns department, and then adding to them, we could support local 'ground war' efforts, particularly in our held and target seats, throughout the four years after the 1997 breakthrough. This helped to ensure that at the end of the general election campaign in 2001, we retained twenty-six of the twenty-eight seats that we had gained in 1997. Monitoring the key performance indicators of the seats meant that we were able to prove that the campaigns of twenty-six of the twenty-eight seats had followed both the style and the scale that the campaigns department had recommended. It was not a coincidence that the two seats where MPs opted out of this approach were the two that were lost. Peter Brand lost his parliamentary seat in the Isle of Wight, having previously been successful there as an independent councillor, and having been unwilling to sustain the campaigns department approach that had helped him to become an MP. Whilst most of our MPs chose to persuade people why they should vote to re-elect them, Peter chose to tell his voters why some of them were wrong to oppose his views on capital punishment and fox-hunting, amongst other controversial subjects. His main election leaflet featured his arguments about these issues combined with policy extracts from the national manifesto. When I saw it, I offered to pay for something else to be printed instead, but my offer was declined. Jackie Ballard's defeat in Taunton was only by the narrow margin of 235 votes, but her campaign had been very complacent; she had discontinued production of the kind of tabloid newspapers and leaflets that had helped her to win, and it fell well short of the then campaigns department model.

It was a major challenge for us to finance the national campaign as well as provide sufficient support for both the held and target seats. Many of the donations that Tim Razzall had been able to attract for the 1997 general election campaign were one-off donations given to help defeat the Conservatives. With new rules making all donations publicly known, and prohibiting those from abroad, our overall budget for the 2001 campaign was only £2.4 million, compared to budgets of around £3 million in both 1992 and 1997. This meant that I had to be incredibly careful with spending, which was becoming more difficult as many more people came to expect financial support for their campaigns.

The situation was particularly critical a few months before the campaign formally began, when it looked as if we were going to have less than £2 million to spend. Fortunately, I was able to help secure two very significant donations. Our director of communications, David Walter, introduced me to a friend from his Oxford days, and after some discussion over the course of a week, Duncan Greenland sent me a cheque for £100,000. My main hopes, however, still rested, as was so often the case with the party, on the Joseph Rowntree Reform Trust. Tim and I had persuaded them to invest significantly in the 'mid-term' election campaigns of 1999, but they had not yet made any commitment for the Westminster general election. Three of their directors, including their chair, a longstanding Lib Dem councillor and former parliamentary candidate, David Shutt, met with Charles Kennedy privately to discuss the funding issue. Unfortunately, the meeting was a disaster. In a very angry state David and the other directors met me immediately afterwards to explain their disappointment that Charles 'had been in such bad form' and not really able to deal with them. It was one of those occasions when Charles's health problems came close to costing the party very dearly. In response to this, I sat down in a small private room with the three Rowntree directors and, after calming them down, laid out the election battle plans and potential budgets, and pleaded for their help. I ascertained that if the meeting with Charles had gone well, they had been authorised to make a grant of up to £300,000, but that they had left the earlier meeting not wanting to give us anything. David, in particular, understood the problems that I was now facing, and eventually it was agreed that he would go back to his fellow directors and persuade them that they needed to make a grant of £500,000. They agreed. With these contributions, our budget grew to £2.4 million; still a very modest amount compared to the budgets of the other parties that we knew would be close to £20 million.

By making savings compared to previous budgets on things like advertising (our main advertising agency 'banc' provided their services for a token fee), by spending very little on professional poster hoardings and by printing the manifesto as a newspaper, we were able to retain funding for the key seats at the same level as in 1997, in spite of the reduced overall budget. We had shown in that campaign the effect of allocating around 33 per cent of the £3 million budget to effectively supporting what we were doing in the target seats. I was able in 2001 to increase the proportion of the budget spent supporting them again to around 40 per cent of the budget (i.e. around £1 million again). Spending on target seats had only been 4 per cent of the budget in 1992 (£120,000). These funds, however, had to be spread over the course of much more of the parliament, for more staff and for more seats than was previously the case. Cash was still a major constraint on our capacity to expand the number of seats we could target through the ground war.

Our 2001 manifesto, headlined 'Freedom Justice Honesty', was published for the first time in tabloid newspaper format. This was not a popular innovation with all members of the Federal Policy Committee, many of whom clearly expected a traditional book format to place on their bookshelves at home next to previous manifestos. It was, however, a great improvement in communication, helping to make our messaging priorities clearer, and journalists liked it. We were able to distribute many more copies more quickly than ever before (providing a number of free copies to all candidates), and producing it in this way resulted in a financial saving well in excess of £100,000. The front page was professionally designed and, using a style guide, some of our own party's most brilliant leaflet designers completed the layout, with Richard Grayson overseeing the text. One of the greatest problems with the design was getting a suitable photograph of Charles for the front page. In the end, we opted for the head from one photograph and the body from another, but it worked well and nobody noticed.

In choosing a newspaper format for the manifesto, I was also mindful of the need for us to be able to launch it at short notice once we had identified a separate weekday to when the two other main parties launched theirs, but within the same week. This was in order to make sure that we were seen to be part of the 'big three' and that our manifesto was included in all the comparisons of those from the main parties. I wanted to avoid any repetition of the problems in 1997, when we only received the first 100 copies of the manifesto an hour before we launched it.

During the last four weeks of the campaign, I was always at Cowley Street before 5 a.m. I wanted first to study the daily polling analysis that we were conducting through a rolling sample of 400 voters across our key seats. In order to do this, 100 voters in these seats were called each day by telephone and the four-day sample was updated. Tim and I then discussed the results at 6.30 a.m., with Julian Ingram[58] when possible, before the first 'management team' meeting of the day at 6.45 a.m. The management team then heard from Julian about the tracking polling in more detail later in the day at our 5 p.m. meeting.

This polling methodology had been used by Ronald Reagan in his Presidential campaigns, and it proved to be most effective for us at seeing what was happening in our battleground. Prior to the campaign, Julian had assisted us with several waves of 'baseline' research across the seats, which confirmed the most important issues within them, the most powerful messages for us, and the growing standing of Charles Kennedy. These ratings increased during the course of the campaign, based on Charles's outstanding media performances.

The polling was very sensitive in picking up changes in opinion and quickly showed, for example, problems for our campaign when the issue of immigration came more to the fore. The message from it was clear that we should not seek ourselves to make immigration an election issue, even though it was an area in which Charles felt comfortable in attacking the Tories. By the end of the campaign, we could demonstrate that, in our key seats at least, we were seen to have the best policies on health and education (the two biggest issues) and that we had the most popular party leader. Our spokespeople on these issues (Nick Harvey and Phil Willis) had done very well for us, and Charles had been the outstanding figure of the campaign overall. He was able to articulate our values effectively, often using distinctive phrases that had popular appeal. When he said: 'What you see is what you get', this

---

58   Julian is a leading commercial market research expert, former parliamentary candidate and also a friend from my Liberal student days.

contrasted strongly with the impressions people held about both other main parties and their leaders.

Our early-morning press conferences each weekday provided a successful, but stressful, platform for our campaign. We had to begin them at 8 a.m. in order to avoid clashing with those of the other parties. I had persuaded Olly Grender, our former director of parliamentary communications, and her husband David Thomson (who had also worked in the Lib Dem Commons Whips' Office) to run the overnight team, and they produced an excellent analysis of what was running in the media, with some suggested lines to take in response. Their team's report, together with the polling analysis, provided me with the material that I needed as soon as I arrived at Cowley Street. The report was discussed at a strategy meeting chaired by Tim at 6.45 a.m., and which confirmed our 'lines to take' on the issues that were running. Some of us then walked over to Local Government House in Smith Square where we held a briefing meeting with Charles and the various spokespeople on the platform for that day's press conference, and at which Tim explained what we had agreed earlier. It was important for his performance that Charles did not hear conflicting opinions and he trusted Tim's presentation of our conclusions.

We stuck to a 'grid' of themes for each morning press conference based on a process that I had overseen with each of the parliamentary teams. This involved holding several rounds of meetings with them to ascertain what would be in most cases their two or three best messages for these events. I ensured that there was clear agreement on these messages and statements prior to the campaign, with only last-minute tweaks permitted to take into account developing news.

The themes of the press conferences reflected the priorities shown in the polling. Health and education were the themes to which we returned most frequently, whilst other themes included the economy, crime and the environment. Charles's campaign visits for each day were themed according to the subject of the morning press conference, but we had to recognise that what Labour, as the governing party, chose to make as their theme of the day would always be more dominant in the news. Tim Razzall's private dialogues with Charlie Falconer helped us ensure that we included relevant comments in our press conferences to fit in with Labour's agenda (as well as our own) in order to make what we said feature more prominently in the news bulletins. This was 'two against one' in practice, and it worked well for us in terms of keeping up the attack on the Tories, whilst not compromising our principles or independence.

It was also very important to me to ensure that the platform panel every morning reflected our principles of diversity by balancing Charles and Tim on the platforms with the inclusion of some of our most effective female candidates and members of the House of Lords, as well as party president Lord Dholakia (who often spoke on policing issues). Those on the platform, apart from Charles, were generally not clipped in the main news programmes. This disappointed some of them, who complained to me about their appearance seeming tokenistic. I had to explain that it was inevitable that media concentration would be on the leader, but I at least wanted to ensure that our diverse teams were always seen to be reflected in the wide shots on the TV news and during the live coverage, which had grown considerably in importance since previous elections, and I never allowed us to only have three white men on the platform.

I had learned in many parliamentary by-election campaigns how important it could be to serve journalists a good breakfast, especially if holding the first press conference of the morning. In a side room at Local Government House, we therefore served excellent quality sausage and bacon rolls (with vegetarian alternatives) and really good coffee and tea. The breakfast room also provided us with the first opportunity of the day for me and the press team to mingle with journalists and endeavour to manipulate the mood there so that the positive morale amongst the Lib Dem team was made obvious before the press conferences even began. The whole press team, well-led by the head of media Liz Peplow, worked hard on this so that whilst media expectations were very low about our prospects at the outset of the campaign, the journalists present soon came to realise that we were positive about our campaign and optimistic about our prospects.

As the formal start of the campaign approached, one of the greatest private fears that Tim and I harboured was in relation to what Charles later referred to in his resignation statement as his 'drink problem'. This had become more apparent as the run-up to polling day approached, and Charles was visibly more stressed. It meant, for example, that when we planned a full dress rehearsal of our election press conferences at Local Government House, Charles was unable to attend. When I announced that Malcolm Bruce would stand in for him at the mock press conference, most people assumed incorrectly either that Charles had never planned to be there, or that this was simply a matter of his unreliability when it came to diary commitments. When discussing with him the campaign ahead, Charles was most upset that he was not allowed to stay in his flat just off Victoria Street during the course of it. Tim explained to him the nature of 24-hour Special Branch protection and their strict rules, which deemed his flat to be an unsafe location in which to protect him if necessary. This was very convenient because it ensured that Charles stayed in another flat during the campaign, where Tim was also able to stay, remaining close to him. This helped to ensure that Charles made it to every press conference, even though Tim had to leave somewhat earlier in the morning to chair the first strategy meeting of the day. There was only one occasion when we received a message at Local Government House to say that Charles was not feeling well and wanted to cancel his campaign plans for the day. After speaking to Tim, however, Charles turned up a little late for his pre-press conference briefing and the day continued as planned.

Immediately before the 8 a.m. news headlines each day (which delayed the start of press conferences by two minutes), Charles would step outside the back of the building for what he famously called 'a breath of fresh air'. This cigarette calmed his nerves before walking onto the press conference platform to make his statement on the message of the day, as had been agreed well in advance and tweaked the day before. He then listened to one of his colleagues follow it up before the panel took questions. This discipline at the start of the day, I believe, helped to keep us on message, and keep us to time for Charles's planned series of campaign visits to a different constituency each morning and then each afternoon, before either evening rallies or major set-piece interviews. The visits again precisely targeted those of our most marginal seats and those that we were most likely to gain, and were well received by everyone in the constituencies that he visited. There was, of course, disappointment in other places that he could not visit. We managed expectations by letting all the constituencies know in advance about his tour as it concerned them. Niall Johnston[59] oversaw the tour logistics superbly with support teams across the country checking out everything in advance of Charles's arrival.

In 1987, I had seen how the Alliance leaders had appeared to create energy at the start of their campaign by criss-crossing the country in a small plane, and I was keen that Charles was seen to have a similar 'flying start'. He needed to counter the impression that he might somehow lack determination and drive, which had arisen partly as a result of planned events that he had previously missed. This aspect of the tour was planned by Garry White.[60] We arranged three or four regional press conference events for each of the first few days of the campaign. By using a small plane and staying at the relevant airport hotel the night before an early-morning press conference it was not so difficult for us to successfully convey the desired impression. Charles also had carefully prepared and agreed scripts.

One of Charles's significant early statements was nevertheless made off the cuff and caught both Tim and I unawares. Charles admitted, quite truthfully, that he was not going to become Prime Minister at the end of the election campaign. This statement went against the

---

59   An ex-army officer who had also been the principal aide to Lord Alderdice when he was
       Speaker of the Northern Ireland Assembly.
60   A former member of the campaigns department.

previous conventional wisdom that no major party leader should ever concede defeat. But Charles endeared himself to many people with his very candid approach to the election and was able to suggest why people should vote to support what we stood for, to 'send a message' and elect more Lib Dem MPs in support of what he was saying. The implication of this was that the more of them who voted for us, the more seats that we would win, and the more votes that there would be in the House of Commons to support what we were proposing, and oppose what we were against. Together with Charles's skilful handling of the set-piece interviews, it helped to lift our national share of the vote in the campaign, as Paddy had done four years earlier.

Charles handled the rallies well in spite of much nervousness on his part. Speeches from him and Shirley Williams at our final election rally in London warned against the dangers of a large Labour majority, high-lighted the failure of the present government to deliver and described us as 'the party of the NHS', calling for a boost in pay and recruitment for the lowest paid in it. Charles also avoided being distracted by the inter-vention of a male streaker who rushed onto the stage from a few rows in front of me, quickly removed his tracksuit (which was held together with Velcro), and revealed a large 'V' on his left buttock and 'TE' on his right buttock. I had the job of explaining to Shirley Williams, when she asked at the next morning's pre-press conference briefing, why he had not had the letter 'O'. Our own stewards had been much quicker in acting to remove the streaker from the stage than the Special Branch officers tasked with protecting the party leader. Charles told me that he was not really aware of what was happening as it occurred so quickly, but he had understood enough to make a quip about the heat in the hall: 'If you can't stand the heat, get out of the kitchen.' It proved to be only a minor distraction as the news bulletins fortunately focused on the message more than this intervention.

At the end of the election campaign, Ipsos MORI asked 1,010 adults: 'Which political party, if any, has impressed you most in the election campaign?' The responses were: Liberal Democrats 30 per cent, Labour 20 per cent and Conservatives 11 per cent. There had been a very low expectation amongst many of the media commentariat about our prospects in advance of the campaign. Sir Robert Worcester had forecast, on the basis of a MORI poll, that we would be down (from forty-seven) to thirty-two seats, and *The Sun*, reporting this on its front page, said that Simon Hughes and Steve Webb would be amongst our leading casualties (they both won). *The Guardian*, somewhat unwisely applying the principles of uniform national swing from the last election result to subsequent pre-election polls, reported month after month before the election that we would be down to around twenty-five seats. Many people assumed that our gains in 1997, with Paddy as leader, were a 'flash in the pan', and would not be repeated with Charles. This was not my view, and in December 2000, Deirdre Razzall, the editor of *Liberal Democrat News*, had asked leading party figures to make private forecasts as to how many seats we would win in the general election. Her entry for me shows that my forecast was for fifty-two/fifty-three seats. We won fifty-two. This total gave us our largest number of MPs 'in the Liberal tradition' (as Charles referred to it) since Lloyd George's last campaign as Liberal leader in 1929.

Our share of support in 2001 increased by 1.6 per cent compared to 1997 and was the first increase in support that we achieved compared to the previous general election since 1983. We had begun the campaign on about 13 per cent and this had risen to 18.8 per cent by the end. Opinion polling showed that only 25 per cent of those who voted had not decided how to cast their vote prior to the election being called. This suggested, therefore, that our campaign had won the support of around 36/37 per cent of these floating voters.

We had targeted to try to win seats in every region in England and Paul Holmes's gain in Chesterfield (where I had been involved in campaigning since the 1984 by-election) was particularly pleasing. Our young agent there at the previous general election[61] repaid her student

---

61   Jo White, who was the agent for Don Foster's re-election campaign in Bath this time and
       then Chris Huhne's at the following election.

debt as a result of a bet on this outcome that she had placed immediately after the 1997 election. We also made breakthroughs in Surrey,
Dorset and Shropshire, electing our first MPs in these counties for
fifty years. In Scotland, for the first time ever, we outpolled the Conservatives and came within 4 per cent of the SNP's share of the vote.
Of the eight gains that we made across Great Britain (compared to the
previous general election), four of them were with women candidates
(including Sandra Gidley, who retained Romsey). Charles had been
flown to Cheadle on the eve of poll, where I had said that Patsy Calton
could win. She did so by thirty-three votes, whilst Sue Doughty gained
Guildford and Annette Brooke gained Mid Dorset & North Poole.

After the campaign, I ensured that a full and detailed report of the
campaign was made available to all those who had been involved in
it at national level, to senior party officers, and to the entire Federal
Executive. I favoured transparency and considered it essential to document carefully everything that had been done. This was in order to
ensure that all relevant lessons were learned for the future. The report
(written by the members of the management team) comprised 190
pages and 67,000 words. Rereading this report highlighted to me the
huge number of people involved in the campaign and the great skill,
judgement and professionalism that they brought to it. It is quite impossible to recognise all of them in my own personal account of these
and other events spanning several decades, but I remain immensely
proud of having worked so well with so many of them. In Charles's
own contribution to the general election report of 2001, he was kind
enough to say that 'all those who put up with my truculence, periods
of silence and increasing irritation with the bug that just would not go
away deserve medals'. Our feeling was that he deserved a medal for his
own performance. But some of us were also very aware of the personal
health issues that he had had to fight in the run-up to and during the
course of the campaign.

Charles's nervousness about public events such as press conferences,
and in particular the five major rallies, caused him great stress. He had

even sought to avoid doing any election rallies at all (we argued about this at a meeting) and he showed his lack of self-confidence when he subsequently suggested to me, quite incredibly, that he did not think he could speak well at them. In many ways, it was largely down to Anna Werrin that Charles was able to function on the tour, with her constant presence by his side, ability to reassure him and to make sure that he had a drink when needed, but in ways that she managed carefully and discreetly. This often involved a pre-mixed gin and tonic in her handbag. I was always extremely careful not to tolerate any damaging gossip on this issue. In response to my concerns, however, Tim said that Charles would take a long break over the summer and that this would provide him with the necessary cover to help him to deal with the problem professionally. Sadly, however, as was so often the case, Charles's commitment to this course of action was not sustained and the issue remained a major source of concern to me, even though I suspect that Charles was unaware of how many of us knew of its true nature.

CHAPTER 10

THE IRAQ WAR

AFGHANISTAN AND A LABOUR MP'S DEFECTION

In the summer of 2001, I expected September's Lib Dem conference to be a celebratory event, marking further advances on top of our major gains in 1997. My confidence in public speaking had grown significantly, partly as a result of speaking in the House of Lords. I was happy, therefore, to speak in an early debate during the conference. In it I successfully urged the rejection of a constitutional amendment attempting to reverse the decision early in the last parliament that had put the Campaign and Communications Committee (CCC) in charge of the major election campaigns. I think that this proposed change to replace the CCC role with something controlled more by the English party and the English regions would not have been nearly so successful. But it was clear from the debate that there had been significant resentment amongst some people in the English party about the existing 'centralised' arrangement and some of this was directed at me. For my part, I felt frustrated about the time spent trying to negotiate with the English regions about how they spent the money that the party HQ raised for them and of course I wanted more of it to be spent supporting candidates directly.

Our MPs and candidates were in overwhelming agreement with me, as were the major donors supporting the election campaigns (which could not be financed by the day-to-day income that came from membership subscriptions etc.). I often felt that election campaigns were in some ways akin to a wartime situation, and I wondered how the D-Day landings, for example, could ever have taken place successfully if control over the planning process and resources had been subject to each county regiment deciding for themselves on which beach they would land. Some regional parties were immensely cooperative, but their officers could change frequently, and there were always people within them who either wanted to hoard resources or had very different approaches to spending money. The MPs wanted there to be some sort of overall command rather than find that support for many of them depended, for example, on the internal processes of the eleven regional parties in England. The vote was won, but the tension always remained.

Normal party conference business had to be conducted that week, but the nature of the event was changed dramatically by what happened in the USA on 9/11. We obviously had to tone down significantly the celebratory aspects of the parade that was planned for our recently elected fifty-two MPs in the aftermath of the attack on the World Trade Center in New York. Charles had even wondered if it was appropriate to hold the conference at all in the light of the terrorist attack. But prior to it there had been a House of Commons debate in which the parties' different responses to the attack began to emerge, and it became clear that we would need to properly debate the issues as a party ourselves, and this could only really be done at the conference.

There was strong support in the country for action to be taken against those responsible for the recent atrocity. Tony Blair spoke in the Commons debate about acting on the warning that had been provided by the events of 11 September. Whilst not generally recognised at the time, his agenda for the years ahead was being set as he warned of the dangers of people and states who could 'go further and use chemical, biological or even nuclear weapons of mass destruction'. Iain Duncan Smith, who had only become Conservative leader the day after 9/11, immediately offered unequivocal support to Tony Blair and the US in their future actions.

It was clear that the Lib Dems would want to show solidarity with the people who Charles described as 'our American cousins' and express strong condemnation of terrorism. But there was also much scepticism about the history of US foreign policy, and an overwhelming belief in the principles of the United Nations. The party would never support what Ming Campbell referred to in the Commons debate as 'a blank cheque for military action'. At the party conference, Charles skilfully and successfully argued for a position which largely achieved consensus in the party by endorsing a military response; provided that it was precise, proportionate and consistent with international law. The subsequent bombing campaign in Afghanistan, and the British contribution to the fighting there, was clearly authorised by the United Nations and therefore presented the Lib Dems with few difficulties.

It was, nevertheless, opposition to the invasion of Afghanistan which triggered the first ever defection of a Labour MP to the Lib Dems. Paul Marsden had unexpectedly won the Shrewsbury & Atcham constituency in Labour's 1997 landslide. He subsequently had a series of fallouts with the Labour hierarchy and with his party over issues including the way in which he spent the resources allocated to him as a constituency MP. He now called in the Commons for a vote over military action in Afghanistan, subsequently complaining about being told that 'war was not a matter of conscience'. Whilst publicising his 'dressings down' with the Labour whips (much to their annoyance), he frequently met for drinks with the Lib Dem MPs representing nearby constituencies; Lembit Öpik, Matthew Green and Paul Keetch. Rumours of a potential defection quickly spread and I was soon made aware of the possibility, but was unable to attend a meeting with senior party figures and Paul Marsden to discuss his potential defection. The crucial Friday night when this meeting was held coincided with when I was speaking at the Westmorland & Lonsdale's Liberal Democrat annual dinner in support of their prospective candidate Tim Farron. Tim had succeeded in replacing the party's previous candidate Stan Collins in a fierce selection contest for the marginal seat and had cut the Conservative majority from 4,521 to 3,147. Tim now wanted me to show my personal support to his constituency members for the campaigning methods that had already proved so successful in helping to win other seats as he sought to win next time. On the day after speaking at Tim's dinner, I received a message to call Paul Marsden. He told me that Charles had now agreed that he would be joining us, and he had been advised that a letter announcing his switch to the Lib Dems should be issued across the constituency when the news was made public. I was then a little taken aback by his apparent assumption that I could write such a letter to his constituents without him having any involvement in the drafting of it. He had been given a most flattering account of my skills by his new friends in the party, and over several conversations conducted over my mobile phone whilst I was still in the Lake District, I persuaded him that I needed some information from him about his constituency campaigns, as well as his national ones, in order to reassure his constituents about how he would be serving their interests in his new party. The letter was duly sent out, and a few weeks later I was the guest speaker at his new party's constituency dinner in Shrewsbury, which was attended by the small but very decent group of Lib Dems now committed to supporting him. I had travelled there in haste having spent two days at the Welsh Lib Dems' conference in Llandudno (and acquiring a speeding ticket whilst getting lost on the way). The party nationally then helped to support Paul and the Shrewsbury Lib Dems as best it could, and it provided some finance for a re-election campaign, including paying for an organiser.

The Blair government's response to 9/11 in terms of domestic policy outraged many people concerned with civil liberties issues. This included everyone in the Liberal Democrats, as well as many in the Labour and Conservative parties, who also believed that terrorism would not be defeated by trampling upon civil liberties at home, and that such action could be seriously counter-productive.

The Labour MP Bob Marshall-Andrews QC (a close friend of Tim and Deirdre Razzall), later wrote a brilliant book, *Off Message*,[62]

---

62   Bob eventually joined the Liberal Democrats for the 2017 general election.

which explained his own principled opposition to Blair's readiness to indulge in foreign adventures in support of the US, rather than the UN, and to try to undermine civil liberties that had been enshrined in our laws for centuries. When some Lib Dem friends were later to have their doubts about the party having to vote with the Conservatives during the coalition period, I sometimes lent them my copy of Bob's book to remind them of how appallingly Labour had behaved when they were in government. The Anti-Terror, Crime and Security Act of 2001 sought to allow the Home Secretary (David Blunkett) to certify individuals as 'foreign terrorists' and to arrange for their indefinite imprisonment without trial. This power of 'certification', which could not be challenged in any court or by any judge, would give unprecedented power to the Home Secretary. Bob called it 'a signpost to tyranny' and cited Lewis Carroll claiming that the government's logic would have been well understood in Wonderland, where words are what you certify them to be.

After Labour's second general election landslide had given them another huge majority in the House of Commons, it was ironic that the unelected House of Lords had to take upon itself the role of defending people from what even the newly elected Tory MP for Tatton, George Osborne, said would 'drive a coach and horses through 800 years of legal history, stemming from habeas corpus'. The Lib Dem peers, including Tom McNally, Navnit Dholakia and many of our lawyers in the House, spoke eloquently against such abuse of due process and I felt very proud to sit amongst them during these debates. Willie Goodhart spoke for us when he said that:

The government should be ashamed of this Bill. It introduces detention without trial, admittedly in special circumstances, but without enough safeguards. It extends police powers not only over terrorism but over ordinary crime. It extends the powers of the state to obtain and use information over a wide spectrum and for purposes not limited to terrorism. It gives the executive power to push important legislation through

Parliament by statutory instrument. The Bill does all these things on the basis of legislation which has been considered for no more than three days in the other place[63] and is being considered in an extreme hurry in your Lordships' House. This is not the way to deal with important legislation which is contentious and much of which does not warrant the urgency which would justify this exceptional procedure.

The House of Lords' power to delay legislation forced the government to offer a concession to let the Special Immigration Appeals Commission (SIAC) review the Home Secretary's decisions, but this would have meant nothing as this body was a government-appointed tribunal. In the end, the government was forced to let the constitution of this body be altered to make it a court of law itself, with greater involvement by High Court judges, and this curbed to some extent the extraordinary powers being granted to the Home Secretary. The Conservatives initially showed considerable willingness to use their position of power in the House of Lords to prevent the Labour government abusing its power in the House of Commons. But they eventually backed down and accepted this compromise, whilst Liberal Democrats continued to object to any politician having such powers over any individual.

In early 2002, it became clearer that George Bush's initial focus on Afghanistan was moving towards Iraq, which he identified, together with North Korea and Iran, as being part of an 'axis of evil'. There was speculation throughout the year about the potential of another military invasion with UK involvement and this prospect could easily have divided the Liberal Democrats. Ming Campbell had been highlighting the failures of existing containment policies towards Saddam Hussein. Paddy Ashdown's initial support for Tony Blair's position on Iraq lasted for some years and this support was not made public by him in order to avoid embarrassing his successor, but was leaked by Labour.

---

63   'The other place' is how members of the House of Lords may officially refer to the House of Commons.

It was later to become a significant myth that Charles Kennedy himself was immediately and unequivocally opposed to military action in Iraq. I witnessed how in fact he took a strongly evidence-based approach to the issue, wanting to see if any military action could be justified before declaring his view on it. At times, Blair tried to take him into the government's confidence 'on Privy Council terms', but his reports of these conversations to our internal meetings indicated that he had not really learned anything from them that was more confidential than he could read in the newspapers. Charles's instinct about anything that Blair told him was always significantly more sceptical than Paddy's.

Parliament was recalled during the Lib Dems' autumn conference in 2002 and the situation in Iraq was the dominant theme of the week. Tony Blair spoke to the House of Commons about Iraq's possession of weapons of mass destruction (WMD). Iain Duncan Smith backed military action. But Charles maintained a distinctive position, seeking to establish the facts before committing himself, or the Liberal Democrats, to supporting any course of action. The party felt comfortable that he emphasised the supremacy of the United Nations and the need for any military action to be supported by a vote in the House of Commons. Many Conservative MPs protested angrily in the debate about Charles's position, and we later used some footage of this debate in party broadcasts. It showed Charles pointing out: 'I'm only asking questions unasked by the leader of the Conservative Party.' This contrasted his position as Lib Dem leader with the acquiescence of the Tory leadership in whatever Blair was planning. At conference, Charles was again able to steer through a motion making it clear that military action was acceptable only as a last resort; if Iraq refused to allow the return of UN weapons inspectors, if there was proof that Iraq could deliver weapons of mass destruction, and if it was approved following a full debate and a vote in the House of Commons.

The party was by and large comfortable with this position and felt confident about challenging the Blair government on an issue of huge principle and importance in a way that the Conservatives were not.

During the conference, we also sought to talk up our long-term prospects of being able to overtake the Conservatives nationally. Despite being the official opposition, the Conservatives had made no real progress in the polls since they left government, providing us with an opportunity to provide what we called 'the effective opposition'.

The UN weapons inspectors returned to Iraq in November, and their work should have determined whether or not we would be committed to war. I was amongst the many Lib Dems who felt very sceptical that they would find evidence to justify invasion. At this point, Charles was relying heavily on advice from Tim Garden, a former Air Vice-Marshal with extremely good military contacts, and who Charles made a peer in 2004. Tim was also sceptical that there was a real threat from weapons of mass destruction. Charles was under great pressure as to how to respond to the prospect of war as the Bush–Blair axis continued to push towards invasion with considerable determination. Whilst he may have suffered the consequences of stress and his drink problem at other points in his leadership, he appeared to me throughout this period to be very well focused on the issue at hand. He chaired our own Iraq Advisory Team, providing him with a forum for informed and rational debate discussing the pros and cons of the issues, and at which he listened carefully. He took advice from many quarters and kept in regular touch with Ming Campbell, our highly respected foreign affairs spokesman, but who was in the middle of a lengthy enforced absence from Westminster whilst receiving and recovering from treatment for cancer. Paul Keetch, a trusted friend of Charles's, and our defence spokesman, helped to liaise between Ming and Charles. Throughout his leadership, Charles's patience in listening carefully to many representations, and allowing those making them to feel that their views were properly considered, was a great strength. It helped him with this particular issue to ensure that the party achieved consensus, and it was a source of great satisfaction for him when the crucial vote came in the House of Commons and every single Lib Dem MP voted in the same lobby, opposing the invasion of Iraq.

THE IRAQ WAR

The final stages of the decision-making process which led to the Lib Dems opposing the war were not straightforward. Whilst Charles was clearly moving in the direction of saying that the war was not justified (on the basis claimed for it), and that invasion could not be supported without being endorsed by a specific UN resolution, many others in the party had already made up their minds to oppose it. The party's Federal Executive was asked in late January to support a motion put forward by former mayoral candidate Susan Kramer and radical activist James Graham encouraging party members to participate in the 'Stop the War' demonstration planned for 15 February. The motion was somewhat ambiguous as it encouraged members to 'voice their concerns about the Iraq situation' but fell short of demanding unequivocal opposition to the use of military force. It asked the Parliamentary Party to send a representative to speak at the rally. The motion was not in itself a great problem for Charles as he sought to resolve any remaining conflict within the party about the stand that it would finally take if asked to endorse military action. The main focus of attention of those closest to Charles that night appeared to me to be the annual elections for party officers. Tim Razzall's position as chair of the Campaign and Communications Committee was being challenged by another radical activist, Gareth Epps. Whilst I knew that the Federal Executive would vote overwhelmingly for Tim (Charles's choice), I think that the Leader's Office concentrated that night on ensuring Tim's re-election (he won with around twenty votes, compared to four for Gareth). This meant that the implications of the Iraq resolution, and Charles's desire to keep the party united, were not properly considered. Participation in the rally on an individual basis and expressing concerns about the Iraq situation was certainly not a problem (and I intended participating in the march myself). But Charles did not want the involvement of Lib Dems to be taken to indicate outright opposition to any military action, irrespective of facts that might yet emerge, or a UN decision.

I therefore found myself promoting participation in the march through the party's various internal communication mechanisms, but seeking direction as to how far to go in doing this from Tim Razzall as my line manager, and Navnit Dholakia as president (and chair of the Federal Executive). They obviously did not want to compromise Charles's position negotiating with some MPs who might still need to be won round if we opposed the invasion. The HQ now came under pressure from the most radical activist on the Federal Executive, Donnachadh McCarthy, to immediately mobilise the HQ's resources in support of the march. There were, however, quite a few senior people in the party, including Ming Campbell, who had strong reservations about some of the people who appeared to be planning the peace march, and the image that might result from Charles's unequivocal endorsement of it.

One of Charles's favourite sayings in private was 'to govern is to choose' and it was now time for Charles to choose. *The Guardian* was strongly urging him to put himself at the head of public opposition to British participation in the likely war, whilst he faced some internal criticism for apparently prevaricating about the issue. Tony Greaves used his column in *Liberal Democrat News* to promote participation in the anti-war march, but the HQ was expected to hold back from unequivocal support for it until we knew whether or not Charles was really in favour of formal Lib Dem participation. On the Sunday before the march, Charles finally made his position known on *Breakfast with Frost*. His sudden decision to take part in the rally came in answer to a question and caught some of us unawares, but we were not surprised by his conclusion. He emphasised strongly that he was making a pro-United Nations case, and not opposing military action in all circumstances. This meant that he wanted our message at the march the following Saturday to be 'Give Peace a Chance'. I arranged for some banners to be printed with his chosen message for Lib Dem supporters to carry at the march, but the display of them was barely significant compared to the hundreds more 'Lib Dems say NO' placards that Donnachadh had organised. More than 3,000 Lib Dem members marched together, having assembled by the Royal Festival Hall and been addressed by Charles at the outset of the march. He told us that it was his proudest moment as a Liberal Democrat. I also felt great pride standing with him as he spoke, together with Sarah Kennedy, fellow peers Navnit Dholakia and Tim Razzall, and Lib Dem MPs including Simon Hughes, Liz Lynne, Matthew Taylor, Don Foster and Chris Huhne. I actually thought Donnachadh McCarthy had done Charles and the party a favour by pushing the issue, and his tenacity had brought about a proud day in the party's history. The size of the crowd meant that it was more of a shuffle than a march, and I dropped out after about three hours, feeling that the point had been well made by more than a million people demonstrating the scale of opposition in the country to Blair's apparently pre-determined course of action.

Charles used the event to restate his longstanding position that he had yet to be persuaded of the case for war, and that in any event the Lib Dems could only support it if it had UN backing. Blair was clearly furious about the march and in his own speech to a Labour conference that day he went so far as to imply that those people who did not support toppling Saddam Hussein would be responsible for bloodshed. The Tories were particularly vicious about Charles's participation in the rally, with Iain Duncan Smith calling him 'an appeaser'. A column in the *Daily Mail* now called him 'Charlie Chamberlain', which I considered to be ironic, as that newspaper's owner in the 1930s had admired Hitler and his papers gave support to Moseley's Blackshirts. When it came to the crucial Commons vote on 18 March, all fifty-three Lib Dem MPs (together with fifteen Conservative and 139 Labour MPs) voted for an amendment, saying:

> This House ... believes that the case for war against Iraq has not yet been established, especially given the absence of specific United Nations authorisation; but, in the event that hostilities do commence, pledges its total support for the British forces engaged in the Middle East,

expresses its admiration for their courage, skill and devotion to duty, and hopes that their tasks will be swiftly concluded with minimal casualties on all sides.

Just over a third of the Parliamentary Labour Party voted against the war, with Robin Cook publicly resigning from the Cabinet to much very rare applause in the Chamber of the Commons, and Philip Hunt resigning as a minister in the House of Lords, also in order to express opposition to the war. With about a third of all Labour MPs being on the 'payroll vote', and forced to vote for the war or resign their government positions, Blair's elegant but flawed arguments were only able to win over about half of the Labour Parliamentary Party that was free to vote according to its conscience.

The Lib Dem position was an extremely tricky one for Charles to have negotiated. Alone amongst the major party leaders he had led his entire Parliamentary Party in the Commons through the same division lobby, with Ming Campbell returning to the Commons in order to vote for the first time after his five-month enforced absence. In the end, Charles's greatest difficulty in achieving unanimity had been with John Burnett, the Lib Dem MP for Torridge & West Devon, who was an ex-Royal Marine and who was most anxious not to be seen to let down our troops if and when they were in combat. In the end, John felt able to support this amendment, but he abstained when the other Lib Dems MPs opposed the final vote authorising military action after the amendment failed.

The day after the Commons vote on 18 March, the bombing campaign began. Charles and the party had now done as much as they could to prevent the UK supporting the invasion of Iraq. But the party's position had also been clearly expressed that if British troops were authorised by the House of Commons to take military action, then, as I put it to our MPs, 'we could not be seen to be on the side of Saddam Hussein's Republican Guards when firing at them'. A somewhat different position was adopted by a small number of party activists, such as Donnachadh McCarthy, who continued to believe that the party's position was best represented by participation in various peace vigils, whilst there were also a very small number of members who were positively enthusiastic about the invasion. Fortunately, the period in which it was most difficult to reconcile opposition to the war in principle, with support for British troops in conflict, was very short. Baghdad was occupied on 9 April and major combat operations were declared over on 1 May.

The invasion of Iraq had taken place before a UN-backed weapons inspection team led by Hans Blix had been allowed to complete its work. Blix later said that he had only really required another two weeks in order to determine whether or not Saddam Hussein really did pose a threat of being able to use weapons of mass destruction, which was the pretext for invasion. But he was not given that time. When Saddam was defeated, without having used any such weapons, there was even more scepticism as to whether or not the purported threat of WMD had ever really existed. At the end of May, the BBC was to trigger a major confrontation between it and the Blair government by broadcasting an interview on the *Today* programme with its then defence and diplomatic correspondent, Andrew Gilligan. He claimed that the government had arranged for its infamous dossier about the threat of WMD to be 'sexed up, to be made more exciting, and ordered more facts to be … discovered'. Gilligan's report was based on a briefing by Dr David Kelly, a government scientist and weapons expert, whose name then emerged and who died in mysterious circumstances two days after he was subjected to questioning on the WMD issues by the Foreign Affairs Select Committee. An inquiry later concluded that he had committed suicide.

Even before the death of David Kelly, it was clear that there had been a major turning point in public opinion on the issue of trust in Tony Blair. In June 2003, I worked with Julian Ingram on a major qualitative market research project aimed at assessing the feelings of our potential voters in some of the constituencies where we believed that we could advance. The approach taken in this research was to interview individual voters in some depth, rather than to risk them being influenced by other people's opinions, as could sometimes happen in a focus group. I worked closely with Julian for many years and the party found that this research process greatly helped us in shaping messages to explain our policy issues and principles. Our resulting presentations to what Charles now called the Lib Dem shadow Cabinet were particularly dramatic about the issues of Iraq and trust. We showed a number of PowerPoint slides paraphrasing what people said in the interviews:

THE WAR: If opinion expressed, it was anti the war
- Blair subservient to Bush
- Bush is power crazy
- 'ulterior motives' e.g. control of oil
- has led to severe distrust of Blair: suspicion of lies
- Kennedy is the only party leader to oppose the war, yet this has not always done him good (+ve – Not opportunist)
- if money and resources are so scarce for other purposes, how come money could be found to fight this war?
- has taken resources away from domestic issues
- Blair too concerned with world stage, neglects home country

BLAIR: Reputation has taken severe battering
- was admired as clever, young and of promising competence
- but now viewed as dishonest
- under thumb of Bush
- has lied to us about Iraq and other matters
- 'worse than Thatcher', 'understudy of Thatcher'
- out of touch with people, does not consult, more interested in fat cat businessmen and powerful people
- does not care about concerns of ordinary people
- has not delivered on election promises

LABOUR: Many feel let down – hopes not fulfilled
- high hopes damaged by lack of progress and preoccupation with 'spin'
- no ideological (socialist) values; now artificial, shallow, dishonest, not true to historical Labour principles

The bell curve chart showing the rise and then fall in the level of trust for Tony Blair was particularly dramatic. I felt that this finding now showed that there was a real opportunity for the Lib Dems to advance against Labour in a way that had not seemed possible since Blair became their leader and New Labour had been created.

The findings also showed that Charles was not yet well established in the public mind, whilst they were particularly damning for Iain Duncan Smith. Several people interviewed did not know who the Tory leader was, and those who did were unimpressed by him. There were comments about his 'lack of charisma', 'being worthy but useless, and not a good speaker' and 'not dynamic enough'. The Conservatives generally were still associated with 'many class-based connotations'; they were seen as an 'ineffective opposition', 'out of date and past it' and 'still to blame for many things'.

I was always extremely keen that all the market research I was commissioning was widely shared amongst our parliamentarians, party committees, candidates, key staff and others. I wanted them all to be able to act on the basis of it so I made a series of presentations to these groups throughout the course of that summer. Controlling market research, and the presentation of it, is obviously an important tool in controlling a party. Rick Ridder once told me that 'whoever has the numbers, has the power', referring to how private opinion polling can be used. I felt that I was always objective in managing this process, but I was also aware of how much power it gave me in crafting what the party was saying. This occasionally caused some internal resentment, but the research really proved to be very useful to us in developing effective messages and constantly increasing our electoral base. It also helped at this time to convince the rest of the party that there really was a major opportunity ahead for us, and I was determined that we would seize it.

A CAREER CHANGE?

Before the Iraq War, in early 2003, I had begun to consider privately that I could not really continue performing the same role that I had developed for the party over the previous fourteen years. I did not think that my health could sustain it indefinitely, nor did I feel as comfortable in the role as it probably appeared within the party, and so I thought of doing other things. My role as director of campaigns and elections had grown considerably, and I felt that it had been hugely successful for the party, but I was never completely within Charles's inner circle. I had detected some resentment after the 2001 general election over the way in which I had pushed Charles into a busier schedule, including more events such as campaign rallies, than he'd wanted, even though it was very much lighter than for previous leaders. I found that Charles's office began trying to deal with people such as the advertising agency that had helped us during the general election directly, cutting me out of the process. A meeting was held to plan Charles's involvement in the 2002 local elections without me being invited. Once assembled, however, those at the meeting realised that nobody in attendance even knew where these elections would take place, and they had to agree that I had better be included again in any election-related meetings. I think that a factor in this was that Charles had some feelings of paranoia resulting from his health issues, and he feared exposure of them beyond his innermost circle. He did not seem to be aware of how many of us knew about them anyway and about much earlier attempts at rehab even before he became party leader. Those closest to him, however, generally knew that I knew.

The personal stresses all of this caused me were often enormous. I felt that I needed some change, and possibly new challenges. Almost ten years after first being diagnosed with diabetes, and having for a long time maintained reasonable control of it, the stress and lifestyle meant that I was no longer doing so, and I was put on insulin in addition to a lot of other medication for the condition and the associated high blood pressure. There was never any respite in the role as I spent many weeks and months, as well as almost every weekend, away at by-elections, conferences and training events. This generally involved either eating out or relying on unhealthy takeaways, whilst taking very little physical exercise. I started early, finished late, generally worked seven days a week, had meetings most evenings, and I was constantly 'on call' for staff, MPs, candidates and others about their various problems and issues at almost every hour of the day and night.

Charles had not followed the approach that I had wanted of making a public statement about his 'drink problem' after the 2001 campaign in order to help him tackle it more effectively with medical support. My previous doubts about Charles's capacity to lead the party without dealing with this problem returned. He later allayed them again to some degree by performing brilliantly in the Brent East by-election, but he had been far from his best earlier in 2003 when we fought the second round of Scottish Parliament and Welsh Assembly elections, and we had had council elections in much of England. I had drawn up with his office various timetables for Charles to campaign in the different areas with elections during the month of April, but many of these visits simply didn't happen or only took place in a very limited way. On one campaign day, for example, he should have been campaigning across Wales and in the Welsh media in support of the Assembly election campaign. At the last minute, however, this became a one-hour visit to Brecon at 9 a.m. on a Wednesday morning when he was driven over from Hereford by Paul Keetch, as Charles had been there the night before. It was impossible to get any of the Cardiff-based media up to Brecon for that time in the morning, and there was no coverage in the Welsh media of his 'campaign day' in Wales. Tim Razzall was on holiday for much of that Easter recess, so I had to tell him on his return that much of Charles's election programme had not been undertaken. In general elections Tim had a major role in managing Charles to help ensure that there were no such problems, but he could not do this every week or for every round of elections.

Nevertheless, the party still did very well in the mid-term elections of 2003. I spent time helping Jim Wallace and his team in the Scottish Liberal Democrats to successfully defend our position there after four years in coalition with Labour (we again elected seventeen MSPs, as in 1999). I also spent time in Wales and provided support to Mike German, our party leader in the Welsh Assembly, and the campaign there, which was ably organised by the Welsh Liberal Democrat chief executive Chris Lines and supported by my former Cowley Street colleague Mark Soady. In Wales, we had also to defend our record in coalition and we again did this successfully, retaining all six of our seats on the Welsh Assembly (although the coalition there came to an end, in spite of some efforts to recreate one, as Labour had now won thirty of the sixty seats). In the local elections in England that year we gained control of another five councils (so that we now controlled twenty-eight principal local authorities) and we won 2,586 council seats (gaining an extra 189).

Throughout Charles's leadership, his office, closest advisers and friends were constantly concerned about his health and sought to support him, very loyally. Most of the party, including most MPs, were unaware of the nature of the problem, but for those of us who knew, it was a great source of stress. We lived in almost constant fear that it would be exposed publicly in a way that would be very damaging to Charles and the party. In June 2003, Charles failed to make it to the Chamber of the House of Commons for Gordon Brown's statement about Britain's prospects of joining the euro. He was simply not well enough, and the explanation that he had chosen to watch the statement in his office upstairs set alarm bells ringing. Later that month, I held two training weekends at the Great Northern Hotel, Peterborough, for our target seat agents and candidates. Late on the Friday evening of the agents' training weekend, I received a call from Anna Werrin. She said that Charles had finally agreed to make a public admission about his problem, and acknowledge that he was seeking treatment for it. There had been a meeting that night of his closest advisers. I could not attend it because I was in Peterborough, and was now surprised at the speed of events as Anna sought advice as to how best this could be announced the following day. I agreed that it should be done immediately, and I said that I could make all the arrangements for Cowley Street to be opened in the morning for a press conference. In the meantime, I had to maintain my normal calm composure with all the constituency agents and campaign staff who were completely unaware of what was happening. On the Saturday morning, however, having arranged to open the HQ, I received a further call from Anna to say that Charles had now decided not to make a public statement, but she assured me that he was now dealing with the problem with medical support. My instinct remained that only a public declaration would give Charles the support that he needed from everyone to stand any realistic chance of overcoming it, but this was a very difficult decision for both Charles and Sarah, who had been married the previous year. I knew that Ming Campbell had been asked to travel down to London from his Edinburgh home in order to be at Charles's side and support him when he made this announcement. Only later on did I discover that Ming had made it as far as Peterborough on the train before receiving his call from Anna about Charles's change of mind. We were only yards apart at the time, with him on the train and me in the station hotel.

Ming later met with Charles and Sarah, together with Jackie Rowley, Tim Razzall and Dick Newby, to discuss the issue. It was one of many such occasions when Charles provided assurances about steps that he was taking to deal with the problem. It was of course very difficult to do this publicly, and Charles had rejected the idea of doing so. The party was, however, able to help ensure that discreet financial arrangements were made to facilitate medical treatment. In later reports of Charles's tragic death, I was upset by some suggestions (also made at the time of his resignation) that the party had not been sufficiently supportive of him over this issue. This was certainly not the case. The fact is that alcoholism is an extremely difficult issue to deal with, made more difficult by the desire to preserve confidentiality. Meanwhile, more people in the party were becoming aware that Charles was occasionally drunk in public. That summer marked twenty years since he had first been elected as an MP in the 1983 general election. He was the guest of honour at a garden party, attended by several hundred party supporters, hosted at the Harrow home of Ramesh Dewan, a longstanding party member who was very supportive of Charles. Many of the guests present could see that Charles was barely able to stand up and shake hands with people. After dinner, Tim Razzall and I sat next to each other at the far end of the enormous marquee from where Charles spoke. I had provided Ramesh with some key bullet points for his speech, highlighting the tremendous progress that the party was making. Charles then followed and Tim and I witnessed an extremely painful and embarrassing event as everyone listened to Charles's very drunken speech as he tried to explain how 'we would make great progress on my watch' and that he was 'up for the fight ahead', whilst appearing to be anything but ready for it.

I shared my feelings of stress about Charles with nobody, but Ann was aware that I continued to suffer from bouts of depression, probably made worse by the stress. With hindsight, and in the process of writing this book, I realise that I should have sought more medical support for my mental health at the time, but I too was fearful of public exposure of such a condition and the effect that it might have on my career and the party, in a way that I should not have been. I had had some private counselling and been on anti-depressants as prescribed for me. They helped, but I still felt quite isolated, having very little time for friends or family outside of my very demanding work environment and my constant attention to it.

This was partly why I had made an attempt in the earlier part of 2003 to look for alternative employment which would also be compatible with my hopes of doing rather more in the House of Lords. But this was not easy, as I found that a number of jobs that might use my political skills could also have been in conflict with my membership of the Lords. Similarly, there would have been some problems with other roles on offer to me that were very highly paid (compared to being director of campaigns and elections for the Liberal Democrats), but which would lack the sort of mental stimulation that came from working for a cause in which I passionately believed. I had a few meetings discussing potential opportunities, and I could have increased my salary considerably (and also provided for a very comfortable retirement) but some of them would have been in conflict with my conscience. My immediate focus then had to return to elections when the Labour MP for Brent East died in the middle of June, and the public reaction to the invasion of Iraq was about to be tested. There were also to be significant changes at HQ that I had not expected, and which would change my role considerably.

BRENT EAST

In spite of my fears about Charles's health, he rose to the challenge of the first real electoral opportunity to test opinion post the Iraq War most effectively. The constituency was to become the scene of the first ever Lib Dem gain in a parliamentary by-election from Labour, but I did not see that prospect immediately. It seemed to me that Labour would almost certainly call the by-election for the end of July and that it would take a big effort on our part just to move up from our previous third place in the constituency and overtake the Conservatives. I also underestimated Sarah Teather, who I hoped would fight a target seat somewhere, but did not think that she could switch from being an Islington councillor to being the champion of Brent East in only a few weeks. Her energy and skill in personally canvassing sixty-one of the sixty-three local party members meant that, somewhat to my surprise, she won the selection. My immediate aim was then to ensure that the campaign was fought as well as possible to try to get us into second place, ahead of the Conservatives, by the end of July.

I was also determined not to continue taking the same degree of responsibility as I had in most of the by-elections that we had won between Eastbourne in 1990 and Romsey in 2000. I'd helped to recruit, train and manage some excellent campaigners, and I really wanted them to undertake the key roles in future by-elections. I wanted not to go beyond some strategic oversight of the campaign messages and ensuring that there were adequate funds and helpers available for our campaigns. I also enjoyed reverting to knocking on doors. Whilst canvassing in Brent East in July, it became very clear to me that there was now a much stronger reservoir of goodwill for Charles Kennedy and the Liberal Democrats than I had originally anticipated.

The launch of our campaign was also helped by a major gaffe by the Conservative candidate, who told the *Daily Telegraph* at the start of her campaign that she knew she couldn't win, and that her aim was to be able to find a better seat to fight in future. Shaun Roberts, an excellent leaflet designer and in charge of the by-election literature, was able to make much of this quote in our leaflets.

My canvassing, sometimes alongside Sarah Teather, reflected the findings of our recent market research showing that the tide of opinion amongst many people who had previously supported Tony Blair had now finally turned against him. Brent East had one of the largest ethnic minority populations in the country (48 per cent according to the census, with Hindus being the largest group amongst them, followed by Muslims). The party had not previously had much significant support amongst ethnic minority communities, but these were now often the people who were most inflamed by Blair's decision to back Bush on Iraq. I had not myself experienced such strong and enthusiastic support amongst these communities since I had helped with campaigning in Leicester twenty years previously. We were now also winning support from many 'middle-class' white residents who appeared to live in very comfortable homes, had voted for 'New Labour' but were now not just disappointed, but really angry with Tony Blair. People simply did not believe the claims that he made to justify the invasion of Iraq.

After a few weeks, we dared to hope that we might have a chance to campaign in the constituency throughout the summer, in which case the contest could become potentially winnable for us. We encouraged people we knew in Labour to think that our assumption was that we could not win, but that given time we could inflict a humiliating result on the Conservatives, who had been within just 1,653 votes of winning the constituency in 1987.[64] Labour may have taken the bait about our suggestion that we could not win. They eventually moved the writ for the by-election to be held on 18 September, giving us at least six weeks more to campaign than we had expected.

Whilst in France on holiday with some of my Liverpool friends that August, they were somewhat bemused about how I spent every afternoon with my mobile phone hooked up to my laptop looking at the very effective literature that Shaun was writing. Charles was most anxious that we stuck to the lines that he and Ming Campbell had been using about the Iraq War, and that we avoided any potential attacks on us over any inconsistency in our approach, and we made sure of this. The campaign newspapers were designed to have the look and feel of the red-top tabloids that were most popular locally. The large photographs of Sarah Teather campaigning against Labour's neglect of that part of the borough were helping to build her reputation quite rapidly. These papers also featured prominently a photograph showing George Bush and Tony Blair standing together, smiling broadly. The photograph required little explanation and we used it frequently in the campaign and subsequently.

We were able to mobilise thousands of party activists for the campaign more easily than ever before because for some time at HQ we had prioritised collecting their email addresses, a relatively recent

---

64 This was when Ken Livingstone had first stood there and when Danny (now Lord) Finkelstein had been the SDP candidate.

innovation. We used my name, and those of many other well-known by-election activists, in emails to urge our members to seize the opportunity ahead in the way that we had done in previous by-election successes. The Brent East HQ was very small and cramped, as it had first been identified for a much smaller and much shorter campaign. Behind a temporary screen towards the back of the former WH Smith shop, Victoria Marsom, the by-election agent, oversaw a brilliantly efficient organisation. Mark Pack, who I had recruited to the HQ three years earlier as our first full-time internet and social media campaigner, oversaw the database operations, and the analysis that he provided showed our growing level of support as we closed the gap on Labour and squeezed the Conservative vote.

The by-election was not, however, the only thing on my mind when I returned from holiday that summer. Donnachadh McCarthy had been making sustained attacks through social media about the HQ's allegedly slow response to the Federal Executive resolution about the peace march. He was very persistent. All party members had access to the 'CIX' online conference where he was posting his comments, and it was therefore a very public way of discussing people's jobs and some very sensitive employment issues. He sought to propose alternative structures, changing the lines of management at HQ in a way that I believed was aimed at strengthening his own power over it. Donnachadh thought that there should no longer be a director of campaigns and elections position, or that any member of staff should report to the chair of campaigns and communications. He believed that all campaign staff should now come under the direct line management of the chief executive, who should take over direct responsibility for managing our election campaigns (even though he had not been appointed for such a role). This would have reversed the post-1997 'mid-term review' structure that had put me in charge of the professional campaign structure for our elections (reporting to the chair of campaigns and communications). He made public his proposal, saying that the two jobs of director of campaigns and elections and chief executive should be combined, and

I was sure that he didn't intend me occupying the position. The almost 'dual leadership' at HQ would thereby be brought to an end, and I was sure that his assumption would be that Hugh Rickard would take over responsibility for elections, as well as admin, HR, IT etc. In the event of Hugh's appointment, the new job might have involved working more closely under Donnachadh's own direction as, in the absence of other candidates, he had become deputy chair of the Federal Executive and sought to be very assertive in the role.

I also understood some of the frustration that Hugh Rickard may have felt by having the title of chief executive, but having been appointed on the basis that someone else would be in charge of the high-profile election campaigns. He was responsible for some significant achievements at HQ, including IT improvements, but he had no significant election experience. I also recognised that the political events in which I was engaged may have appeared to be much more interesting than many aspects of party administration. In discussing all this, he told me that he was not sure if he wished to continue at all, but that if he did it would be only on the basis that the new job did put him in charge of the party's elections and political campaigning. On my part, I had never sought to bring about a structure in which I would have to be chief executive in order to retain my leading role with regard to the party's election campaigns. The Federal Executive, and the party's Federal Finance and Administration Committee (FFAC) discussed the restructuring at length, and after much deliberation agreed the proposed job description for the new chief executive.

I made it plain to all concerned that if I was the one who became chief executive, I would immediately appoint a deputy, or HQ director, who would then be largely responsible for much of the previous chief executive's role in relation to management, HR, IT and administration. Whilst I would be that person's line manager, I would expect to retain overall responsibility for the party's major elections. The single most important power held by the party's Federal Executive, according to the party's Constitution, is the appointment of a chief executive. In the summer of 2003, it took this responsibility seriously, and it decided on an interview panel of twelve people in order to make sure that it was broadly representative of the many diverse parts of the party. But at this point, I think that Donnachadh suddenly realised that the panel was not likely to make the appointment that he had expected, and he made a last-minute attempt at the FFAC the night before the panel was due to meet to pull the plug on the whole reorganisation. He failed, however, in this attempt to reverse his own proposals. Interviews with both Hugh and I (an external candidate dropped out) took place in Charles Kennedy's House of Commons office on a Friday evening in early September. They were chaired by Charles, who was one of the eight panel members able to attend.

My feeling at the time was that if the party wanted to appoint Hugh, and make me redundant, then it had a perfect right to do so. I was also very aware that many people in the party were alarmed by this prospect. The panel met with each of us for over an hour. I felt pleased with my performance at interview, particularly since I had not been interviewed for a job since being appointed director of campaigns and elections in 1989. I therefore lacked interview experience and was grateful to Don Foster who very kindly met me privately to help me prepare, and I felt much better about my interview as a result.

I could not wait for the outcome of the interviews as I needed to get back up to Brent East as soon as possible that evening. I was asked to keep my phone to hand whilst at the by-election HQ. I had not, however, reckoned on there being such poor mobile phone reception within it. When I stepped outside (into the pouring rain) to make a couple of calls myself, I picked up the message to ring David Griffiths, the chair of the FFAC. They wanted me to do the job. There was a little negotiation over my salary and I agreed to settle for slightly less than was paid to my predecessor, even though the new job had much greater responsibilities. I did so on the basis that I knew the party could not afford to pay many of my colleagues what they were worth, and I also received allowances as a working peer in the House of Lords.

That evening I was grateful for some early feedback from Tim Razzall, who told me that I had given a really excellent interview, a message wishing me good luck in the new job from Charles Kennedy, and confirmation from David Griffiths that the panel vote had been eight nil in my favour. There was then a small celebration in the by-election HQ. We cleared the tables of the leaflets being bundled up for delivery the next day, and old newspapers had to serve as tablecloths as we ordered in from a local Indian takeaway, where the staff were most supportive of our campaign. As was often the case in by-election HQs, I was very happy for the opportunity to personally treat everyone there to a meal, although I had not expected that the team would also kindly produce some nicely chilled wine for the occasion. At the end of the evening, Ann and I returned to south London from the by-election HQ feeling content in many ways, but also apprehensive about the challenges ahead, including the first priority of winning the by-election. Hugh was also kind enough to get in touch to offer me his congratulations.

The momentum for our campaign in Brent East grew, and the enthusiasm within the small HQ was as great as I can ever recall in a by-election. I visited most evenings and spent most weekends there, largely canvassing, sometimes delivering, and occasionally offering advice, particularly in relation to drafting the many letters we sent out to different groups of voters, including one of our famous 'blue letters'. Labour's campaign in contrast was quite complacent. Their candidate, Robert Evans, was an MEP who continued with many of his responsibilities within the European Parliament, whilst Sarah Teather was frequently working in the constituency to the point of complete physical exhaustion. The printing machine at the back of the HQ ran virtually 24/7 and every time it stopped, Victoria would shout at Erlend Watson, one of our legendary by-election helpers, to get it running again. He printed leaflets as fast as people could deliver them.

Charles performed brilliantly. I often phoned him fairly late at night when we thought that there would be significant media presence the following morning and we wanted him to front as much of it as possible. He led by example in urging his 'shadow Cabinet' and fellow MPs to head up the Jubilee line from Westminster to Willesden on what he later said should have been called the 'Victory line'. At one point, when pressed at a 'shadow Cabinet' meeting as to whether or not we really could win, I read out Mark Pack's canvassing analysis showing our support on each of the previous ten days. This showed how it was growing in the way that Sir Trevor Jones would have approved. The party's weekly newspaper, *Liberal Democrat News*, was also a very important vehicle for party communication, and the editor, Deirdre Razzall, did the campaign proud. We did everything we could by way of emails, letters and phone calls to mobilise the party to seize the opportunity of our first gain from Labour (making it their first loss of a parliamentary by-election since Greenwich in 1987).

Over the final weekend, the other parties finally hit back in an attempt to halt the momentum behind Sarah's campaign. They pointed out, as I had feared they might at the outset, that she was still an Islington councillor, and not yet resident in Brent. We sought to muddy the water and defuse this attack by constantly pointing out that she 'would be a local MP', relying on this use of the future tense as she would obviously move into the constituency if elected. On the eve of poll, Lib Dem activists travelled from all over the country, often driving through the night, in order to arrive at the Willesden HQ in time to deliver the early-morning leaflets. I had shown Shaun how in many previous by-elections we had managed to get helpful content from the national newspapers published on polling day into the early-morning leaflets. This had previously involved getting early editions of the papers, but could now be done via the internet, and we found helpful quotes on this occasion pointing towards our potential victory that day.

We had so many helpers that we were continuously printing more leaflets throughout polling day. I was particularly proud of one which again used the photograph of George Bush and Tony Blair and was headed: 'You can help these two men today...' suggesting that voting

Labour would make them smile even more, whilst the reverse side of the leaflet featured strongly Sarah's pledges if she became the local MP.

In previous by-elections I had often tried to get candidates to have a rest on the afternoon of polling day, in order to be at their best for a speech and interviews at the count and afterwards. To give Sarah a break from knocking on doors, we set aside two hours in the HQ on the afternoon of polling day for me to work with her on her speech for the count. Drafting the speeches for newly elected victorious Lib Dem MPs was one of the things that always gave me most pleasure in by-elections. Sarah asked me at the start of our session to just outline what I would say if I was in her shoes that night, and if she won.

I quickly outlined roughly what I thought she should say in that event. As I spoke, she jotted down some notes on a side of A4 that she had divided into eight squares in order to break up the sections. After not much more than five minutes of me talking, she simply said that she would use it if she won, and it was to be the speech that she delivered that night. Whilst she then went for a brief rest, I jotted down a few notes for the 'other speech' in the event that it might prove necessary.

With the many different leaflets for delivery on polling day printed, Victoria drove me around the committee rooms where there was an incredible sense of excitement amongst all those working on the campaign, and a perception that the role of trying to drag out voters would really make the difference. Victoria had picked up on the fact that many of our newly identified ethnic minority supporters were actually new to the voting process, so she carefully ensured that specific detailed notes were provided for them about exactly where they had to go to vote, and how to support 'Sarah' when they got to the relevant polling station. When the polls closed at 10 p.m., Victoria then drove me to the count. Charles Kennedy was at his flat in Victoria with Anna Werrin and Jackie Rowley nervously waiting for any news. On previous such occasions I had tried to keep the party leader in some state of suspense when I thought that we would win in order to make their public reaction as spontaneous and as emotional as possible. I knew that there was no need for that with Charles on this occasion. I spoke to him on my mobile and he pressed me on what I now thought as to the likely outcome. I wanted to downplay my expectation very slightly so as to allow for a margin of error, so I told Charles that I thought we would win by about 500 votes. As a forecast, this was to understate our majority by just over 600 votes. The early stages of the count had not looked encouraging for us as the votes came in first from Labour's stronger areas, but I knew that we were soon catching up and should overtake them. Whilst the counting agents who attended on behalf of the Labour and Conservative candidates were reluctant to concede defeat at an early stage, I was able to secure confirmation from people on their teams that their analysis also showed that we were going to win. This meant that we quickly went into top gear with the media to make the most of what would be seen as an incredible result.

When the declaration came, Labour's previous majority of 13,047 votes had been overturned as we gained the seat by 1,158 votes (having come from third place with just 10.6 per cent of the vote at the previous general election). The swing to us from Labour was 29 per cent. I remembered the impact of David Owen's apparently spontaneous appearance at the celebrations on the night of Rosie Barnes's victory in Greenwich in 1987. So, I asked Charles and Navnit Dholakia to come over to the Willesden HQ that night to appear with Sarah for all the pictures, and for them to address our jubilant supporters as they crowded into the HQ and the street outside.

Our by-election press officer Richard Stokoe (on leave from Paul Burstow's office) and I then spent the following twenty-four hours without a break ensuring that we maximised the media coverage of our success. Sarah conducted dozens of interviews throughout the night and the following morning when Charles returned for a victory walkabout in front of our supporters holding our very recognisable diamond poster boards. The phone went mad in the HQ with a combination of media calls, messages of congratulation and constituents now seeking help from their new MP. The campaign team were all exhausted and so Ann took over dealing with the phone calls. She also had the job of finding a dry cleaner who could cope with cleaning all of Sarah's clothing within the day, as she literally had nothing left to wear, and had to leave that night to be at our conference in Brighton. She and the campaign team were shown live on the Friday evening national news bulletins meeting commuters at the local tube stations, and thanking them personally for their support.

Sarah immediately became the star of the conference, which began that evening, and the by-election triumph was the theme of the week. The media coverage was greatly enhanced by the fact that our conference immediately followed it. Our activists were euphoric about the victory and the way in which it represented an emphatic endorsement of our principled opposition to the Iraq War. For the first time in nearly ten years, there was much critical comment of Tony Blair in the media. But it was Iain Duncan Smith who suffered most as a result of the Brent East by-election because of his incredibly inept reaction to the result, describing our victory as being 'a strategic error' for us. In the immediate aftermath of the by-election, the three main parties were at level pegging in the national opinion polls (ICM put all three of us on 31 per cent). Duncan Smith's response, with his party genuinely fearing being overtaken by the Lib Dems, was bizarre. Presumably he meant that we should have continued trying to advance in Tory seats, without challenging Labour in theirs. Over many years I had tried to explain to anyone that would listen that any successful Lib Dem strategy would always have to aim to win seats from both other parties in the long run. Labour then held over 400 seats. Our ambitions required winning some of them if ever we were to help reduce that majority and one day get into a position of power nationally. Brent East showed that we could now win seats from Labour, pushing the Conservatives from second into third place in some of them in order to do so. It was far from a 'strategic blunder' for us, and some Conservative MPs now took their party leader's comments to be the last straw when evaluating his political judgement and reflecting on this very ineffective period of op-position for them. Iain Duncan Smith was defeated in a no-confidence vote by his MPs on 25 October by ninety votes to seventy-five, just five weeks after the by-election. With hindsight, there were parallels with Mrs Thatcher's downfall immediately after the Conservative per-formances in the Eastbourne and Bradford North by-elections. These leadership coups showed how utterly ruthless the Conservative Party was in getting rid of their leaders when their position of power was at stake. As a consequence of these coups, their party recovered from the low points of 1990 and 2003. The effect of Michael Howard replacing Iain Duncan Smith after the Brent East by-election, in an unopposed 'coronation', was both a Conservative recovery and almost certainly the end of any real prospect that we had of overtaking the Conservatives in that Parliament.

CHAPTER 11

CHIEF EXECUTIVE

NEW JOB

I had been asked to undertake the position of chief executive by the unanimous vote of the panel appointed by the Federal Executive, but I was also anxious that the whole of the FE properly exercised its right to vote to approve my appointment, which it subsequently did (almost unanimously).

I had a tremendous reception at the 2003 conference, and there was much enthusiasm about my appointment, which had been announced during the Brent East campaign. Prior to all this, the Parliamentary Candidates Association (PCA) had planned a dinner in my honour at the conference. This was to mark twenty years since I had been a constituency agent. Over 200 people attended, Charles Kennedy spoke at the outset, and it was another very emotional occasion in which I in turn thanked everyone present for their encouragement and support, and paid tribute to some of the people who had encouraged me in my early days of campaigning but were no longer with us, including Cyril Carr and David Penhaligon. A special souvenir edition of *Liberal Democrat News* circulated at the dinner included tributes to my past election successes from David Steel, Paddy Ashdown and David Alton.

There was clearly a little nervousness amongst some of the party staff that the campaigns department would remain too much my personal priority, whilst other departments might be neglected by their new chief executive. At my first staff meeting, I therefore emphasised that I wanted every one of my staff colleagues to feel proud to be part of a political project guided strongly by Liberal Democrat values, and which would grow, become more successful, and help to achieve our ideals, as I promised more of my own 'blood, sweat and tears'.

Having worked for the party all my professional life in a campaigning role, I knew that some people might question my management experience as its new chief executive. But I could point out to them that as director of campaigns and elections, I had been directly responsible for managing more people in the campaigns department (twenty plus) than had been employed by the entire Federal Party when I was appointed to that role in 1989 (sixteen). I had also described to the appointment panel how I had already held significant administrative and budgetary responsibilities, including all those connected with the most recent and successful general election campaign. I could also demonstrate to them that there had been very good adherence to best-practice management principles within the department for which I had been responsible than generally existed in much of the party at the time, particularly in Parliament.

I sought advice and support where I most needed it, and tried to make sure that the senior management team complemented my skills and covered gaps in them. I arranged to do some senior management training with ACEVO (the Association of Chief Executives of Voluntary Organisations), which I found helpful, and I also asked a number of members or party sympathisers who had been chief executives of other organisations to offer me advice and support.

I had said that I would appoint a deputy chief executive, or HQ manager, to undertake some of the more traditional roles of chief executive on my behalf. I was fortunate in being able to persuade Ben Stoneham, who had been a very successful and popular interim chief executive a few years previously, to become the interim 'HQ director' on a voluntary basis for some months, whilst he was in between employment roles. He had until recently run much of the business side of

News International within the UK, and his experience, particularly in HR issues and contractual negotiations with suppliers, was invaluable to me and to the party. We quickly conducted a review of all staff contracts to bring them up to date with best HR practice and employment law. We then reviewed the Staff Handbook (which was sensibly negotiated with the very experienced staff representative Doug Janke). We also looked carefully at all of our existing contracts with suppliers of equipment and services. Whilst Sarah Morris continued to deal with my diary and liaise with everyone in the campaigns department, I was also keen to appoint a really good executive secretary; and Kate Heywood was very strongly recommended by many parliamentarians and staff. She was very quickly able to help me to manage the party business effectively and soon became office manager/committee administrator, before further promotion into management.

I was keen to see some quick wins and to identify and deal with any areas of significant complaint made by party members about the HQ. The single biggest issue at the time was the long delay in receiving party membership cards once payment had been made to either join the party or renew membership. This was generally an unacceptable six weeks. With his agreement, I moved David Allworthy, then the head of membership services, out of this area and into a new role focused on ensuring that individual donations made to the party came from people who were on the electoral register, in accordance with recent legislation governing donations to political parties, and giving basic advice to local parties on matters such as complying with that legislation. The senior team working with me, including Ben, David Loxton and Nigel Bliss (who I made director of finance), then changed the cumbersome way in which HQ had previously struggled to bank cheques in a timely fashion (so much so that they were sometimes out of date by the time that they were banked). Instead, we got the Royal Bank of Scotland, who were our bankers, and who handled this function for a number of charities and other voluntary organisations, to process the banking and recording of payments directly. I promoted an excellent staff member, Ernest Baidoo-Mitchell, to work under David Loxton's guidance and he and his team then received the data about payments on the same day as the bank received them, and it was able to issue membership cards to party members within a couple of days.

As Ben initially expected only to be able to donate a few months of his time, my major priority was to appoint a permanent deputy or HQ director. There was no shortage of people within the party (and some even willing to join it!) who considered that they were ideally suited for what was then seen to be the only well-paid job in the HQ (at about the level of an MP), apart from that of chief executive. There were many unlikely expressions of interest from people who lacked sufficient experience of senior management in the commercial, public or voluntary sector. There was also a lack of self-awareness on the part of some people who told me that they (or their partner) were so obviously suitable for the job that we need not advertise at all, and that I should simply give the job to them! A defector from the Conservatives joined us with his application for the job already completed. Even one of the most junior members of staff applied, thinking that they could immediately become the second highest paid member of it. I later learned how much making such appointments could cause great jealousy and make you enemies.

We advertised the position in the *Sunday Times* and elsewhere, and the appointment panels led to me offering the job to two different people, but who subsequently turned it down after careful consideration, comparing the remuneration and benefits packages we could offer with those available elsewhere. Re-advertising then brought forward new applications from people who could clearly do a part of the job at least, but none of whom came close in ability or experience to Ben Stoneham, who was still actively seeking a senior role elsewhere. I therefore went to David Griffiths as chair of the Federal Finance and Administration Committee (FFAC), and who had served on the appointment panels, to suggest that we made an approach to Ben to offer him the permanent job and the salary that went with it, but on the basis that he would still be allowed to undertake some of the other roles that he was interested in on a one-day-per-week basis. Ben is an extremely committed party member, and he particularly liked working with me as he had done at various times since we first met at the Warrington by-election in 1981. I persuaded Ben, and the party's FFAC formally approved the proposal to employ him in this way.

Having witnessed several cycles of sudden and unplanned redundancies amongst party staff over the previous twenty years, particularly after general elections, I was determined to try and avoid them. I wanted the party to be very clear about its priorities in business plans that were properly approved by it and I wanted the party to focus on trying to achieve power in order to implement our principles by increasing our electoral success at all levels. A mantra that I often used was that we would focus on what won us seats, won us votes and raised money.

Our agreed financial strategy meant confining the party's 'day-to-day' expenditure to what we realistically knew that we could raise in 'day-to-day' income. I was always under pressure to get the party committees to breach this principle and to start paying for activities that people considered desirable in the hope of future income arriving to pay them. But I had seen the very damaging consequences to the party of doing so in the past. Previous cycles of redundancy had deprived the party's organisation of skilled staff, been costly in terms of paying them off, and even more costly in the long run as it always took a long period of time recruiting and training their eventual replacements when money could again be found. I wanted to avoid any repetition of these cycles during my tenure as chief executive and ensure delivery of the agreed priority to concentrate as much support as possible on the party's candidates and campaigns, even if this was at the expense of having more staff to undertake administrative tasks at HQ for the party and its associated organisations. This meant that campaign funds provided by donors for specific purposes could sustain the party's growing electoral success at many levels. But this financial discipline also made me some enemies.

THE JUNE 2004 ELECTIONS

After some months finding my feet and feeling a little nervous as the new chief executive, I began to feel more comfortable with my new role, and I was now much more 'on the inside' of Charles's office. Six months after being appointed, we faced a very important round of elections in June 2004 for the European Parliament, for many local councils in England, and for the London Mayor and Assembly. Whilst coordinating preparations for all these elections, I also had to ensure that the party kept a strong focus on preparing to defend our now fifty-three parliamentary seats at Westminster, as well as making more gains, in a general election expected the following year.

Concerns about Charles's drink problem persisted, but were largely confined to the still relatively few people with significant knowledge of it. A year after Charles had failed to attend Gordon Brown's statement about the euro, he failed to make the March 2004 Budget itself. On that day, I went over to the House of Lords for a meeting and immediately saw Matthew Oakeshott at the Peers' Entrance, who told me that Charles had been unable to attend Prime Minister's Questions, which preceded the Budget, and that Vince Cable would later be making the party's response to it in the Chamber instead of the party leader. The party was very fortunate to have someone like Vince who would be able to undertake the role without advance notice. Charles had done a large number of media interviews the day before in anticipation of the Budget and I ascertained from a TV journalist I knew well that he had become 'much the worse for wear' as the day had progressed. There was inevitably a lot of media speculation about the reasons for his non-attendance, and a persistent pattern of questioning his drinking habits had now been established by journalists both formally and privately. Many of them were asking about attempted rehab as though they knew about it.

The spotlight continued to focus on Charles's health in the run-up to the party's spring conference in Southport the weekend after the

Budget. Whilst telling everyone that he had recovered from a 'stomach bug', it was clear that he was still very unwell. During his closing conference speech, he sweated profusely and constantly had to dab his face with a handkerchief. The television pictures looked extremely poor. All efforts to try and expose a 'drinking scandal' had been rebutted firmly, but it was increasingly hard to maintain his official position that there was no such issue.

More and more senior figures in the party were talking to me about Charles's problem and to people like Tim Razzall and Anna Werrin. After the conference, Anna called me to say that there was now agreement amongst the senior people in Charles's office that there must be a renewed, and more determined attempt, to help Charles address the problem. She asked me to be part of a group to see Charles that would now include Ming as deputy leader, Matthew Taylor as chair of the Parliamentary Party, and Andrew Stunell as Chief Whip. A few days later, the four of us entered the Lib Dem Leader's Office, just off the Committee Room Corridor in the House of Commons, and were ushered upstairs into Charles's private office, whilst Anna remained immediately outside. Anna was clearly doing everything that she could to help Charles, and she had been very firm in telling him how he would need to conduct himself in future, whilst advising me not to hold back in the discussion.

Ming, who had been part of a conversation with Charles a year earlier on the same subject, explained that he could not say too much as deputy leader in the meeting in case anyone was later to suggest that he was acting from a point of self-interest. Andrew Stunell also said little. I felt it was down to me to do the 'heavy lifting' in the meeting, knowing that others had tried and failed before. I explained to Charles that I had some knowledge of the issues because of two very close friends who had suffered from problems with alcohol. One of them had been able to recover by giving up alcohol completely some years ago, having got himself into enormous personal difficulties prior to that. My other friend had been unable to do this and continued to have major problems in his life. I had learned a lot about the Alcoholics Anonymous approach as a result of their experience, and I knew that the first step to recovery was to admit the nature of the problem. I therefore pressed Charles very hard as to whether or not he was an alcoholic. He tried several times to avoid a direct answer, but I would not let the question go. I saw no prospect of his recovery without his acknowledgement of the nature of his illness. Eventually, when it became clear that he would have to answer the question, he said 'yes'. He spoke quietly, and was clearly most uncomfortable in making this admission, but it was very significant. I then explained that I was very aware of the tremendous personal support for him throughout the party, but that what it really wanted 'was Charles Kennedy without alcohol'.

Matthew Taylor then followed up by saying to Charles that 'the next time he picked up a drink, was the time that he would give up being leader'. We all made it clear that we really wanted to support Charles, but that the problem could not continue. We were pleased and relieved that Charles had acknowledged to us the nature of the problem, said that he was following medical advice, and that he agreed we would meet again in a few weeks to review the situation. Anna had prepared him well and was determined to impose new office rules and routines to help him, including there being no alcohol in the office, and him arriving there at a reasonable time each morning. The whole conversation should, in my view, have always remained entirely private, and I kept it so. I was perturbed, therefore, to find out that within a week, one MP not present was able to tell me about exactly who had been there. Two years later, it was a leak about this meeting (which I refused to substantiate) which proved to be the trigger for Charles's downfall as leader. At the end of the meeting, however, the four of us were very pleased with the progress that we felt we had made. I was grateful to Ming in particular for his praise for the way in which I had handled the most difficult parts of it. But when the group met again a few weeks later, Charles was clearly not feeling in the same weak position that he had been in immediately following the Southport conference. He now felt stronger and no longer wanted this group to convene again to consider the issue with him and it was a very short follow-up meeting. I was much less convinced that he would be able to deal with the problem than I had hoped after our original meeting.

The local, London Mayoral and Assembly, and European elections were all to be fought on 10 June 2004. I had had some involvement in how all these elections had come to be combined on a single day, as opposed to being held on two days five weeks apart as in 1999. I believed that this was very much in the party's interest, but my view was not universally shared by everyone in it, especially by some councillors. My experience of the local elections in May 1999, followed by the European elections five weeks later, was that it was practically impossible to mobilise party activists to do very much in the European campaign once the local election campaigns had concluded. In spite of the Liberal Democrats being the most enthusiastically pro-European party, few of its members were prepared to knock on many doors or deliver leaflets in Euro-elections, compared to their efforts in local elections; nor did they have additional funds at their disposal after the conclusion of the council election campaigns. I therefore took the view that we could maximise our level of support in the European elections (conducted under PR) by holding them on the same day as the local elections, whilst our local election share of the vote would not suffer in the wards that we were seeking to win. At the same time, the Labour government was aware that it faced a potential 'mid-term' backlash in both the local and the European elections, and it did not want two sets of bad headlines five weeks apart. The Labour Party chairman at the time was Charles Clarke, and he met with Tim Razzall and me on a number of occasions, usually over a substantial English breakfast at a Westminster Indian restaurant called The Cinnamon Club. I made the case to Charles that all of the elections should be combined that year. The turnout in the 1999 European elections had fallen to 24 per cent, as there had been an element of voter fatigue with a second campaign five weeks after the local elections, as well as a general lack of interest in the outcome. We considered that it was in the best interest of democracy to try to improve turnout in the European elections. The Labour Party chairman accepted this proposal and, after some consultation within our own party, we supported the legislation to enable it to happen. At the same time, I also explained to Charles Clarke our strong opposition to all postal vote elections. Where these had been piloted, there had been many problems. Some of the postal votes had been collected unopened from voters, and then returned in the post by people acting on behalf of particular candidates. Some of the ballot mailing envelopes had even been redirected so that the voters entitled to receive them never saw them. Some were stolen from communal entrances and recycling boxes. Nevertheless, Labour felt that their own supporters were the least likely to turn out to polling stations in the traditional manner, and they were enthusiastic about 'piloting' postal-only elections on a widespread basis, and particularly in their strongest regions.

This put the Labour government at loggerheads with the recently formed Electoral Commission, who considered that changing the election rules in this way and on a very widespread basis was far from safe. They recommended that a postal-only election should only be conducted on a pilot basis in two regions of the country where there were few local elections and some existing experience of postal ballot mailings. The Labour government, with John Prescott in charge of a powerful department responsible for local government and the regions, decided instead that it wanted to force postal-vote-only elections to be conducted in four regions (North East, North West, Yorkshire and the Humber, and the East Midlands). This provoked a protracted confrontation between the House of Lords and the House of Commons. I led opposition to this plan from the Lib Dem benches, and worked closely with Lord MacKay of Ardbrecknish[65] and other Conservative peers to

---

65   A former Conservative MP for Argyll & Bute, and previously a Liberal.

oppose it. We saw it as the Labour Party trying to change the electoral rules unilaterally and unfairly to their advantage. In the debates in the House of Lords I highlighted (with the Conservatives agreeing) the entitlement of the House (provided for by the Parliament Acts) to block attempts by a government to use its Commons majority to abuse its powers to determine the rules for the conduct of elections unfairly. We defeated the government three times on the issue. Many Conservative peers wanted to oppose them again, but the Conservative front bench caved in on the fourth occasion, when I and the Lib Dems sought again to defy the majority Labour vote in the House of Commons.

The London mayoral and London Assembly elections were problematic for the Liberal Democrats because they required London-wide organisation, whilst we were only strong in relatively few parts of the capital. We had struggled in 2000 to fight a serious campaign across a city which then had seventy-four Westminster constituencies, only six of which were held by Liberal Democrats. The London campaign also appeared to be dominated by the mayoral contest, and most people believed that doing well in the Assembly elections would require us maximising our vote in the mayoral election campaign. Thoughts therefore turned to Simon Hughes standing for us, as he was the best-known London Lib Dem. Ever since the leadership election, in which Charles had defeated Simon, Charles's office appeared to me to remain fearful of a further challenge from Simon. There was obviously also some discontent within the party about Charles's recent performances, and Simon was generally seen at the time as the only alternative candidate for leader. I felt that this was a factor in Charles's office's enthusiasm for Simon standing to be Mayor of London, but their relations were understandably delicate. Charles's office therefore pressed me to persuade Simon to stand, knowing that we had a good longstanding relationship. It was assumed, I think, that Simon could not combine this role with making another leadership bid. At the same time, it was my view that Simon was the most popular and well-known Lib Dem in London and that it would probably be best for us if he stood. In the likely event of a rerun of the 2000 contest (which the media saw as being between Ken Livingstone and Steve Norris), Simon would inevitably have a higher profile than Susan Kramer had enjoyed. The London members chose the party's mayoral candidate, and they voted for Simon. Susan was clearly disappointed by this outcome, but I had in the meantime been talking to Jenny Tonge, who had taken me into her confidence about her decision not to stand again in Richmond Park in 2005. Jenny sought my advice as to how and when to announce this decision, given that she wanted to see another woman, and preferably Susan, fight the seat next time. I advised that her announcement that she was standing down should be made immediately following the result of the mayoral selection ballot. This sent an obvious signal from her about who should be selected to take over in Richmond Park, and Susan was later chosen overwhelmingly by the members there.

Simon's mayoral campaign was chaired by Tim Clement-Jones, who had some significant success in fundraising for the campaign, and this meant that there was money to pay for an advertising agency to come up with creative ideas. Sadly, however, there were still only very limited party funds with which Simon's agent, Victoria Marsom, could promote either the agency's ideas, or those of anybody else working on the campaign. Simon remained extremely busy in Parliament during the run-up to the election dealing with legislation and as a constituency MP. This may be part of the reason he struggled to identify a clear and distinctive message as to why he was the best candidate to be Mayor of London. We did some polling which showed that if he could get into second place, then either he would be within the margin of error of beating Ken Livingstone, or he would more easily defeat Steve Norris if Livingstone came third. The polling showed that Simon had the highest net favourable rating of the three main mayoral candidates; most people thought that Ken Livingstone spent too much time (and public money) promoting himself, and that Steve Norris had a conflict of interest as a director of Jarvis. This company was still facing an investigation over the Potters Bar rail disaster of 2002 in which seven people had been killed.

There was a strong case to be made for Simon as a powerful and effective Mayor of London. Our campaign election broadcast featured how he had bravely helped to put three murderers behind bars by persuading a very frightened sixteen-year-old girl in his constituency that she should testify against them. As a result, Simon allegedly had a contract taken out against him seeking his murder in retaliation for his involvement in the case. For some months Simon had to be accompanied everywhere by Metropolitan Police close protection officers (armed bodyguards), until the threat appeared to have been lifted. This was apparently as a result of some of the female partners of the gang members, who knew what a fantastic MP he was, putting pressure on them. But Simon's evident bravery was not sufficient for him to be seen as one of the two main contenders. Our vote was therefore squeezed, particularly as the *Evening Standard* featured the choice as being a very close one that was just between Livingstone and Norris. We were disappointed with Simon's 15.3 per cent share of the vote (only 3.4 per cent more than Susan Kramer four years earlier), and which compared to 37 per cent for Ken Livingstone (now standing as an official Labour candidate) and 29 per cent for Steve Norris.

The local elections across much of England that year proved to be significantly more successful for us, even with postal-vote-only elections in four regions. We continued our steady increase in our number of councillors (winning 1,293 of the council seats up for election that year, a gain of 123) and we remained in control of thirty local authorities. More significantly, we narrowly outpolled the Labour Party in the estimated national share of the vote across the country (27 per cent to their 26 per cent). The Conservatives, now led by Michael Howard, polled an estimated 37 per cent national share of the vote.

The second European election fought under the party list system of proportional representation was seen on 10 June 2004. We were defending our ten seats won in 1999 (by five men and five women).

The system of 'zipping' was relaxed to provide for at least one person of each gender within the top three candidates (despite significant reservations about doing so being expressed by both Shirley Williams and me). This change to the zipping scheme was made partly because gender balance had been achieved in the previous set of elections, and partly because the party was extremely keen to try to elect an ethnic minority MEP. We expected that Saj Karim would come second on the list for the North West, where we hoped to win a second seat, whilst also retaining the one held by Chris Davies. In these elections, I also thought (and was right) that with additional financial support we could gain a twelfth MEP seat by electing Fiona Hall (later leader of our group in the European Parliament) in the North East region.

There was always internal controversy about the degree to which the party focused on purely European issues in European elections. Previous polling in European elections had shown five out of six voters failing to take into account a single European issue in considering how to cast their votes. My own approach to all elections was to try to follow the maxim of addressing the voters' concerns, rather than believing that the Liberal Democrats were really in a position to tell voters what should be important for them. But this principle also encouraged a myth to develop that we did not also fight European elections on strongly pro-European principles. In 2004, with Charles's enthusiastic agreement, I ensured that we sought to explain *why* we were in favour of those European principles, and *how* people benefited from them, rather than appearing simply to state repeatedly that we were in favour of the EU institutions.

Crafting messages was always the aspect of politics that I most enjoyed. I gained a real sense of excitement from things like drafting Charles's words for the opening of the European election campaign and for our main European election broadcast. Of course, Charles would always approve any scripts and there was occasionally some robust discussion about them. I was particularly keen on the use of an autocue to assist him in adhering to an agreed script. Without this device, and even sometimes with it, he had what I considered to be an unfortunate habit of drifting away from the text to add in a number of superfluous expressions, which then meant that other carefully constructed phrases had to be omitted due to time constraints. He disliked the autocue for exactly this reason. We got the very best performances from him when he was most involved in agreeing the script before it would appear on the autocue, and when he was therefore more comfortable in the delivery of it.

In this broadcast, he emphasised the contrast between the two halves of the twentieth century and the importance of Europe in preventing war and tackling new threats of terrorism. We argued for Europe to take a lead in environmental issues, particularly because of George Bush's reluctance to do so, and emphasised our vital trading relationship that depends on being within the European Union. Charles did not pull any punches and he condemned the Conservatives for their uncritical support for Bush and Blair. He said that 'Saddam Hussein was a brutal dictator. And our forces did their job brilliantly. But it was profoundly wrong to go to war without the support of the United Nations, with no urgent threat and with diplomacy still in play.'

When the results were declared on the Sunday night, we had elected twelve Lib Dem MEPs. This was our highest ever total, winning for the first time two seats in the North West, including Saj Karim,[66] whilst Fiona Hall also gained one of the only three MEP seats in the North East region. The new group of twelve Lib Dem MEPs comprised six women and six men.

LEICESTER SOUTH

Two weeks before polling day in the 2004 European elections, the Labour MP for Leicester South, Jim Marshall, died. On the same day,

---

66   Who later defected to the Conservatives when he feared that he would not be re-elected.

fifty new members apparently joined Leicester South Lib Dems. Their subscriptions were all sent to HQ by one of our local councillors, and the former parliamentary candidate for the seat, Parmjit Singh Gill. The surge in membership, and the apparent winnability of the seat, made it obvious that there would be a selection battle to be our candidate. We had finished third in Leicester South in 2001, but we had won almost all the local council seats within the constituency in the 2003 local elections when controversy about the Iraq War was at its height.

I knew the seat well as I had lived there for four years in the 1980s. It was at that time the most marginal constituency in the country as the Conservatives had won it in 1983 by just six votes. We won our first council seats for many years when I lived there, but Labour had since regained the parliamentary seat, and now had a 13,253 majority.

Since I had moved away, the Lib Dems had gone on to become the main opposition to Labour on Leicester City Council, and we eventually took minority control of the council in 2003. Following Brent East, and with Leicester South also having a large ethnic minority population, it was immediately assumed that we would be able to obtain a large vote in the by-election on the basis of our opposition to the Iraq War. Many of us in the Lib Dems were also very conscious of the fact that we still had an all-white Parliamentary Party at Westminster, were embarrassed by this, and wanted our parliamentary representation to become more reflective of the country. Whilst the party could not control selections, it was obvious that we would hope for an ethnic minority candidate in such a seat. But Parmjit was a controversial figure within the local party and there was a lot of opposition to his selection, whilst he had strong support from the local Sikh community and many members of it now joined the party. At the same time, many local Muslims joined in order to support Zuffar Haq, who was well known in Leicester and had previously fought the next-door Harborough constituency. Other local party members favoured our previous Leicester East candidate, Harpinder Athwal, a former member of staff for the region's Lib Dem MEP Nick Clegg, or Jon Ellis, who had been a very good local member, but had moved away.

My own view was that in any hustings meeting in front of the members, Harpinder might well prevail and that as a highly intelligent and articulate young Asian woman she would have become a prominent and popular figure in the media if we had been able to win the by-election with her. But the party's national organisation could not determine the outcome of a selection, and certainly I couldn't. The local party's selection committee largely comprised Parmjit's supporters (he was chair of the local party) and in what seemed a very unfair process to me, they excluded his main rival, Zuffar Haq, from the shortlist. Party rules provided for hustings to be held for local party members to hear and question those people who did make the shortlist. Postal votes were not allowed, and attendance at a selection meeting at which all the candidates spoke was required if you were to vote. I was shocked, therefore, to arrive at the selection meeting to find that something akin to a polling station had been established some hours before the meeting was due to begin, and that many votes had already been cast, without those people having listened to or questioned the candidates. A returning officer, appointed by the English party, was in charge and, together with a staff member from HQ acting without my knowledge, they had been persuaded to permit this arrangement. This was on the basis of claims made about local Asian women being unwilling to attend a hustings meeting in the evening, and wanting to exercise their vote during the day. Having lived locally, I considered this claim about a sunny June evening to be ridiculous. At the meeting itself, there was a very small proportion of the local membership present to listen to the speeches. Meanwhile, many more of Parmjit's supporters attended for only a few minutes in order to cast their votes. A few of them chatted at the back of the room for a while, distracting the candidates to whom they paid no attention.

I considered this whole process to be grossly unfair, but the rapid by-election timetable meant that it could not be challenged properly without causing considerable delays in the candidate selection, thereby destroying our prospects of winning. The campaign, therefore, began with significant bitterness in the local party, and which continued after the by-election and probably contributed to Parmjit's defeat in the 2005 general election, in spite of very considerable financial help and professional support provided to him by the party.

Our frontrunner status in the by-election was not a comfortable one, and the campaign was far from straightforward. I appointed Stuart Bray as the agent and he had a great deal of experience successfully running elections for the party in Leicester, and other nearby areas, in his role as regional organiser. We worked hard to promote Parmjit, who had been a Leicester councillor for a year, as part of the team taking up many different local issues and working with the other local Lib Dem councillors who now represented most of the very diverse parts of the constituency. As our canvassing confirmed, it was very much harder for us to win the by-election than appeared to be the case if you simply looked at the previous year's local election results. Labour's by-election candidate was Peter Soulsby, who was very well established in Leicester politics, having been a councillor there for thirty years, and who had previously been the Labour leader of the city council. He was also known as an opponent of the Iraq War and had been on the anti-war march.

Anti-war sentiment had helped us in 2003 to gain council seats in the most inner-city and strongly Muslim part of the constituency. It soon became clear in the by-election, however, that there was now strong support in those areas for Respect. Their candidate was Yvonne Ridley, a journalist who became well-known as a result of having been kidnapped by the Taliban, and her agent was George Galloway.

We also had to contend with an unexpectedly vigorous Conservative campaign. Michael Howard made at least five visits to the constituency and was determined to avoid a repeat of the Brent East result in which the Conservatives had fallen from second to third place. They hoped that the split in Labour and Lib Dem votes might enable them to win back a seat which they had held until 1987.

The Leicester South by-election soon became an even harder fight for us to win when the resignation of the Labour MP for Birmingham Hodge Hill, Terry Davis, triggered a second parliamentary by-election. This was also a seat with a large ethnic minority population. We had only polled 8 per cent there in the previous general election, but it was another by-election which we would have to fight to win. It had long seemed likely that this by-election might occur if the sitting Labour MP became general secretary of the Council of Europe. Anticipating this possibility, I had discussed the potential by-election with John Hemming, our leader on the council (and MP from 2005 for Birmingham Yardley). Based on John's information, I was extremely pleased that one of our local Asian members, Tariq Khan, would stand for us if the by-election occurred. Tariq was very well known locally and, when John and I discussed the potential by-election, was planning to stand in a council ward within the Hodge Hill constituency that we expected to gain in the May elections of that year.

The problem was that Tariq would not agree to become the parliamentary prospective candidate before the local elections, as he wanted to win his ward without Labour targeting him in the knowledge that he would be our candidate in a by-election. Once, however, he had gained his council seat with a very large majority, and the by-election occurred, he then decided that he wanted to fight the general election in a different part of Birmingham, and refused to put his name forward for the by-election. I found this most frustrating as I have no doubt that he would have won. Instead, the local party was left without an ethnic minority choice. Their eventual choice, Nicola Davies, proved to be an excellent candidate, and had the support in the selection of the party's Gender Balance Task Force (which was seeking to increase the number of female candidates), but had no real Birmingham connections and lived in Warwickshire. Labour's candidate, Liam Byrne, was not local either, but we were deprived of the local choice argument that had often been crucial for us.

We now had to contest two winnable parliamentary by-election campaigns on the same day for the first time in Lib Dem history. I was very mindful of our narrow failure in Liberal Party days to win 'a doubleheader' in 1986 when I had been the agent in West Derbyshire and we lost by 100 votes, but won Ryedale by 4,940. I believed that both Leicester South and Birmingham Hodge Hill could now be won, but I also had to recognise that there was the danger that we might win neither. The Conservatives fought very vigorous campaigns and started in second place in both constituencies. This made it much harder for us to present ourselves in each constituency as the clear alternative to Labour. We were also threatened with a third parliamentary by-election on the same day as rumours spread that Peter Mandelson might resign his Hartlepool seat in order to become a European Commissioner. I was determined to rise to the challenge of three by-election campaigns if necessary, and we printed a Lib Dem newspaper for Hartlepool attacking the potential closure of the local hospital in readiness. Fortunately, rumours of a pending appointment soon faded, leaving us with just two contests.

The Leicester South and Birmingham Hodge Hill by-elections were both called very quickly for 15 July as Labour sought to divide our resources and give us little time to develop momentum in our campaigns and squeeze the Conservative votes. I spent as little time as possible in London, occasionally attending early-morning meetings in Cowley Street, and usually then heading to Leicester on the train to spend most of the day there, travelling across to Birmingham for the evening, and then back to Leicester on the last train. I would stay overnight in the same house that I had lived in during the 1980s, and which had since been bought by a friend and local member. The HQ and parliamentary staff were immensely supportive of the approach that I was taking to try to win both by-election campaigns, and many of them also travelled frequently to the by-election battlegrounds.

Charles Kennedy was very prominent in both campaigns, making about six visits to each of them. He featured very strongly in our leaflets and in numerous carefully targeted letters that I wrote for different groups of voters in each of the two constituencies. In Leicester, with a little more time to prepare for the by-election campaign, we held a public meeting with Charles and Parmjit. Instead of holding such a public event themselves, Labour decided to try and disrupt ours by staging a protest outside using a powerful loudspeaker to try to drown out what was being said in the hall where we held our meeting. They were claiming, as usual, that the Lib Dems were 'soft on crime', and one of their members was dressed in a chicken suit as their supporters chanted loudly that we were 'chicken on crime'. I went outside for a short while and enjoyed a vigorous discussion with them, arguing that they were the 'chickens' – they were afraid to hold any public meetings because their leader was so unpopular. Indeed, they wouldn't even let Tony Blair visit Leicester during the campaign! I also accused them of anti-democratic tactics in trying to disrupt a meeting at which voters could hear from and ask questions of our leader and candidate, whilst holding none of their own.

Unfortunately, we had not handled control of the city council well, and it had taken some effort to get our councillors to reverse earlier decisions to reduce the provision of pensioners' free bus passes in an era before they were provided universally. We were also attacked over £2 million of cuts to community organisations in the city, many of whom were supportive of Labour as a result of funding having been given to them when Labour ran the council. We hit back by pointing out that Labour had closed six schools and a swimming pool when their candidate had been the council leader. One of the school closures had been in the heart of the constituency, and it had been particularly unpopular. The empty and boarded-up school buildings served as a constant reminder of the Labour candidate's local record. One of our campaign newspapers led with a large picture of the boarded-up school and the headline 'Shame on you, Sir Peter' (he had been knighted for services to local government in 1999).

In the end, the result of the campaign in Leicester South was probably more determined by tactical voting than anything else. There were large areas of the constituency which had traditionally been very Conservative in general elections. Over 150 Conservative MPs campaigned in Leicester South during the by-election. The Conservative candidate, Chris Heaton-Harris, one of the region's MEPs, was forecast by the Conservatives to be 'on the brink of victory' and was possibly not too far off this a week out from polling day. But in the last week of the campaign his level of support collapsed, as many voters in those areas decided that the choice was, as we portrayed it, between the local Lib Dem councillor and Tony Blair's candidate. I had been briefing the media a week before the election that there would be less than 2,000 votes between us and Labour on polling day, and then in the last few days that there might only be 1,000 votes between us and Labour in both by-elections. Some of my previous claims about likely by-election results had been treated with scepticism by political journalists, but they were now respected and reported extensively. The resulting newspaper quotes were, of course, extremely helpful in reinforcing the tactical message in our leaflets and letters during the last few days of the campaign.

Meanwhile, in Birmingham, we also fought hard to establish ourselves as the challengers. The work done in the local elections helped enormously in this regard, and whilst he did not stand as our candidate, Tariq Khan and the local Asian community rallied very strongly behind Charles Kennedy, Nicola Davies and our anti-war message. The whole campaign was incredibly short (approximately three weeks). We had, since Brent East, continued to improve our campaigning skills with Asian communities, and Ed Fordham, who had greatly helped with local campaigning in Brent, took a lead in building relationships with the community there, including helping to identify people with translation skills to assist with leaflets to be distributed outside mosques, and to produce advertisements in various ethnic publications.

Labour were clearly very threatened by our campaign and feared losing. Newspapers reported how the two by-elections might be decisive in determining Blair's future. In the last week of the campaign, the Butler Report was published, which showed that the intelligence that had supposedly justified the Iraq War was in fact 'flawed'. But it was not the killer blow that many people hoped for in terms of exposing the manipulation of that intelligence. Nevertheless, the report served to remind many people of how they could protest about being misled over the way in which Blair had backed Bush in what we considered to be an immoral, and probably illegal, war. Once again, the picture of Bush and Blair smiling together featured prominently in our campaigns.

Labour's campaign in response was both nasty and very aggressive. Whilst claiming that Lib Dems were 'soft on crime', their own campaign at some points was quite thuggish. There was one occasion when Labour activists surrounded the car in which Charles Kennedy and Nicola Davies were sitting, rocking it severely from side to side. Nicola worked in the telecoms industry, which sometimes involved liaising with local communities over applications for phone masts. This led Labour to claim in their leaflets that 'scandal hits phone mast Lib Dem' as they sought to play upon people's fears about the alleged dangers of mobile phone masts. In both campaigns, we were very worried about the potential abuse of the postal vote system. The ease with which postal votes could now be applied for meant that many people were effectively surrendering their right to vote in proper conditions of privacy in a polling station. In Birmingham, there were a number of legal actions following the local elections that year and which led the judge concerned to conclude that aspects of our electoral process were open to the sort of abuse that he might have expected in a 'banana republic'. We devoted considerable effort to advising people with postal votes to avoid handing them over to anybody else, and to make sure that they completed them themselves and returned them promptly before the possibility of anybody approaching to 'assist them' with returning their votes. I was also mindful of my experience in Leicester in the 1980s, when Labour workers would surround people approaching polling stations and harangue them with instructions about who to vote for. We asked for a strong police presence on polling day to try to prevent this.

I was desperate to try and win both by-elections, and for Charles Kennedy to gain credit for whatever success we could achieve. We made private arrangements for him and his key office staff, including Tim Razzall, to travel up on polling day to a hotel in the Midlands. If we won Birmingham Hodge Hill, he would go there for an election night victory party, as this would have been the biggest story. If we didn't, but we did manage to win Leicester South, then he would go to Leicester to make sure that he was pictured celebrating with our new MP. But if we won neither by-election, the plan was that he and his team would return to London without anybody knowing that he had ever been in the Midlands that night. Unfortunately, somebody from his office revealed that evening that he was on a train heading towards the Midlands, and I feared that we would be subject to some embarrassment if we won neither campaign.

I spent polling day in Leicester South, where much of my time was taken up dealing with the police, who had to investigate a break-in at our campaign HQ the night before the polls opened and the theft of a number of computers, including my own laptop. When the polls closed, our team of counting agents, including Sarah Teather, who would be commenting with me on TV programmes that night, arrived at the counting centre resplendent with the yellow rose buttonholes that Ann had thoughtfully arranged to have sent to our HQ on polling day. As the ballot boxes opened, I remained optimistic after my first glances at the ballot papers indicating our share of the vote. We were not, however, winning in very many polling districts at all. The inner-city Spinney Hill ward and neighbouring polling districts had voted heavily for Respect. The wealthy (and more white areas) still showed a strong Conservative vote, and in some of these places they were actually ahead of us. Sarah told me that we had not won a single box that she had seen opened and she feared that we had lost. I told the team that we were okay, but that it was close. Unlike the other parties, we were achieving a strong vote almost everywhere, which I thought would be enough to win overall. It was too close to make any firm prediction until about midnight, when I was live on the BBC election night programme and said that 'it was close, but the right side of close'. Sarah repeated this line live on Sky News a few moments later. Based on what I had been hearing from Birmingham, I also suggested that there would be a recount at Hodge Hill. But by then I knew that we would be asking for it, and that we would not quite make the double gain. Parmjit was declared the winner in Leicester South by a majority of 1,654 votes (34.9 per cent to 29.3 per cent, a swing of 21 per cent to us from Labour). Following the recount in Hodge Hill, Nicola Davies lost by just 460 votes (36.5 per cent to 34.2 per cent, a swing of 27 per cent to us from Labour). Charles and his entourage then headed over to Leicester to be pictured with the Lib Dems' first ethnic minority MP. It was another joyous scene, and we repeated it the following week outside the House of Commons when Parmjit took his seat. I felt delighted that we had now won the constituency where I had helped us win our first council seats nearly twenty years previously, that we were no longer an all-white Parliamentary Party at Westminster, and that we were maintaining the momentum of our challenge to Labour, whilst preventing the Conservatives establishing their own. But I was also very frustrated that we had not elected Nicola, and that 'the double' had eluded us. I went over to Birmingham on the day after polling day to commiserate with team members and persuaded some of the key people who had done so well there, including Hilary Stephenson, to come across to Leicester for the team's victory meal the Friday evening after polling day.

BOSTON AND HARTLEPOOL

In the summer of 2004, I had once again arranged to go to the US Democrat Convention in Boston. Tim Razzall and I were both keen that Charles Kennedy came with us and saw something of how the Democrats did things at the biggest event in their four-year election cycle. We were the guests of the National Democratic Institute for International Affairs (NDI) and, together with Ming Campbell, attended events addressed by Madeleine Albright, Bill Clinton and others before the start of the convention. During one of these seminars, I was able to show Charles a news alert on my phone showing the latest UK polls. On the back of the Leicester and Birmingham by-elections, we had reached level pegging with the Conservatives on 28 per cent, only 2 per cent behind Labour on 30 per cent.

The Democrat conventions were always a great experience for me, and I considered it well worthwhile paying personally to attend it. Boston was a brilliant venue; I liked the city and in particular visiting the Kennedy Museum to see and hear about the Kennedys and their extraordinary influence on American politics. Many great speeches were made and Bill Clinton demonstrated, once again, why I thought that he was the best political orator in the world at the time. Charles was particularly impressed that he could make the equivalent of a brilliant leader's speech in just twenty-two minutes, speaking on live TV, and finishing just before they would break for the news. There is generally also great musical entertainment at the conventions, this year provided by the likes of Carole King, of whom I discovered that Charles was also a fan. The events in the main hall are a series of speeches in which leading Democrats are allocated slots according to their status and usefulness to the forthcoming general election campaign. The runners-up in the primary contest always get a good slot if they promise to endorse the successful candidate, in this case John Kerry. Howard Dean had run an effective 'insurgent' campaign[67] based on the need for universal health care coverage, and when he came to the platform there were demonstrations of wild enthusiasm from the so-called 'Deaniacs' amongst the 20,000 or so people in the hall. The noise was such that it was difficult for him to begin speaking. Ed Fordham was watching the live TV coverage in London (in the small hours of the morning) and

---

67   Initially managed by Rick Ridder and which might well have been successful if Rick had continued in the role.

texted me to say that if we all shut up, we would be able to hear Dean speak! I texted back to advise that he stay up for four or five more speeches to hear the bloke they'd chosen to stand for the Senate in Illinois: 'They say that Barack Obama is a great speaker.' Obama then made one of the most impressive and moving speeches that I have ever heard. 'There is not a black America, there is not a white America, there is the United States of America' was his theme. Ed texted back: 'Wow!' I turned to the delegates around me and said: 'That man will be the first black President or Vice-President of the US!' They were a bit surprised by the confidence of my assertion given my English accent and, of course, I thought Vice-President more likely.

Charles was accompanied by Sarah; they had by now been married for two years and clearly enjoyed the break in Boston. Charles liked being recognised in the street, and was much surprised by this, as he didn't realise the popularity of Prime Minister's Question Time on US TV. They stayed on in Boston for the weekend after the convention. Ann also came out as term finished at her Early Years Centre in Islington, and we had decided to have a holiday on the east coast of the US. I could generally work very hard, seven days a week, but needed my holiday in August. We and the Kennedys went out to dinner on the Saturday night at a branch of Legal Seafood, a favourite Boston chain. We all had lobsters. Sarah, Ann and I enjoyed the wine, whilst Charles drank Coca-Cola. We were all in a very relaxed and cheerful mood. Ann and I then set off for Long Island, New York and New Jersey as the Kennedys began their journey to Italy for a holiday there. It was nine months before the 2005 general election, and also before Donald Kennedy was born.

Whilst I was in New England, the early preparations were also taking place for the by-election that now followed Peter Mandelson's resignation to become a European Commissioner. Richard Pinnock was the agent and Ed Fordham, along with his partner Russell Eagling, were already helping in the crucial early stages and keeping me informed of progress. A barrister, Jody Dunn, who lived not far away from the constituency, had been chosen as our candidate. The future of the Hartlepool hospital was still considered to be under threat, and so the newspaper that we had printed in June was now being delivered. As with Brent East, Leicester South and Birmingham Hodge Hill, we began in third place. We had polled just 15 per cent of the vote in Hartlepool in 2001.

I ran up very large bills on my mobile phone talking to the campaign team from the US. I also later felt some guilt about my absence from Hartlepool during this crucial period, but I felt that we really needed the holiday. When I returned to the UK, I went straight up to Hartlepool. Our campaign leaflets focusing on local issues such as the future of the hospital had gained traction immediately, particularly in the areas where the Conservatives had previously been strong. Jody was an inspirational speaker, and really stood out in the campaign. We considered the Labour candidate, Iain Wright, to be very weak in comparison. The *Hartlepool Mail*, however, appeared now to be under the thumb of the Labour Party. A previous editor had been dismissed after making strident criticisms of Peter Mandelson and supporting the election of 'H'Angus the Monkey' as Mayor of Hartlepool in a challenge to Labour's dominance of the town. When Jody triumphed over the Labour candidate in a local debate over issues such as the future of the hospital, the *Hartlepool Mail* had virtually nothing to say about it. It should have been a great story as Labour's candidate was torn to shreds. It now appeared to us that we were seeing an example of Labour's 'machine politics' control in such places, and we were determined to challenge it. For much of the campaign it seemed to me that we should win, and in spite of Peter Mandelson's 14,571 majority over the Conservatives, it was, almost, our campaign to lose.

The penultimate week of the by-election clashed with our annual conference in Bournemouth. We used the conference effectively to promote Jody, who came down to speak at it on the day before the leader's speech. She gained some very good national publicity and at the end of the conference was flown back up to Hartlepool, together with Charles Kennedy, by Lembit Öpik in his private plane. I felt positive about the by-election outcome until I heard whilst in Bournemouth about a blog posting that Jody had made. Some of my campaign colleagues had been very keen on the candidate communicating directly with people about the by-election via a personal blog. This was a good idea in principle. But, unfortunately, the safeguards that would normally be in place to check the sense of a press release, a speech or a leaflet, or even to prepare for media questions, were not there for Jody's blog. Those who saw what Jody proposed to post as a light-hearted joke about one night's canvassing in which she had encountered 'a man who was drunk, a man who was semi-naked and a man with an angry dog' did not see how this could obviously be portrayed as being a very poor representation of Hartlepool people. Nor could Jody. Labour quickly seized upon her unfortunate remarks and implied that this was her description of Hartlepool people in general. Whilst I was busy with the Bournemouth conference, the situation span out of all control as Jody was pressed on the *Today* programme to apologise for her remarks, and she was unable to put them in proper context. Nor were we, and Labour had a recording of her *Today* interview blaring out from loudspeakers in a bus that was touring the constituency.

Our momentum against Labour was halted. The row coincided with the large number of postal voters receiving their ballot papers and we were doing very badly at that point. We would have needed a very large majority on polling day itself to overcome the likely large deficit from the postal votes. Nevertheless, we came within 2,033 votes of winning (40.7 per cent to 34.2 per cent, with a swing to us from Labour of 18.9 per cent), and we pushed the Conservatives into a humiliating fourth place behind UKIP.

Hartlepool proved to be the last parliamentary by-election before the 2005 general election. We had come close, but hadn't won. In just over a year, in four parliamentary by-elections in previously 'safe' Labour seats in London, Leicester, Birmingham and Hartlepool, we had come from third place to win two and nearly win two others. In each case we had pushed the Conservatives from second place to third or fourth. Michael Howard's election as Conservative leader in place of Ian Duncan Smith had given his party a major boost, but we stopped him making any real progress in these by-elections, and we had shown that Lib Dems could be effective challengers to Labour even in their heartlands.

By-election results of this scale cannot be easily repeated in general elections. But I felt that we had created an atmosphere in which people would see Charles Kennedy's Liberal Democrats challenging Labour effectively in many places where the Conservatives would not be able to do so. I knew also, however, that the seats in which we were facing Labour at the general election often had very large majorities, and that our resources on the ground in many of them were not nearly strong enough for us to be able to win them. Nevertheless, I was confident that we would now make the biggest advance against Labour in a general election that we had ever made as either the Liberal Party, the Alliance, or the Liberal Democrats. The success of the by-elections, however, meant that many other people now had quite unrealistic expectations about the scale of the advance that we could make as and when the general election came the following year, and this was to make life much harder for Charles Kennedy after the 2005 election than it might otherwise have been.

CHAPTER 12

HIGH WATERMARK

MICHAEL BROWN

Fridays at Cowley Street were usually kept clear from meetings in my diary in order to help me to catch up with paperwork, or more usually so that I could prepare for and travel to the many weekend party activities and events that took place all over the country. Shortly before Christmas 2004, I was surprised to see that a meeting appeared in my diary for a Friday morning with a Mr Michael Brown. He had evidently been persistent in requesting a meeting with the chief executive, I understood, to discuss Liberal Democrat policies. It turned out not to be a very convenient Friday for me, so I asked Ben Stoneham if he would be willing to meet him on that day. Apparently, Mr Brown was somewhat disappointed not to meet me personally, but Ben chatted to him in my office and noted that when he left it was in a very smart car apparently driven by a personal chauffeur. He had left his impressive-looking business card for me. This said that he represented a company called '5th Avenue Partners'. There had been no obvious motive for his visit to Cowley Street, but Ben thought it worthwhile passing on his details to the party treasurer Reg Clark.

I heard no more of Michael Brown until the middle of January, when a lunch was organised for a few of the people who we hoped would be amongst our most significant financial backers for the general election expected within a few months. He had been invited to it and I was immediately struck by his somewhat eccentric appearance (he was sporting a ponytail) and I also noted his polite and very softly spoken manner. As the lunch broke up, and a few of us were chatting with him, I found it strange that what he appeared to want to know most was the size of our largest previous donation. We told him that it had been £250,000 and the inference that he might make a sizeable donation was obvious.

The possibility of him becoming a major new donor was discussed at several of the chief officers' meetings held in the Leader's Office, and chaired by Charles. These meetings brought Charles together with some of the major party committee chairs, officers of the party, and his senior office staff. Since the lunch, Reg had maintained contact with Michael Brown and there was a sense of excitement at these meetings that we might have a major new donor. Reg reported that Michael Brown had a business based in the UK which was able to make a donation and that he seemed willing to make one. He also appeared to be entitled to be on the electoral register, based at an apartment in Dover Street, Mayfair, where he was now resident and running his business. I felt that it would look strange if a large personal donation was made within a few months of first being included on the electoral register, so the company donation seemed to be the better route if he wanted to help us. We were all delighted when he gave Reg a cheque from the company for £100,000. The party had fewer than a dozen people at that time able and willing to make donations of that size and so, of course, we discussed whether or not we could persuade him to make further contributions.

Given all the subsequent controversy, it is important to note that to the very best of my knowledge, nothing was ever sought by Michael Brown from the party, nor was anything ever offered or given to him, and there was collective responsibility amongst this group over his donations. What I learned from the discussions was that he appeared to be a strong supporter of Charles Kennedy as a fellow Highlander. Soon after his first donation, however, his discussions with Reg clearly became problematic, as he appeared also to be examining the possibility of investing in Reg's company as well as in the party. Our new donor was a persuasive character, as well as appearing to be extremely rich, so I can see how Reg may have been led to believe that he was seeking businesses to invest in, as well as supporting his chosen political party. In the end, Brown decided not to make any investment in Reg's company, but indicated that he was prepared to make a further sizeable donation of £151,000 to the party in order to exceed in total our previous largest single donation. Anna Werrin went with another member of the Leader's Office staff to Dover Street to collect this cheque personally. Meeting him there confirmed the impression of his business being in operation as he monitored various financial transactions on computer screens. Of course, we were aware that we needed to make some more checks upon him in case there was any hidden agenda behind his motives for contributing. In the meantime, Reg had decided to step down as party treasurer.

A political party has very limited means with which to investigate people's personal financial backgrounds, or those of companies that they control, especially if, as in this case, the UK company had not yet filed accounts at Companies House. We knew that Michael Brown had very respectable and well-known lawyers, accountants and bankers with many more powers of investigation than we had, and that they had legal responsibilities (and powers) to make checks upon him. But we did not just want to rely upon them. With the general election approaching, we were frequently in touch with Special Branch, who were responsible for issues such as Charles's personal security during the campaign. We were considering, at my suggestion, using Michael Brown's private jet for some of Charles's election tour, and this would have necessitated him being accompanied on the plane by Special Branch officers. Anna therefore made an approach to see if Special Branch could help to check out any security or other concerns for us about Michael Brown and provided them with a photocopy of his initial £100,000 cheque. Through this process, I was quite staggered to discover what powers they had. We were informed that there was more than £10 million in the account from which the cheque was drawn and that millions of pounds were regularly flowing through it, but without there being any activity that should worry us. We were told that he had made money relatively quickly, but that there was no gun running, drug dealing or any other illegal activities going on. We were also assured that they had no concerns whatsoever about their officers flying with Charles in Michael Brown's jet. This information was, of course, given in strict confidence, but it provided us with significant reassurance, and we used it later to help demonstrate to the Electoral Commission, with the help of an opinion that I obtained from a leading QC, that this and other evidence showed that we had done what we reasonably could to check the provenance of Michael Brown's company and that no court could reasonably expect us after we had spent his donations during the election to pay an equivalent sum to all his donations to the Treasury. This is what happened with impermissible donations that had been accepted and not returned within twenty-eight days. The Political Parties, Elections and Referendum Act (2000) provided for companies to be able to make donations to political parties, providing that they did business in the UK. In considering the issue during the debates in Parliament, the level, or type, of business conducted was not considered to be relevant to the permissibility of the donation. There was very little more, beyond checking that the company had been registered at Companies House, and was not 'dormant', that we could have done ourselves, especially in the very short period of twenty-eight days allowed by the legislation for parties either to accept donations as being permissible, or to return them. Amidst all the later controversy, few people realised how short a timescale parties have to check the permissibility of donations, or their limited means of doing so. We felt confident, however, to proceed on the basis of the convincing information that we had, and the Special Branch information in particular.

In the run-up to the pre-election spring conference that year in Harrogate, I suggested that we tried to use Michael's private jet to demonstrate to him how it could help us to obtain media coverage in two different regions in one day, whilst efficiently getting Charles up to North Yorkshire. This was agreed, and on the Friday that the conference was to begin, he flew up with Michael via Rochdale in order to make a campaign visit there and do interviews with the north west media, and then on to Leeds Bradford airport and to do further interviews from Harrogate. On the Saturday night of the conference, I organised a private dinner for just over a dozen of our most significant donors to enjoy Charles's company, be briefed privately about the imminent campaign, and be thanked for their generous contributions. It was important for me to also show to the Rowntree Reform Trust directors present that the party had some significant financial backers as well as themselves. Held in a private dining room of the White Hart Hotel, the donors, including Michael Brown, all seemed to think that it had been a good occasion.

The conference went extremely well in terms of internal confidence-building, but media coverage was very limited, as was often the case with spring conferences. On the Sunday that it finished, Tim Razzall approached me to say that, following the dinner, Michael Brown was now making an extraordinary offer in terms of additional financial help to the party for the election campaign that we expected would formally begin in about two weeks. He had been asking about how much the other parties spent on their election campaigns, and how this compared with our budget. I provided information showing that I expected both other major parties to spend to the £20 million national limit, whilst I showed the breakdown of our own budget at around £2.5 million. Whilst expressing the hope that he would really have liked to create a level playing field in party funding, Michael Brown had indicated that he might enable us to double the size of our budget. Two days after the conference, I was attending a regular meeting of the party's Finance and Administration Committee, knowing that at the same time Tim and Anna were meeting with Michael Brown to discuss this potential donation. I had provided the briefing as to exactly where we stood in relation to our general election budget, so that he knew exactly what we were already committed to. He was clearly unwilling to pay for anything already budgeted for in the existing plan. Nor was he going to allow us to use any additional funds as we most wanted, but his aim, I understood, was to help us to make a significant impact during the election in terms of things like national advertising. Our aim was to get him contributing and see what he might pay for in future.

My immediate problem then was that we would need to sign contracts very quickly if we were to spend a donation in excess of £2 million and undertake the sort of advertising campaign that he wanted. I was not prepared to sign anything committing us to expenditure until the funds were received and fully cleared, which was only days before the start of the campaign. I therefore had to work rapidly to make tentative preparations to spend the expected donation. With a lot of help from Julian Ingram, I investigated the possibilities for spending on advertising. In the process, we discovered that the agencies responsible for professional poster board hoardings had at this point given up on the prospect of any further election advertising being booked. We were therefore able to book around £1.4 million worth of sites for less than £700,000. Our advertising agency, banc, led by Robert Bean, worked superbly well (after some initial difficulty in agreeing messaging) in organising the production and distribution of the chosen poster designs across the country and they were to become amongst the top four most recognised advertising posters in the last fortnight of the campaign. We were very quickly able to produce and commercially distribute 10 million copies of a special eight-page tabloid newspaper promoting Charles and our national campaign and which was designed in house by Duncan Borrowman. I was also able to book some national and local newspaper advertising, in accordance with what I understood that he wanted to pay for, as well as significant social media advertising. With more time and greater flexibility, we would have used this £2 million-plus donation rather differently. But given that it had to be spent on specific additional projects, my immediate concern was to make sure that the donor felt that we did what had been agreed with him. Tim and I were both very mindful of the importance of trying to secure similar funding for future projects on a regular basis and which would be consistent with a long-term strategy that could transform our prospects of competing in national elections.

2005 GENERAL ELECTION

Michael Brown's plane helped Charles to repeat the 'Flying Start' of his last campaign, so that he was seen to tour every region in the country in the four days that followed Tony Blair's announcement that he had gone to Buckingham Palace to seek a dissolution. The start of our campaign was, however, much more difficult for us than that of 2001, largely because of events outside our control. The death of Pope John Paul II had postponed the Prime Minister's planned visit to the Palace from 4 April to 5 April, and then led to the suspension of campaigning for his funeral on 8 April. Knowing that Tony Blair would be at Buckingham Palace some time on the 5th, we decided that Charles's main election launch statement would be delivered in Newcastle city centre, which was the scene of one of his three campaign visits planned that day. We felt this would symbolise our challenge to Labour and our optimism for the campaign. Charles seemed, however, to be somewhat lacking in confidence that day. At the last minute, he insisted somewhat impractically that a lectern be flown up in the plane with him so that it could be set up in the street, allowing him to rest the notes for his very short speech on it. He then had some difficulty with these notes as he wanted to add what I considered to be an unnecessarily 'flowery' but typical Charles style of introduction that would have been more appropriate for a debate. His speechwriter, Greg Simpson, assisted him in revising the bullet points and, inevitably, this list appeared in the television pictures, but sadly without any real meaning being obvious from reading them. The Pope's funeral on the third day of the campaign meant that the wedding of Prince Charles and Camilla Parker Bowles was in turn put back to 9 April, and this again had to be a non-campaign day. It was therefore very difficult for us to establish the early momentum for which we had hoped, and in the 'war room' at HQ we felt frustrated and in trying to explain our difficulties to a briefing of Sunday press reporters, Tim actually referred to the 'Pope's wedding and Charles's funeral'.

Our manifesto launch, perhaps the most important day of the campaign, and the 24-hour period when we could expect our greatest share of media coverage, was planned for Tuesday 12 April. On the Monday morning before this, I signed off the operational note to be sent out to the media inviting them to the launch. Just twenty-five minutes after this was emailed out, we received a call from Sarah Kennedy's brother, James Gurling, to say that Sarah's waters had broken. Journalists waiting for Charles's plane to take off for campaigning that day eventually had to be told why he was instead returning immediately to London, and I had to rescind the note to the media convening the manifesto launch.

We had planned all along for Ming Campbell, as deputy leader, to take over all the leader's responsibilities from this point until after the baby's birth. The year before, I had to go so far as to warn Ming privately that there was at least a one in five chance in my view that he would have to take over as leader for the whole campaign in view of Charles's health problems. But we got to the start of the campaign without this, and prior to it beginning, my understanding was that Charles and Sarah's baby was not likely to be born until later in the campaign, so I hoped that Charles would have completed the bulk of his campaign engagements by then. But this was not to be, and we now found that our political campaign coverage became much more limited than we had hoped, as media interest in the Lib Dems focused more on St Thomas's Hospital than on events such as Ming meeting pensioners in Westmorland & Lonsdale.

There was, of course, much delight when Donald was born in the early hours of the Tuesday morning and there were wonderful pictures of Sarah and Charles with him outside St Thomas's later that day. An enormous Harrods hamper of gifts for the Kennedys arrived at Cowley Street, courtesy of Michael Brown. On the following afternoon (Wednesday), Tim, Anna and I went to see the new baby at the Kennedy's Kennington home. We also had to take the tricky decision as to whether or not to go ahead with the revised plan to launch the manifesto the following morning (Thursday). It was clear when we went that Charles was in good form, and very happy of course. I asked him if he felt up to speed with all the election issues, and he said that he had seen much of the 24-hour TV coverage whilst in the hospital, and had been able to follow political events more easily than was generally possible when he was campaigning around the country. It was about 4.15 p.m. and we felt confident that we could launch the manifesto as now planned.

Having held our usual series of pre-press conference meetings at Cowley Street, Tim and I, together with Matthew Taylor, Ming Campbell and Sarah Teather, who were to be part of the manifesto launch, walked over to Local Government House in Smith Square for our meeting with Charles as part of the final preparation before the launch. Alarm bells soon rang, however, when we received a call to say that Charles would not make this meeting as 'the baby had kept him awake much of the night, he had not slept well and was running late'. The Bevin Hall in Local Government House was completely packed with media. Charles arrived only a few minutes before he was due to appear on the platform, in time for his ritual pre-press conference cigarette in the small courtyard just outside the otherwise 'no smoking' building. A member of our team, and longstanding friend of his, kissed him to congratulate him on Donald's birth, after which she immediately warned me and others about the smell of alcohol that we had feared might be the more likely cause of his delayed arrival.

Charles did not look well as he gave a too-lengthy ten-minute introduction to the event. He then sat down with the rest of the panel and immediately looked relieved to have got through his speech. We had deliberately tried to create a 'Breakfast TV' look for the press conference (generally held at 7.30 a.m.) as we believed that Charles would perform best in a more relaxed setting than that usually used for formal press conferences. But, on this occasion, he appeared to be too relaxed. He had previously spoken in party discussions about local income tax, showing a good grasp of the facts about at what point 'two-income taxpaying households' might be net losers if council tax was replaced by local income tax. On this occasion, however, he struggled painfully with an answer to a question about this, and nobody else on the platform felt able to intervene easily without suggesting that he didn't know the answer. Financial statistics were never Charles's strong point and he kept quoting different figures in answer to this question whilst slowly moving his hands around as though this was helping him to do the calculation. It was the most embarrassing few minutes that I have ever witnessed in a press conference. Most of the HQ team was stony-faced, whilst Vince Cable was actually striking his head with the palms of both hands and muttering in the hearing of those nearby about Charles's performance.

I feared at this moment that Charles might suddenly have become a huge liability to the campaign, in contrast to the great public asset that he had been in 2001. The immediate job for us now was to somehow try to restore some apparent self-confidence to the campaign. We had to explain emphatically that his hesitancy had simply been the result of lack of sleep, and that he would now be quickly and effectively promoting the key messages of the manifesto, demonstrating that the Liberal Democrats were 'The Real Alternative – putting patients first, promoting ambitions for every child, prepared to tackle crime and build prosperity for Britain'.

After much coffee in Norman Lamb's flat close to Smith Square, Charles's recovery was indeed quite rapid as he began a series of interviews, spelling out these themes. His broadcast media communication skills again came to the fore, if a little less effectively than on other occasions. For the next four days, however, it was the clips of his hesitancy and strange hand movements whilst trying to answer the question about local income tax that dominated media coverage of the Lib Dems' general election campaign. The British Election Study tracking public opinion during the campaign was available online and I saw how Charles's personal ratings plummeted as a result, before recovering strongly a few days later. I showed Ming the graph indicating the recovery, provoking him to remark on Charles's extraordinary 'Houdini capacity' in these circumstances.

Having had such a difficult start to our campaign, recovery from this point was certainly not inevitable. A degree of liaison between our campaign and Labour's had continued via telephone calls between Tim Razzall and Sally Morgan in Tony Blair's office. Tim very rarely referred to them, even to me, and I do not think that either campaign was changed significantly as a result of this communication. But the plane back from the Pope's funeral in Rome provided an opportunity for Tony Blair and Charles to speak privately together. The Labour leader was very keen to debate the Tory arguments being made in the campaign about immigration. He knew that it would be better for him to do so if Charles was making similar arguments at the same time, and Tim and I were shocked to discover that Labour appeared to think that the two leaders had agreed that this would happen on the Friday of that week. We both knew that the Tories would be delighted if immigration was brought to the top of the agenda in this way. We knew that arguments about it could not be won within a few days, and that every time controversy over immigration became more salient in the campaign we suffered significantly in our private polls, with the Tories gaining at our expense. Charles was a little sheepish about what had been agreed, but then understood that we had to stick to our own plans and our most effective messaging. Labour were subsequently furious that Charles did not join in raising the profile of immigration when they expected him to. The Tories would have been delighted if Charles had also decided to major on the issue. When he was asked about it in the campaign, Charles simply said that his starting point on the issue was to talk about the benefits of immigration, but he said little more.

Our pre-election market research, interviewing voters individually in our target constituencies, had revealed considerable cynicism in response to our various attempts to package between three and five of our major policies into some sort of 'pledge card', along the lines that Labour appeared previously to have done successfully. Much to my surprise, a longer list, packaging together our top ten proposals, was shown to have rather more appeal. Robert Bean had helped us to develop a potential approach based on simply suggesting 'what we opposed' and 'what we proposed' instead. This 'sloganised' approach to policy was itself fairly crude, but it proved effective when we said, for example: 'We oppose: tuition fees and top-up fees. We propose: scrapping student fees.' We listed on the back page of our manifesto, and in newspaper adverts, the 'Ten Good Reasons to Vote Liberal Democrat', concluding with: 'We oppose: Bush and Blair on Iraq. We propose: never again.' It worked well in the research, and with voters in the election.

The manifesto was drawn up under the oversight of Matthew Taylor (who had been treasury spokesperson when the process of writing it began) and the party's Federal Policy Committee. Their work was helped initially by Richard Grayson (who left the party's employ in the autumn of 2004) and then received very valuable input from Sandy Walkington. Sandy was a former director of communications for BT, and many years before had been the most senior staff member for the Liberal MPs. He became director of policy and communications for the party almost exactly 100 days before polling day, as part of a reorganisation in which I had sought to bring together the party's research, policy and communications functions in a more streamlined process. The manifesto – 'Freedom, Fairness, Trust' – attempted to set out our political vision in the same tabloid newspaper format that had proved to be an effective and popular campaigning document in 2001. One problem, however, that we never seemed to overcome was our difficulty in obtaining good-quality photographs of Charles; either because he was often not looking at his best, or because he was not available for long enough whenever suitable photographers could be found. The document, with a front-page photograph of Charles surrounded by a diverse array of party supporters taken at the spring conference prior to the election, outlined our major – and carefully costed – proposals. We offered to cut class sizes in primary schools by abolishing Labour's Child Trust Fund. We said that we would abolish tuition fees and introduce free personal care for elderly and disabled people, and cut local government tax bills. This would all be paid for by increasing the level of income tax to 50p in the pound for earnings in excess of £100,000 per year. I was personally doubtful that these proceeds might stretch to cutting local government tax bills on top of the other commitments, but the 50p rate was in itself a popular proposal, as well as providing the finance to scrap tuition fees across the UK, as we had already done in Scotland. The persuasive messages certainly helped to support our 'ground war' campaigns in the constituencies, and our poll ratings began to rise significantly in spite of the difficult start to our campaign. This helped to restore Charles's self-confidence as he continuously emphasised in the campaign what were the key differences between us and both of our main rivals.

Our tracking polls in the target seats were also giving me some confidence as I came into Cowley Street about 4.30 a.m. every morning in order to review them and to prepare for the 6.30 a.m. strategy meeting. We were also getting canvassing data from these seats on a regular basis, and I could see familiar patterns forming as I had seen in the data from many of the same seats in our three previous general election campaigns. Much would again depend on tactical voting, which tended only to show up in the polling in the closing few days of the campaign, and there was real excitement amongst the candidates and agents that I spoke to.

My telephone calls, however, had to be severely curtailed halfway through the campaign when I lost my voice. A throat infection hit me at the worst possible time and I found that by early afternoon for the last two weeks of the campaign I could barely speak. The run-up to the formal period of the campaign was probably more exhausting for me than the campaign itself, in which there was a much bigger support team at HQ. I ended up feeling immensely frustrated at having to lie down and rest during many of the afternoons towards the end of the campaign. This meant that I missed some of the excitement, including the immediate preparations for the defection to us of Brian Sedgemore, a sitting Labour MP until the dissolution of Parliament. Originally a quite left-wing Labour MP, Brian was very strongly pro-European and had told his friend Tim Razzall prior to the campaign that he would join us during it. His defection to us, during one of our morning press conferences, incensed the Labour Party; though our job was not to help Labour, but to demonstrate why so many decent people now opposed them because of their support for Bush's war in Iraq in particular. With hindsight, we should probably have been more careful about the words accompanying Brian's defection as he appealed to 'the centre and left in British politics' to unite behind us, whilst ignoring the fact that we were also trying to appeal to more Conservative-minded voters who would no doubt be uncomfortable with such labelling.

I had initially assumed that we would raise the issue of the Iraq War strongly at the start of our campaign. But Charles, I felt afterwards, was right to have judged instead that we should leave it for later in the campaign in order to reduce the risk of us being seen as a 'one-trick pony'. Brian Sedgemore's defection now brought the Iraq War issue into a prominent position and lifted our campaign immediately prior to the leaking of the advice by the Attorney General about the legality of the invasion. This advice was significantly different to the claims that had been made about it at the time, suggesting that Blair's government had been disingenuous, to say the least, about what it said. The actual advice suggested that the government, as demanded by the Liberal Democrats, should have sought a second resolution from the United Nations Security Council specifically authorising military action. We regarded the apparent alteration or falsification of legal advice very seriously. Whilst Charles was always extremely careful in his choice of words, and unlike Michael Howard avoided the word 'lie', he was able to articulate the concerns of everyone who felt misled by Tony Blair about his support for Bush's war. In turn, Michael Howard was forced to admit that he would have also supported the Iraq invasion if he had been Prime Minister, but claimed that he would have been more honest than Tony Blair about the reasons for doing so. I was always most comfortable with the positioning of the Liberal Democrats when we supported a popular cause that was also principled, and over which we could bracket both other main parties as being on the wrong side of public opinion. Issues such as Iraq and the abolition of student tuition fees across the UK, therefore, worked extremely well for us in the campaign and particularly in many of our target constituencies with significant student and ethnic minority populations.

Charles did not have the great advantage of the 2010-style leaders' debates, which benefited Nick Clegg considerably, but he triumphed in the nearest equivalent, which was the main *Question Time* debate on BBC One. In this, the three main party leaders were in turn interviewed by David Dimbleby and then subjected to questions from a studio audience. Charles's personal charm on such occasions, and his considerable debating skills when feeling confident and relaxed, could put him on the right side of both the studio audience and the viewers. As the first of the three leaders to perform that night, Charles possibly had an audience in a better mood, and in cooler temperatures, than when his rivals faced them. His skill was shown in the way that he alone chose to chat with the audience informally prior to the programme. When he was in good form, he could be one of the most polite and courteous people you could ever meet, and he demonstrated this as he asked members of the audience where they had travelled from and sympathised with them about their journeys. They took to him immediately and the applause when he walked out for the start of recording his section of the programme was very strong, in contrast to the indifference or hostility shown when Howard and Blair appeared later. Charles also had the skill to challenge David Dimbleby effectively when being questioned, and to get the audience on board with him, rather than with his sometimes too-acerbic interviewer.

The manifesto and our ten-point programme gave Charles sufficient ammunition to sustain our campaign through to polling day, whilst emphasising a small number of popular and principled causes that highlighted differences with both our major opponents. We sought in the ten points to demonstrate our concern about environmental issues and climate change, but what we said about them never attracted the same attention as other issues.

Our tracking polls and canvas analysis from the target seats showed that the campaigns on the ground and our 'air war' messaging were helping us to increase support significantly within them during the course of the campaign, as had happened during those of 1997 and 2001. The internal polling showed that we increased our support in the target seats by an average of 16 per cent during the campaign, which was vital to our results because at the outset of the campaign we had been a long way behind in many of them (including in held seats). The focus of our attention in the target seat constituency campaigns was on the benefits of having a Lib Dem MP standing up for the popular principles in Parliament that were so effectively articulated by Charles. We saw how this was having a significant effect, putting us within striking distance of the approximately sixty-five seats that I believed we could win; but there remained a quite unrealistic expectation promulgated by some people within the party that we could win many more.

Our prospects of advancing at constituency level depended largely on what we did within those seats in the four years prior to the election. In many of those that we targeted, we had been campaigning effectively for at least a decade, generally with the same candidate. But this also had the downside of making many of the target seats fairly obvious to our rivals who were now seeking to combat the effects of our grassroots campaigning by undertaking much more of it themselves in these places. For this reason, we kept the fact that we were targeting Solihull as secret as we could, knowing that the Conservatives were complacent with their 20 per cent lead in 2001 over us there. Lorely Burt, advised by the director of campaigns, Paul Rainger, ran what was probably the best campaign in the country in order to gain that seat. Labour had been third in the constituency with 25 per cent of the vote in 2001, and this was reduced to just 15 per cent in 2005.

I was under some pressure prior to the campaign to make much more of internet-based campaigning. I was keen, but considered some of this thinking to be premature in 2005. I looked carefully at how it had developed so far in the US primarily as a means of mobilising and communicating with supporters, as opposed to winning converts amongst voters, as became the case later with the creation and expansion of Facebook, for example. We therefore sought to do as much as we could to ensure that the public and media could engage with our campaign via our website, internet advertising and the nascent social media, whilst recognising that most people who were not supporters would be unlikely to seek out our website. We used some of our advertising budget to pay for online adverts. We even hoped that we might raise some money from them, and we had some success from *The Independent*'s webpage, raising about 80p for every £1 spent. But I rejected any idea (as suggested to me) that we should try to launch anonymous viral cartoons that would have made fun of scandalous revelations concerning the private lives of some of Blair's ministers on the basis that neither Charles nor I would countenance this sort of campaigning.

We managed, under the leadership of our internet campaign 'guru' Mark Pack, to achieve a level playing field in online campaigning between the three major parties, and we ensured that all of our candidates had an online presence. Charles Kennedy's blog from his battle bus was written on it by James Lundie, who was trusted by all concerned to make it effective, whilst avoiding any embarrassments, and some of Charles's words at key events were made available for the first time as podcasts.

As ever in the last week, both our main rivals sought to squeeze our vote. The Conservative campaign, advised by Lynton Crosby, had seized upon Lib Dem support for some prisoners to be allowed to vote in elections in order to imply that we were enthusiastic about letting people like Soham murderer Ian Huntley take part in the election. Young Conservatives were sent on bus trips round the country trying to surround Charles wherever he went, wearing T-shirts saying that the Lib Dems wanted 'votes for murderers'. This message was also delivered in phone calls to Lib Dem supporters in our target seats in an effort to dissuade them from voting for us. We failed to rebut this charge effectively, and should probably have done more about it before the campaign rather than make the issue more prominent during it. One of the campaign myths that arose after the election was that weaknesses in our manifesto in terms of such policies did us damage. The truth was that manifestos were always subject to so much scrutiny for potential 'hostages to fortune' before campaigns that they were rarely the problem. We did sometimes, however, have difficulty with occasionally clumsy statements by party spokespeople that could be taken out of context. In the same campaign, the Conservatives quoted Mark Oaten as our home affairs spokesman speaking about penal reform and alternatives to prison, in order to suggest that we were wholly opposed to the concept of ever detaining anyone.

Tony Blair sought to warn those of his former supporters thinking of switching to the Lib Dems that doing so would have the same effect as voting Conservative. In our target seats against Labour we could counter this in local campaigning by pointing out the irrelevance of the Conservatives locally, but we failed to deal with Labour's tactic effectively at national level. In my view, Charles should have strongly stated that there was no prospect at all of the Conservatives winning the 2005 general election or any Lib Dem vote helping them. Charles's style, however, was sometimes such that he resented being asked to make simple and effective statements without explaining fully the context of them in the manner that he might have done in a formal debate. He chose to describe in his interviews how Tony Blair was claiming that voting Lib Dem was the same as voting Conservative, before seeking to rebut this claim, and without realising that the only part of what he was saying that was likely to be understood by those listening to it was his own repetition of Tony Blair's claim.

Another mistake in the campaign was allowing too much focus on our so-called 'decapitation strategy'. In the 2001 campaign, five of our candidates had come particularly close to winning seats held by prominent Conservatives. Charles had decided to change the pre-campaign programme that I had planned for him in order to visit all these seats and highlight our prospects in them. Unfortunately, this then became known as the 'decapitation strategy'. With hindsight, we should have abandoned realistic hopes of gaining Folkestone & Hythe when its MP Michael Howard became Conservative Party leader, and it was my fault that we did not. Theresa May, David Davis, Tim Collins and Oliver Letwin had also nearly lost to us in 2001. Their campaigns were now much more prepared, and the expectation of them being specifically targeted by the Lib Dems did not help us. Tim Farron was the only candidate who succeeded in winning one of the 'decapitation seats', when he beat Tim Collins in Westmorland & Lonsdale by 267 votes, whilst Justine McGuinness also came close to beating Oliver Letwin in Dorset West.

Winning sixty-two seats achieved a new 'high watermark' for the Lib Dems, and Charles boasted of leading the largest presence in the House of Commons in what he called 'the Liberal tradition' since 1923. We gained twelve seats from Labour (more than we ever gained from them in any one election during their entire history of just over 100 years), three from the Conservatives and one from Plaid Cymru. We lost five of our previous gains back to the Conservatives. Overall, the result meant that we were now in first or second place in 40 per cent of the seats in Great Britain and well-placed to make further advances. We lost our deposit in only one constituency. Our vote share was 22.1 per cent (which was our highest since 1987). We had closed the gap against

Labour from 26.4 per cent at their peak in 1997 to just 13.1 per cent in 2005. We had narrowed the gap between ourselves and the Conservatives from 24.1 per cent (when they last won a general election in 1992) to just 10.2 per cent.

As in 2001, half of our net gains were with female candidates. The Lib Dem Parliamentary Party had been just 6.5 per cent female in 1997. This had risen to 11.5 per cent in 2001 and our ten women MPs in 2005 now made up 16.1 per cent of the total (compared to 19.8 per cent of the membership of the Commons at the time). When I joined the Liberal Party, it had just over half a dozen MPs, all of whom were white men. I had had to fight very hard to change party strategy fundamentally to support campaigning effectively in target seats, and this was significant in winning more seats and improving gender balance amongst our MPs. In my early days in the party, I had seen how it took a huge amount of time and effort over many years, and generally a lot of money (often their own), for any of our candidates to win a seat in a parliamentary election. Women often had less available time, money and support than men and so lost out. Without 'safe' seats to allocate to candidates, or the stronger and richer party organisations belonging to our rivals, we had to try to overcome the problems of trying to win under first past the post by targeting much more effectively in order to give candidates who might win more support and to try to improve our gender balance in Parliament. In the 2005 general election, targeted support on a scale that had not existed in the early days of the Lib Dems helped candidates including Julia Goldsworthy, Jenny Willott, Lynne Featherstone, Lorely Burt and Jo Swinson to gain their seats (and Sarah Teather to retain the seat that she had won in a by-election). I thought that a future party leader could well be amongst these women. We had also narrowly failed to win another five seats with women candidates.

I felt very proud of the campaign, the organisation of it and the way in which we brought together a very skilled and dedicated team of people. We were not able to use the sudden large influx of money from Michael Brown as we might have wished, but we used it effectively given the constraints upon us, including time. We used resources that were still very limited compared to those of the other parties to prioritise promoting effective messaging in the seats that mattered most to us. To have spread our targeted support much more thinly across many more seats (as some people wanted) would have resulted in far fewer seats being won and would have done very little to benefit the vast majority of candidates outside our target seats. The results showed, however, that they did all benefit considerably from the national campaign, including the coverage of Charles's election tour, our advertising campaign (including more than 2,000 professional billboards) and our extremely well-received party election broadcasts (the last one of which was viewed by sixteen million people).

Tim and I were both extremely grateful for the very effective role played by Alison Suttie in overseeing many of the organisational, practical and technical aspects of the campaign. I had persuaded Alison to return from Brussels, where she had been working for the President of the European Parliament Pat Cox, to undertake the job of election manager. I had realised some years previously that the kind of organisational skills that Alison brought were no longer my strong points and we complemented each other well. She found the detailed archive of planning materials left by Kate Fox from the previous general election to be extremely useful and this helped to make sure that lessons learned from 2001 were not forgotten. We again ensured that there was a very detailed management report available to all members of the federal and state party executives.

On rereading our 2005 management team's 147-page report, it was clear that we all assumed then that we would fight the next election with Charles Kennedy as party leader. I could not believe that the problems which had caused such difficulties on days such as when we launched the manifesto would not now be dealt with by Charles. But I was less confident than Tim Razzall appeared to be that Charles could be seen in the years ahead as a potential Prime Minister. I did believe, however, that we were moving closer to power at Westminster than we had been for almost a century. The post-election photograph with sixty-two newly elected Lib Dem MPs outside Local Government House showed a very happy scene. With Labour's majority reduced from 167 to sixty-six, we believed that we now had the base from which to complete the transition that Paddy had frequently spoken about, of 'moving from protest to power'. It was the achievement of our campaign in 2005 that eventually enabled us to enter government in 2010.

CHAPTER 13

THE DOWNFALL OF CHARLES KENNEDY

PATSY CALTON DIES

It was concern about the need for a new pedestrian crossing following the death of one of her daughter's school friends in a road accident that brought Patsy Calton into politics. She had asked neighbours who to go to in order to get something done about this, and they all said that 'it's the Liberal Democrats who get things done around here'. This was how many people joined the party, and within a few years Patsy was a local councillor, and then deputy leader of Stockport Council, which was Liberal Democrat run. She then fought her local constituency of Cheadle, coming 16,000 votes behind in 1992 and reducing the majority to just 3,189 in 1997. Her gain of the constituency by just thirty-three votes in 2001 had been one of our election highlights. I had expected her to win again in 2005, and she had done so with a majority of 4,020. Whilst many people knew that she'd been fighting cancer since shortly after her first parliamentary election contest, and had undergone a double mastectomy, few people knew the cancer had returned to her spine in early 2005. Patsy was a very brave and popular person and was determined to be re-elected and take her seat in Parliament for the last time. She died a few days afterwards.

This was the first time since the creation of the Lib Dems that we had to defend a parliamentary seat in a by-election following the death of one of our MPs. Whilst Patsy was personally irreplaceable, I knew that we would now need a candidate who could stand as a strong local champion for the area. The local party had decided not to shortlist the only councillor within the constituency who applied for the nomination[68] and would have considered candidates from outside the area. Peter Carroll (who had some local connections, but who lived in Folkestone where he had stood a few weeks earlier) initially put his name forward. But when I spoke to him, Peter and then the national party's by-election panel recognised that you could not easily be Folkestone's local champion in one month and Cheadle's in the next. Our council leader, Mark Hunter, who represented a ward in the next-door Hazel Grove constituency, thereby emerged as our candidate. My own early canvassing was very positive and made obvious to me the tremendous sympathy and support that had existed for Patsy and her family. Her husband, Clive, had worked closely with her on local casework issues.

During July, I travelled up to Cheadle for a day or two each week whilst Ann (now retired) spent the entire campaign there as we were worried about the lack of help from the party, which was possibly complacent about our prospects. My canvassing, however, became more worrying as I found that the 'sympathy vote' declined as the campaign went on. Many people admitted that they were 'natural Conservatives' who had voted for Patsy personally, but might now return to their original fold. The Conservative candidate, Stephen Day, had been a very popular Member of Parliament for the seat between 1987 and 2001, when Patsy narrowly defeated him, and he still lived locally. Although he was leader of the local council, Mark Hunter was much less well-known in the constituency and lived some eight miles from its boundary.

The kind of attack that we had previously launched on opposing candidates for 'not being local' was now launched against Mark. Our private poll had shown that Stephen Day was so well established

---

68   Stuart Bodsworth, who also failed to be selected for Oldham East & Saddleworth and eventually defected to Labour.

locally that none of our attacks on his voting record whilst he had been the local MP had any effect. In contrast, Mark was attacked 'as the unpopular local council leader' and, in somewhat contradictory fashion, for 'not being local'. The aggressive Conservative campaign was also strongly echoed by that of Labour, which consisted almost exclusively of attacks on Mark with leaflets headed: 'Hunter Special'.

I left much of the campaign to the direction of Hilary Stephenson (one of the party's best ever organisers) and Shaun Roberts (one of its best ever campaigners), but decided that, in view of what I saw happening there, I had better spend the last week of the campaign in Cheadle. Andrew Stunell, MP for next-door Hazel Grove, was doing the canvass analysis and it was clear on the Sunday before polling day that our lead had slipped away and that we had fallen behind the Conservatives. At the same time, much of the dissatisfaction with Charles Kennedy within the party was spilling into the media. Charles came to the campaign on five occasions, but it was clear to me that his confidence was completely drained as he was struggling with the level of criticism that he was facing in Westminster. He knew that his job was on the line, depending upon the by-election result. When he was in Cheadle on the Friday before polling day, I warned him that he needed to 'pull out all the stops' and ring all sixty-one of our MPs, demanding their presence in the campaign during the last week of it. He rather weakly told me that it would be better if the calls came from me, rather than him.

I felt dreadful about the apparent likelihood of losing and the implosion within the party that would be triggered by the loss of a held seat. The Conservatives sensed their opportunity to make a gain and switched resources from their general election campaign to Cheadle. Fortunately for us, however, the Conservative campaign went 'over the top' in the last week and gave us the chance to use our own campaign skills to turn around our prospects. The Conservatives made some very dubious claims about the costs to people in the constituency of introducing local income tax, as we had proposed during the recent general election. We pointed out that the independent analysis which they quoted from 'CRD' was actually better known as the Conservative Research Department! One particularly obnoxious Conservative leaflet was headed 'Shocking Crime Record of Mark Hunter', about crime generally but juxtaposed with a local newspaper report about a rape. On the eve of poll, a Conservative campaign newspaper led with a completely bogus story that the council, led by Mark, had a 'secret plan' to take away pensioners' free bus passes. This was without foundation and would have been absurd, given that the government was legislating at the time for a free national bus pass scheme for all pensioners. Working through sleepless nights, Shaun and I revamped our leaflets, producing several extra ones highlighting the sheer dishonesty of the Conservative campaign. Over many years I have always found that very little annoys Conservative-minded voters more than being lied to.

The Conservatives' narrow lead on the final Sunday was now reversed. Mark came across extremely well in his media interviews which were concentrated in the last week of the campaign, and the Labour vote was also in decline as their supporters reacted to the desperate dishonesty of the Tory campaign and their own party's failure to make any case for voting Labour. I met some of Labour's campaign team as we waited outside the studio for one of the candidates' TV debates to take place on the Sunday before polling day, and they were quite shocked when I told them that they were about to lose their deposit.

At the count, it quickly became clear that Mark would almost match Patsy's majority, even on a reduced turnout. I had agreed with Charles that he would be in the constituency on the Friday morning for media interviews in the event of us winning. The tremendous relief in his voice was obvious when I rang him from the count to say that he would be coming to Cheadle in the morning. Our majority was 3,657. There was a small swing to us from the Conservatives whilst the Labour vote halved to just 4.6 per cent, costing them their deposit.

The Guardian's coverage of the result picked up on the mounting internal concern about Charles:

MPs had warned that [Charles's] leadership could face renewed pressure if the seat fell to the Conservatives, and earlier this week he admitted that holding the seat was 'very important' for morale. 'This is a stunning defeat for the Tories,' said Chris Rennard, the Lib Dems' chief executive and election supremo. 'In 1992, when [the Tories] had only a slim majority in the country, they had a 16,000 majority here. This was their number one target two months ago and their best chance of a by-election gain for two decades.'

We had seen off the Tory challenge and bought Charles some breathing space.

CHARLES KENNEDY RESIGNS

In spite of experiencing feelings of joy and relief at their own election success, there was significant discontent amongst many Lib Dem MPs in the summer of 2005. Some of the newer ones were shocked and disappointed by how they now found things were managed in Parliament. Many of the new MPs complained about poor induction processes and the time that it took to be allocated offices and computers. They also remarked upon how poorly managed the party's operation then was in Parliament, finding the weekly meetings of the Parliamentary Party most unsatisfactory. There were different issues for some of the MPs who had now been elected three or four times, but had been shocked in the election campaign by much more aggressive campaigning by the Conservatives in their constituencies than they had previously witnessed. To them, I had to defend the strategy in which the party had done very little recently to help those MPs in what were now relatively safe seats for them, in favour of trying to defend their more vulnerable colleagues and make more gains with a more diverse range of candidates. Some of the MPs in the safer seats now seemed angry that they had not had the same level of support and campaign innovation that had first helped many of them to win in 1997. In contrast, the most recently elected felt more awareness that Charles's electoral appeal and campaigns against the Iraq War and student tuition fees had helped them to win. Some of the latter group, however, were now disappointed to find that Charles in Parliament was frequently withdrawn, inaccessible and ineffective.

Attempts were being made by those around Charles to make him seem more like the potential Prime Minister which they hoped that he could become, but he demonstrated few of the requisite skills in this period. An overlong speech to the Parliamentary Party attempting to set out his philosophical vision for the future was cringingly embarrassing as he failed to read his audience and see their dissatisfaction. He angered a number of party members as he sought to blame conference activists for some of the attacks that had been made on us during the campaign, suggesting that all previous conference resolutions should be nullified. Whilst attacking your own party activists is sometimes popular with those around a party leader, it was resented by some of the people whose support he needed, and who felt that the blame for such problems more often lay with leaders failing to prepare properly for party conferences. I thought myself that it was more often the injudicious comments sometimes made by leaders or spokespeople that led to these attacks on us, rather than conference resolutions. His office was very distracted by renewed speculation that stories alleging that he had a problem with alcohol would appear in the media and little real effort was made on Charles's behalf to prepare for the party conference that autumn. Specific denials had to be made to the media by his office in order to prevent publication of stories about his drinking.

After our recent gains, and our third consecutive general election electoral advance, I naively expected the mood at our September conference to be rather more celebratory than it turned out to be. Blackpool was a difficult and unpopular venue for party conferences, but this did not entirely account for the fractious atmosphere. We had not matched the share of the vote in the general election that had been suggested by opinion polls following our best by-election results in the previous parliament when for three periods of time we had been achieving between 28 per cent and 30 per cent in them. We had also fallen significantly below what I considered to be the unrealistic expectations of many people in terms of seat numbers. There were some candidates who unfairly thought that they would have won, rather than lost by a large margin, if only the national campaign had redirected substantially more resources to them and away from more marginal seats. There were also people I spoke to at the conference who clearly thought that we would have won more seats if only they had been given more power and prominence in the national campaign. And there were some people who wanted a party leader to be more focused on taking the party in a policy direction which they considered to be more attractive to Conservative-minded voters.

It didn't seem to take long for people to forget, or fail to understand, that the 2005 general election campaign had been the best ever Liberal Democrat performance in electoral terms. Charles, therefore, had some justification for feeling personally resentful of the attacks upon him. But his battle with alcohol, which was very evident to those closest to him at the conference, possibly helped to fuel his sense of paranoia, anger and frustration about the growing personal criticism of him. As he left his hotel room to make what proved to be his final conference speech as leader, he remarked to Ann (who was minding the young Donald Kennedy for the duration of the speech) that he was going off 'to defend these dreadful election results for which your husband and I were responsible'. Nick Robinson reported on the BBC that night an unhelpful but probably fair assessment by one of Charles's longstanding critics that 'the only thing keeping Charles in position as leader, as far as many MPs were concerned, was the fact that the only evident alternative was Simon Hughes'.

When the conference finished, I planned to have a rest in my room at the Imperial Hotel as I would be staying in Blackpool overnight in order to visit two elderly aunts who lived there, one of whom would be celebrating her birthday. My attempts to sleep, however, were disturbed by a series of phone calls from Tom Baldwin[69] of *The Times* informing me that the paper had become aware that Michael Brown had some years previously been arrested in the United States over a series of three bounced cheques and that the Electoral Commission had been asked to investigate the permissibility of his company's donations to the party. Our own enquiries had earlier established that a cheque of his for $5,000 had indeed bounced in the US some years ago. We had considered this to be unimportant as it seemed to involve a small amount of money and he assured us that this was an accident that would be put right. Incidents of this kind are not taken as seriously in the UK as they appeared to be in the US. We now discovered that there had been three bounced cheques to a total value of up to $7,000. This news dominated the front page of *The Times* the following day and took centre stage across all media, wiping out any coverage that we might have got from Charles's speech. The timing was most damaging. I then began receiving a series of phone calls from journalists seeking to follow up the story and in response issued the following brief statement on behalf of the party:

'We believe that we have acted in good faith and properly in relation to all donations received by the Liberal Democrats, and that all donations we have received are from individuals entitled to donate to British political parties or from companies based and trading in the UK.'

Michael Brown's company had been acquired by him in June 2004, well before his first approach to the party, but it had not leased more permanent offices in London until after his first donations, totalling £251,000, had been made. This meant that there was less evidence of the company trading in the UK when it made its first donations, although we had been assured that it did, and had no reason at the time

---

69   Whom I had helped when he was a local newspaper journalist covering some of the by-elections in which I was involved and who later became press spokesman for Ed Miliband as Labour leader.

to disbelieve Michael Brown. The situation now was made more difficult because relations with him had soured during the general election campaign. This followed his sending of the Harrods hamper on the occasion of Donald's birth, and then his claiming to have been snubbed by a lack of acknowledgement and gratitude for it on Charles's part. Such are the perils of dealing with major donors. Thanking people was not something that Charles always remembered to do instinctively, and at that point he had both a new baby and an election campaign preoccupying his mind.

Details of all donations to the party in the first quarter of 2005 had been published by the Electoral Commission, in accordance with their rules, on 20 May. This was two weeks after the election and had generated some immediate interest in Michael Brown, as well as accusations that the party had been hypocritical in receiving such substantial backing, whilst favouring a ban on such donations for all parties. The media pointed out that I had, in 2000, moved amendments in the House of Lords to cap all donations to political parties at £50,000. My view, of course, was that we should only stop accepting such donations when they were banned for all parties. In August, Michael Brown had asked for a more detailed breakdown as to how his major donation had been spent. I was on holiday at the time, but arranged for him to be given this via Anna Werrin. With hindsight, I think that he wanted to know if it had all been spent, which of course it had been, and in accordance with what was agreed. As controversy about the donations spiralled following *The Times* story, nobody else from the party wanted to comment on the issue. I asked the press office to provide my statement in response to ongoing media enquiries and to say that nobody was available for interview. Whilst checking out of the Imperial Hotel in Blackpool on the Friday morning, I noticed a film crew setting up in the foyer with the obvious aim of trying to get me to add to that statement. I had no intention of doing so, so Ann and I departed from a side entrance of the hotel to visit my aunts. Over many months, *The Times* appeared to become obsessed with the story as questions followed about the provision of Michael Brown's plane to Charles for the first days of the campaign. This had been costed at £30,000 and the charges invoiced to the UK company from which the donation was made. This refuted the suggestion that the provision of the plane had been an illegal foreign donation.

The developing controversy turned what was first suggested as a significant fundraising triumph that we should publicise pre-election, into a question about Charles's judgement. This was somewhat unfair to him as the party's chief officers group had been involved in the discussions about the donations. The party placed legal responsibility in its constitution for determining a view about the permissibility of accepting such donations on its registered treasurer, then David Griffiths, the chair of the FFAC, but the group all discussed it and as explained previously there was a very small amount of time and few powers to investigate. The publicity about the donation came as confidence within the Parliamentary Party was ebbing away from Charles following what was seen to be a significant failure of leadership at the Blackpool conference, with defeats on issues such as the size of the EU budget and potential plans for part privatisation of the Royal Mail. It was also clear that some ideological divisions were opening up within the party between people characterised as 'economic liberals' (also described as the 'orange bookers') and those seen as 'social liberals' (who would have considered themselves to be in the mainstream 'centre-left' of the party). Those most concerned about Charles continuing as leader were not, however, confined to either camp and amongst those MPs I knew to have the greatest concerns and to be discussing them with each other included Sarah Teather, David Laws, Norman Lamb and Ed Davey.

Throughout the autumn, most Lib Dem MPs appeared to me to be still oblivious to the real reasons for some of their other colleagues' concerns about Charles's performance. For some of them it was a simple question of loyalty being expected for the party leader who had helped to bring such success to the party. But a factor in the escalating opposition to Charles was the fact that Ming had now sufficiently recovered from his cancer treatment and was considered by many of those most opposed to Charles to be his desired replacement.

What should have been a personal and private matter was now regularly spilling out into the media, and there was much anger within the party about how this was happening. Party members contacting Cowley Street were furious about criticism of Charles being made anonymously and regularly in many newspapers. In the view of Charles and his office, the MPs wanting a change were out of step with opinion in the party, as indeed they were at the time. Members generally, however, had no idea about the nature of Charles's problem and its consequences.

Throughout these most controversial times, I was speaking privately to those people most opposed to Charles continuing as leader as well as to his strongest supporters. I explained as best I could to both sides that members were extremely angry with press coverage that damaged the party, that this should be avoided, but that in the long run they would want the issue resolved. Either Charles had to somehow show that he had the confidence of his MPs, and his own chosen shadow Cabinet in particular, or his critics had to show that a majority of the latter group now favoured a change, in which case, Charles's position was untenable. Charles was defiant, whilst his critics hoped that Andrew Stunell as Chief Whip might become the discreet recipient of a list of names of those seeking a change, and whose job it would be to inform Charles if and when he lost the support of a majority of his shadow Cabinet and would have to go.

Whilst they were greatly annoyed by the opposition to him becoming public, I did not sense any feeling from Charles (or from his office) that they thought that this was the endgame of his leadership. I think they felt that as they had been through so much before, this was just another crisis that would pass. Their sense of anger about what they considered to be plotting increased when a prominent party figure, aware of what was happening and hoping to back Ed Davey as leader, thought that he was ringing the Kingston MP to offer his support for the prospect, but rang the wrong number and ended up leaving a voicemail message on Mark Oaten's mobile telephone. The gist of this call was immediately relayed to Anna Werrin, who then spoke firmly to some of the alleged plotters about the risks that they were taking with their own political careers if they went against Charles.

In the meantime, attempts continued to develop new policies and to try to break free of the internal controversy. A great deal of work on new pension policies had been done by David Laws, and Charles was to endeavour to lead the presentations of them personally in order to show how he was proposing to tackle big issues facing the country. At the shadow Cabinet meeting to unveil the plans, however, Charles was clearly unwell and he laboured terribly over his presentation of them. Through the meeting, I sat next to Anna Werrin, who thought that Charles might fall off his chair whilst he was speaking, and I considered that he might fall asleep. Charles's next engagement that morning was with students at the LSE, accompanied by the recently elected MP for Falmouth & Camborne, Julia Goldsworthy. At this event, Charles appeared to need to prop himself up, leaning on the lectern, whilst he once again had difficulty with his script, after which he left rapidly without holding the expected Q&A session. Charles should probably have called it a day at this point, but instead headed up to Newcastle on the train for a campaign visit. He never made it there, returned to London, and a private media briefing had to be given by his office that he had returned for a 'family situation'. Talk about the events of this day quickly spread round many concerned MPs.

Those around Charles now began to realise the gravity of the situation, and in some cases the threat to their own positions if he had to stand down as leader. I think that it was then poor judgement for Charles's office to brief the media, in advance of a shadow Cabinet meeting to be held early that December, that Charles would use it to face down his critics. This briefing ensured that whatever happened at the meeting would inevitably become much more public, and not to

Charles's advantage. I received several media calls asking me what was going on just before it took place. Charles opened the meeting on a Tuesday morning by inviting anyone who lacked confidence in him to let him know immediately so they could be replaced by the time of the Parliamentary Party meeting the following afternoon. He paused, and was preparing to move on when Sandra Gidley was the first member present to suggest that this was not an acceptable way forward to resolve any issues. Several shadow Cabinet members present, including Ming, suggested that it would be more appropriate for people to make known any concerns that they had privately via Andrew Stunell. Some of them had been expecting the Chief Whip to be the one who would have to step up to the plate and tell Charles that he had finally lost the confidence of most of his senior colleagues. Andrew, however, went on to suggest that anyone with concerns should meet him and Charles together, thereby constraining considerably anything that they might want to say. Andrew was, I think, anxious not to bring matters to a head at this point, and certainly not before the local elections the following May. Inevitably, reports of the meeting reached the media and Greg Hurst in *The Times* wrote a fairly full account of it.

Later that evening, the '2001 group' of Lib Dem MPs elected in that year held their annual Christmas dinner in a private Commons dining room. Discussion inevitably included the leadership once Charles had departed after a brief diplomatic visit with Simon Hughes (then party president) to wish them well. When talk then moved as far as consideration of a possible alternative to Charles, Sarah Teather immediately told the group: 'It's got to be Ming.' There was much unhappiness, however, about how events were unfolding. Chesterfield MP Paul Holmes was chair of the Parliamentary Party and later pointed out that nobody had sought to involve him in resolving the issue that was now dividing the MPs. He was particularly angry about the constant leaks to the media. The Parliamentary Party meeting the next evening followed much discussion during the day about the 'if you don't back me, you must resign from the shadow Cabinet' approach now being taken by Charles. After months, if not years, of showing little willingness or acceptance of the need to fight for his position, he was now doing so very strongly. The meeting was raucous and followed several widely gossiped 'private meetings' in the intervening period at which a number of Charles's colleagues, including Ming Campbell and Sarah Teather, told him privately that he should stand down. The MPs always met on a Wednesday evening and Alistair Carmichael spoke at it of how 'there was an elephant in the room'; Lynne Featherstone said she'd been 'hearing concerns about Charles's personal habits'; whilst Mark Hunter responded furiously in support of Charles, and others such as Bob Russell expressed their dismay about perceived disloyalty and the media coverage. Mark Oaten spoke very emotionally in support of Charles, describing him as 'my friend', whilst many of his colleagues were aware that his own campaign to become the next leader had been established.

On the Thursday morning, and just before Parliament broke up for the Christmas recess, I met Andrew Stunell in my office at Cowley Street to swap notes prior to his meeting with Charles. I prepared a memo for him with the intention that he gave it to Charles, or at least used it to brief him. This note explained the differing positions I had heard described by our MPs, from 'Charles has had his last chance' to 'this is his last chance', and how quite possibly over half the shadow Cabinet was now in the former category. Charles's support was actually dwindling as more of his MPs were becoming aware of his alcohol problem. Many of those most loyal to him, however, remained in ignorance of it. Andrew set off to see Charles.

I later spoke to Charles myself saying that if he wanted to survive, he really needed to use the recess to ring round and speak personally to all his MPs and establish for himself whether or not he really could demonstrate majority support. I was away in the Lake District over the New Year, and out of mobile phone reception, but picked up messages from Charles suggesting that he might do this in the New Year. In the meantime, some calls were being made on his behalf trying to stave off resignations or a rebellion.

On 4 January that year, my mother-in-law celebrated her ninetieth birthday, so I had stayed in Liverpool for a family lunch with her before driving back down to London on Thursday 5 January. As we stopped at a motorway service station, I checked my mobile phone to pick up a message from Daisy McAndrew (formerly Sampson) of ITN, whom I knew well from her time as Charles's former press secretary. When I rang her back she asked me to confirm a story that in 2003 I had had a meeting with Charles, along with Ming Campbell, Matthew Taylor and Andrew Stunell, which confirmed his alcohol problem and that he was receiving medical support in relation to it. I refused, as always, to confirm the basis of any private meeting, but I knew that the story was clearly very well sourced and that, in the absence of me and others being able to sustain a categorical denial about it, it was likely to run that evening. Many of those close to Charles, and some others, regarded Daisy's role at this point as a betrayal of him and an unprofessional act. But I think that this was grossly unfair to her, as she clearly maintained absolute discretion as a journalist about what she personally knew from all the time when she was working for Charles and in relation to which she maintained professional confidentiality. She knew a great deal that would have caused Charles major embarrassment and she spurned opportunities to reveal any of it. The story that she was now about to break was almost certainly given to ITV over the Christmas period by someone who thought that it was now time that it should be broken, and would have gone elsewhere if Daisy had not now pursued it.

Ann took over the driving and I spent the rest of the journey down to London on the phone. Charles's office was aware of the impending story, as, it appeared, were a considerable number of people. I learned that the strategy in response would be to pre-empt the ITN story by giving a live statement in time for the earlier BBC News in which Charles would admit to 'a drink problem' and say that he was seeking support to deal with it. It had always been my view that such a statement was necessary and that it should have been made some years previously. Only this would have enabled Charles to get the understanding and support that he needed to try to deal with this very difficult issue. I could not get back to London in time for the crucial meeting with Charles and his closest advisers that took place in his house that afternoon in order to work out exactly what he would say. Ben Stoneham attended in my place and rang me from Charles's house to say that the plan would be for Charles to call a leadership election that would supposedly either force any potential opponent to stand against him or force his critics to desist. The tremendous stress on those around Charles was obvious, and they were relying on the then widespread support for him amongst most party members who had little idea about what the controversy was really all about. I knew, however, that a leadership election, if it happened, would be a very bloody affair, and that if there was no leadership election, Charles's critics would simply feel the need to step up the pressure. With hindsight, I still feel that if Charles had thrown himself on the mercy of the party and the public without calling a leadership election, he might have survived as party leader for some months at least, until his 'drink problem' was either resolved or not. It would have been much harder for his critics to show him no mercy in that event. But Charles's determination that there would be a leadership election now led many MPs to believe that the issue had to be resolved within the next twenty-four hours, and not over the six weeks of a potential leadership election campaign. Ben relayed to Charles my firm advice against the leadership ballot strategy, citing for me a phrase about the need to show 'grace under pressure' used by Roy Jenkins, which I knew would appeal to Charles, but his mind was made up.

I arrived back in London, just in time to see Charles's press conference being broadcast live, with him acknowledging his 'drink problem', saying that he had 'not touched a drop for six weeks', and 'did not intend to do so again'. He said that he would now be using his constitutional powers to call a leadership election and challenged anyone who would oppose his leadership to do so publicly and let the members vote. As a bloodbath began to unfold in the media, one of my first concerns back at Cowley Street on the morning after Charles's Thursday evening broadcast was, as it was so often, the morale of party staff. Many of them were watching the rolling television coverage in their offices as a different Lib Dem MP appeared every half hour or so to say that Charles should stand down. At HQ, we were carefully monitoring phone calls and emails from members. They had previously been enthusiastically and overwhelmingly in support of Charles, but the tone of most of this communication now changed dramatically as many members became aware for the first time of the nature of his problem. Over twenty-five MPs, many of them quite senior, were soon saying that they could not serve as spokespeople if Charles Kennedy continued as party leader. Charles sensibly stayed out of sight, whilst frantic but futile efforts continued to be made by his office to get those MPs still most sympathetic to Charles, such as Phil Willis, to appear in the media to try to counter his detractors.

Announcing that there would be a leadership election, possibly to be conducted against this background over the next six weeks, forced the hand of Ed Davey and those now believing that Charles would have to resign. They had hoped that private representations to Charles would show him that he no longer had the confidence of his shadow Cabinet and his MPs, and that it would be best for him to resign with dignity and without a public row. But Charles had been encouraged by some people to fight back, based on strong support amongst the wider membership but which was unaware of the alcohol issue. Others had tried to find different routes and timescales for addressing the problem. Andrew Stunell thought that it could all be postponed to a 'soft landing' after May's local elections. Simon Hughes had sought to negotiate independently with Charles for the leader to take a 'leave of absence' during which Ming would have become acting leader, and Charles could later return. The media was dominated by reports about how virtually half of the Parliamentary Party would now refuse to serve as spokespeople under Charles's leadership if it continued.

I got up early on the Saturday to get the day's papers. As I arrived at my newsagents in Stockwell, he said to me straight away that 'it doesn't look good for Mr Kennedy'. After perusing them, I resolved to ring Anna Werrin, Tim Razzall and James Gurling in that order before speaking to Charles to say that he would sadly have to bring an end to all this that day. But before I could begin that round of phone calls, Anna rang me in tears at 7.45 a.m. to say that Charles would be resigning that afternoon, and please could I make all the arrangements. I knew that it was important to try to seize control from the chaos and not to let it continue to spin out of control. We agreed that Charles would make a resignation statement at 2 p.m. in the Cowley Street boardroom, where he had made his statement on the Thursday evening, and that complete confidentiality was needed to avoid any prior leak of the news in order to preserve his personal dignity, and that of the party.

I needed help to set up the press conference, so I rang a small number of most trusted colleagues, including Ben Stoneham, Kate Heywood and Sarah Morris, to say that I needed them to come into Cowley Street as soon as possible, without explaining the reason, but they were of course aware of the crisis engulfing the party. It was not unusual for me to be in Cowley Street on a Saturday morning and there were a small number of people in the HQ for various meetings, including the executive of the Liberal Democrat Women. I suggested to them that I needed to hold a meeting with the press team in the boardroom that afternoon, that I had unfortunately failed to book this properly in the system, and asked if they would mind moving their meeting to a downstairs room. Charles's personal director of communications, Jackie Rowley, told me that Charles was okay and working on his resignation statement, but she expressed strong reservations about allowing Mark Littlewood[70] and the press office to know what

---

70   Who had been appointed by the Parliamentary Party to be head of the media office shortly before the 2005 general election (after he had defected back to the party from the 'Pro-Euro Conservative Party).

was happening for fear of leaks. I explained that I would need them in Cowley Street with me to convene the press conference and issue statements, but that I could get them to come into the HQ without telling them what was really happening until twelve noon. My plan was for an operational note to be issued at 1 p.m. saying that Charles would be making a personal statement at Cowley Street at 2 p.m. The team working with me also had a list of key party people's pager and mobile numbers, including those of all MPs, so that they could also be informed at 1 p.m. about an impending statement. Its meaning would be fairly obvious.

Also that morning I had to ring Ming to advise him that he would that afternoon become acting leader of the party and that Charles would shortly be ringing him to say that he was resigning with immediate effect. Ming had previously assumed that if he resigned, Charles would continue as party leader until the election of his successor. Charles sensibly realised that this would be an impossible position for him, having lost the confidence of his parliamentary colleagues. I told Ming that he would need to be ready to make a statement at 3 p.m. to try to 'steady the ship', pay appropriate tribute to Charles, and show that the party was not now without leadership. Ming's declaration of his candidacy in that statement was of course not an entirely spontaneous event. It was his availability for the job that had led many MPs to demand a change, and it was generally considered that he should now make it plain publicly that he was willing to be the next leader in order to avoid the impression that the party might have any difficulty finding a permanent leader. The 'coronation' of Michael Howard had certainly not harmed the Conservatives when they had ditched Iain Duncan Smith just over two years previously, and it did not seem inevitable that there would be a contested leadership election now.

I had also rung Simon Hughes that morning to advise him as party president of what was happening, and to ensure that he agreed with me that the deputy leader (Ming) would become the acting leader in these circumstances. This was not necessarily straightforward because of the absence of any reference to the position of deputy leader in the party's constitution. We had to refer, therefore, to the Standing Orders of the Lib Dem MPs. I contacted Andrew Stunell, who had a copy of them to hand, and we agreed that one of the duties of the deputy leader, elected by the MPs, was to stand in for the party leader.

That morning, Mark Oaten (having just returned from holiday) was giving interviews to the TV cameras outside Cowley Street in support of Charles continuing as party leader. In between his interviews, I suggested to him that he might pop inside for a discreet cup of coffee. He knew that I was checking whether or not he was aware of what was really happening. He told me that Anna had let him know of Charles's plans, but said that he was 'maintaining the line' until the official statement. I asked Mark directly what his own intentions would now be. I knew of a campaign in support of his leadership, but wasn't sure if those involved in it realised that Mark might struggle to get the nomination of seven parliamentary colleagues required for him to stand. Mark thought that there would be problems with Ming's image as party leader, but was quite adamant that he would not now stand himself. He was thinking about what he would say to the media, as Charles's friend, at the conclusion of the press conference and told me that he would make it clear that he was not standing, and that he would say that he would be 'ringing Ming Campbell', with the obvious inference that he would be supporting him as the new party leader.

By 2 p.m., Cowley Street's first floor boardroom was completely packed with journalists and TV crews. I met Charles outside to escort him through the media scrum awaiting his arrival. As we went inside, the staircase was lined by the members of the executive of the Liberal Democrat Women, who had now realised the real reason why I needed the room which they had booked that afternoon, and they were all very supportive. Charles had spent the morning writing his statement and it was to be one of the most impressive that he ever gave. He pointed out defiantly that no challenger had come forward to stand against him in the leadership election that he had requested two days earlier. But he recognised his 'personal, political and constitutional duty', and would be standing down as leader 'with immediate effect'. He spoke of how leadership personalities change from time to time, but that 'principles should not'. He emphasised the party's commitment to civil liberties, justice, the rule of international law, and the country's commitment within Europe, the United Nations and the Commonwealth, together with environmental challenges and the need for 'a far fairer social deal for the have-nots in our society'. It was principled and very dignified. Several journalists discussed with me afterwards how if Charles had been able to deliver that kind of performance throughout his party leadership, then it would not have just ended.

A LEADERSHIP ELECTION, CRISIS MANAGEMENT AND RECOVERY

Lembit Öpik was on the M4 driving back to his home in Wales when he got the pager message telling him about Charles's 'personal statement'. He hastily turned around, returning to central London to show his continued personal support for Charles at Cowley Street. On arrival, he quickly conferred with Mark Oaten in my office. It was just before Charles's statement and they discussed what they would be saying in response to it. Mark made it clear again that he would not be standing to be the next leader, at which point Lembit gripped him in a kind of bear hug and persuaded him that he should not make any such announcement at this stage. Mark subsequently paid tribute on camera to Charles without speculating about his own position. This interview, not ruling out a leadership bid, surprised Ming, who I had earlier told to expect a call from Mark. Whilst I had to deal with the aftermath of the press conference, some of those closest to Charles then gathered for what must have been something of a wake at the Kennedys' Kennington home. It was there that anger about the media's suggestion of a potential coronation for Ming helped drive the decision that Mark would stand for the leadership, which was announced a couple of days later.

In the few days after Charles's resignation there was also speculation that Simon Hughes might stand. He was in a potentially difficult position because he was the party's president and he was speaking to the media about responsibility for the running of a leadership election campaign in which he might be a candidate himself. He spoke of favouring a long campaign lasting at least four months, with a new party leader being elected sometime after the May local elections. The Federal Executive had a regular meeting scheduled for the Monday two days after Charles's resignation and prior to which concern was expressed to me about Simon's position if he sought to chair a meeting to agree the election timetable. Simon understood this, and it was therefore agreed that I should chair all the deliberations about the election campaign in his place. Considerable concern was also expressed at this meeting about the idea of a lengthy contest, and after an hour's reasonable discussion, the meeting agreed on a timetable to elect a new party leader immediately prior to the party's spring conference at Harrogate in mid-March.

There were then some private negotiations as Simon Hughes was prepared not to put his name forward for the leadership if he had Ming's support to be deputy leader (a post chosen by the MPs). Simon's calculation was obviously that he would then be 'presumptive heir' and at least very well placed to become leader after Ming. The same logic meant, however, that some of Ming's most ambitious supporters would not let him agree to this, so a contest was becoming inevitable, even without Mark Oaten's intervention, which soon followed. The party appeared to want a contest of some kind and John Hemming at one point suggested that he would stand if that was necessary to ensure that there would be an election, and he did some polling of party members, but his intervention was not needed.

In quite chaotic fashion, Mark Oaten's team then launched his bid to be leader. The event was in the car park of a Westminster Hotel and a small group of potential supporters, including Lembit, huddled around Mark to shelter him from the windy conditions. Private negotiations having failed, Simon Hughes also formally launched his candidacy. Rumours then began to reach me (and the betting markets) that Chris Huhne might also enter the fray.

Ming's first experience as acting leader at Prime Minister's Question Time had been disappointing when he had asked about the lack of permanent headteachers, thereby drawing attention to the party's own problems. A meeting at Lynne Featherstone's house led to pressure on Chris Huhne to put his name forward. Chris had been an MP for less than a year, but had been an MEP for six years before that, had been a parliamentary candidate in the 1980s, and saw an opportunity to stand before the field might become more crowded in future. Chris's candidature was much to Ming's annoyance, as Chris had previously promised to support him. It was also a source of considerable frustration to Nick Clegg, who strongly backed Ming in the campaign. Nick did not feel able to stand at the time, but saw himself as better placed to become leader within a few years as successor to Ming than if Chris Huhne was elected now and led the party for longer than was likely to be the case with Ming.

There was, however, to be only one event in which all four potential candidates appeared together publicly. The agenda of a planned policy conference at the LSE on Saturday 14 January was changed in order to permit leadership hustings to be held just a week after Charles's dramatic resignation. Mark Oaten's campaign had incurred very considerable expenditure renting offices and equipment, but it lasted only another five days. Mark, as I had expected, had been struggling to get the seven nominations required to show that he had the support of 10 per cent of his parliamentary colleagues, especially since Charles was maintaining the tradition within the party that retiring leaders did not publicly endorse anyone to succeed them. Lembit appeared to be Mark's only public backer amongst the MPs. Several more of them were prepared to nominate Mark in order to allow him to stand, provided it was clear that they would not be voting for him. In some desperation, I received representations from Mark's campaign suggesting that MPs who nominated other candidates should be allowed to nominate him in addition to the person that they were supporting. The rules were silent on the issue of how many different nomination papers an MP could be permitted to sign. My instinct was that the rules should be permissive where possible, but that nominations for such a public office should not be kept secret, and that if Mark had seven signatures on a nomination paper, then their names should be made public. I confirmed that this should be the case with the chair of the Federal Appeals Panel (who was the returning officer for the election) and this decision about publicly listing the nominations effectively made Mark's candidature untenable. Amongst his seven nominators would have been several MPs identified as voting for other candidates, or not necessarily supporting Mark, and on Thursday 19 January he announced that he was withdrawing from the contest.

I was worried about Mark, and even considered the possibility that in a depressed state he might defect to the Conservatives. I made sure that I and others kept in touch with him, but I didn't expect what followed. Just before 8 a.m. on the Saturday morning, I had a phone call from Anna Werrin. Anna asked me to ring Mark immediately, as he had *News of the World* reporters outside his house, and they were asking him about a male prostitute. When I rang Mark, he was clearly very distressed. He told me that he had seen people sitting in two cars outside his house when he woke up and that he had been out to challenge them. One of them showed him a photograph of a male prostitute that he clearly recognised. He had then had to go back into the house in order to explain this to his wife, Belinda, whilst their children were having breakfast in the next room. I advised him to say nothing more, that he might soon find his house surrounded by reporters questioning him, and that it was best for them to get away from the house if possible without commenting. This was the first of fourteen conversations that I had with Mark that day as I remained very conscious of his shocked and distressed condition, and the need to try to arrange personal support. In my second call, Mark and Belinda had agreed that they would leave the house with their children and go and stay with family out of sight of the media, if we could devise a plan for arranging this. By now, very kind neighbours had come into the house to help mind the children whilst Mark and Belinda spoke to each other, and I spoke to Mark. I confirmed that Mark had clearly acknowledged the young man in the photograph.

When I next spoke to Mark, he said that Belinda and the children would not now accompany him away anywhere, and would seek to go somewhere on their own. I understood the position and advised Mark to try to get away somewhere discreetly himself to avoid further media questioning. It was now a case of damage limitation from every perspective. I was seriously worried about Mark and I knew that he had suffered from periods of stress previously. He had been trying to negotiate with the Home Secretary over hugely controversial anti-terrorist legislation, cope with all the issues associated with Charles, and pursue his own potential ambitions. He was now anxious that he might have to resign as an MP, and feared the consequences for him and his family of losing his job and his income. I told him that I did not feel that this should happen and sought to reassure him on this point, providing that he had done nothing illegal. He assured me that the young man concerned was not underage and that therefore there was no question of illegality. I advised, however, that his position as home affairs spokesman would be very difficult to maintain at this point as it would keep him in the media spotlight and make him vulnerable in the face of difficult questions, just when he did not want to be. I suggested that it would be best, therefore, to protect himself and others, for him to step down as the party's home affairs spokesman, but not until we were ready to make any statement, the content of which would depend on any specific allegations put to him. Mark agreed.

It was, of course, very difficult for Mark, in this condition, to talk through the issues with me. Our MPs knew that I could be trusted as a friend and confidential adviser, and in Mark's case I had guided him through the traumatic events of being declared the victor in his constituency by just two votes, then having the result challenged legally and having to fight a by-election in order to retain it. I sensed that Mark would find it very difficult to explain his resignation to Ming Campbell, who had been his rival for the leadership until two days previously, and was now acting leader. So, I offered to talk to Ming on his behalf and Mark was most grateful. It was still quite early on the Saturday morning when I rang Ming at his home in Edinburgh to tell him why his home affairs spokesman would be resigning. Ming was getting dressed when I called and shared the detail of our conversation with Elspeth as we spoke. Ming's sharp legal brain also immediately focused on the issue of the age of the man concerned (he was twenty-three) and whether or not any of Mark's actions might have been illegal (they were not). I knew that Ming was due to go over to Dunfermline to support our by-election campaign there that day.[71] I was determined that, notwithstanding Charles's resignation and today's developments, we would make every effort to try to win this by-election. Questions would have been asked in the media if Ming had suddenly cancelled his pre-announced campaign visit, and I was very keen to ensure good coverage of Ming's acting leader's visit on the Scottish TV bulletins that night and in the next day's Scottish Sunday papers before the news about Mark broke. I advised, therefore, that he must stick with the plan, but return to his home in Edinburgh by 3 p.m., and make sure that his front door remained firmly closed for the rest of the day.

By now, Mark had received the offer from a neighbour with a flat in Cornwall to drive him there. I advised that he accept this offer, conscious of the fact that he would not be alone during the long drive. Mark was able to scramble over the back wall of his garden and escape

---

71   The Labour MP for Dunfermline & West Fife had died the day before Charles Kennedy's
       resignation.

with the neighbour unnoticed by the *News of the World* reporters at the front of the house. A plan we had considered for neighbours to use their cars to block those of the reporters and prevent them following Mark was therefore unnecessary. My immediate concerns now were Mark's state of health and the fact that he would almost certainly need to make a statement later that day, but not before at least 3 p.m., as I wanted to minimise coverage in other papers. I was able, via Anna, to get a message to Mark's doctor expressing my serious concern about him. I considered that there was a real prospect of self-harm and that this issue took precedence over everything else. His doctor was able to speak to him whilst he was being driven and arrange for a prescription to be collected from a chemist in Cornwall that evening.

I spoke about the developing situation to Ben Stoneham, who had previously been responsible for the print production of the *News of the World* and who knew about their final deadlines and policies for printing anything that might be challenged legally. He advised that they would feel confident of publication if it appeared that Mark had indeed recognised the photograph that he was shown and acted as though the basis of the allegation about a relationship was correct. In order to minimise what was therefore their inevitable coverage, we agreed that normal crisis management rules should be followed with the most minimal written statement issued as late in the day as possible, and all efforts made to prevent any other comment from Lib Dem sources. We hoped that Mark's stepping down as home affairs spokesman would take some of the sting out of the story by reducing his media exposure and inevitable questions about retaining that position, as opposed to him remaining as an MP.

I helped Mark to draft his statement apologising for 'errors of judgement in personal behaviour and for the embarrassment caused, firstly to my family but also to my friends, my constituents and my party'. It also said: 'I will not be commenting further at this time and would now ask for some space and personal privacy for me and my family.' This gave nothing away about the details of any allegations so that any reports would have to be careful about relying on anything unsubstantiated and not admitted.

Mark was happy with my advice and felt able to contact a small number of friends whilst on the way to Cornwall to forewarn them about the story that would break. I got the press office to give the statement to the *News of the World* at about 4 p.m. and to be ready to issue it on request, whilst making it clear that nobody from the party would be commenting. The storm broke on the TV news bulletins that evening, when the story on the inside pages of the *News of the World* became known. I did not like the fact that references were constantly made to a 'rent boy' (he was a male prostitute, aged twenty-three) and to a 'Lib Dem sex scandal', as allegations featuring politicians in other parties would generally be reported in more personal terms about them, rather than their respective parties.

In a statement, the *News of the World* justified publishing their story about Mark's private life on the supposed basis that he had campaigned for election 'as a family man' and that they considered this to be hypocritical. It appears that they had known of the story for some considerable time and had been holding it back, possibly with the intention of publishing it if Mark became leader. Mark's resignation from the leadership contest was unconnected with the story, although it provided the trigger for publication of it.

On the Saturday morning that I began talking to Mark, I was also very mindful that the party had a duty of care towards Belinda and the children. I spoke to Belinda privately once it was clear that she did not wish to accompany Mark. She wanted, of course, to get the children away from the maelstrom that I warned her was likely to develop. I knew that the girls might have to face unpleasant comments at school as soon as their father's picture became prominent in the papers. As we discussed potential plans, there seemed to be nowhere that Belinda could feel comfortable and safe. The family had just recently returned from a skiing holiday in Austria and she felt that the children might best appreciate another week back at the same resort, but she could not afford to take them back there. I therefore spoke to a party donor, with whom I could be completely discreet, explained the problem and said that we really needed to finance Belinda and the girls getting away. At the back of my mind was also the fact that Belinda could justifiably have been critical of the party if it had not acted to support her and her family in these circumstances. I was able to tell her that I had raised the funds for them to go back to the resort. The children were aware of very strange goings-on as photographers tried to picture them departing with Belinda in her car, but they were happy to be going skiing again.

On the Saturday evening, I had arranged with Mark Littlewood to pick up the earliest printed edition of the *News of the World* and bring me a copy. I then had the difficult task of reading the story over the phone to Mark in Cornwall. As I read it out, I chose to omit a couple of sentences that I thought he would find most difficult to cope with. Over the next two weeks, I kept in constant contact with him, knowing that it was important to ensure that he was never alone and always had somewhere safe to stay where he was unlikely to be 'doorstepped' by the media. Having left for Austria without him, Belinda was then willing for Mark to visit them there to see the children, who were obviously missing him. I did not want him to travel alone and his mother, who still lived in Watford where he had grown up, was willing to travel with him. He arrived at his mother's house, checking, as I advised, for any journalists or photographers who might be waiting outside the house or in cars in the road before knocking on the front door. But as he did this, a photographer emerged from the bushes to take a picture of him knocking on the door of his mother's house. After ringing me, he explained to his mum that they had better leave immediately before news of his whereabouts spread. They were relieved to make it to Heathrow without anyone appearing to recognise him, in spite of his picture being on the front page of national newspapers that day. Mark's spirits were lifted by being with his children and his few days there largely passed without incident, although one of them answered his mobile phone to an enquiring journalist whilst they were on the ski slopes. Mark was again able to evade recognition as he returned to the UK and stayed with various friends, one of whom lived further down the road from our Stockwell house, enabling us to meet discreetly to discuss his next steps over breakfast there.

In the meantime, the media harassment of anyone connected with the Oatens was considerable. Belinda asked me to help with advice on how her family should try to deal with this and cope with the pressure. At one point, a reporter was calling at the door at one of her sisters every twenty minutes seeking news and opinions about Mark. I spoke to her sister several times suggesting that she use the simple form of words: 'I'm sorry, I have nothing to say to you' in response to any enquiries and that the party could, if necessary, raise a complaint with the Press Complaints Commission.

After a week away, Belinda was due to return home. I was in Dunfermline at this point and staying in a hotel when woken by a phone call before 7 a.m. from Belinda, who was trying to check out of the hotel in Austria. Whilst I had promised that the costs of her family's trip would be covered, her credit card balance would not allow this payment to be taken from it, and I asked her to put the hotel management on the line to me and paid the bill on my personal credit card, to be reclaimed from the donor later. Belinda was, of course, most grateful.

For some weeks, I continued to maintain daily contact with Mark as he began to try to recover, and I remained anxious about his welfare and that of his family. I suggested that his first public statement should be by way of an interview with his local paper, the *Hampshire Chronicle*, and I sat with him in the interview, having first tidied his office to remove sight of anything unwanted in photographs. At my suggestion, his first public activity was then his advice centre, which was of course also attended by many representatives of the media, and he rang me in horror when he arrived to find the venue locked as the caretaker did not open it until his surgery was due to start. He also began making speeches in Parliament, where coverage could of course be carefully controlled, and he was welcomed back into the parliamentary group. He also began doing some television commentary and wrote two books,[72] but subsequently chose not to stand again at the next general election.

It was a new experience for me to be the acting returning officer for the leadership election, and it came at the same time as I was in charge of the party's crisis management following Charles's resignation and the outbreak of publicity following Mark's admission, and whilst I was also trying to ensure maximum support for our by-election campaign in Dunfermline, which I had personally determined would be fought to win. Whilst the party's media coverage was relentlessly negative, and opinion polls showed that we were down to 13 per cent nationally, I tried to calm the nerves of the party and its staff for whom I had a particular responsibility. I held a series of staff meetings endeavouring to reassure them that we would get back on track. I asked all of our parliamentarians to do as much as they could to support their own staff and to ensure that party members saw them all behaving in a dignified fashion, maintaining a sense of unity. I wanted the party to focus on choosing its permanent leader and on the Dunfermline campaign, which I still believed could be won, although there was, of course, much scepticism about this objective.

Four days after Mark's resignation as home affairs spokesman, I was sitting in my normal place at the back of our weekly MPs' meeting ready to brief them on the leadership election and the Dunfermline campaign, when I received a text message from Paul Holmes, who was acting as Simon Hughes's agent for the leadership election, asking me to come to his office immediately. The media had been pursuing any potential Lib Dem scandal story with great determination and rumours abounded about further potential revelations. Some malicious and obviously false claims had been made about Ming, and we

---

72 *Screwing Up: How One MP Survived Politics, Scandal and Turning Forty* and *Coalition: The Politics and Personalities of Coalition Government from 1850.*

had tracked down the source of them. A number of people contacted me fearing that there might be vulnerabilities concerning Simon and I discussed them with him. Media interest in Simon had increased since he had given an interview to Andy McSmith of *The Independent* ten days earlier in which he was asked if he was gay. He had replied that 'the answer is no, as it happens, but if it were the case, which it isn't, I hope that it would not be an issue'. He would soon have to admit that this had been 'misleading'. His team, including his personal lawyer, and I were told that *The Sun* had somehow obtained telephone records of calls to a gay chatline showing that Simon's phone had been used to call them. We understood that they did not have any details of Simon's calls, but were threatening to expose transcripts of other calls made to the chatline if Simon did not give an interview to them admitting that he was gay. Simon had sought to protect his privacy, but *The Sun* was about to 'out' him.

Simon gave his interview to Trevor Kavanagh of *The Sun* that evening. Many of us felt outraged at the manner of his 'outing' and about this breach of personal privacy. Simon had never been remotely hypocritical about his own views concerning homosexual equality, but the controversy surrounding the Bermondsey by-election in 1983 was now bound to return. Fortunately, and greatly to his credit, Peter Tatchell was very supportive of Simon's position. There was a brief discussion at the meeting with Simon about whether or not he should continue in the leadership race. Although I was acting returning officer, I spoke up as chief executive very strongly to insist that it was essential that he continued his campaign, as it was particularly important for a party with our values for him not to be intimidated out of standing as a result of being outed in this way. I feared that his withdrawal might have sent out a signal that someone who was gay could not stand for the leadership of a party which had been the first to promote homosexual equality. His campaign team, including the very politically experienced Nick Carthew, knew, however, that their hopes of him winning had been effectively dashed. The leadership election involving Simon and Charles seven years earlier had been fairly close, and so until now Simon might have thought seriously about his prospects of winning. An ICM poll of Lib Dem voters had put him ahead prior to this, but his support now fell substantially in response to the perception that because of the initial denial that he was gay, he had not handled the issue well. Simon later told the Leveson Inquiry how he had been informed by the police in October 2006 of evidence that Glenn Mulcaire had hacked his mobile phone whilst working for the *News of the World*. It later transpired that Mulcaire also had a great deal of private data relating to him and some of his friends. Simon told the inquiry that the *News of the World* had also tried to stand up stories about him 'based on a salacious assumption'.

As *The Sun* prepared to go to press, it was necessary to batten down the hatches again and prepare for another wave of damaging publicity. As with Mark, I was now concerned with ensuring that Simon was protected as well as possible and that the party would remain focused on conducting the leadership election in a civilised fashion and on the Dunfermline campaign. I spoke to Ming and Chris, as the other leadership candidates, to tell them what was happening and that a statement would be made later. They were both very supportive of Simon. During the evening, a media scrum developed outside Simon's house. Neighbours had called out the police and contacted Simon to express concern about it. Paul Holmes arranged for Simon to stay at his Dolphin Square flat which could be accessed via the underground car park in order to avoid media detection. In the meantime, I waited in my Cowley Street office for news of how *The Sun* would handle Simon's interview whilst drafting a potential statement for him in response to it. I had learned that I needed to always carry a note with me showing contact details for key party figures. I now had to alert them to what was happening, whilst advising them not to comment any further and that the party would rely at this stage solely on a statement that would be issued later. It was only in a late edition of *The Sun* that the story ran, and the first version of it had to be changed following demands made by Simon's lawyer to remove inaccuracies. I spoke to Simon about his statement and there was quite a lot that he wanted to say. I advised him, however, to stick with my short draft based on acknowledging that he had had 'both homosexual and heterosexual relationships in the past' and that he would continue his campaign and his job in public life, which should not be affected by this.

Chris Huhne's entry to the leadership election campaign had been quite unexpected, as all those who had agreed to the statement saying that they would not serve under Charles Kennedy were expected to back Ming. But he knew that he would have a chance as he had fought a vigorous selection contest with Emma Nicholson in the south-east region as to which of them would top the party's list there for the 2004 European Parliament elections, and he had been an MEP there with the largest party membership for six years. He had the support of most of the party's well-established campaigners in the region, including Keith House, who had previously run the party's membership department. Many of them had worked closely with me in the past and they all understood the power of effective direct mail as we had used it in our major parliamentary by-election successes and in target seats. Chris also had strong networks of support based on his SDP days.

In contrast, Ming had significantly more support amongst the party's MPs, but he struggled to establish an effective election machine with so many MPs (and some peers) appearing to fall over each other in their attempts to take charge of his campaign. When nominations opened, I had calls from six different people telling me that they were in charge of ensuring that Ming was nominated and that they were coming to see me to collect the necessary papers.

Odds on Chris Huhne becoming leader obviously fell dramatically when he actually entered the race, having previously been considered a non-runner. They then fell further as there was undoubtedly some betting market manipulation by his supporters. Chris also benefited considerably from the leaking from within Ming's camp of their private poll. In all the polls I was responsible for overseeing in parliamentary by-elections, none of them ever leaked and very few people ever knew the result of the voting intention questions. But a poll conducted on behalf of Ming's campaign in order to 'steady their nerves' in the face of evidence of growing support for Chris Huhne backfired badly. Instead of maintaining confidentiality, the fact that Ming was only narrowly ahead of Chris was widely gossiped about, prompting the Huhne campaign to have the confidence to commission and publish their own poll confirming this.

Simon's campaign never really recovered from him being outed just two weeks after he had said that he was 'not homosexual'. Simon explained in relation to this that he was simply seeking to avoid being pigeonholed by a label that did not fit him and now told the *Pink News* that he was bisexual. He was not dishonest, but was forced to admit 'that he had not handled matters well'.

Whilst overseeing the leadership election, and dealing with the aftermath of the controversies surrounding Charles, Mark and Simon, I was also working on trying to rescue the party from its current troubles with the sort of spectacular by-election win that had saved us on previous occasions. Very few people in the party considered that winning Dunfermline & West Fife was a serious prospect in these circumstances, but our Scottish leader, Nicol Stephen (who I'd helped to elect in his 1991 by-election), was very supportive and trusting of my judgement based on his own experience of working closely with me. I was also taking a major gamble in deciding that the party could raise and spend £100,000 on the campaign, and I knew that there would be a lot of flak directed at me personally if this investment did not pay off.

In the autumn of 2005, Willie Rennie had been to see me and Paul Rainger to talk about what many people knew was a potential parliamentary by-election, as the MP for Dunfermline & West Fife, Rachel Squire, was seriously ill. The strength of our 2005 general election campaign and a good local candidate (who had sadly died subsequently) had narrowly given us second place in the seat. Great discretion was, of course, required in such circumstances as you could not possibly campaign in anticipation of someone dying, and we were sensitive to the fact that we had been unfairly accused of this a number of times in the past. Willie lived just outside the constituency, but had firm Fife roots. He was not the only potential candidate for us, as local councillor Jim Tolson might well also put his name forward. I anticipated that it would be very difficult for us to mount a potential challenge if there was a by-election and the campaign was very short. I therefore proposed that we should proceed to the selection of our prospective candidate for the Scottish Parliament Constituency of Dunfermline West, which was based on very similar boundaries to those for the Westminster seat. I suggested that there would have to be an informal, and somewhat unconstitutional, agreement amongst potential candidates that whoever was selected for the Scottish Parliament Constituency would be unopposed, in the event of it being necessary to select a Westminster parliamentary by-election candidate. This was agreed, and Willie was chosen and began to raise his profile on local campaign issues and he appointed Peter Barrett as his agent. Willie had acquired years of campaign experience working within the campaigns department, especially in parliamentary by-elections including Christchurch, where he had been the agent and we had worked very closely together.

I was happy with how Willie's campaign for the Scottish parliamentary constituency had been progressing when the by-election now occurred for the Westminster seat. But when Charles Kennedy resigned the next day and media coverage of the Liberal Democrats was dominated by revelations about his alcoholism and the private lives of Mark Oaten and Simon Hughes, most people assumed that any prospect that we might have had of winning had vanished. A national opinion poll putting us on 13 per cent was widely reported as meaning the end of the party. I was also annoyed at the time that the discussion of a meeting of Scottish Lib Dem MPs at Westminster, at which I was not present, and where they considered that we had no prospect of winning the by-election, leaked to the media.

I was mindful of how we had previously sometimes managed to win parliamentary by-elections in spite of very low national standings, and that this was what the party now desperately needed. The key ingredients in these circumstances had always been a strong local candidate and local campaign issues that engaged people within the constituency sufficiently strongly for them to believe that we should and could win. Labour's planned toll charges on the Forth Bridge Road provided us with one such major issue, together with several others concerning the provision of schools in West Fife and a hospital, and Willie campaigned on them brilliantly. A great deal of casework was undertaken by a very dedicated team from across Scotland, including Caron Lindsay, who I had known from my East Midlands days when she was a party member there, and Ed Maxfield, who I had worked with as Norman Lamb's agent. They worked closely with Paul Rainger and Mark Pack to ensure that we were communicating effectively about those issues within the constituency. My own canvassing, and that of other people I trusted, confirmed that local residents were discussing the issues that we were campaigning on, as opposed to the problems of the party far away in Westminster.

It remained very difficult, however, to persuade party members in Scotland or elsewhere that we had any chance of winning, and that they should come and help in order to make this happen. On the penultimate weekend before poll, there were very few of us at the by-election HQ and I was helping to draft an optimistic 'Set to Win'-type newspaper of the kind that we produced in previous successful campaigns. But it was clear that we were lacking the volume of help that had been necessary to win in the past as well as the kind of media profile that could give us sufficient credibility for Willie to win.

Something big had to happen to establish momentum for us and I could only think of one thing that might do that. Charles had sensibly gone abroad, and out of sight, for a holiday after his resignation. But I knew that he would want to re-engage politically at some point, and I felt that now should be the time, and that Dunfermline should be the place. There was always a particularly strong affection for Charles in Scotland, and there was perhaps also more understanding of his problem in a country with a higher level of alcohol consumption. Many senior party figures went further than expressing concern about my plan, suggesting I was quite mad to ask Charles to make his first public appearance after his resignation in the Dunfermline by-election. I knew, however, that it was an absolutely necessary gamble, as I thought that we could win, but not without it. Charles was very understanding of my view, and willing to take my advice. He had certainly not given up on politics, and I think welcomed the opportunity for some early political rehabilitation. He agreed to be in Dunfermline on the final Thursday before polling day.

One of the most politically effective and personally emotional scenes that I have ever witnessed in an election then took place in Dunfermline High Street on that day. Charles's route was very carefully planned to avoid any embarrassment, such as being pictured outside off-licences. I had asked for the entire Scottish Liberal Democrat membership to be emailed inviting them to Dunfermline High Street to show support for Charles that Thursday afternoon. A large contingent of our MPs from all over Great Britain also came to support him. Those who had called for his resignation generally went campaigning elsewhere in the constituency that day, whilst many of those closest to him provided significant support at his side as we marched down the high street. The reaction to him from members of the public was immensely supportive, as I believed that it would be, and he was at his campaigning best standing next to Willie, urging people to vote for him and explaining why Willie should be the next MP and what the choice was for local voters. There were, of course, attempts by journalists to ask Charles about his resignation, rather than the by-election. At one point, the Scottish party's press officer, Neil MacKinnon, placed his foot on the cable for *Newsnight*'s TV camera, making it difficult for them to get close enough to Charles to ask questions. I stood in the way of an aggressive SNP-supporting radio journalist who was shouting at

Charles, blocking his questions and directing Charles towards more sympathetic shoppers. In all the resulting pictures it looked like Willie, Charles, Jim Wallace and others were surrounded by enthusiastic local supporters. In fact, we only met eleven local shoppers who were not there in some capacity as party supporters or reporters etc., but eight of them were backing Willie and that was sufficient evidence of our support for the media, much of which had significant goodwill and sympathy towards Charles, and so the event was extensively reported as a triumph. Towards the end of the walkabout, I saw Gordon Brown leave Labour's by-election HQ at the bottom of the high street, and his jaw dropped at the sight of the huge Lib Dem procession he was witnessing as our bandwagon was rolling. It was an amazing turna-round. Earlier that morning, I had been with Willie, who had had his head clasped in his hands in despair as he looked at the papers report-ing bad polls for his campaign, and he had thought that his prospect of winning was over. I had done my best to reassure him that it would turn around, and it did.

It still remained very difficult convincing all the leadership candi-dates that they should be prepared for a possible by-election victory for us in these circumstances. I met with Michael Moore on Ming's behalf, who conceded that based on what I had said about previous by-elections, Ming had better prepare his diary for the option of being in Dunfermline on the Friday morning after the by-election. Simon Hughes would not make any definite diary commitment (although he later arrived at Cowley Street at 5.30 a.m. on that Friday to book a flight up to Edinburgh in order to get to Dunfermline). Chris Huhne's campaign told me that he would be sticking to his planned engage-ment with business people in Manchester.

Late on the eve of poll I found myself in a Millbank TV studio debating prospects for the next day's by-election with Alex Salmond, amongst others. I cheekily offered him a bet on air about the result in order to show how my confidence contrasted with his, and he responded better than I could have hoped by taking off his headphones and saying that he couldn't hear me anymore! I decided to base myself at Cowley Street on polling day to help encourage the many volunteers there (including Ann, who had never undertaken telephone canvassing before) to assist with the polling day calling operation for the by-election and then to help handle the London-based media. When Willie was declared the winner by 1,800 votes, it was the first ever Lib Dem (or Liberal or SDP) gain from Labour in a parliamentary by-election in Scotland, and the first that Labour had lost there since 1988.

Ming was most prominent in the extensive coverage of Willie's victory throughout that weekend, having taken part as acting leader in the follow-up victory parade along Dunfermline High Street. I believe this coverage was a significant factor in helping Ming secure victory in the leadership election.

When the ballot for the leadership was over, I asked former party president Navnit Dholakia to declare the result of it in the same room at Local Government House, where we had held the general election press conferences. He declared the first preference votes as follows:

Sir Menzies Campbell	23,264
Chris Huhne	16,691
Simon Hughes	12,081

When Simon Hughes's votes were transferred, this left the final result as:

Sir Menzies Campbell	29,697
Chris Huhne	21,628

More than 52,000 members voted (72.2 per cent of them). Charles Kennedy sat in the front row for the declaration and was there to shake Ming's hand (something which Ming acknowledged to me was most magnanimous in the circumstances). I spoke to Simon's mum, who was there to support her son, and was pleased to discuss the pride which we both had for him, and she spoke of her disgust about how the newspapers had behaved. Chris Huhne's team thought they had done well, and I think were satisfied that he was well placed for the future. After the declaration, a walk back to Cowley Street became something of a victory parade involving most of the party supporters who had been at the press conference. Then, from the staircase outside the boardroom, Ming as the new leader addressed everyone, including the party staff.

It was less than two months since Charles Kennedy had resigned. It had been an incredibly turbulent time. But the constant sense of crisis in the party had passed, and the party's self-confidence and external reputation was restored. As we celebrated winning our sixty-third seat in the House of Commons, some of the media commentators there remarked to me that if we could win by-elections such as Dunfermline in these circumstances, we could win elections in any circumstances. 'Winning Here' had really mattered.

INDEX